AF631238

THE MÁRCANDEYA PURANA

other recent books from Cosmo Publications . . .

THE HINDUS. *Bestseller*
Encyclopaedia of Hinduism in 5 Volumes
Edited by Subodh Kapoor

ENCYCLOPAEDIA OF INDIAN HERITAGE. in 90 Volumes
A Descriptive Work of Indological Research in Philosophy, Religion, Sacred Literature, Society, Thought, Traditions, and Ancient Sciences.
Edited by Subodh Kapoor

ENCYCLOPAEDIA OF VEDIC PHILOSOPHY. *Bestseller*
The Age, Literature, Religion, Pantheon, Philosophy. Traditions and Teachers of the Vedas
in 9 Volumes
Edited by Subodh Kapoor

ENCYCLOPAEDIA OF INDIAN PHILOSOPHERS. *Bestseller*
Philosophers, Saints, Sages, Thinkers, Acharyas, Rishis, and great Religious Leaders
in 9 Volumes
Edited by Subodh Kapoor

ENCYCLOPAEDIA OF VEDANTA PHILOSOPHY.
in 5 Volumes
Ed. S. kapoor

Also Available . . .

INDIAN HISTORICAL RESEARCHES *Bestseller*
By Several Authors of International Repute
in 78 Volumes

REDISCOVERING INDIA *Bestseller*
INIDAN PHILOSOPHY LIBRARY
By Several Authors of International Repute
in 71 Volumes

BIBLIOTHECA INDICA

a

COLLECTION OF ORIENTAL WORKS

published by the

ASIATIC SOCIETY OF BENGAL

THE MÁRCANDEYA PURANA

IN THE ORIGINAL SANSCRIT

Edited By

K. M. Banerjea

VOLUME 1

Cosmo Publications

2004 New Delhi

All rights reserved. No part of this publication may be reproduced, or stored in retrival system, or transmitted in any form or by any means without the prior permission of Cosmo Publications.

THE MARCANDEYA PURANA

First Published by COSMO 2004

ISBN 81-7755-857-9 (set)
81-7755-858-7 (volume 1)

Published by
MRS. RANI KAPOOR
for COSMO PUBLICATIONS
Publishing Division of
GENESIS PUBLISHING PVT. LTD.
24-B, Ansari Road, Darya Ganj,
New Delhi-110 002, INDIA

Printed at
Mehra Offset Press

INTRODUCTION

TO THE

Márcandeya Purána.

The Márcaṇḍeya Puráṇa of which a complete edition is now presented to the public may be considered under two divisions. The first is that in which the Ṛishi whose name it bears takes scarcely any part, the second is that in which he is the principal speaker. The former comprises the first forty four chapters and extends to page 255, the latter consists of ninety three chapters, from the 45th to the 137th, with which the Puráṇa concludes.

It would appear that this Puráṇa, if indeed it was the work of one person, originally comprised only that portion in which Márcaṇḍeya is the principal narrator. The section called *Deví-Máhátmya,* contained in what we have called the second division, was probably an interpolation, Márcaṇḍeya himself scarcely appearing in it. And the first division was afterwards prefixed with a view to introduce certain extraordinary characters, and new doctrines, not contained in the original compilation.

The two divisions, again, we may subdivide into five sections, allotting two to the first, and three to the second.

I, 1. The first section, although it makes some reference to Mārcaṇḍeya, was really intended to propound the *Bhágavata* doctrine of the Supreme Being subsisting in four forms, and to appease the Brahminical mind by the solution of certain moral difficulties presented in the ancient mythology of the Hindús.

Jaimini the disciple of Vyása comes to the Ṛishi Márcaṇḍeya with a string of queries, or rather theological and moral problems, which he had not been able to solve for himself, and which consequently very much disturbed his inquisitive mind. The *first* question was, Why, or how, was Vásudeva, himself *nirguṇa*, or devoid of qualities, endued with humanity? The *second* related to the *polyandry* in the case of Draupadí, Why, or how, did Kṛishná, the daughter of Drupada, become the common wife of the five sons of Páṇḍu? The *third* had scarcely any pith in itself, though it no doubt represented a difficulty felt at the time by Vaishṇava Brahmins. Why, or how, did the great Baladeva who, be it known, was the *second* form of the Supreme Divinity in Bhágavata theology, expiate, by a pilgrimage, the sin of Brahmincide which he had committed under the influence of liquor? The *fourth* was still more insignificant. Why did the five sons of Draupadí meet with violent deaths, while yet unmarried and infants, as if they had no protectors?

When asked for a solution of these theological problems, Márcaṇḍeya told Jaimini he was about to engage in the celebration of certain religious solemnities, and had not the time to satisfy his friend's curiosity. But as the questions appeared to possess some gravity, the Ṛishi referred the querist to certain *oviparous* sages, inhabiting one of the peaks of the Vindya mountains, and competent, fully, to remove the doubts which distracted the mind of Jaimini. This reference to *oviparous* sages, however, served only to detain the Ṛishi Márcaṇḍeya, the longer, from his contemplated ceremonies,—longer, than the solution of the original questions, as given in the sequel, could have done. Curious as Jaimini was on the theological points already mooted, he became still more inquisitive on the *physical* wonder, now disclosed by Márcaṇḍeya. Birds endowed with the power of articulation and with the wisdom of learned sages ! In his eagerness to explain this wonder, Márcaṇḍeya forgot for a moment the call of his religious rites, and, without any more complaint on the score of time, entered into a long explanation from which it appeared that certain Brahmins had in a previous state of life, incurred the wrath of their father, and were now passing their days as *birds* under parental malediction, tempered, however, by the merciful allowance of articulation, and a large addition of transcendental knowledge.

Jaimini went to these learned birds and proposed his questions. The winged Ṛishis, after an eloquent salutation to the Supreme Vásudeva, to Brahmá, and to I'sána, proceeded to resolve his doubts. The salutation itself contains ideas and sentiments which appear to be foreign to the portion we have supposed to be the original Márcaṇḍeya Puráṇa. The first question, the most difficult of the four, the very question on which Sankaráchárya and others have written volumes, is, by an adroit evasion, summarily disposed of in a few words, but apparently to the querist's satisfaction. "Nara means "water, as has been said by sages conversant with truth; "it was originally his receptacle; hence he is called Ná-"ráyaṇa. The illustrious lord, the divine Náráyaṇa, per-"vading every thing, lives, O Bráhmaṇa, permeant in a "quadruple form. He is possessed, as well as devoid, of "attributes. His first form is inscrutable ; the wise (alone) "see it in its fairness. It is enclosed in a blaze of light, "and is the supreme object of contemplation with devotees. "It is far, and it is near, and is known to be beyond the "attributes. It is called Vásudeva and can be seen (only) "in the absence of egotism. Its shape and colour are not "real, they are fictitious. It is always pure, and the only "form laudable.

"His second form, called Sesha, suppor from below "the earth with its head (or hood); it is designated as "composed of Tamas or the quality of darkness, and has "passed to the brute creation. His third form is active "and devoted to the preservation of creatures; it is con "sidered as mainly of the quality of goodness, and is the "instituter of virtue. His fourth form, abiding in water, "lies on a serpent as its bed; its attribute is passion, and "it always creates.

"The third form of Hari, which is constantly employed "in the conservation of creatures, always preserves virtue "on the earth. It destroys the haughty Asuras, the ex-"terminaters of virtue, and protects the gods and holy "men who are intent on the maintenance of righteous-"ness. Whensoever, O Jaimini, the depression of virtue "and the prevalence of vice take place, it creates itself. It "became a Varáha, in former times, and repelled the "water with its face. The earth was rescued by a single "one of his tusks like lotus flowers; it detroyed Hirany-"akas'ipu in the incarnation of Nrisinha. Viprachitti "and other demons his followers, were also destroyed. His "other incarnations, such as the Dwarf, I cannot venture "to enumerate now. This, his recent incarnation was in "Mathurá. In this manner that form of goodness becomes "incarnate. It is designated Pradyumna and is given to "the act of preservation. By Vásudeva's will, it remains "divine and human, as well as in the state of a brute, and "continually partakes of their several natures.

"Thus have we told you why the Lord Vishṇu, "though successful, assumed human forms: hear now the "sequel thereof."

The feathered philosophers thus left the question exactly where it was. They simply repeated the dogma that Vásudeva was both devoid and possessed of qualities, and that he was both *nirguṇa* and *saguṇa*. How the two characters could consist in the same individual,—and which was the very question that troubled the imagination of Jaimini—they did not undertake to solve.

The above description of the Supreme Vásudeva and his quadruple form shows that the section under review was composed by a disciple of the school of the *Nárada-pancha-rátra,* which propounds the same doctrine, and to which S'ankaráchárya has given an eleborate reply in his commentary on the Brahma Sútras. It involved a theory in theosophy of which no traces can be found in the second division of the Puráṇa.

The second question is also disposed of in a few words. Indra, the king of the gods, had on various occasions committed diverse atrocities, and had consequently lost portions of his personal energy, which had got into other divinities. The five sons of Páṇḍu were no other than sons of himself and the other deities which had thus been pervaded by his energy. The Páṇḍavas were therefore themselves pervaded by Indra's personality, and their common wife Draúpadí could not be guilty of polyandry, since she married but one personality of which her five husbands were only portions. The question and the answer only show that the Hindus were rather uncomfortable under the notion that there should be, in one of their most respected families, such a gross case of conjugal impropriety, and it is not at all improbable that the stringent rules, subsequently introduced, against the marriage of widows, were dictated by their feverish anxiety to prevent the possibility of an imitation of Draupadí's example, and to vindicate the purity of their moral code.

The third question had but little significancy in itself, and could not call for an elaborate reply. Certainly nothing could possibly be urged in extenuation of a gross atrocity committed by one who personated the second form of the Supreme Brahma. Balarãma felt he was placed in a delicate situation when his brother Krishṇa was going to interfere in the domestic quarrel between the Kurus and the Pãṇḍavas. He was unwilling, by siding with either party, to give umbrage to the other. He accordingly resolved to go on a pilgrimage and thereby avoid the difficulty of choosing his side in the unnatural contest. But just on the eve of his departure, he indulged rather freely in spirituous liquor, and—"when drunk he went to the luxuriant Raivata forest, holding by the hand the exhilarated Revatí (his wife) resembling an Apsaras (in beauty). The intoxicated hero walked in the midst of a number of women with unsteady steps, and saw the charming and most excellent great forest which was filled with fruits and flowers of all seasons, crowded with monkeys, holy, and furnished with beds of lotus flowers, and pools of waters." He went from forest to forest until he encountered certain Brahmins who were reading the Vedas. The sacred fraternity, terrified at the sight of a strong man in a state of intoxication, provided for their safety by soothing him with a courteous salutation. One of them, however, Súta by name, refused to prostrate himself before a *drunkard*, on which Balaráma was so infuriated that he struck him dead on the spot. Such an atrocious Brahmincide filled the murderer himself with remorse. "Fie on anger, said he, fie on wine!" He accordingly undertook a pilgrimage to the Pratilomá Saraswatí with a view to expiate his guilt.

The fourth question gave the birds an opportunity of recounting the story of Haris'chandra, a king of the Solar race, who had been put to great trouble by the Ṛishi Vis'wámitra. The Vis'we-devás, five in number, indignant at the hardships inflicted on the good king, heaped reproaches on the proud priest who had caused such sufferings. Brahmins are never forbearing when harshly spoken to. Vis'wámitra punished the insolence of the five gods by pronouncing a malediction to the effect that they should have to endure the disgrace of *human* existence on the earth. A Brahmin's malediction strikes terror even into gods. The Vis'we-devas, accordingly, humbled by such a tremendous curse, entreated the Ṛishi to withdraw the anathema. But this was simply impossible, for a word, once uttered by a Brahmin, must have its fulfilment. Vis'wámitra so far consoled the terrified gods as to promise that, though condemned to live as men, they would be freed from the defilement of human matrimony. When therefore they were subsequently born of Draupadí, they were suffered to fall in infancy as victims to an assassin's barbarity. Thus were the problems solved which had distracted the mind of Jaimini. But he now propounded fresh questions, relating to the conception, preservation, and growth of animal life in the mother's womb—and to the separation of body and soul at death. The experience of good and evil as the fruits of actions was also referred to, but it was mixed up with the physical question why those fruits could not be consumed in the womb.

The feathered sages considered these questions to be "immensely heavy," and, without attempting any answers that might pretend to originality, began to recount a dialogue which once had taken place between a father and a son, both Brahmins, but the latter transcendentally wise, and therefore far superior to his parent. Here commences, in our opinion, the *second* section, for it introduces characters, and treats of subjects, altogether different from the first. In the conversation between father and son, we lose sight, almost completely, of Jaimini and his winged friends. The birds are indeed supposed to be the narrators, but there is no further notice either of them or of Jaimini until toward the end of the section, and then they reappear only to call in the hero of the next division. The first section accordingly finds its completion at the end of chapter 9 page 73.

2. The second section, although it introduces other interlocuters, who at times long occupy our attention, professes to be a dialogue between the Brahmins just referred to. This conversation between father and son was occasioned by the former calling upon the latter to study the Vedas as became a young Brahmin. The boy declared he had no need of the Vedas. He was already perfected in knowledge. He knew all the previous stages of life through which he had passed. He had existed as a Brahmin, a Kshetriya, a Vais'ya, and a S'údra, as a beast and a worm, as a deer and a bird, as a king's courtier and a king's enemy. He had experienced servitude as well as lordliness, he had killed many and had in turn

been killed by many. "Therefore, said he, to me, already grown wise, of what use are the Vedas?" (p 75)

The father was struck by his son's wisdom and asked him various questions which the boy readily undertook to answer. He treated of physics, morals, and theology. "The corporeal air, or gas, called *udána*, determines upward."—"He who has distributed food with a pure mind is then (at the time of death) gratified even without food. He that has not spoken untruth, nor caused a breach of amity, the faithful believer, meets a happy death. Those who have been intent on the worship of gods and Brahmins, the fair, the charitable, and the shamefaced, die happily." "Those who have not given away water, nor distributed food, endure, on the approach of death, burning thirst and hunger." A terrific description follows of the pangs and sufferings of wicked and irreligious men inflicted by the officers of Yáma. The false witness, or perjurer, has his portion in a hell called *Raurava*. "There a hole is dug to the depth of a man's knee for sixteen thousand miles. It is filled up with burning coals to the level of the ground. The officers of Yama cast the wicked man on that ground, thus blazing with fire. Scorched and burnt by the terrific flames, the wretched man has no rest, but runs frantic over the place, the soles of his feet being at every step scalded and bruised. Day and night he thus goes on, alternately setting and taking off his feet. When he has gone over eight thousand miles in this way, he is released from the torment, but only to enter another infernal region for the purging of his sins." After these sufferings he is allowed once more to experience terrestrial life. But he has to begin as a worm, an insect, a cricket, or a musquito, and rises gradually to be an ox or a horse. If he attains afterwards to the state of humanity, he commences career humpbacked, deformed, or a dwarf, is then promoted to the condition of a Chaṇḍâla or Pukkasha, and may at last become a S'ùdra, a Vais'ya, or a Kshetriya,—and perhaps ultimately a Brahmin.

It is remarkable that the S'ùdra is here classed with the Vais'ya and Kshetriya, and the Brahmin distinguished by a broad line from all three. In the primitive age of Brahminism, the priests, warriors, and merchants were classed together as the three regenerate classes, and the S'ùdras were far-distanced from them all as serfs. It is comparatively in recent times that the Sùdras rose to consequence and importance, and began to be classed with the Vais'yas and Kshetriyas, while the Brahmins were further distanced from the two intermediate orders by reason of the latter not caring for privileges which once had excited the ambition of a Vis'wâmitra and a Janaka.

The description of the *enjoyments* of those who practise virtue is equally graphic with that of the sufferings of the wicked. They are regaled with the songs af Gandharvas and the dances of Apsarases, and are conducted in chariots amid the sweet sounds of anklets, adorned with sparkling necklaces and garlands. And after these enjoyments, when they return to this land of the living, they are born in one of the superior castes.

The all-sapient boy goes on describing other scenes of torment where specific crimes meet with specific punishments. He introduces, among other interlocuters, an officer of Yama himself, who gives fearful details of his master's penal code. "Those who have looked on their neighbours' wives with an evil eye, or have cast avaricious glances on their neighbours' goods, have their eyes plucked from their sockets by birds with bills as hard as thunderbolts." This pain is not once inflicted for all, for directly one pair of optics is thus wrenched away, another is immediately produced to undergo the same torment. This process of torture continues "as many thousands of years as were the winks of the sinner's eyelids, while committing the crime for which he is punished." Those, again, "who either gave or instigated instruction of wicked Śástras, those who contradicted the (true) śástras, or uttered wicked words, who reviled the Vedas or the gods, Brahmins or their *gurus*, have their tongues plucked away (by the birds mentioned before) and reproduced (for the continuance of the torture)." Some crimes are punished by sawing, others by splitting the body in two, others again by splitting the tongue. The descriptions are terrific, and, in many cases, shockingly indelicate.

This little hero of a Brahmin goes on instructing his father until the end of the 44th chapter (p 254) when he disappears, and Jaimini acknowledges his obligations to his winged friends for the edification he had received by the recital.

And now Jaimini propounds other questions again. "How was this world with its moveables and immoveables created? How again at the dissolution they all pass away. Whence were the gods, Ṛishis, fathers, and other creatures produced?" He inquires into chronology, geography and history—the duration of *manwantaras* and *kalpás*,—the earth, its dimensions, and the mountains rivers and forests on its surface,—the upper and the lower worlds, together with "the motions of the sun, moon, stars planets, and other luminaries."

The birds, all-sapient as they were, felt the *weight* of

these questions to be unusually heavy, perhaps still more so than the second set that Jaimini had proposed. Geography, astronomy, chronology were all involved in them. They did not however shrink from an answer. They told the querist that the great Ṛishi Márcaṇḍeya had on a previous occasion unfolded to one Kraushṭuki the very mysteries which Jaimini was desirous of learning. They did not refer him back to Márcaṇḍeya who had originally sent him to them, but offered to relate all that the latter had spoken. Thus was introduced as an interlocuter the Ṛishi from whom the Puráṇa derived its name.

In the first forty four chapters Márcaṇḍeya bears scarcely any part in the acts of this Puráṇa. He comes in properly at the forty-fifth chapter, and, notwithstanding the episode of the Deví-Máhátmya, continues the principal speaker to the end of the book. Indeed the birds who introduced him disappear altogether after this. We hear nothing of them or of Jaimini when Márcaṇḍeya has once begun his narration, as far at least as the *Gauḍíya* manuscripts are concerned. This narration forms, in our opinion, another section in which commences the second division of the work.

II, 3. Márcaṇḍeya begins with Brahmá himself, the first-born among the gods. "As soon as Brahmá of mysterious origin was produced, this Puráṇa and the Vedas issued from his heads. The great Ṛishis compiled many *Puráṇa-sanhitás.* Sections of the Vedas were also made by them a thousand fold."

Márcaṇḍeya then makes his salutation to Brahmá before he enters in detail on the subject of Kraushṭuki's inquiry. This salutation differs in one essential respect from that of the first section. The principal god saluted by the birds was Vásudeva. That divinity is not recognized at all in this invocation. It is addressed to "the uncreated and indestructible origin and support of the universe, the upholder of the world with its moveables and immoveables, to Brahmá, the primeval *purusha*." Brahmá alone is here addressed, plainly showing that the sections preceding were composed, or at least recast, at a later period, when the doctrine of the supreme Vásudeva was introduced. The solemn invocation at the commencement of the section is a further proof of this division having originally been considered as complete in itself.

The account of the creation given in this Puráṇa is, like that of most others, highly tinctured with the Sánkhya theory of Prakṛiti. "The *Pradhána*, or chief cause, is called Invisible; it is the same which the great Ṛishis have styled the subtle and eternal prakṛiti, both an entity and a non-entity. It is true, indestructible, undecaying, incomprehensible, and independent or devoid of other support. It is destitute of smell colour, taste, sound, and feeling. It is the origin of the world, without beginning and without end, itself composed of the three Guṇas, and inscrutable. It existed before Brahmá. After the general dissolution, the world was formed by it. In consequence of the equableness of the guṇas, of the intelligent one presiding over it, of the production of the guṇas again at the creation, the wonderful element pradhána contains the *mahán* or great principle." This theory of the creation is manifestly based on the Sánkhya philosophy and almost involves the very atheism of Kapila. The whole is traced to prakṛiti or nature. The process of creation is also in accordance with that system. From Prakṛiti, otherwise called pradhána, we have the Mahat; from mahat, Ahankára; from ahankára, the five *tanmátras,* and the five elements. From the same ahankára, again, proceed the understanding and the senses. From these products of nature proceeds "an egg which gradually increases like a water bubble." It is the great egg of the creation, lying in water. "In that prákṛita or natural egg, the intelligent one called Brahmá grows. He is the first embodied person, he is called purusha. He is the original creator of all things, subsisting in the beginning." "In that egg remained the whole universe, with gods, demons, and men, continents, mountains, oceans, and luminaries."

Márcaṇḍeya further explains the process of creation: "When the whole of this universe finds its dissolution in prakṛiti, it is called by the learned a resolution in nature. The Invisible subsisting then by itself, and the development being then re-enveloped, prakṛiti and purusha remain in their own proper states. Then the qualities of darkness and goodness continue in a state of equability, neither in excess nor in deficiency. As oil subsists in the sesamum, or butter in milk, so does the quality of activity in darkness and in goodness. As many as are the days of Brahmá, that is two parárdhas,* so many are the days of the supreme Lord, and of such duration also is his night in the state of dissolution. But the incomprehensible Supreme Spirit, the cause of all things, subsisting before the universe, himself without beginning, "awaking at the commencement of his day, he, the Lord of the world, the great God, quickly entering Prakṛiti and Purusha, excited them by means of his great *yoga,* or contemplation. As

* 200000000000000000.

exhilaration in the case of young women, as the vernal breeze of Vaiśákha, when once entered, tends to excitement, so is that incarnation of yoga. On Pradhána being excited, the divinity styled Brahmá is produced in the egg as already related to you. He, the lord of Prakṛiti, is the original exciter, he is also himself excited. He remains as Pradhána by contraction and expansion. That origin of the world being produced, though himself without qualities, yet partaking of the quality of passion, is moved to the act of creation, subsisting as Brahmá. Having, as Brahmá, created the world, he obtains an excess of the quality of goodness, and, becoming Vishṇu, maintains the universe in justice. And at last the quality of darkness becoming excessive, he becomes Rudra, and having drawn in (i. e. destroyed) the whole universe of three worlds, lies down, endowed with the three qualities, and yet devoid of them. As first expanding, then maintaining, then again destroying, he obtains successively the names of Brahmá, Vishṇu, and I'śa. As Brahmá he creates the world, as Rudra he destroys, as Vishṇu he is inactive. These are the three states of the Self-existent."

We cannot help noticing in this place the dignity imparted to the work under review. It is classed in the same category with the Vedas, and described as an immediate product from Brahma's mouth. Although a Puráṇa, it is not attributed to Vyása, whom other Śástras consider as the author of all works bearing that title. The Márcaṇḍeya however does not acknowledge him as its composer, editor, or compiler. It claims equal honor in this respect with the Vedas themselves.

Professor Wilson says in the Preface to his translation of the Vishṇu Puráṇa: "The Puráṇas are uniformly "stated to be eighteen in number. It is said that there "are also eighteen Upa-purāṇas, or minor Purāṇas; but "the names of only a few of these are specified in the "least exceptionable authorities, and the greater number "of the works is not procurable. With regard to the "eighteen Purāṇas, there is a peculiarity in their specifica-"tion, which is proof of an interference with the integrity "of the text, in some of them at least; for each of them "specifies the names of the whole eighteen. Now the "list could not have been complete whilst the work that "gives it was unfinished, and in one only therefore, the "last of the series, have we a right to look for it. As "however there are more last words than one, it is evident "that the names must have been inserted in all except "one after the whole were completed: which of the "eighteen is the exception, and truly the last, there is no "clue to discover, and the specification is probably an in-"terpolation in most, if not in all."

As far as we have seen *Bengal Manuscripts*, the Márcaṇḍeya presents a singular exception to this hackneyed enumeration of the eighteen Purăṇas, and the celebration of Vyăsa's name as the author of them all. The Maithila manuscripts, as they are commonly called, are not so chaste. We have appended the concluding section from a manuscript of that class which recounts, in the ordinary way, the number of the eighteen Purăṇas.

But to return to our Digest. After relating the production of Brahmă, Mărcaṇḍeya goes on with the procession of all other creatures from him. The Asuras issued from his loins receiving bodies pervaded by darkness. The gods were produced from his head by the predominance of the quality of goodness. Men were created by the prevalence of the quality of activity, or rather *passion*. The bodies of the gods, demons, *pitṛis*, and men were severally emblematic of Day, Night, Twilight, and Moonlight. "The gods by day, the demons by night, men by moonlight, and the *pitris* by twilight are therefore most powerful, and become invincible."

After dwelling at large on the productions of men, gods, and demons, Mărcaṇḍeya gives the periods of time called *Yugas* and *Manwantaras*. Six of these manwantaras, he says, have already passed, viz. those of Swă yambhuva, Swarochis, Auttama, Tămas, Raivata, and Chăkshusha. We are now in that of Vaivaswata. Seven more are yet in the womb of futurity. The learned sage proceeds to relate the most important events that occurred in the manwantaras which are passed. He says the seven continents were parcelled out between the seven sons of Piryavrata in the first manwantara. This leads him to settle the geography of the seven continents and of their subdivisions, the *varshas*. He defines the land in which we are breathing at this moment as the Jambudwipa, and the Bhăratavarsha.

Many mountains and rivers are here named, most of which appear to be different peaks and branches of some noted ranges and streams. It is impossible to identify them all. Many countries nations and towns are also given of which we possess no information as to their history or locality. The unknown are however so mixed up with the known that at times we feel quite tantalized in our efforts to discover the former by means of the latter.

Coming down, in order, to the Săvarṇa manwantara, the Ṛishi takes occasion to introduce the *Devi-măhătmya*. This is an episode altogether unconneced with what precedes and follows it. There is also a transition from Mărcaṇḍeya to another Ṛishi as the chief interlocuter. Here therefore we must mark a new Section.

4. The Deví-Măhátmya bears the most evident marks of an interpolation. A Rájā is abruptly introduced going in company with a Vais'ya, whom he had accidentally encountered in a forest, to put certain questions to a Ṛishi on the mysteries of human passions and affections. The Vais'ya is represented as a person, once possessed of immense wealth but since despoiled by dependents, and expelled from home by his wife and children. Notwithstanding the ill treatment to which he was thus subjected, his heart still beat with a father's and a husband's affection. In the midst of his personal sufferings his chief concern was, not for self, but for the ungrateful household that had, by their unnatural conduct, turned him from a wealthy citizen into a homeless exile. He could not be happy in the absence of those for whom his bowels continued to yearn as before. He had for a long time remained without tidings of his family. This ignorance of their welfare rendered him extremely uneasy. " I can not tell why, said he, but my mind is still moved by lovefor those whom I know to be wicked and undeserving." The Raja's philosophical curiosity was excited. Why should human nature be subject to such mental perturbations ? Why should an injured man be in such a moral plight ? He was conscious in his own case of the attachment he bore to his kingdom and its members, well knowing that such attachment was not for the tranquillity of his mind. He accordingly asked the Ṛishi what could be the secret of such moral anomalies.

The Ṛishi told the king that the world is under the

fascination of the great Delusion of Hari by which human passions and affections are created. The illustrious goddess captivates the minds even of the wise. She is at the same time both the eternal wisdom by which liberation may be effected, and the delusion by which the bondage of the world is encompassed. The Raja then inquires: "Who, O Lord, is that goddess whom you call the Great Delusion? How was she produced, and what are her acts? Of what nature is she, what essence, and from whom did she emanate"?

The Ṛishi replies, "Eternal is she, the form of the world, by whom is all this universe stretched out. She has still been produced in many ways. Whensoever for accomplishing the objects of the gods, she manifests herself, she is said to be produced, though eternal." We are then told how this goddess had originally saved Brahmá from the destructive rage of two demons Madhu and Kaiṭabha. This story is followed by a narrative of the death of Mahishásura, a demon who had discomfited all the gods and expelled them from paradise. The gods, thus forced to wander like mortals on the face of the earth, had recourse to Brahmà, Vishṇu, and S'iva, and these were filled with the greatest indignation at the audacity of the demon. A fiery light issued from their faces when in this state of fury. A similar light or energy simultaneously proceeded from all the other divinities. "This unprecedented energy, emanating from the bodies of all the gods, produced, by concentration, a female, filling the three worlds with her brilliance." The sage describes in detail the different limbs produced by processions from the different gods, who then severally furnished the creature of their joint emanations with the weapons and implements peculiar to each. Thus produced, furnished, and equipped, and riding on a lion, the goddess gave free exercise to her risible sensibilities. "The whole sky was filled with the sound of her laughter, and the echoe was tremendous. All the worlds were thereby moved, and the seas were agitated. The earth quaked, and so did all the mountains. To her, thus riding on a lion, the gods joyfully said, 'prosper.' The Munis, meekspirited by faith, paid their adorations. The enemies of the gods seeing the three worlds thus agitated, armed themselves, and advanced with their forces in battle array. Mahishásura, crying out in his rage, 'Ah what is this'! ran in the direction of the sound, surrounded by innumerable demons."

The demons soon encountered the Deví, when a terrible conflict took place. On the one side fought the goddess, single-handed, if the phrase may be used in the case of a ten-armed combatant—assisted only by her favourite beast the lion. On the other, were demons whose numbers in men, chariots, horses, elephants, and arms baffled the highest terms in European numeration. But the goddess prevailed to the unspeakable joy of the celestials. The rout of the enemy was as complete as was their destruction terrific. "Some were cut asunder by strokes of sharp swords, others, felled by blows of clubs, were buried in the earth. Some were throwing up blood under repeated strokes of the pestle, others fell pierced in the chest by the javalin, others again sank under showers of darts. Some lost their arms, others their heads, others again were cut asunder in the middle. Some great asuras fell, their legs being carried off, some were split in two by the Deví, each (oblong) part having one hand one eye and one leg." "Thus did the Deví destroy in a moment the great army of the Asuras, even as fire consumes in a moment a heap of straw and fuel."

The next encounter was with the chief of the demons, Mahishásura himself. He advanced furious with rage, assuming different forms, now an elephant, now a buffaloe. The goddess fought him with the aid of her lion. She called up her energies by copious drink, and, laughing with reddened eyes, railed at him, thus; "Roar, roar, thou fool, while I drink my wine. The gods will presently roar in turn on my slaying thee." She then sprang upon him and after a short struggle cut off his head.

This struggle of the goddess with Mahishásura is annually commemorated in Bengal at the festival called the Durgá-pújá. The goddess is there represented with ten arms, trampling upon the demon, who is also attacked by her lion, and wounded in the chest by her spear. She has also laid hold of him by the hair, and is about to chop off his head.

The most popular commemoration of this event takes place in the autumn about the time of the equinox, and if the practice may be supposed to be eight hundred or a thousand years old, it is not inconceivable that it was originally fixed *at the equinox*, though the *precession* has since made it a few days later. The calculation of the day depends however on a certain lunar day. But it can never be earlier than the seventh of A'swin, which is about the time of our present equinox, nor can it be more than a month later than that date

The idea of the possible connection of the Durgá-pújá with the equinox is suggested by the fact that there is a corresponding festival about the time of the vernal equinox too, in which, though it is not so popular as the autumnal púja, the same group of figures is constructed, and the image of the goddess is in the same attitude, with the same attendants and the same enemy. It is her struggle with Mahishásura that is then commemorated too. The two pùjás, called respectively the vernal and the autumnal, are performed with the same rites and ceremonies, occupying each the same same number of days—although the former is less known, because it has not attained the popularity enjoyed by the latter. And the calculations of the days in the two cases have precisely the same relation to the two equinoxes.

The *Deví-máhátmya* goes on relating another contest in which the goddess engaged with two demon-kings called S'umbha and Nis'umbha. These asuras had likewise discomfited the gods and reduced them to utter destitution. The gods presented their supplications to her for relief. The struggle was brought about by her displaying the elegance of her form and the attractions of her person before Chaṇḍa and Muṇḍa, two servants of S'umbha and Nis'umbha. These men went and reported to their masters that they had seen on the Himálaya a handsome female whose beauty added splendour to the whole mountain. S'umbha on hearing this report of her beauty sent a messenger to call her into his palace. The goddess told the messenger that she had formed the resolution of giving herself away to none but him that could overpower her in personal strength. When this was related to the king, he felt indignant at the impertinence of a weak delicate woman, and sent a hero named *Dhumralochana* with stringent orders to bring the goddess into the palace. The goddess made quick work of the hero, reducing him to ashes by a single turn of her eyes, while her lion destroyed and feasted on the whole army which he had brought with himself. Then came, at the head of a large force, the two servants who had originally seen her at the mount. The appearance of this army threw the Deví into a tremendous passion, when from her head issued a sable goddess, as black in her person as she was furious in her character. This goddess, thus produced, destroyed the army of Chaṇḍa and Muṇḍa, and cut off their heads. The story is annually commemorated in Bengal at the *Kálí-pújá*, which takes place three weeks after Durgá's festival. The sable goddess is represented holding the severed head of Chaṇḍa in her hand, with the heads of his soldiers formed into a garland suspended from her neck, and their hands wreathed into a covering round her loins—the only covering she has, in the image constructed for the pújá.

The worship of Kálí, to which the above narrative has given rise is considered by the Hindus themselves as embodying the principle of *tamas* or darkness. She is represented as delighting in the slaughter of her foes, though capable of kindlier feelings to her friends. She is however styled the black goddess of terror, frequenting cemeteries and presiding over terrible spirtes, fond of bloody sacrifices, and her worship taking place in the darkest night of the month.

After the death of Chaṇḍa and Muṇḍa, the Deví had to fight a demon of the name of Raktavíja, who had a sort of charmed life. Each drop of blood shed from his body had the singular virtue of producing hundreds of demons like himself. The strokes of the goddess's weapons began, therefore, to harrass her own self more than her malignant enemy, and that exactly in proportion to her success. "The demons produced by the Asura's blood infested the whole universe. The gods were sore afraid. Seeing them affrighted, Chaṇḍiká (their heroine) thus spake to Kălí: 'O Chặmuṇḍá, widen your mouth. Drink up quidkly the drops of blood as they are shed by my weapons, and go about the battle-field devouring the great asuras produced by blood. Thus will the demon, exhausted of blood, come to destruction. When these are all devoured, no others can then arise.' Thus saying the goddess struck him (Raktavíja) with the spear, when Kálí received his blood into her mouth. The wounded hero bled profusely, and Chámuṇḍá received all the blood into her mouth. As to those demons produced by the blood in her mouth, she ate them up and drank their blood. Thus fell Raktavíja, the great Asura, on the earth, wounded by various weapons, his blood drunk up by Chámuṇḍá."

Two more contests, still more furious than the preceding, were entered into by the goddess. They were with the brother chiefs, S'umbha and Nis'umbha, with whose death the Deví-máhátmya concludes after a long doxology to the goddess.

5. Márcaṇḍeya now resumes his narration which turns on the annals of kings and heroes. The legends are dry and uninteresting. One peculiarity is that we miss the accounts, usually given in other works, of the two royal families of ancient renown, named respectively after the *sun* and the *moon*. It is interesting however to notice the sort of hold which the transcendental doctrines of the Hindu philosophy had in possession at that time on the Brahminical mind. We are told that the patriarch Ruchi had been troubled with certain ascetic notions in-

compatible with the undisturbed enjoyment of worldly life. He was bent too much on the mortification of the senses. For the cure of his melancholy, the *pitṛis,* or deceased ancestors, found it necessary to pay him a preternatural visit on the earth. "Why, O child, said they, hast thou not entered into the holy state of matrimony? That is the true cause of Heaven and emancipation. Without it, there must be perpetual bondage. The house-holder, by his adoration of gods, pitṛis, ṛishis, and strangers, gets into happy worlds." The pitṛis concluded with an eloquent appeal to their surviving son to discharge the duties of terrestrial life. Ruchi said in reply that marriage was a cause of trouble and sin, that the subjugation of the spirit, so necessary for attaining emancipation, was incompatible with the state of matrimony, that the soul, though besmeared with the mud of selfishness, is daily washed by the waters of the understanding in single life, that the wise, with their senses subdued, should clear with the waters of pure ideas the soul already soiled with the works of many previous worlds."

The fathers rejoined: "It is indeed proper that men with subdued senses should purify the soul, and your way may be for emancipation. But evil is averted by gifts free from aims, and past actions are requited by good and evil fruits and experiences. Thus there is no bondage to one who performs merciful acts. Nor are such acts for bondage, if done without aims. Virtuous and vicious acts of past existences are consumed, O child, by the experience of happiness and misery. In this manner the wise cleanse their souls and save themselves from bondage, nor are they defiled by non-discrimination and the stain of sin."

Ruchi again said, "O Fathers, the way of works is called *avidyá,* or ignorance, in the Vedas. How then can you exhort me to enter that path ?"

The fathers thus solved this problem : "True it is that works are ignorance, this is not a false saying. Nevertheless works are necessary for the acquisition of knowledge. The mortification practised, with a view to emancipation, by wicked men who neglect the prescribed duties, leads them at length to infernal regions. Thou thinkest, O child, that thou art cleansing thy soul, but in truth thou art being soiled with sin from the neglect of prescribed duties. Even ignorance, like poision, is for the good of men." Arguments, such as these, produced conviction in the mind of Ruchi, and the deceased fathers vanished at once, "like a lamp blown out by the wind," and their terrestrial son succeeded, after the most gallant efforts, in obtaining a bride, and became the father of a hero named Rauchya.

The remainder of the Puráṇa is a repetition of the process of creation, and the rise of the early patriarchs, interspersed with devotional addresses, after the Magian model, to the sun and to fire, and giving the legendary annals of the age, until the time of a king named Dama. Professor Wilson considers this as rather an abrupt termination, and suggests the possibility of its being only the first part of the Puráṇa, though there is no second or supplementary part extant.

We incline to the opinion that no Puráṇa was composed in its integrity in the same age, or by the same person, excepting only the sectarian ones like the Srí Bhágavata. That the Márcaṇḍeya, which is certainly not sectarian, was not composed in its integrity by the same person and in the same age, appears from the different sentiments and the different characters introduced in the several sections into which we have divided it. In the first section the Supreme divinity is Vásudeva, a name unknown in the other sections, and never occurring on the various occasions on which different heroes invoked their several objects of faith, reverence, or fear. In the second section we do not notice any effort to magnify a particular divinity, although fearful torments are described as awaiting the revilers of gods, Brahmins, and Vedas. This was probably one among many attempts made by the Brahmins to resist the influence of Buddhism or prevent a relapse on the part of those whom they had reclaimed. The third section is principally devoted to chronology, history, and geography, and the supreme divinity that appears in it is no other than ancient Brahmá. This section appears to us to be the oldest part of the Puráṇa. It may be, for aught we know to the contrary, very old. The Deví máhátmya which is our fourth section, is as we have already said evidently an interpolation. The fifth section is, like the third, chiefly historical.

To what extent these historical annals contain any thing that is true is a question of no small difficulty. Authentic history of course there is none. That is out of the question here. There is nothing in any of the Puráṇas to which we can give credence on the *authority* of the narrators. The accounts are far more incredible, and have far less authenticity, than the most incredible portions of early Roman history. Still the question is whether these incoherent and extravagant annals were absolute fabrications, or whether any facts may be found embedded in them.

We are disinclined to believe that they were absolute fabrications. What could be the meaning—what the objects of the authors in such a case? They are not tales such as are those of Rasselas and the vicar of Wakefield. There is no plot—no finish—no humor—no wit in them. What object could the authors propose to themselves when they took up their pens to compose such voluminous unpoetical *poems*—for the Puráṇas are poetry, if mere versification can entitle a work to such a dignified appellation.

On a question beset with so many difficulties even a possible theory may be entertained. We incline to the belief that the Puráṇas were composed in detached pieces by various persons, who exercised their poetical genius, or rather their powers of versification, after the manner of bards in Anglo-Saxon times, on the events of the day, or on past events reported by tradition. These they embellished, or rather distorted, as taste or interest dictated. In this manner were the historical portions composed. The ethical and theological sections were, after the fashion of Vishṇus'arma's Hitopades'a, often illustrated by tales without the slightest element of truth in them. Such appears to have been the story of the *satí*, or dutiful wife, who herself carried her loathsomely diseased and perfectly unprincipled husband to a harlot, his mistress, thinking that the duty of a wife was to please her husband in everything.

In respect of chronology the bards thought it but a moderate exaggeration to turn an unit into a million. This idea is found to influence all their numerical descriptions. Whether it be the equipments of an army, or the furniture of a palace, or gifts made at a wedding or a solemn sacrifice, the animals and chariots are more than the products of the soil could sustain, or human labour manufacture. Of all the descriptions of the Purāṇas it is in their numerical delineations that the smallest element of truth is found.

It may here be asked who were the gods, demi-gods, and demons, spoken of in all Brahminical writings. Of the gods some were personifications of the elements and heavenly bodies, and some were perhaps certain highly favoured and opulent A'rya monarchs. The demi-gods were probably such among the aboriginal inhabitants of the country as were in alliance with the A'ryas, and the demons were no doubt their enemies. The Gandharvas, Kinnaras, Yakshas, Siddhas were among the former, while the Daityas, Asuras, and Rákshases were among the latter.

But who were the Nágas? In some respects they are represented as men, and in some as snakes. They had corporeal constitutions capable of (sexually) attracting and being attracted by human beings, and yet they were not without the serpentine furniture of the hood and the venomous fang. The word *nágas* is evidently the same as the *náchas* of Genesis, and we feel no difficulty in recognizing, in the Brahminical mythology, a confirmation of the Biblical account of the serpent, which was originally perhaps a species corresponding to the nága of the Brahmins, before the sentence was pronounced by which it became a creeping reptile.

Of the allegorical descriptions in the Purāṇas, the Deví-máhátmya presents a singular example. It is difficult to imagine what the Brahmins could mean by representing the discomfiture of the asuras by a single youthful lady. It has been supposed that the appearance of Semiramis on the banks of the Indus probably suggested the tale. But, to say nothing of the mythical character of Semiramis herself, the retreat of a foreign enemy was not likely to be commemorated by the fabrication of a triumphant goddess. If the Brahmins had thought of preserving some recollections of the Babylonian queen in their literature, they would more probably have given her the sort of celebrity which Táḍaká, or Súrpanakhá the sister of Rávaṇa, enjoys in the Rámáyaṇa, or Putaná in the S'rí Bhágavata.

The Deví-máhátmya appears to be altogether allegorical. The goddess was produced by the concentration of the energies of all the gods, and furnished with the weapons for which they were severally conspicuous. Supposing that the etherials had a quarrel with the demons and that after many signal defeats, separately sustained, they had thought of the wisdom of uniting their forces, and had formed a general confederacy by which the Asuras were vanquished,—how could an imaginative Brahmin describe the fact more felicitously than by means of the allegory of the Deví-máhátmya. The union of their forces and resources furnished the gods with a *power*, (the goddess has among other names that of Sácti) which the demons could not resist.

We have followed the *Gauḍíya*, or Bengal manuscripts, in this edition. The Maithila manuscripts present in many instances various readings of which the most remarkable is that which we have placed separately at the end. From the 28th s'loka of chapter 135 that reading entirely diverges from Bengal manuscripts. We find no more convergence between the two even to the end of the book.

This divergence is a remarkable fact and may afford important evidence as to the extent to which the Puráṇa is genuine. We have already referred to the opinion of of Professor Wilson that the Puráṇa is incomplete because of its abrupt conclusion. He must have based his opinion on a consideration of Bengal manuscripts, for therein the conclusion is certainly abrupt. Take the various lection, however, with which Maithila manuscripts supplement the Puráṇa, and the conclusion is not so abrupt.

The abrupt conclusion of Bengal manuscripts is to us an evidence of their comparative purity. If our theory be correct that the Puráṇas are compilations of detached memoranda, their abrupt conclusion can be no more wonderful than the abrupt conclusion of a person's journal, in which the diaries were entered at different times and on different occasions; and the greater the abruptness of the conclusion, the less is the suspicion of after-embellishment.

The Bengal manuscripts, as we have already said, do not contain the foolish and hackneyed enumeration of the eighteen Puráṇas, and of Vyása their common parent, which can serve only to detract from their value as historical guides. There are however seven slokas at the end on the glory of the Márcaṇḍeya which are no doubt an interpolation. Setting these aside, the Puráṇa concludes with the words, "Dama (the king) said nothing to his father's enemies when they were put to the flight." This may have been the last entry of the annalist who worte this Puráṇa. If we accept it as the conclusion, and discard the supplement of the Maithila manuscripts, we may, again, have some light thrown on the introductory part of the Puráṇa.

The introductory part, or what we have called our

first section, brings before us doctrines and characters of an after age to which no allusion is made in the body of the Puráṇa. In this interpolation Bengal manuscripts concur with the Maithila. But the simplicity of the Bengal interpolater, not sufficiently drilled in the manœuvres of Mithilá, betrays the secret. The introductory interpolation was evidently made without advertence to the conclusion. The winged sages and Jaimini were brought in for the purpose of broaching the doctrine of the quadruple form of Vásudeva, and for pacifying the Brahminical conscience still smarting under the polyandry of Draupadí, and the outrageous conduct of Balaráma. The interpolaters however forgot to wind up the conclusion consistently with their introduction. The birds are the living speakers, according to that introduction, and Jaimini the auditor. To make the interpolation complete and consistent, the birds and Jaimini ought to take leave of us when the curtain drops. Of them, however, there is no trace in Bengal manuscripts at the end.

The Maithila writers afterwards discovered and rectified the error, in the supplement of which we have spoken. But the omission in Bengal manuscripts, while it testifies to their comparative purity, opens our eyes to the whole interpolation. We are thereby emboldened to hazard the assertion that the Puráṇa, or compilation of legends, which has become noted under the name of Márcaṇḍeya commenced originally at chapter 45, where Márcaṇḍeya himself appears as the living speaker, and extends to chapter 137, where that living speaker removes from our sight. The first two sections, where the birds are the speakers and Jaimini the auditor, are interpolations, like the Deví-Máhátmya.

KUMAR NARENDRA KRISHNA * RAI BAHADUR *

मार्कण्डेय पुराणं ॥

प्रथमोऽध्यायः ।

श्रोंनमोभगवते वासुदेवाय ॥

यद्योगिभिर्भवभयार्त्तिविनाशयोग्य-
मासाद्य वन्दितमतीव विविक्तचित्तैः ।
तद्वः पुनातु हरिपादसरोजयुग्म-
माविर्भवत्क्रमविलङ्घितभूर्भुवःस्वः ॥ १ ॥
पायात् स वः सकलकल्मषभेददक्षः
क्षीरोदकुक्षिफणिभोगनिविष्टमूर्त्तिः ।
श्वासावधूतसलिलोत्कणिकाकरालः
सिन्धुः प्रनृत्यमिव यस्य करोति सङ्गात् ॥ २ ॥

नारायणं नमस्कृत्य नरञ्चैव नरोत्तमं ।
देवीं सरस्वतीं व्यासं ततो जयमुदीरयेत् ॥

तपःस्वाध्यायनिरतं मार्कण्डेयं महामुनिं ।
व्यासशिष्यो महातेजा जैमिनिः पर्य्यपृच्छत ॥ १ ॥
भगवन् भारताख्यानं व्यासेनोक्तं महात्मना ।
पूर्णमस्तमलैः शुभ्रैर्नानाशास्त्रसमुच्चयैः ॥ २ ॥
जातिशुद्धिसमायुक्तं साधुशब्दोपशोभितं ।
पूर्व्वपक्षोक्तिसिद्धान्तपरिनिष्ठासमन्वितं ॥ ३ ॥

त्रिदशानां यथा विष्णुर्द्विपदां ब्राह्मणो यथा।
भूषणानाञ्च सर्वेषां यथा चूड़ामणिर्वरः॥ ४ ॥
यथायुधानां कुलिशमिन्द्रियाणां यथा मनः।
तथेह सर्व्वशास्त्राणां महाभारतमुत्तमं॥ ५ ॥
अत्रार्थश्चैव धर्मश्च कामो मोक्षश्च वर्ण्यते।
परस्परानुबन्धाश्च सानुबन्धाश्च ते पृथक्॥ ६ ॥
धर्मशास्त्रमिदं श्रेष्ठ मर्थशास्त्रमिदं परं।
कामशास्त्रमिदं चाग्र्य मोक्षशास्त्रं तथोत्तमं॥ ७ ॥
चतुराश्रमधर्माणामाचारस्थितिसाधनं।
प्रोक्तमेतन्महाभाग वेदव्यासेन धीमता॥ ८ ॥
तथा तात कृतं ह्येतद्व्यासेनोदारकर्मणा।
यथा व्याप्तं महाशास्त्रं विरोधैर्नाभिभूयते॥ ९ ॥
व्यासवाक्यजलौघेन कुतर्कतरुहारिणा।
वेदशैलावतीर्णेन नीरजस्का मही कृता॥ १० ॥
कलशब्दमहाहंसं महाख्यानपराम्बुजं।
कथाविस्तीर्णसलिलं कार्ष्णं वेदमहाह्रदं॥ ११ ॥
तदिदं भारताख्यानं बह्वर्थं श्रुतिविस्तरं।
तत्त्वतो ज्ञातुकामोऽहं भगवंस्त्वामुपस्थितः॥ १२॥
कस्मान्मानुषतां प्राप्तोनिर्गुणोऽपि जनार्दनः।
वासुदेवो जगत्सूतिस्थितिसंयमकारणं॥ १३ ॥
कस्माच्च पाण्डुपुत्राणामेका सा द्रुपदात्मजा।
पञ्चानां महिषी कृष्णा ह्यत्र नः संशयोमहान्॥ १४ ॥

भेषजं ब्रह्महत्यायाबलदेवो महाबलः ।
तीर्थयात्राप्रसङ्गेन कस्माच्चक्रे हलायुधः ॥ १५ ॥
कथञ्च द्रौपदेयास्तेऽकृतदारा महारथाः ।
पाण्डुनाथा महात्मानो बधमापुरनाथवत् ॥ १६ ॥
एतत् सर्वं विस्तरशो ममाख्यातुमिहार्हसि ।
भवन्तो मूढबुद्धीनामवबोधकराः सदा ॥ १७ ॥
इति तस्य वचः श्रुत्वा मार्कण्डेयो महामुनिः ।
दशाष्टदोषरहितो वक्तुं समुपचक्रमे ॥ १८ ॥

मार्कण्डेय उवाच ॥

क्रियाकालोऽयमस्माकं संप्राप्तो मुनिसत्तम ।
विस्तरे चापि वक्तव्ये नैष कालः प्रशस्यते ॥ १९ ॥
ये तु वक्ष्यन्ति वक्ष्येऽद्य तानहं जैमिने तव ।
तथा च नष्टसन्देहं त्वां करिष्यन्ति पक्षिणः ॥ २० ॥
पिङ्गाक्षश्च विबोधश्च सुपत्रः सुमुखस्तथा ।
द्रोणपुत्राः खगश्रेष्ठास्तत्त्वज्ञाः शास्त्रचिन्तकाः ॥ २१ ॥
वेदशास्त्रार्थविज्ञाने येषामव्याहता मतिः ।
विन्ध्यकन्दरमध्यस्थास्तानुपास्य च पृच्छ च ॥ २२ ॥
एवमुक्तस्तदा तेन मार्कण्डेयेन धीमता ।
प्रत्युवाचर्षिशार्दूलो विस्मयोत्फुल्ललोचनः ॥ २३ ॥

जैमिनिरुवाच ॥

अत्यद्भुतमिदं ब्रह्मन् खगवागिव मानुषी ।
यत् पक्षिणस्ते विज्ञानमापुरत्यन्तदुर्लभं ॥ २४ ॥

तिर्य्यग्योन्यां यदि भवस्तेषां ज्ञानं कुतोऽभवत्।
कथञ्च द्रोणतनयाः प्रोच्यन्ते ते पतत्रिणः ॥ २५ ॥
कश्च द्रोणः प्रविख्यातो यस्य पुत्रचतुष्टयं।
जातं गुणवतान्तेषां धर्म्मज्ञानं महात्मनां ॥ २६ ॥

मार्कण्डेय उवाच ॥

शृणुष्वावहितो भूत्वा यद्वृत्तं नन्दने पुरा।
शक्रस्याप्सरसाञ्चैव नारदस्य च सङ्गमे ॥ २७ ॥
नारदो नन्दनेऽपश्यत् पुंश्चलीगणमध्यगं।
शक्रं सुराधिराजानं तन्मुखासक्तलोचनं ॥ २८ ॥
स तेनर्षिवरिष्ठेन दृष्टमात्रः शचीपतिः।
समुत्तस्थौ स्वकञ्चास्मै ददावासनमादरात् ॥ २९ ॥
तं दृष्ट्वा बलवृत्रघ्नमुत्थितं त्रिदशाङ्गनाः।
प्रणेमुस्ताश्च देवर्षिं विनयावनताः स्थिताः ॥ ३० ॥
ताभिरभ्यर्च्चितः सोऽथ उपविष्टे शतक्रतौ।
यथार्हं कृतसंभाषः कथाश्चक्रे मनोरमाः ॥ ३१ ॥
ततः कथान्तरे शक्रस्तमुवाच महामुनिं।

शक्र उवाच ॥

देह्याज्ञां नृत्यतामासां तव याभिमतेति वै ॥ ३२ ॥
रम्भा वा कर्कशा वाथ उर्वश्यथ तिलोत्तमा।
घृताची मेनका वापि यत्र वा भवतो रुचिः ॥ ३३ ॥
एतच्छ्रुत्वा द्विजश्रेष्ठोवाचं शक्रस्य नारदः।
विचिन्त्याप्सरसः प्राह विनयावनताः स्थिताः ॥ ३४ ॥

युष्माकमिह सर्वासां रूपौदार्य्यगुणाधिकं ।
आत्मानं मन्यते या तु सा नृत्यतु ममाग्रतः ॥ ३५ ॥
गुणरूपविहीनायाः सिद्धिर्नाट्यस्य नास्ति वै ।
चार्व्वधिष्ठानवन्नृत्यं नृत्यमन्यद्विडम्बनं ॥ ३६ ॥

मार्कण्डेय उवाच ॥

तद्वाक्यसमकालञ्च एकैकास्ता नतास्ततः ।
अहं गुणाधिका न त्वं न त्वं चान्याब्रवीदिदं ॥ ३७ ॥
तासां सम्भ्रममालोक्य भगवान् पाकशासनः ।
पृच्छ्यतां मुनिरित्याह वक्ता यां वो गुणाधिकां ॥ ३८ ॥
शक्रच्छन्दानुयाताभिः पृष्टस्ताभिः स नारदः ।
प्रोवाच यत्तदा वाक्यं जैमिने तन्निबोध मे ॥ ३९ ॥
तपस्यन्तन्नगेन्द्रस्थं या वः क्षोभयते बलात् ।
दुर्व्वाससं मुनिश्रेष्ठं तां वो मन्ये गुणाधिकां ॥ ४० ॥

मार्कण्डेय उवाच ॥

तस्य तद्वचनं श्रुत्वा सर्व्वा वेपितकन्धराः ।
अशक्यमेतदस्माकमिति ताश्चक्रिरे कथाः ॥ ४१ ॥
तत्राप्सरा वपुर्नाम मुनिक्षोभणगर्व्विता ।
प्रत्युवाचानुयास्यामि यत्रासौ संस्थितो मुनिः ॥ ४२ ॥
अद्य तं देहयन्तारं प्रयुक्तेन्द्रियवाजिनं ।
स्मरभ्रस्तगलद्रश्मिं करिष्यामि कुसारथिं ॥ ४३ ॥
ब्रह्मा जनार्दनो वापि यदि वा नीललोहितः ।
तमप्यद्य करिष्यामि कामबाणक्षतान्तरं ॥ ४४ ॥

इत्युक्ता प्रजगामाथ प्रालेयाद्रिं वपुस्तदा ।
मुनेस्तपःप्रभावेण प्रशान्तश्वापदाश्रमं ॥ ४५ ॥
सा पुंस्कोकिलमाधुर्य्यं यत्रास्ते स महामुनिः ।
क्रोशमात्रं स्थिता तस्मादगायत वराप्सराः ॥ ४६ ॥
तद्गीतध्वनिमाकर्ण्य मुनिर्विस्मितमानसः ।
जगाम तत्र यत्रास्ते सा बाला रुचिरानना ॥ ४७ ॥
तां दृष्ट्वा चारुसर्व्वाङ्गीं मुनिः संस्तभ्य मानसं ।
क्षोभणायागतां ज्ञात्वा कोपामर्षसमन्वितः ॥ ४८ ॥
उवाचेदन्ततो वाक्यं महर्षिस्तां महातपाः ॥ ४९ ॥
यस्माद्दुःखार्जितस्येह तपसो विघ्नकारणात् ।
आगतासि मदोन्मत्ते मम दुःखाय खेचरि ॥ ५० ॥
तस्मात् सुपर्णगोत्रे त्वं मत्क्रोधकलुषीकृता ।
जन्म प्राप्स्यसि दुष्प्रज्ञे यावद्वर्षाणि षोडश ॥ ५१ ॥
निजरूपं परित्यज्य पक्षिणीरूपधारिणी ।
चत्वारस्ते च तनयाः निष्पन्तेऽधमाप्सरः ॥ ५२ ॥
अप्राप्य तेषु च प्रीतिं शस्त्रपूता पुनर्दिवि ।
वासमाप्स्यसि वक्तव्यन्नोत्तरन्ते कथञ्चन ॥ ५३ ॥
इति वचनमसह्यं कोपसंरक्तदृष्टि-
श्चलकलवलयान्तां मानिनीं श्रावयित्वा ।
तरलतरतरङ्गां गां परित्यज्य विप्रः
प्रथितगुणगणौघां संप्रयातः खगङ्गां ॥ ५४ ॥

इति मार्कण्डेयपुराणे वपुश्शापः प्रथमः ॥

द्वितीयोऽध्यायः ॥

मार्कण्डेय उवाच ॥

अरिष्टनेमिपुत्रोऽभूद्गरुडो नाम पक्षिराट् ।
गरुडस्याभवत् पुत्रः सम्पातिरिति विश्रुतः ॥ १ ॥
तस्याप्यासीत् सुतः शूरः सुपार्श्वोवायुविक्रमः ।
सुपार्श्वतनयः कुन्तिः कुन्तिपुत्रःप्रलोलुपः ॥ २ ॥
तस्यापि तनयावास्तां कङ्कः कन्धरएव च ॥ ३ ॥
कङ्कः कैलासशिखरे विद्युद्रूपेति विश्रुतं ।
ददर्शाम्बुजपत्राक्षं राक्षसं धनदानुगं ॥ ४ ॥
आपानासक्तममलस्रग्दामाम्बरधारिणं ।
भार्य्यासहायमासीनं शिलापट्टेऽमले शुभे ॥ ५ ॥
तद्दृष्टमात्रं कङ्केन रक्षः क्रोधसमन्वितं ।
प्रोवाच कस्मादायातस्त्वमितो ह्यण्डजाधम ॥ ६ ॥
स्त्रीसन्निकर्षे तिष्ठन्तं कस्मान्मामुपसर्पसि ।
नैष धर्म्मः सुबुद्धीनां मिथोनिष्पाद्यवस्तुषु ॥ ७ ॥

कङ्क उवाच ॥

साधारणोऽयं शैलेन्द्रो यथा तव तथा मम ।
अन्येषाञ्चैव जन्तूनां ममता भवतोऽत्र का ॥ ८ ॥

मार्कण्डेय उवाच ॥

ब्रुवाणमित्थं खड्गेन कङ्कं चिच्छेद राक्षसः ।
क्षरत्क्षतजबीभत्सं विस्फुरन्तमचेतनं ॥ ९ ॥

कङ्कं विनिहतं श्रुत्वा कन्धरः क्रोधमूर्च्छितः ।
विद्युद्रूपबधायाशु मनश्चक्रेऽण्डजेश्वरः ॥ १० ॥
स गत्वा शैलशिखरं कङ्को यत्र हतः स्थितः ।
तस्य सङ्कलनञ्चक्रे भ्रातुर्ज्येष्ठस्य खेचरः ।
कोपामर्षविवृद्धाक्षो नागेन्द्र इव निःश्वसन् ॥ ११ ॥
जगामाथ स यत्रास्ते भ्रातृहा तस्य राक्षसः ।
पक्षवातेन महता चालयन् भूधरान् वरान् ॥ १२ ॥
वेगात् पयोदजालानि विक्षिपन् क्षतजेक्षणः ।
क्षणात् क्षयितशत्रुः स पत्ताभ्यां क्रान्तभूधरः ॥ १३ ॥
पानासक्तमतिं तत्र तं ददर्श निशाचरं ।
आताम्रवक्त्रनयनं हेमपर्य्यङ्कमाश्रितं ॥ १४ ॥
स्रग्दामापूरितशिखं हरिचन्दनभूषितं ।
केतकीपत्रगर्भाभैर्दन्तैर्घोरतराननं ॥ १५ ॥
वामोरुमाश्रितां चास्य ददर्शायतलोचनां ।
पत्नीं मदनिकां नाम पुंस्कोकिलकलस्वनां ॥ १६ ॥
ततो रोषपरीतात्मा कन्धरः कन्दरस्थितं ।
तमुवाच सुदुष्टात्मन्नेहि युध्यस्व वै मया ॥ १७ ॥
यस्माज्ज्येष्ठो मम भ्राता विश्रब्धो घातितस्त्वया ।
तस्मात्त्वां मदसंसक्तं नयिष्ये यमसादनं ॥ १८ ॥
विश्वस्तघातिनां लोका ये च स्त्रीबालघातिनां ।
यास्यसे निरयान् सर्व्वांस्तांस्त्वमद्य मया हतः ॥ १९ ॥

मार्कण्डेय उवाच ॥

इत्येवं पतगेन्द्रेण प्रोक्तं स्त्रीसन्निधौ तदा ।
रक्षः क्रोधसमाविष्टं प्रत्यभाषत पक्षिणं ॥ २० ॥
यदि ते निहतो भ्राता पौरुषं तद्धि दर्शितं ।
त्वामप्यद्य हनिष्येऽहं खड्गेनानेन खेचर ॥ २१ ॥
तिष्ठ क्षणं नाच जीवन् पतगाधम यास्यसि ।
इत्युक्त्वाञ्जनपुञ्जाभं विमलं खड्गमाददे ॥ २२ ॥
ततः पतगराजस्य यक्षाधिपभटस्य च ।
बभूव युद्धमतुलं यथा गरुडशक्रयोः ॥ २३ ॥
ततः स राक्षसः क्रोधात् खड्गमाविध्य वेगवत् ।
चिक्षेप पतगेन्द्राय निर्वाणाङ्गारवर्च्चसं ॥ २४ ॥
पतगेन्द्रश्च तं खड्गं किञ्चिदुत्प्लुत्य भूतलात् ।
वक्त्रेण जग्राह तदा गरुडः पन्नगं यथा ॥ २५ ॥
वक्त्रपादतलैर्भङ्क्त्वा चक्रे क्षोभमथाण्डजः ।
तस्मिन् भग्ने ततः खड्गे बाहुयुद्धमवर्त्तत ॥ २६ ॥
ततः पतगराजेन वक्षस्याक्रम्य राक्षसः ।
हस्तपादकरैराशु शिरसा च वियोजितः ॥ २७ ॥
तस्मिन्विनिहते सा स्त्री खगं शरणमभ्यगात् ।
किञ्चित् सञ्जातसन्त्रासा प्राह भार्य्या भवामि ते ॥ २८ ॥
तामादाय खगश्रेष्ठः स्वकं गृहमगात् पुनः ।
गत्वा स निष्कृतिं भ्रातुर्व्विद्युद्रूपनिपातनात् ॥ २९ ॥

कन्धरस्य च सा वेश्म प्राप्येच्छारूपधारिणी ।
मेनकातनया सुभ्रूः सौपर्णं रूपमाददे ॥ ३० ॥
तस्यां स जनयामास तार्क्षीन्नाम सुतान्तदा ।
मुनिशापाग्निविप्लुष्टां वपुमप्सरसां वरां ।
तस्या नाम तदा चक्रे तार्क्षीमिति विहङ्गमः ॥ ३१ ॥
मन्दपालसुताश्चासंश्चत्वारोऽमितबुद्धयः ।
जरितारिप्रभृतयो द्रोणान्ता द्विजसत्तमाः ॥ ३२ ॥
तेषां जघन्यो धर्म्मात्मा वेदवेदाङ्गपारगः ।
उपयेमे स तान्तार्क्षीं कन्धरानुमते शुभां ॥ ३३ ॥
कस्यचित्त्वथ कालस्य तार्क्षी गर्भमवाप ह ।
सप्तपक्षाहिते गर्भे कुरुक्षेत्रं जगाम सा ॥ ३४ ॥
कुरुपाण्डवयोर्युद्धे वर्त्तमाने सुदारुणे ।
भावित्वाच्चैव कार्य्यस्य रणमध्यं विवेश सा ॥ ३५ ॥
तत्रापश्यत् तदा युद्धं भगदत्तकिरीटिनोः ।
निरन्तरं शरैरासीदाकाशं शलभैरिव ॥ ३६ ॥
पार्थकोदण्डनिर्मुक्तमासन्नमतिवेगवत् ।
तस्या भल्लमहिश्यामं त्वचं चिच्छेद जाठरीं ॥ ३७ ॥
भिन्ने कोष्ठे शशाङ्काभं भूमावण्डचतुष्टयं ।
आयुषः सावशेषत्वात्तूलराशाविवापतत् ॥ ३८ ॥
तत्पातसमकालञ्च सुप्रतीकाद्गजोत्तमात् ।
पपात महती घण्टा बाणसञ्छिन्नबन्धना ॥ ३९ ॥
समं समन्तात् प्राप्ता तु निर्भिन्नधरणीतला ।

छादयन्ती खगाण्डानि स्थितानि पिशितोपरि ॥ ४० ॥
हते च तस्मिन्नृपतौ भगदत्ते नरेश्वरे ।
बह्वन्यहान्यभूद्युद्धं कुरुपाण्डवसैन्ययोः ॥ ४१ ॥
वृत्ते युद्धे धर्मपुत्रे गते शान्तनवान्तिकं ।
भीष्मस्य गदतोऽशेषान् श्रोतुं धर्मान्महात्मनः ॥ ४२ ॥
घण्टागतानि तिष्ठन्ति यत्राण्डानि द्विजोत्तम ।
आजगाम तमुद्देशं शमीको नाम संयमी ॥ ४३ ॥
स तत्र शब्दमशृणोच्चिचीकुचीति वाशतां ।
बाल्यादस्फुटवाक्यानां विज्ञानेऽपि परे सति ॥ ४४ ॥
अथर्षिः शिष्यसहितो घण्टामुत्पाट्य विस्मितः ।
अमातृपितृपक्षाणि शिशुकानि ददर्श ह ॥ ४५ ॥
तानि तत्र तथा भूमौ शमीको भगवान्मुनिः ।
दृष्ट्वा स विस्मयाविष्टः प्रोवाचानुगतान् द्विजान् ॥ ४६ ॥
सम्यगुक्तं द्विजाग्रेण शुक्रेणोशनसा स्वयं ।
पलायनपरं दृष्ट्वा दैत्यसैन्यं सुरार्द्दितं ॥ ४७ ॥
न गन्तव्यं निवर्त्तध्वं कस्माद्व्रजत कातराः ।
उत्सृज्य शौर्य्ययशसी क्व गता न मरिष्यथ ॥ ४८ ॥
नश्यतो युद्ध्यतो वापि तावद्भवति जीवितं ।
यावद्धातासृजत् पूर्व्वं न यावन्मनसेप्सितं ॥ ४९ ॥
एके म्रियन्ते स्वगृहे पलायन्तोऽपरे जनाः ।
भुञ्जन्तोऽन्नं तथैवापः पिबन्तो निधनं गताः ॥ ५० ॥
विलासिनस्तथैवान्ये कामयाना निरामयाः ।

अविक्षताङ्गाः शस्त्रैश्च प्रेतराजवशङ्गताः ॥ ५१ ॥
अन्ये तपस्यभिरता नीताः प्रेतनृपानुगैः ।
योगाभ्यासे रताश्चान्ये नैव प्रापुरमृत्युतां ॥ ५२ ॥
शम्बराय पुरा क्षिप्तं वज्रं कुलिशपाणिना ।
हृदयेऽभिहतस्तेन तथापि न मृतोऽसुरः ॥ ५३ ॥
तेनैव खलु वज्रेण तेनैवेन्द्रेण दानवाः ।
प्राप्ते काले हता दैत्यास्तत्क्षणान्निधनं गताः ॥ ५४ ॥
विदित्वैवं न सन्त्रासः कर्त्तव्यो विनिवर्त्तत ।
ततो निवृत्तास्ते दैत्यास्त्यक्त्वा मरणजं भयं ॥ ५५ ॥
इति शुक्रवचः सत्यं कृतमेभिः खगोत्तमैः ।
ये युद्धेऽपि न संप्राप्ताः पञ्चत्वमतिमानुषे ॥ ५६ ॥
क्काण्डानां पतनं विप्राः क्क घण्टापतनं समं ।
क्क च मांसवसारक्तैर्भूमेरास्तरणक्रियाः ॥ ५७ ॥
केऽप्येते सर्व्वथा विप्रा नैते सामान्यपक्षिणः ।
दैवानुकूलता लोके महाभाग्यप्रदर्शिनी ॥ ५८ ॥
एवमुक्त्वा स तान् वीक्ष्य पुनर्व्वचनमब्रवीत् ।
निवर्त्तताश्रमं यात गृहीत्वा पक्षिबालकान् ॥ ५९ ॥
मार्जाराखुभयं यत्र नैषामण्डजजन्मनां ।
श्येनतो नकुलाद्वापि स्थाप्यन्तां तत्र पक्षिणः ॥ ६० ॥
द्विजाः किं वातियत्नेन मार्य्यन्ते कर्मभिः स्वकैः ।
रक्ष्यन्ते चाखिला जीवा यथैते पक्षिबालकाः ॥ ६१ ॥
तथापि यत्नः कर्त्तव्यो नरैः सर्व्वेषु कर्मसु ।

कुर्व्वन् पुरुषकारन्तु वाच्यतां याति नो सतां ॥ ६२ ॥

इति मुनिवरचोदितास्ततस्ते
मुनितनयाः परिगृह्य पक्षिणस्तान् ।
तरुविटपसमाश्रितालिसंघं
ययुरथ तापसरम्यमाश्रमं स्वं ॥ ६३ ॥

स चापि वन्यं मनसाभिकामितं
प्रगृह्य मूलं कुसुमं फलं कुशान् ।
चकार चक्रायुधरुद्रवेधसां
सुरेन्द्रवैवस्वतजातवेदसां ॥ ६४ ॥

अपाम्पतेर्गोष्पतिवित्तरक्षिणोः
समीरणस्यापि तथा द्विजोत्तमः ।
धातुर्विधातुस्त्वथ वैश्वदेविकाः
श्रुतिप्रयुक्ता विविधास्तु सत्क्रियाः ॥ ६५ ॥

इति मार्कण्डेयपुराणे चटकोत्पत्तिर्द्वितीयः ॥ २ ॥

तृतीयोऽध्यायः ॥

मार्कण्डेयउवाच ॥

अहन्यहनि विप्रेन्द्र स तेषां मुनिसत्तमः ।
चकाराहारपयसा तथा गुप्त्या च पोषणं ॥ १ ॥
मासमात्रेण जग्मुस्ते भानोः स्यन्दनवर्त्मनि ।
कौतूहलविलोलाक्षैर्दृष्टा मुनिकुमारकैः ॥ २ ॥

दृष्ट्वा महीं सनगरां साम्भोनिधिसरिद्वरां ।
रथचक्रप्रमाणां ते पुनराश्रममागताः ॥ ३ ॥
श्रमक्लान्तान्तरात्मानो महात्मानो वियोनिजाः ।
ज्ञानञ्च प्रकटीभूतं तच्च तेषां प्रभावतः ॥ ४ ॥
ऋषेः शिष्यानुकम्पार्थं वदतो धर्म्मनिश्चयं ।
कृत्वा प्रदक्षिणं सर्व्वे चरणावभ्यवादयन् ॥ ५ ॥
ऊचुश्च मरणाद्घोरान्मोक्षिताः स्मस्त्वया मुने ।
आवासभक्ष्यपयसां त्वं नो दाता पिता गुरुः ॥ ६ ॥
गर्भस्थानां मृता माता पित्रा नैवापि पालिताः ।
त्वया नो जीवितं दत्तं शिशवो येन रक्षिताः ॥ ७ ॥
क्षितावक्षततेजास्त्वं कृमीणामिव शुष्यतां ।
गजघण्टां समुत्पाट्य कृतवान् दुःखरेचनं ॥ ८ ॥
कथं वर्द्धेयुरबलाः खस्थान् द्रक्ष्याम्यहं कदा ।
कदा भूमेर्द्रुमं प्राप्तान् द्रक्ष्ये वृक्षान्तरं गतान् ॥ ९ ॥
कदा मे सहजा कान्तिः पांशुना नाशमेष्यति ।
एषां पक्षानिलोत्थेन मत्समीपविचारिणां ॥ १० ॥
इति चिन्तयता तात भवता प्रतिपालिताः ।
ते साम्प्रतं प्रवृद्धाः स्मः प्रबुद्धाः करवाम किं ॥ ११ ॥
इत्यृषिर्वचनं तेषां श्रुत्वा संस्कारवत् स्फुटं ।
शिष्यैः परिवृतः सर्व्वैः सह पुत्रेण शृङ्गिणा ॥ १२ ॥
कौतूहलपरो भूत्वा रोमाञ्चपटसंवृतः ।
उवाच तत्त्वतो ब्रूत प्रवृत्तेः कारणं गिरः ॥ १३ ॥

कस्य शापादियं प्राप्ता भवद्भिर्विक्रिया परा।
रूपस्य वचसश्चैव तन्मे वक्तुमिहार्हथ ॥ १४ ॥

पक्षिण ऊचुः ॥

विपुलस्वानिति ख्यातः प्रागासीन्मुनिसत्तमः।
तस्य पुत्त्रद्वयं जज्ञे सुकृषस्तुम्बुरुस्तथा ॥ १५ ॥
सुकृषस्य वयं पुत्त्राश्चत्वारः संयतात्मनः।
तस्यर्षेर्विनयाचारभक्तिनम्राः सदैव हि ॥ १६ ॥
तपश्चरणशक्तस्य शाम्यमानेन्द्रियस्य च।
यथाभिमतमस्माभिस्तदा तस्योपपादितं ॥ १७ ॥
समित्पुष्पादिकं सर्व्वं यच्चैवाभ्यवहारिकं।
एवं तत्राथ वसतां तस्यास्माकञ्च कानने ॥ १८ ॥
आजगाम महावर्ष्मा भग्नपक्षो जरान्वितः।
आताम्रनेत्रः स्रस्तात्मा पक्षी भूत्वा सुरेश्वरः ॥ १९ ॥
सत्यशौचक्षमाचारमतीवोदारमानसं।
जिज्ञासुस्तमृषिश्रेष्ठमस्मच्छापभवाय च ॥ २० ॥

पक्ष्युवाच ॥

द्विजेन्द्र मां क्षुधाविष्टं परित्रातुमिहार्हसि।
भक्षणार्थी महाभाग गतिर्भव ममातुला ॥ २१ ॥
विन्ध्यस्य शिखरे तिष्ठन् पक्षिपक्षेरितेन वै।
पतितोऽस्मि महाभाग श्वसनेनातिरंहसा ॥ २२ ॥
सोऽहं मोहसमाविष्टो भूमौ सप्ताहमस्मृतिः।

स्थितस्तत्राष्टमेनाह्ना चेतनां प्राप्तवानहं ॥ २३ ॥
प्राप्तचेताः क्षुधाविष्टो भवन्तं शरणं गतः ।
भक्ष्यार्थी विगतानन्दो दूयमानेन चेतसा ॥ २४ ॥
तत् कुरुष्वामलमते मत्त्राणायाचलां मतिं ।
प्रयच्छ भक्ष्यं विप्रर्षे प्राणयात्राक्षमं मम ॥ २५ ॥
स एवमुक्तः प्रोवाच तमिन्द्रं पक्षिरूपिणं ।
प्राणसन्धारणार्थाय दास्ये भक्ष्यं तवेप्सितं ॥ २६ ॥
इत्युक्त्वा पुनरप्येनमपृच्छत् स द्विजोत्तमः ।
आहारः कस्तवार्थाय उपकल्प्यो भवेन्मया ।
स चाह नरमांसेन तृप्तिर्भवति मे परा ॥ २७ ॥

ऋषिरुवाच ॥

कौमारं ते व्यतिक्रान्तमतीतं यौवनञ्च ते ।
वयसः परिणामस्ते वर्त्तते नूनमण्डज ॥ २८ ॥
यस्मिन्नराणां सर्व्वेषामशेषेच्छा निवर्त्तते ।
स कस्माद्वृद्धभावेऽपि सुनृशंसात्मको भवान् ॥ २९ ॥
क्व मानुषस्य पिशितं क्व वयश्चरमं तव ।
सर्व्वथा दुष्टभावानां प्रथमो नोपपद्यते ॥ ३० ॥
अथवा किं मयैतेन प्रोक्तेनास्ति प्रयोजनं ।
प्रतिश्रुत्य सदा देयमिति नो भावितं मनः ॥ ३१ ॥
इत्युक्त्वा तं स विप्रेन्द्रस्तथेति कृतनिश्चयः ।
शीघ्रमस्मान् समाहूय गुणतोऽनुप्रशस्य च ॥ ३२ ॥
उवाच क्षुब्धहृदयो मुनिर्वाक्यं सुनिष्ठुरं ।

विनयावनतान् सर्व्वान् भक्तियुक्तान् कृताञ्जलीन् ॥३३॥
कृतात्मानो द्विजश्रेष्ठा ऋणैर्युक्तामया सह ।
जातं श्रेष्ठमपत्यं वो यूयं मम यथा द्विजाः ॥ ३४ ॥
गुरुः पूज्यो यदि मतो भवतां परमः पिता ।
ततः कुरुत मे वाक्यं निर्व्यलीकेन चेतसा ॥ ३५ ॥
तद्वाक्यसमकालञ्च प्रोक्तमस्माभिरादृतैः ।
यद्वच्यति भवांस्तद्वै कृतमेवावधार्य्यतां ॥ ३६ ॥

ऋषिरुवाच ॥

मामेष शरणं प्राप्तोविहगः क्षुत्तृषान्वितः ।
युष्मन्मांसेन येनास्य चणं तृप्तिर्भवेत वै ॥ ३७ ॥
तृष्णाक्षयश्च रक्तेन तथा शीघ्रं विधीयतां ।
ततो वयं प्रव्यथिताः प्रकम्प्योद्भूतसाध्वसाः ।
कष्टं कष्टमिति प्रोच्य नैतत् कर्म्मेति चाब्रुवन् ॥ ३८ ॥
कथं परशरीरस्य हेतोर्देहं स्वकं बुधः ।
विनाशयेद्घातयेद्वा यथाह्यात्मा तथा सुतः ॥ ३९ ॥
पितृदेवमनुष्याणां यान्युक्तानि ऋणानि वै ।
तान्यपाकुरुते पुत्रो न शरीरप्रदः सुतः ॥ ४० ॥
तस्मान्नैतत् करिष्यामो नो चीर्णं यत् पुरातनैः ।
जीवन् भद्राण्यवाप्नोति जीवन् पुण्य करोति च ॥ ४१ ॥
मृतस्य देहनाशश्च धर्म्माद्युपरतिस्तथा ।
आत्मानं सर्व्वतो रक्ष्यमाहुर्धर्मविदो जनाः ॥ ४२ ॥
इत्थं श्रुत्वा वचोऽस्माकं मुनिः क्रोधादिव ज्वलन् ।

प्रोवाच पुनरप्यस्मान् निर्दहन्निव लोचनैः॥४३॥
प्रतिज्ञातं वचो मह्यं यस्मान्नैतत् करिष्यथ।
तस्मान्मच्छापनिर्दग्धास्तिर्य्यग्योनौ प्रयास्यथ॥४४॥
एवमुक्त्वा तदा सोऽस्मांस्तं विहङ्गममब्रवीत्।
अन्त्येष्टिमात्मनः कृत्वा शास्त्रतश्चौर्द्ध्वदेहिकं॥४५॥
भक्षयस्व सुविस्रब्धो मामत्र द्विजसत्तम।
आहारीकृतमेतत्ते मया देहमिहात्मनः॥४६॥
एतावदेव विप्रस्य ब्राह्मणत्वं प्रचच्यते।
यावत् पतगजात्यग्र स्वसत्यपरिपालनं॥४७॥
न यज्ञैर्दक्षिणावद्भिस्तत्पुण्यं प्राप्यते महत्।
कर्मणान्येन वा विप्रैर्यत् सत्यपरिपालनात्॥४८॥
इत्यृषेर्वचनं श्रुत्वा सोऽन्तर्विस्मयनिर्भरः।
प्रत्युवाच मुनिं शक्रः पक्षिरूपधरस्तदा॥४९॥
योगमास्थाय विप्रेन्द्र त्यजेदं स्वं कलेवरं।
जीवज्जन्तुं हि विप्रेन्द्र न भक्षामि कदाचन॥५०॥
तस्यैतद्वचनं श्रुत्वा योगयुक्तोऽभवन्मुनिः।
तं तस्य निश्चयं ज्ञात्वा शक्रोऽप्याह स्वदेहभृत्॥५१॥
भो भो विप्रेन्द्र बुध्यस्व बुद्ध्या बोध्यं बुधात्मक।
जिज्ञासार्थं मयाऽयं ते अपराधः कृतोऽनघ॥५२॥
तत् क्षमस्वामलमते का चेच्छा क्रियतां तव।
पालनात् सत्यवाक्यस्य प्रीतिर्मे परमा त्वयि॥५३॥
अद्य प्रभृति ते ज्ञानमैन्द्रं प्रादुर्भविष्यति।

तपस्यथ तथा धर्म्मे न ते विघ्नो भविष्यति ॥ ५४ ॥
इत्युक्त्वा तु गते शक्रे पिता कोपसमन्वितः ।
प्रणम्य शिरसास्माभिरिदमुक्तो महामुनिः ॥ ५५ ॥
बिभ्यतां मरणात्तात त्वमस्माकं महामते ।
क्षन्तुमर्हसि दीनानां जीवितप्रियता हि नः ॥ ५६ ॥
त्वगस्थिमांससंघाते पूयशोणितपूरिते ।
कर्त्तव्या न रतिर्यत्र तत्रास्माकमियं रतिः ॥ ५७ ॥
श्रूयताञ्च महाभाग यथा लोको विमह्यति ।
कामक्रोधादिभिर्दोषैरवशः प्रबलारिभिः ॥ ५८ ॥
प्रज्ञाप्राकारसंयुक्तमस्थिस्थूणं पुरं महत् ।
चर्म्मभित्तिमहारोधं मांसशोणितलेपनं ॥ ५९ ॥
नवद्वारं महायासं सर्व्वतः स्नायुवेष्टितं ।
नृपश्च पुरुषस्तत्र चेतनावानवस्थितः ॥ ६० ॥
मन्त्रिणौ तस्य बुद्धिश्च मनश्चैव विरोधिनौ ।
यतेते वैरनाशाय तावुभावितरेतरं ॥ ६१ ॥
नृपस्य तस्य चत्वारो नाशमिच्छन्ति विद्विषः ।
कामः क्रोधस्तथा लोभो मोहश्चान्यस्तथा रिपुः ॥ ६२ ॥
यदा तु स नृपस्तानि द्वाराण्यावृत्य तिष्ठति ।
तदा सुस्थबलश्चैव निरातङ्कश्च जायते ॥ ६३ ॥
जातानुरागो भवति शत्रुभिर्नाभिभूयते ॥ ६४ ॥
यदा तु सर्व्वद्वाराणि विवृतानि स मुञ्चति ।
रागो नाम तदा शत्रुर्नेत्रादिद्वारमृच्छति ॥ ६५ ॥

सर्व्वव्यापी महायामः पञ्चद्वारप्रवेशनः।
तस्यानुमार्गं विशति तद्वै घोरं रिपुत्रयं॥ ६६॥
प्रविश्याथ स वै तत्र द्वारैरिन्द्रियसंज्ञकैः।
रागः संश्लेषमायाति मनसा च सहेतरैः॥ ६७॥
इन्द्रियाणि मनश्चैव वशे कृत्वा दुरासदः।
द्वाराणि च वशे कृत्वा प्राकारं नाशयत्यथ॥ ६८॥
मनस्तस्याश्रितं दृष्ट्वा बुद्धिर्नश्यति तत्क्षणात्।
अमात्यरहितस्तत्र पौरवर्गोज्झितस्तथा॥ ६९॥
रिपुभिर्लब्धविवरः स नृपो नाशमृच्छति।
एवं रागस्तथा मोहो लोभः क्रोधस्तथैव च॥ ७०॥
प्रवर्त्तन्ते दुरात्मानो मनुष्यस्मृतिनाशकाः।
रागात् क्रोधः प्रभवति क्रोधाल्लोभोऽभिजायते॥ ७१॥
लोभाद्भवति सम्मोहः सम्मोहात् स्मृतिविभ्रमः।
स्मृतिभ्रंशाद्बुद्धिनाशो बुद्धिनाशात् प्रणश्यति॥ ७२॥
एवं प्रणष्टबुद्धीनां रागलोभानुवर्त्तिनां।
जीविते च सलोभानां प्रसादं कुरु सत्तम॥ ७३॥
योऽयं शापो भगवता दत्तः स न भवेत्तथा।
न तामसीं गतिं कष्टां व्रजेम मुनिसत्तम॥ ७४॥

ऋषिरुवाच॥

यन्मयोक्तं न तन्मिथ्या भविष्यति कदाचन।
न मे वागनृतं प्राह यावदद्येति पुत्रकाः॥ ७५॥
दैवमत्र परं मन्ये धिक् पौरुषमनर्थकं।

अकार्य्यं कारितो येन बलादहमचिन्तितं ॥ ७६ ॥
यस्माच्च युष्माभिरहं प्रणिपत्य प्रसादितः ।
तस्मात्तिर्य्यक्त्वमापन्नाः परं ज्ञानमवाप्स्यथ ॥ ७७ ॥
ज्ञानदर्शितमार्गाश्च निर्द्धूतक्लेशकल्मषाः ।
मत्प्रसादादसन्दिग्धाः परां सिद्धिमवाप्स्यथ ॥ ७८ ॥
एवं शप्ताः स्म भगवन् पित्रा दैववशात् पुरा ।
ततः कालेन महता योन्यन्तरमुपागताः ॥ ७९ ॥
जाताश्च रणमध्ये वै भवता परिपालिताः ।
वयमित्थं द्विजश्रेष्ठ खगत्वं समुपागताः ।
नास्त्यसाविह संसारे यो न दिष्टेन बाध्यते ॥ ८० ॥

मार्कण्डेय उवाच ॥

इति तेषां वचः श्रुत्वा शमीको भगवान् मुनिः ।
प्रत्युवाच महाभागः समीपस्थायिनो द्विजान् ॥ ८१ ॥
पूर्व्वमेव मया प्रोक्तं भवतां सन्निधाविदं ।
सामान्यपक्षिणो नैते केऽप्येते द्विजसत्तमाः ।
ये युद्धेऽपि न संप्राप्ताः पञ्चत्वमतिमानुषे ॥ ८२ ॥
ततः प्रीतिमता तेन तेऽनुज्ञाता महात्मना ।
जग्मुः शिखरिणां श्रेष्ठं विन्ध्यं द्रुमलतायुतं ॥ ८३ ॥
यावदद्य स्थितास्तस्मिन्नचले धर्मपक्षिणः ।
तपःस्वाध्यायनिरताः समाधौ कृतनिश्चयाः ॥ ८४ ॥
इतिमुनिवरलब्धसत्क्रियास्ते
मुनितनया विहगत्वमभ्युपेताः ।

गिरिवरगहनेऽतिपुण्यतोये
यतमनसो निवसन्ति विन्ध्यपृष्ठे ॥ ८५ ॥

इति मार्कण्डेयपुराणे विन्ध्यप्राप्तिः ॥ ३ ॥

चतुर्थोऽध्यायः ॥

मार्कण्डेय उवाच ॥

एवन्ते द्रोणतनयाः पक्षिणो ज्ञानिनोऽभवन् ।
वसन्ति ह्यचले विन्ध्ये तानुपास्व च पृच्छ च ॥ १ ॥
इत्यृषेर्वचनं श्रुत्वा मार्कण्डेयस्य जैमिनिः ।
जगाम विन्ध्यशिखरं यत्र ते धर्मपक्षिणः ॥ २ ॥
तन्नगासन्नभूतश्च शुश्राव पठतां ध्वनिं ।
श्रुत्वा च विस्मयाविष्टश्चिन्तयामास जैमिनिः ॥ ३ ॥
स्थानसौष्ठवसम्पन्नं जितश्वासमविश्रमं ।
विस्पष्टमपदोषञ्च पठ्यते द्विजसत्तमैः ॥ ४ ॥
वियोनिमपि संप्राप्तानेतान्मुनिकुमारकान् ।
चित्रमेतदहं मन्ये न जहाति सरस्वती ॥ ५ ॥
बन्धुवर्गस्तथा मित्रं यच्चेष्टमपरं गृहे ।
त्यक्त्वा गच्छति तत् सर्व्वन्न जहाति सरस्वती ॥ ६ ॥
इति सञ्चिन्तयन्नेव विवेश गिरिकन्दरं ।
प्रविश्य च ददर्शासौ शिलापट्टगतान् द्विजान् ॥ ७ ॥

पठतस्तान् समालोक्य मुखदोषविवर्जितान्।
सोऽथ शोकेन हर्षेण सर्व्वानेवाभ्यभाषत ॥ ८ ॥
स्वस्त्यस्तु वो द्विजश्रेष्ठा जैमिनिं मां निबोधत ।
व्यासशिष्यमनुप्राप्तं भवतां दर्शनोत्सुकं ॥ ९ ॥
मन्युर्न खलु कर्त्तव्यो यत् पिचातीवमन्युना ।
शप्ताः खगत्वमापन्नाः सर्व्वथा दिष्टमेव तत् ॥ १० ॥
स्फीतद्रव्ये कुले केचिज्जाताः किल मनस्विनः ।
द्रव्यनाशे द्विजेन्द्रास्ते शबरेण सुसान्त्विताः ॥ ११ ॥
दत्वा याचन्ति पुरुषा हत्वा वध्यन्ति चापरे ।
पातयित्वा च पात्यन्ते त एव तपसः क्षयात् ॥ १२ ॥
एतद्दृष्टं सुवहुशो विपरीतं तथा मया ।
भावाभावसमुच्छेदैरजस्रं व्याकुलं जगत् ॥ १३ ॥
इति संचिन्त्य मनसा न शोकं कर्त्तुमर्हथ ।
ज्ञानस्य फलमेतावच्छोकहर्षैरधृष्यता ॥ १४ ॥
ततस्ते जैमिनिं सर्व्वे पाद्यार्घ्याभ्यामपूजयन् ।
अनामयञ्च पप्रच्छुः प्रणिपत्य महामुनिं ॥ १५ ॥
अथोचुः खगमाः सर्व्वे व्यासशिष्यं तपोनिधिं ।
सुखोपविष्टं विश्रान्तं पक्षानिलहतक्लमं ॥ १६ ॥

पक्षिण ऊचुः ॥

अद्य नः सफलं जन्म जीवितञ्च सुजीवितं ।
यत् पश्यामः सुरैर्वन्द्यं तव पादाम्बुजद्वयं ॥ १७ ॥
पितृकोपाग्निरुद्भूतो यो नो देहेषु वर्त्तते ।

सोऽद्य शान्तिं गतो विप्र युष्मद्दर्शनवारिणा ॥ १८ ॥
कच्चित्ते कुशलं ब्रह्मन्नाश्रमे मृगपक्षिषु ।
वृक्षेष्वथ लतागुल्मत्वक्सारतृणजातिषु ॥ १९ ॥
अथवा नैतदुक्तं हि सम्यगस्माभिरादृतैः ।
भवता सङ्गमो येषां तेषामकुशलं कुतः ॥ २० ॥
प्रसादश्च कुरुष्वाच ब्रूह्यागमनकारणं ।
देवानामिव संसर्गो भवतोऽभ्युदयो महान् ।
केनास्मद्भाग्यगुरुणा आनीतो दृष्टिगोचरं ॥ २१ ॥

जैमिनिरुवाच ॥

श्रूयतां द्विजशार्दूलाः कारणं येन कन्दरं ।
विन्ध्यस्येहागतो रम्यं रेवावारिकणोक्षितं ।
सन्देहान् भारते शास्त्रे तान् प्रष्टुं गतवानहं ॥ २२ ॥
मार्कण्डेयं महात्मानं पूर्व्वं भृगुकुलोद्वहं ।
तमहं पृष्टवान् प्राप्य सन्देहान् भारतं प्रति ॥ २३ ॥
स च पृष्टो मया प्राह सन्ति विन्ध्ये महाचले ।
द्रोणपुत्रा महात्मानस्ते वक्ष्यन्त्यर्थविस्तरं ॥ २४ ॥
तद्वाक्यचोदितश्चेममागतोऽहं महागिरिं ।
तत् शृणुध्वमशेषेण श्रुत्वा व्याख्यातुमर्हथ ॥ २५ ॥

पक्षिण ऊचुः ॥

विषये सति वक्ष्यामो निर्व्विशङ्कः शृणुष्व तत् ।
कथं तन्न वदिष्यामो यदस्मद्बुद्धिगोचरं ॥ २६ ॥
चतुर्ष्वपि हि वेदेषु धर्मशास्त्रेषु चैव हि ।

समस्तेषु तथाङ्गेषु यच्चान्यद्वेदसम्मितं ॥ २७ ॥
एतेषु गोचरोऽस्माकं बुद्धेर्ब्राह्मणसत्तम ।
प्रतिज्ञान्तु समावोढुं तथापि न हि शक्नुमः ॥ २८ ॥
तस्माद्वदस्व विश्रब्धं सन्दिग्धं यद्धि भारते ।
वक्ष्यामस्तव धर्मज्ञ न चेन्मोहो भविष्यति ॥ २९ ॥

जैमिनिरुवाच ॥

सन्दिग्धानीह वस्तूनि भारतं प्रति यानि मे ।
शृणुध्वममलास्तानि श्रुत्वा व्याख्यातुमर्हथ ॥ ३० ॥
कस्मान्मानुषतां प्राप्तो निर्गुणोऽपि जनार्द्दनः ।
वासुदेवोऽखिलाधारः सर्व्वकारणकारणं ॥ ३१ ॥
कस्माच्च पाण्डुपुत्राणामेका सा द्रुपदात्मजा ।
पञ्चानां महिषी कृष्णा सुमहानत्र संशयः ॥ ३२ ॥
भेषजं ब्रह्महत्याया बलदेवो महाबलः ।
तीर्थयात्राप्रसङ्गेन कस्माच्चक्रे हलायुधः ॥ ३३ ॥
कथञ्च द्रौपदेयास्तेऽकृतदारा महारथाः ।
पाण्डुनाथा महात्मानो बधमापुरनाथवत् ॥ ३४ ॥
एतत् सर्व्वं कथ्यतां मे सन्दिग्धं भारतं प्रति ।
कृतार्थोऽहं सुखं येन गच्छेयं निजमाश्रमं ॥ ३५ ॥

पक्षिण ऊचुः ॥

नमस्कृत्य सुरेशाय विष्णवे प्रभविष्णवे ।
पुरुषायाप्रमेयाय शाश्वतायाव्ययाय च ॥ ३६ ॥
चतुर्व्यूहात्मने तस्मै त्रिगुणायागुणाय च ।

वरिष्ठाय गरिष्ठाय वरेण्यायामृताय च ॥ ३७ ॥
यस्मादणुतरन्नास्ति यस्मान्नास्ति बृहत्तरं ।
येन विश्वमिदं व्याप्तमजेन जगदादिना ॥ ३८ ॥
आविर्भावतिरोभावदृष्टादृष्टविलक्षणं ।
वदन्ति यत् सृष्टमिदं तथैवान्ते च संहृतं ॥ ३९ ॥
ब्रह्मणे चादिदेवाय नमस्कृत्य समाधिना ।
ऋक्सामान्युग्भिरन्वक्त्रैर्यः पुनाति जगत्त्रयं ॥ ४० ॥
प्रणिपत्य तथेशानमेकबाणविनिर्जितैः ।
यस्यासुरगणैर्यज्ञा विलुप्यन्ते न यज्विनां ॥ ४१ ॥
प्रवक्ष्यामो मतं कृत्स्नं व्यासस्याद्भुतकर्मणः ।
येन भारतमुद्दिश्य धर्माद्याः प्रकटीकृताः ॥ ४२ ॥
आपो नारा इति प्रोक्ता मुनिभिस्तत्त्वदर्शिभिः ।
अयनं तस्य ताः पूर्व्वं तेन नारायणः स्मृतः ॥ ४३ ॥
स देवो भगवान् सर्व्वं व्याप्य नारायणो विभुः ।
चतुर्द्धा संस्थितो ब्रह्मन् सगुणो निर्गुणस्तथा ॥ ४४ ॥
एका मूर्त्तिरनिर्द्देश्या शुक्लां पश्यन्ति तां बुधाः ।
ज्वालामालोपरुद्धाङ्गी निष्ठा सा योगिनां परा ॥ ४५ ॥
दूरस्था चान्तिकस्था च विज्ञेया सा गुणातिगा ।
वासुदेवाभिधानोऽसौ निर्म्ममत्वेन दृश्यते ॥ ४६ ॥
रूपवर्णादयस्तस्या न भावाः कल्पनामयाः ।
अस्त्येव सा सदा शुद्धा सुप्रतिष्ठैकरूपिणी ॥ ४७ ॥
द्वितीया पृथिवीं मूर्द्ध्ना शेषाख्या धारयत्यधः ।

तामसी सा समाख्याता तिर्यक्त्वं समुपाश्रिता ॥ ४८ ॥
तृतीया कर्म कुरुते प्रजापालनतत्परा ।
सत्वोद्रिक्ता तु सा ज्ञेया धर्मसंस्थानकारिणी ॥ ४९ ॥
चतुर्थी जलमध्यस्था शेते पन्नगतल्पगा ।
रजस्तस्या गुणः सर्गं सा करोति सदैव हि ॥ ५० ॥
या तृतीया हरेर्मूर्त्तिः प्रजापालनतत्परा ।
सा तु धर्मव्यवस्थानं करोति नियतं भुवि ॥ ५१ ॥
प्रोद्भूतानसुरान् हन्ति धर्मविच्छित्तिकारिणः ।
पाति देवान् सतश्चान्यान् धर्मरक्षापरायणान् ॥ ५२ ॥
यदा यदा हि धर्मस्य ग्लानिर्भवति जैमिने ।
अभ्युत्थानमधर्मस्य तदात्मानं सृजत्यसौ ॥ ५३ ॥
भूत्वा पुरा वराहेण तुण्डेनापो निरस्य च ।
एकया दंष्ट्रयोत्खाता नलिनीव वसुन्धरा ॥ ५४ ॥
कृत्वा नृसिंहरूपञ्च हिरण्यकशिपुर्हतः ।
विप्रचित्तिमुखाश्चान्ये दानवा विनिपातिताः ॥ ५५ ॥
वामनादींस्तथैवान्यान्न संख्यातुमिहोत्सहे ।
अवतारांश्च तस्येह माथुरः साम्प्रतं त्वयं ॥ ५६ ॥
इति सा सात्त्विकी मूर्त्तिरवतारान् करोति वै ।
प्रद्युम्नेति च सा ख्याता रक्षाकर्मण्यवस्थिता ॥ ५७ ॥
देवत्वेऽथ मनुष्यत्वे तिर्य्यग्योनौ च संस्थिता ।
गृह्णाति तत्स्वभावञ्च वासुदेवेच्छया सदा ॥ ५८ ॥
इत्येतत्ते समाख्यातं कृतकृत्योऽपि यत्प्रभुः ।

मानुषत्वं गतो विष्णुः शृणुष्वास्योत्तरं पुनः ॥ ५९ ॥

इति मार्कण्डेयपुराणे चतुर्व्यूहावतारः ॥ ४ ॥

पञ्चमोऽध्यायः ॥

पक्षिण ऊचुः ॥

त्वष्टृपुत्रे हते पूर्व्वं ब्रह्मन्निन्द्रस्य तेजसः ।
ब्रह्महत्याभिभूतस्य परा हानिरजायत ॥ १ ॥
तद्धर्मं प्रविवेशाथ शाक्रतेजोऽपचारतः ।
निस्तेजाश्चाभवच्छक्रोधर्मे तेजसि निर्गते ॥ २ ॥
ततः पुत्रं हतं श्रुत्वा त्वष्टा क्रुद्धः प्रजापतिः ।
अवलुञ्च्य जटामेकामिदं वचनमब्रवीत् ॥ ३ ॥
अद्य पश्यन्तु मे वीर्य्यं त्रयो लोकाः सदेवताः ।
स च पश्यतु दुर्बुद्धिर्ब्रह्महा पाकशासनः ॥ ४ ॥
स्वकर्माभिरतो येन मत्सुतो विनिपातितः ।
इत्युक्का कोपरक्ताक्षो जटामग्नौ जुहाव तां ॥ ५ ॥
ततो वृत्रः समुत्तस्थौ ज्वालामाली महासुरः ।
महाकायो महादंष्ट्रो भिन्नाञ्जनचयप्रभः ॥ ६ ॥
इन्द्रशत्रुरमेयात्मा त्वष्टृतेजोऽपवृंहितः ।
अहन्यहनि सोऽवर्द्धदिषुपातं महाबलः ॥ ७ ॥
बधाय चात्मनो दृष्ट्वा वृत्रं शक्रो महासुरं ।
प्रेषयामास सप्तर्षीन् सन्धिमिच्छन् भयातुरः ॥ ८ ॥

सख्यञ्चक्रुस्ततस्तस्य वृत्रेण समयांस्तथा।
ऋषयः प्रीतमनसः सर्व्वभूतहिते रताः॥ ९॥
समयस्थितिमुल्लङ्घ्य यदा शक्रेण घातितः।
वृत्रो हत्याभिभूतस्य तदा बलमशीर्य्यत॥ १०॥
तच्छक्रदेहविभ्रष्टं बलं मारुतमाविशत्।
सर्व्वव्यापिनमव्यक्तं बलस्यैवाधिदैवतं॥ ११॥
अहल्याञ्च यदा शक्रो गौतमं रूपमास्थितः।
धर्षयामास देवेन्द्रस्तदा रूपमहीयत॥ १२॥
अङ्गप्रत्यङ्गलावण्यं यदतीवमनोरमं।
विहाय दुष्टं देवेन्द्रं नासत्यावगमत्ततः॥ १३॥
धर्म्मेण तेजसा त्यक्तं बलहीनमरूपिणं।
ज्ञात्वा सुरेशं दैतेयास्तज्जये चक्रुरुद्यमं॥ १४॥
राज्ञामुद्रिक्तवीर्य्याणां देवेन्द्रं विजिगीषवः।
कुलेष्वतिबला दैत्या अजायन्त महामुने॥ १५॥
कस्यचित्त्वथ कालस्य धरणी भारपीडिता।
जगाम मेरुशिखरं सदो यत्र दिवौकसां॥ १६॥
तेषां सा कथयामास भूरिभारावपीडिता।
दनुजात्मजदैत्योत्थं खेदकारणमात्मनः॥ १७॥
एते भवद्भिरसुरा निहताः पृथुलौजसः।
ते सर्व्वे मानुषे लोके जाता गेहेषु भूभृतां॥ १८॥
अक्षौहिण्योहि बहुलास्तद्भारार्त्ता व्रजाम्यधः।
तथा कुरुध्वं त्रिदशा यथा शान्तिर्भवेन्मम॥ १९॥

पक्षिण ऊचुः ॥

तेजोभागैस्ततो देवा अवतेरुर्दिवो महीं ।
प्रजानामुपकारार्थं भूभारहरणाय च ॥ २० ॥
यदिन्द्रदेहजं तेजस्तन्मुमोच स्वयं वृषः ।
कुन्त्यां जातो महातेजास्ततो राजा युधिष्ठिरः ॥ २१ ॥
बलं मुमोच पवनस्ततो भीमो व्यजायत ।
शक्रवीर्य्यार्द्धतश्चैव जज्ञे पार्थो धनञ्जयः ॥ २२ ॥
उत्पन्नौ यमजौ माद्रयां शक्ररूपौ महाद्युती ।
पञ्चधा भगवानित्थमवतीर्णः शतक्रतुः ॥ २३ ॥
तस्योत्पन्ना महाभागा पत्नी कृष्णा हुताशनात् ॥ २४ ॥
शक्रस्यैकस्य सा पत्नी कृष्णा नान्यस्य कस्यचित् ।
योगीश्वराः शरीराणि कुर्व्वन्ति बहुलान्यपि ॥ २५ ॥
पञ्चानामेकपत्नीत्वमित्येतत् कथितं तव ।
श्रूयतां बलदेवोऽपि यथा यातः सरस्वतीं ॥ २६ ॥

इति मार्कण्डेयपुराणे इन्द्रविक्रिया ॥ ५ ॥

षष्ठोऽध्यायः ॥

पक्षिण ऊचुः ॥

रामः पार्थे परां प्रीतिं ज्ञात्वा कृष्णस्य लाङ्गली ।
चिन्तयामास बहुधा किं कृतं सुकृतं भवेत् ॥ १ ॥

कृष्णेन हि विना नाहं यास्ये दुर्य्योधनान्तिकं।
पाण्डवान्‌ वा समाश्रित्य कथं दुर्य्योधनं नृपं॥ २॥
जामातरं तथा शिष्यं घातयिष्ये नरेश्वरं।
तस्मान्न पार्थं यास्यामि नापि दुर्य्योधनं नृपं॥ ३॥
तीर्थेष्वाप्लावयिष्यामि तावदात्मानमात्मना।
कुरूणां पाण्डवानाञ्च यावदन्ताय कल्पते॥ ४॥
इत्यामन्त्र्य हृषीकेशं पार्थदुर्य्योधनावपि।
जगाम द्वारकां शौरिः स्वसैन्यपरिवारितः॥ ५॥
गत्वा द्वारवतीं रामो हृष्टपुष्टजनाकुलां।
श्वोगन्तव्येषु तीर्थेषु पपौ पानं हलायुधः॥ ६॥
पीतपानो जगामाथ रैवतोद्यानमृद्धिमत्‌।
हस्ते गृहीत्वा समदां रेवतीमप्सरोपमां॥ ७॥
स्त्रीकदम्बकमध्यस्थो ययौ मत्तः पदा स्खलन्‌।
ददर्श च वनं वीरो रमणीयमनुत्तमं॥ ८॥
सर्व्वर्त्तुफलपुष्पाढ्यं शाखामृगगणाकुलं।
पुण्यं पद्मवनोपेतं सपल्वलमहावनं॥ ९॥
स शृण्वन्‌ प्रीतिजननान्‌ बह्वन्मदकलान्‌ शुभान्‌।
श्रोत्ररम्यान्‌ सुमधुरान्‌ शब्दान्‌ खगमुखेरितान्‌॥ १०॥
सर्व्वर्त्तुफलभाराढ्यान्‌ सर्व्वर्त्तुकुसुमोज्ज्वलान्‌।
अपश्यत्‌ पादपांस्तत्र विहगैरनुनादितान्‌॥ ११॥
आम्रानाम्रातकान्‌ भव्यान्‌ नारिकेलान्‌ सतिन्दकान्‌।
आबिल्वकांस्तथा जीरान्‌ दाडिमान्‌ बीजपूरकान्‌॥ १२॥

पनसान् लकुचान् मोचान् नीपांश्चातिमनोहरान् ।
पारावतांश्च कङ्कोलान् नलिनानम्लवेतसान् ॥ १३ ॥
भल्लातकानामलकांस्तिन्दुकांश्च महाफलान् ।
इङ्गुदान् करमर्दांश्च हरीतकविभीतकान् ॥ १४ ॥
एतानन्यांश्च स तरून् ददर्श यदुनन्दनः ।
तथैवाशोकपुन्नागकेतकीवकुलानथ ॥ १५ ॥
चम्पकान् सप्तपर्णांश्च कर्णिकारान् समालतीन् ।
पारिजातान् कोविदारान् मन्दारान् बदरांस्तथा ॥ १६ ॥
पाटलान् पुष्पितान् रम्यान् देवदारुद्रुमांस्तथा ।
सालांस्तालांस्तमालांश्च किंशुकान् वञ्जुलान् वरान् ॥ १७ ॥
चकोरैः शतपत्रैश्च भृङ्गराजैस्तथा शुकैः ।
कोकिलैः कलविङ्कैश्च हारीतैर्जीवजीवकैः ॥ १८ ॥
प्रियपुत्रैश्चातकैश्च तथान्यैर्विविधैः खगैः ।
श्रोत्ररम्यं सुमधुरं कूजद्भिश्चाप्यधिष्ठितं ॥ १९ ॥
सरांसि च मनोज्ञानि प्रसन्नसलिलानि च ।
कुमुदैः पुण्डरीकैश्च तथा नीलोत्पलैः शुभैः ॥ २० ॥
कह्लारैः कमलैश्चापि आचितानि समन्ततः ।
कादम्बैश्चक्रवाकैश्च तथैव जलकुक्कुटैः ॥ २१ ॥
कारण्डवैः प्लवैर्हंसैः कूर्मैर्मद्गुभिरेव च ।
एभिश्चान्यैश्च कीर्णानि समन्ताज्जलचारिभिः ॥ २२ ॥
क्रमेणेत्थं वनं शौरिर्वीक्षमाणो मनोरमं ।
जगामानुगतः स्त्रीभिर्लतागृहमनुत्तमं ॥ २३ ॥

स ददर्श द्विजांस्तत्र वेदवेदाङ्गपारगान्।
कौशिकान् भार्गवांश्चैव भारद्वाजान् सगौतमान्॥ २४ ॥
विविधेषु च सम्भूतान् वंशेषु द्विजसत्तमान्।
कथाश्रवणबद्धोत्कानुपविष्टान्महत्सु च ॥ २५ ॥
कृष्णाजिनोत्तरीयेषु कुशेषु च बृषीषु च ।
सूतञ्च तेषां मध्यस्थं कथयानं कथाः शुभाः ॥ २६ ॥
पौराणिकीः सुरर्षीणामाद्यानां चरिताश्रयाः ।
दृष्ट्वा रामं द्विजाः सर्व्वे मधुपानारुणेक्षणं ॥ २७ ॥
मत्तोऽयमिति मन्वानाः समुत्तस्थुस्त्वरान्विताः ।
पूजयन्तो हलधरमृते तं सूतवंशजं ॥ २८ ॥
ततः क्रोधसमाविष्टो हली सूतं महाबलः ।
निजघान विवृत्ताक्षः क्षोभिताशेषदानवः ॥ २९ ॥
अध्यास्यति पदं ब्राह्मं तस्मिन् सूते निपातिते ।
निष्क्रान्तास्ते द्विजाः सर्व्वे वनात् कृष्णाजिनाम्बराः ॥ ३० ॥
अवधूतं तथात्मानं मन्यमानो हलायुधः ।
चिन्तयामास सुमहन्मया पापमिदं कृतं ॥ ३१ ॥
ब्राह्मं स्थानं गतो ह्येष यत् सूतोविनिपातितः ।
तथा हीमे द्विजाः सर्व्वे मामवेक्ष्य विनिर्गताः ॥ ३२ ॥
शरीरस्य च मे गन्धो लोहस्येवासखावहः ।
आत्मानञ्चावगच्छामि ब्रह्मघ्नमिव कुत्सितं ॥ ३३ ॥
धिगमर्षं तथा मद्यमतिमानमभीरुतां।
यैराविष्टेन सुमहन्मया पापमिदं कृतं ॥ ३४ ॥

तत्क्षयार्थं चरिष्यामि व्रतं द्वादशवार्षिकं ।
स्वकर्मख्यापनं कुर्व्वन् प्रायश्चित्तमनुत्तमं ॥ ३५ ॥
अथ येयं समारब्धा तीर्थयात्रा मयाधुना ।
एतामेव प्रयास्यामि प्रतिलोमां सरस्वतीं ॥ ३६ ॥
अतो जगाम रामोऽसौ प्रतिलोमां सरस्वतीं ।
ततः परं शृणुध्वेमं पाण्डवेयकथाश्रयं ॥ ३७ ॥

इति मार्कण्डेयपुराणे बलदेवब्रह्महत्या ॥ ६ ॥

सप्तमोऽध्यायः ॥

धर्मपक्षिण ऊचुः ॥

हरिश्चन्द्रेति राजर्षिरासीत्त्रेतायुगे पुरा ।
धर्मात्मा पृथिवीपालः प्रोल्लसत्कीर्त्तिरुत्तमः ॥ १ ॥
न दुर्भिक्षं न च व्याधिर्नाकालमरणं नृणां ।
नाधर्मरुचयः पौरास्तस्मिन् शासति पार्थिवे ॥ २ ॥
बभूवुर्न तथोन्मत्ता धनवीर्य्यतपोमदैः ।
नाजायन्त स्त्रियश्चैव काश्चिदप्राप्तयौवनाः ॥ ३ ॥
स कदाचिन्महाबाहुररण्येऽनुसरन् मृगं ।
शुश्राव शब्दमसकृत् त्रायस्वेति च योषितां ॥ ४ ॥
स विहाय मृगं राजा माभैषीरित्यभाषत ।
मयि शासति दुर्मेधाः कोऽयमन्यायवृत्तिमान् ॥ ५ ॥

तत्क्रन्दितानुसारी च सर्व्वारम्भविघातकृत् ।
एतस्मिन्नन्तरे रौद्रो विघ्नराट् समचिन्तयत् ॥ ६ ॥
विश्वामित्रोऽयमतुलं तप आस्थाय वीर्य्यवान् ।
प्रागसिद्धाभवादीनां विद्याः साधयति व्रती ॥ ७ ॥
साध्यमानाः क्षमामौनचित्तसंयमिनाऽमुना ।
तावै भयार्त्ताः क्रन्दन्ति कथं कार्य्यमिदं मया ॥ ८ ॥
तेजस्वी कौशिकश्रेष्ठो वयमस्य सुदुर्बलाः ।
क्रोशन्त्येतास्तथा भीता दुष्पारं प्रतिभाति मे ॥ ९ ॥
अथवायं नृपः प्राप्तो माभैरिति वदन् मुहुः ।
इममेव प्रविश्याशु साधयिष्ये यथेप्सितं ॥ १० ॥
इति संचिन्त्य रौद्रेण विघ्नराजेन वै ततः ।
तेनाविष्टोनृपः कोपादिदं वचनमब्रवीत् ॥ ११ ॥
कोऽयं बध्नाति वस्त्रान्ते पावकं पापकृन्नरः ।
बलोष्णतेजसा दीप्ते मयि पत्यावुपस्थिते ॥ १२ ॥
सोऽद्य मत्कार्मुकाक्षेपविदीपितदिगन्तरैः ।
शरैर्विभिन्नसर्व्वाङ्गो दीर्घनिद्रां प्रवेक्ष्यति ॥ १३ ॥
विश्वामित्रस्ततः क्रुद्धः श्रुत्वा तन्नृपतेर्वचः ।
क्रुद्धे चर्षिवरे तस्मिन्नेशुर्विद्याः क्षणेन ताः ॥ १४ ॥
स चापि राजा तं दृष्ट्वा विश्वामित्रन्तपोनिधिं ।
भीतः प्रावेपतात्यर्थं सहसाश्वत्थपर्णवत् ॥ १५ ॥
स दुरात्मन्निति यदा मुनिस्तिष्ठेति चाब्रवीत् ।
ततः स राजा विनयात्प्रणिपत्याभ्यभाषत ॥ १६ ॥

भगवन्नेष धर्म्मो मे नापराधो मम प्रभो ।
न क्रोद्धुमर्हसि मुने निजधर्मरतस्य मे ॥ १७ ॥
दातव्यं रक्षितव्यञ्च धर्मज्ञेन महीक्षिता ।
चापञ्चोद्यम्य योद्धव्यं धर्मशास्त्रानुसारतः ॥ १८ ॥

विश्वामित्र उवाच ॥

दातव्यं कस्य के रक्ष्याः कैर्योद्धव्यञ्च ते नृप ।
क्षिप्रमेतत्समाचक्ष्व यद्यधर्मभयन्तव ॥ १९ ॥

हरिश्चन्द्र उवाच ॥

दातव्यं विप्रमुख्येभ्यो ये चान्ये कृशवृत्तयः ।
रक्ष्या भीताः सदा युद्धं कर्त्तव्यं परिपन्थिभिः ॥ २० ॥

विश्वामित्र उवाच ॥

यदि राजा भवान् सम्यग्राजधर्ममवेक्षते ।
निर्वेष्टुकामो विप्रोऽहं दीयतामिष्टदक्षिणा ॥ २१ ॥

पक्षिण ऊचुः ॥

एतद्राजा वचः श्रुत्वा प्रहृष्टेनान्तरात्मना ।
पुनर्जातमिवात्मानं मेने प्राह च कौशिकं ॥ २२ ॥
उच्यतां भगवन् यत्ते दातव्यमविशङ्कितं ।
दत्तमित्येव तद्विद्धि यद्यपि स्यात् सुदुर्लभं ॥ २३ ॥
हिरण्यं वा सुवर्णं वा पुत्त्रः पत्नी कलेवरं ।
प्राणा राज्यं पुरं लक्ष्मीर्यदभिप्रेतमात्मनः ॥ २४ ॥

विश्वामित्र उवाच ॥

राजन् प्रतिगृहीतोऽयं यस्ते दत्तः प्रतिग्रहः ।
प्रयच्छ प्रथमं तावद्दक्षिणां राजसूयिकीं ॥ २५ ॥

राजोवाच ॥

ब्रह्मंस्तामपि दास्यामि दक्षिणां भवतो ह्यहं ।
व्रियतां द्विजशार्दूल यस्तवेष्टः प्रतिग्रहः ॥ २६ ॥

विश्वामित्र उवाच ॥

ससागरां धरामेतां सभूभृद्ग्रामपत्तनां ।
राज्यञ्च सकलं वीर रथाश्वगजसंकुलं ॥ २७ ॥
कोष्टागारञ्च कोषञ्च यच्चान्यद्विद्यते तव ।
विना भार्य्याञ्च पुत्त्रञ्च शरीरञ्च तवानघ ॥ २८ ॥
धर्मञ्च सर्व्वधर्मज्ञ यो यान्तमनुगच्छति ।
बहुना वा किमुक्तेन सर्व्वमेतत् प्रदीयतां ॥ २९ ॥

पक्षिण ऊचुः ॥

प्रहृष्टेनैव मनसा सोऽविकारमुखो नृपः ।
तस्यर्षेर्व्वचनं श्रुत्वा तथेत्याह कृताञ्जलिः ॥ ३० ॥

विश्वामित्र उवाच ॥

सर्व्वस्वं यदि मे दत्तं राज्यमुर्व्वी बलं धनं ।
प्रभुत्वं कस्य राजर्षे राज्यस्थे तापसे मयि ॥ ३१ ॥

हरिश्चन्द्र उवाच ॥

यस्मिन्नपि मया काले ब्रह्मन्दत्ता वसुन्धरा ।
तस्मिन्नपि भवान् स्वामी किमुताद्य महीपतिः ॥ ३२ ॥

विश्वामित्र उवाच ॥

यदि राजंस्त्वया दत्ता मम सर्व्वा वसुन्धरा ।
यत्र मे विषये स्वाम्यं तस्मान्निष्क्रान्तुमर्हसि ॥ ३३ ॥
श्रोणीसूत्रादिसकलं मुक्त्वा भूषणसंग्रहं ।
तरुवल्कलमाबध्य सह पत्न्या सुतेन च ॥ ३४ ॥

पक्षिण ऊचुः ॥

तथेति चोक्त्वा कृत्वा च राजा गन्तुं प्रचक्रमे ।
स्वपत्न्या शैब्यया सार्द्धं बालकेनात्मजेन च ॥ ३५ ॥
व्रजतः स ततो रुद्ध्वा पन्थानं प्राह तं नृपं ।
क्व यास्यसीत्यदत्वा मे दक्षिणां राजसूयिकीं ॥ ३६ ॥

हरिश्चन्द्र उवाच ॥

भगवन्राज्यमेतत्ते दत्तं निहतकण्टकं ।
अवशिष्टमिदं ब्रह्मन्नद्य देहत्रयं मम ॥ ३७ ॥

विश्वामित्र उवाच ॥

तथापि खलु दातव्या त्वया मे यज्ञदक्षिणा ।
विशेषतो ब्राह्मणानां हन्त्यदत्तं प्रतिश्रुतं ॥ ३८ ॥
यावत्तोषो राजसूये ब्राह्मणानां भवेन्नृप ।
तावदेव तु दातव्या दक्षिणा राजसूयिकी ॥ ३९ ॥
प्रतिश्रुत्य च दातव्यं योद्धव्यं चाततायिभिः ।
रक्षितव्यास्तथा चार्त्तास्त्वयैव प्राक् प्रतिश्रुतं ॥ ४० ॥

हरिश्चन्द्र उवाच ॥

भगवन् साम्प्रतं नास्ति दास्ये कालक्रमेण ते ।
प्रसादं कुरु विप्रर्षे सद्भावमनुचिन्त्य च ॥ ४१ ॥

विश्वामित्र उवाच ॥

किंप्रमाणो मया कालः प्रतीक्ष्यस्ते जनाधिप ।
शीघ्रमाचक्ष्व शापाग्निरन्यथा त्वां प्रधक्ष्यति ॥ ४२ ॥

हरिश्चन्द्र उवाच ॥

मासेन तव विप्रर्षे प्रदास्ये दक्षिणाधनं ।
साम्प्रतं नास्ति मे वित्तमनुज्ञां दातुमर्हसि ॥ ४३ ॥

विश्वामित्र उवाच ॥

गच्छ गच्छ नृपश्रेष्ठ स्वधर्ममनुपालय ।
शिवश्च तेऽध्वा भवतु मा सन्तु परिपन्थिनः ॥ ४४ ॥

पक्षिण ऊचुः ॥

अनुज्ञातः स गच्छेति जगाम वसुधाधिपः ।
प्रव्रज्यामनुचिता गन्तुमन्वगच्छत तं प्रिया ॥ ४५ ॥
तं सभार्य्यं नृपश्रेष्ठं निर्यान्तं ससुतं पुरात् ।
दृष्ट्वा प्रचुक्रुशुः पौरा राज्ञश्चैवानुयायिनः ॥ ४६ ॥
हा नाथ किं जहास्यस्मान् नित्यार्त्तिपरिपीडितान् ।
त्वं धर्म्मतत्परो राजन् पौरानुग्रहकृत्तथा ॥ ४७ ॥
नयास्मानपि राजर्षे यदि धर्ममवेक्षसे ।
मुहूर्त्तं तिष्ठ राजेन्द्र भवतो मुखपङ्कजं ॥ ४८ ॥
पिबामो नेत्रभ्रमरैः कदा द्रक्ष्यामहे पुनः ।
यस्य प्रयातस्य पुरो यान्ति पृष्ठे च पार्थिवाः ॥ ४९ ॥
तस्यानुयाति भार्य्येयं गृहीत्वा बालकं सुतं ।
यस्य भृत्याः प्रयातस्य यान्त्यग्रे कुञ्जरस्थिताः ॥ ५० ॥

स एष पद्भ्यां राजेन्द्रो हरिश्चन्द्रोऽद्य गच्छति।
हा राजन् सुकुमारं ते सुभ्रु सुत्वचमुन्नसं॥ ५१॥
पथि पांशुपरिक्लिष्टं मुखं कीदृग्भविष्यति।
तिष्ठ तिष्ठ नृपश्रेष्ठ स्वधर्ममनुपालय॥ ५२॥
आनृशंस्यं परो धर्मः क्षत्रियाणां विशेषतः।
किं दारैः किं सुतैर्नाथ धनैर्धान्यैरथापि वा॥ ५३॥
सर्व्वमेतत् परित्यज्य छायाभूता वयं तव।
हा नाथ हा महाराज हा स्वामिन् किं जहासि नः॥५४॥
यत्र त्वं तत्र हि वयं तत् सुखं यत्र वै भवान्।
नगरन्तद्भवान् यत्र स स्वर्गो यत्र नो नृपः॥ ५५॥
इति पौरवचः श्रुत्वा राजा शोकपरिप्लुतः।
अतिष्ठत् स तदा मार्गे तेषामेवानुकम्पया॥ ५६॥
विश्वामित्रोऽपि तं दृष्ट्वा पौरवाक्याकुलीकृतं।
रोषामर्षविवृत्ताक्षः समागम्य वचोऽब्रवीत्॥ ५७॥
धिक् त्वां दुष्टसमाचारमनृतं जिह्मभाषिणं।
मम राज्यञ्च दत्वा यः पुनः प्राक्रष्टुमिच्छसि॥ ५८॥
इत्युक्तः परुषन्तेन गच्छामीति सवेपथुः।
ब्रुवन्नेवं ययौ शीघ्रमाकर्षन्दयितां करे॥ ५९॥
कर्षतस्तां ततो भार्य्यां सुकुमारीं श्रमातुरां।
सहसा दण्डकाष्ठेन ताडयामास कौशिकः॥ ६०॥
तां तथा ताडितां दृष्ट्वा हरिश्चन्द्रो महीपतिः।
गच्छामीत्याह दुःखार्त्तो नान्यत् किञ्चिदुदाहरत्॥ ६१॥

अथ विश्वे तदा देवाः पञ्च प्राहुः कृपालवः ।
विश्वामित्रःसुपापोऽयं लोकान् कान् समवाप्स्यति ॥ ६२ ॥
येनायं यज्वनां श्रेष्ठः स्वराज्यादवरोपितः ।
कस्य वा श्रद्धया पूतं सुतं सोमं महाध्वरे ।
पीत्वा वयं प्रयास्यामो मुदं मन्त्रपुरःसरं ॥ ६३ ॥

पक्षिण ऊचुः ॥

इति तेषां वचः श्रुत्वा कौशिकोऽतिरुषान्वितः ।
शशाप तान् मनुष्यत्वं सर्व्वे यूयमवाप्स्यथ ॥ ६४ ॥
प्रसादितश्च तैः प्राह पुनरेव महामुनिः ।
मानुषत्वेऽपि भवतां भविची नैव सन्ततिः ॥ ६५ ॥
न दारसंग्रहश्चैव भविता नच मत्सरः ।
कामक्रोधविनिर्मुक्ता भविष्यथ सुराः पुनः ॥ ६६ ॥
ततोऽवतेरुरंशैः स्वैर्द्देवास्ते कुरुवेश्मनि ।
द्रौपदीगर्भसम्भूताः पञ्च वै पाण्डुनन्दनाः ॥ ६७ ॥
एतस्मात् कारणात् पञ्च पाण्डवेया महारथाः ।
न दारसंग्रहं प्राप्ताः शापात्तस्य महामुनेः ॥ ६८ ॥
एतत्ते सर्व्वमाख्यातं पाण्डवेयकथाश्रयं ।
प्रश्नं चतुष्टयं गीतं किमन्यच्छ्रोतुमिच्छसि ॥ ६९ ॥

इति मार्कण्डेयपुराणे द्रौपदेयोत्पत्तिः ॥ ७ ॥

अष्टमोऽध्यायः ॥

जैमिनिरुवाच ॥

भवद्भिरिदमाख्यातं यथाप्रश्नमनुक्रमात् ।
महत् कौतूहलं मेऽस्ति हरिश्चन्द्रकथां प्रति ॥ १ ॥
अहो महात्मना तेन प्राप्तं कृच्छ्रमनुत्तमं ।
कच्चित् सुखमनुप्राप्तं तादृगेव द्विजोत्तमाः ॥ २ ॥

पक्षिण ऊचुः ॥

विश्वामित्रवचः श्रुत्वा स राजा प्रययौ शनैः ।
शैव्ययानुगतो दुःखी भार्य्यया बालपुत्त्रया ॥ ३ ॥
स गत्वा वसुधापालो दिव्यां वाराणसीं पुरीं ।
नैषा मनुष्यभोग्येति शूलपाणेः परिग्रहः ॥ ४ ॥
जगाम पद्भ्यां दुःखार्त्तः सह पत्न्यानुकूलया ।
पुरीप्रवेशे ददृशे विश्वामित्रमुपस्थितं ॥ ५ ॥
तं दृष्ट्वा समनुप्राप्तं विनयावनतोऽभवत् ।
प्राह चैवाञ्जलिं कृत्वा हरिश्चन्द्रो महामुनिं ॥ ६ ॥
इमे प्राणाः सुतश्चायमियं पत्नी मुने मम ।
येन ते कृत्यमस्त्याशु तद्गृहाणार्घ्यमुत्तमं ॥ ७ ॥
यद्वान्यत् कार्य्यमस्माभिस्तदनुज्ञातुमर्हसि ॥ ८ ॥

विश्वामित्र उवाच ॥

पूर्णः स मासो राजर्षे दीयतां मम दक्षिणा ।
राजसूयनिमित्तं हि स्मर्य्यते स्ववचो यदि ॥ ९ ॥

हरिश्चन्द्र उवाच ॥

ब्रह्मन्नद्यैव संपूर्णो मासोऽम्लानतपोधन ।
तिष्ठत्येतद्दिनार्द्धं यत्तत् प्रतीक्षस्व मा चिरं ॥ १० ॥

विश्वामित्र उवाच ॥

एवमस्तु महाराज आगमिष्याम्यहं पुनः ।
शापं तव प्रदास्यामि नचेदद्य प्रदास्यसि ॥ ११ ॥

पक्षिण ऊचुः ॥

इत्युक्त्वा प्रययौ विप्रो राजा चाचिन्तयत्तदा ।
कथमस्मै प्रदास्यामि दक्षिणा या प्रतिश्रुता ॥ १२ ॥
कुतः पुष्टानि मित्राणि कुतोऽर्थः साम्प्रतं मम ।
प्रतिग्रहः प्रदुष्टो मे नाहं यायामधः कथं ॥ १३ ॥
किमु प्राणान् विमुञ्चामि कान्दिशं याम्यकिञ्चनः ।
यदि नाशं गमिष्यामि अप्रदाय प्रतिश्रुतं ॥ १४ ॥
ब्रह्मस्वहृत् कृमिः पापो भविष्याम्यधमाधमः ।
अथवा प्रेष्यतां यास्ये वरमेवात्मविक्रयः ॥ १५ ॥

पक्षिण ऊचुः ॥

राजानं व्याकुलं दीनं चिन्तयानमधोमुखं ।
प्रत्युवाच तदा पत्नी बाष्पगद्गदया गिरा ॥ १६ ॥
त्यज चिन्तां महाराज स्वसत्यमनुपालय ।
श्मशानवद्वर्जनीयो नरः सत्यबहिष्कृतः ॥ १७ ॥
नातः परतरं धर्म्मं वदन्ति पुरुषस्य तु ।
यादृशं पुरुषव्याघ्र स्वसत्यपरिपालनं ॥ १८ ॥

अग्निहोत्रमधीतं वा दानाद्याश्चाखिलाः क्रियाः ।
भजन्ते तस्य वैफल्यं यस्य वाक्यमकारणं ॥ १९ ॥
सत्यमत्यन्तमुदितं धर्मशास्त्रेषु धीमतां ।
तारणायान्तृतं तद्वत् पातनायाकृतात्मनां ॥ २० ॥
सप्ताश्वमेधानाहृत्य राजसूयञ्च पार्थिवः ।
कृतिर्नाम च्युतः स्वर्गादसत्यवचनात् सकृत् ॥ २१ ॥
राजन् जातमपत्यं मे इत्युक्का प्ररुरोद ह ।
बाष्पाम्बुप्लुतनेत्रान्तामुवाचेदं महीपतिः ॥ २२ ॥

हरिश्चन्द्र उवाच ॥

विमुञ्च भद्रे सन्तापमयं तिष्ठति बालकः ।
उच्यतां वक्तुकामासि यद्वा त्वं गजगामिनि ॥ २३ ॥

पत्नुयवाच ॥

राजन् जातमपत्यं मे सतां पुत्रफलाः स्त्रियः ।
'स मां प्रदाय वित्तेन देहि विप्राय दक्षिणां ॥ २४ ॥

पक्षिण ऊचुः ॥

एतद्वाक्यमुपश्रुत्य ययौ मोहं महीपतिः ।
प्रतिलभ्य च संज्ञां स विललापातिदुःखितः २५ ॥
महद्दुःखमिदं भद्रे यत्त्वमेवं ब्रवीषि मां ।
किन्तव स्मितसंलापा मम पापस्य विस्मृताः ॥ २६ ॥
हाहा कथं त्वया शक्यं वक्तुमेतत् शुचिस्मिते ।
दुर्व्वाच्यमेतद्वचनं कर्त्तुं शक्नोम्यहं कथं ॥ २७ ॥

इत्युक्त्वा स नरश्रेष्ठो धिग्धिगित्यसकृद्ब्रुवन् ।
निपपात महीपृष्ठे मूर्च्छयाभिपरिप्लुतः ॥ २८ ॥
शयानं भुवि तं दृष्ट्वा हरिश्चन्द्रं महीपतिं ।
उवाचेदं सकरुणं राजपत्नी सुदुःखिता ॥ २९ ॥

पत्न्युवाच ॥

हा महाराज कस्येदमपध्यानमुपस्थितं ।
यत्त्वं निपतितो भूमौ राङ्क्वास्तरणोचितः ॥ ३० ॥
येन कोट्यग्रगोवित्तं विप्राणामपवर्जितं ।
स एष पृथिवीनाथो भूमौ स्वपिति मे पतिः ॥ ३१ ॥
हा कष्टं किं तवानेन कृतं देव महीक्षिता ।
यदिन्द्रोपेन्द्रतुल्योऽयं नीतः प्रस्वापनीं दशां ॥ ३२ ॥
इत्युक्त्वा सापि सुश्रोणी मूर्च्छिता निपपात ह ।
भर्त्तृदुःखमहाभारेणासह्येन निपीडिता ॥ ३३ ॥
तौ तथा पतितौ भूमावनाथौ पितरौ शिशुः ।
दृष्ट्वात्यन्तं क्षुधाविष्टः प्राह वाक्यं सुदुःखितः ॥ ३४ ॥
तात तात ददस्वान्नमम्बाम्ब भोजनं दद ।
क्षुन्मे बलवती जाता जिह्वाग्रं शुष्यते तथा ॥ ३५ ॥

पक्षिण ऊचुः ॥

एतस्मिन्नन्तरे प्राप्तो विश्वामित्रो महातपाः ।
दृष्ट्वा तु तं हरिश्चन्द्रं पतितं भुवि मूर्च्छितं ॥ ३६ ॥
स वारिणा समभ्युक्ष्य राजानमिदमब्रवीत् ।
उत्तिष्ठोत्तिष्ठ राजेन्द्र तां ददस्वेष्टदक्षिणां ॥ ३७ ॥

ऋणं धारयतो दुःखमहन्यहनि वर्द्धते।
आप्याय्यमानः स तदा हिमशीतेन वारिणा॥ ३८॥
अवाप्य चेतनां राजा विश्वामित्रमवेक्ष्य च।
पुनर्म्मोहं समापेदे स च क्रोधं ययौ मुनिः॥ ३९॥
स समाश्वास्य राजानं वाक्यमाह द्विजोत्तमः।
दीयतां दक्षिणा सा मे यदि धर्म्ममवेक्षसे॥ ४०॥
सत्येनार्कः प्रतपति सत्ये तिष्ठति मेदिनी।
सत्यञ्चोक्तं परो धर्म्मः स्वर्गः सत्ये प्रतिष्ठितः॥ ४१॥
अश्वमेधसहस्रञ्च सत्यञ्च तुलया धृतं।
अश्वमेधसहस्राद्धि सत्यमेव विशिष्यते॥ ४२॥
अथवा किं ममैतेन साम्ना प्रोक्तेन कारणं।
अनार्य्ये पापसंकल्पे क्रूरे चानृतवादिनि॥ ४३॥
त्वयि राज्ञि प्रभवति सद्भावः श्रूयतामयं।
अद्य मे दक्षिणां राजन्न दास्यति भवान् यदि॥ ४४॥
अस्ताचलं प्रयातेऽर्के शप्स्यामि त्वां ततो ध्रुवं।
इत्युक्ता स ययौ विप्रो राजा चासीद्भयातुरः॥ ४५॥
कान्दिग्भूतोऽधमो निःस्वो नृशंसधनिनार्द्दितः।
भार्य्यास्य भूयः प्राहेदं क्रियतां वचनं मम॥ ४६॥
मा शापानलनिर्द्दग्धः पञ्चत्वमुपयास्यसि।
स तथा चोद्यमानस्तु राजा पत्न्या पुनः पुनः॥ ४७॥
प्राह भद्रे करोम्येष विक्रयं तव निर्घृणः।
नृशंसैरपि यत् कर्त्तुं न शक्यं तत् करोम्यहं॥ ४८॥

यदि मे शक्यते वाणी वक्तुमीदृक् सुदुर्व्वचः ।
एवमुक्त्वा ततो भार्य्यां गत्वा नगरमातुरः ।
बाष्पापिहितकण्ठाक्षस्ततो वचनमब्रवीत् ॥ ४९ ॥

राजोवाच ः

भो भो नागरिकाः सर्व्वे शृणुध्वं वचनं मम ।
किं मां पृच्छथ कस्त्वं भो नृशंसोऽहममानुषः ॥ ५० ॥
राक्षसो वातिकठिनस्ततः पापतरोऽपि वा ।
विक्रेतुं दयितां प्राप्तो यो न प्राणांस्त्यजाम्यहं ॥ ५१ ॥
यदि वः कस्यचित् कार्य्यं दास्या प्राणेष्टया मम ।
स ब्रवीतु त्वरायुक्तो यावत् सन्धारयाम्यहं ॥ ५२ ॥

पक्षिण ऊचुः ॥

अथ वृद्धो द्विजः कश्चिदागत्याह नराधिपं ।
समर्पयस्व मे दासीमहं क्रेता धनप्रदः ॥ ५३ ॥
अस्ति मे वित्तमस्तोकं सुकुमारी च मे प्रिया ।
गृहकर्म्म न शक्नोति कर्त्तुमस्मात् प्रयच्छ मे ॥ ५४ ॥
कर्म्मण्यतावयोरूपशीलानां तव योषितः ।
अनुरूपमिदं वित्तं गृहाणार्पय मेऽबलां ॥ ५५ ॥
एवमुक्तस्य विप्रेण हरिश्चन्द्रस्य भूपतेः ।
व्यदीर्य्यत मनो दुःखान्न चैनं किञ्चिदब्रवीत् ॥ ५६ ॥
ततः स विप्रो नृपतेर्वल्कलान्ते दृढं धनं ।
बद्धा केशेष्वथादाय नृपपत्नीमकर्षयत् ॥ ५७ ॥

रुरोद रोहितास्योऽपि दृष्ट्वा कृष्टान्तु मातरं ।
हस्तेन वस्त्रमाकर्षन् काकपक्षधरः शिशुः ॥ ५८ ॥

राजपत्न्युवाच ॥

मुञ्चार्य्य मुञ्च तावन्मां यावत् पश्याम्यहं शिशुं ।
दुर्लभं दर्शनं तात पुनरस्य भविष्यति ॥ ५९ ॥
पश्यैहि वत्स मामेवं मातरं दास्यतां गतां ।
मां मा स्प्राक्षीराजपुत्र अस्पृश्याहं तवाधुना ॥ ६० ॥
ततः स बालः सहसा दृष्ट्वा कृष्टान्तु मातरं ।
समभ्यधावदम्बेति रुदन् सास्राविलेक्षणः ॥ ६१ ॥
तमागतं द्विजः क्रेता बालमभ्याहनत् पदा ।
वदंस्तथापि सोऽम्बेति नैवामुञ्चत मातरं ॥ ६२ ॥

राजपत्न्युवाच ॥

प्रसादं कुरु मे नाथ क्रीणीष्वेमञ्च बालकं ।
क्रीतापि नाहं भवतो विनैनं कार्य्यसाधिका ॥ ६३ ॥
इत्थं ममाल्पभाग्यायाः प्रसादसुमुखो भव ।
मां संयोजय बालेन वत्सेनेव पयस्विनीं ॥ ६४ ॥

ब्राह्मण उवाच ॥

गृह्यतां वित्तमेतत्ते दीयतां बालको मम ।
स्त्रीपुंसोर्धर्मशास्त्रज्ञैः कृतमेव हि वेतनं ।
शतं सहस्रं लक्षञ्च कोटिमूल्यं तथा परैः ॥ ६५ ॥

पक्षिण ऊचुः ॥

तथैव तस्य तद्वित्तं बद्ध्वोत्तरपटे ततः ।
प्रगृह्य बालकं मात्रा सहैकस्थमबन्धयत् ॥ ६६ ॥
नीयमानौ तु तौ दृष्ट्वा भार्य्यापुत्रौ स पार्थिवः ।
विललाप सुदुःखार्त्तो निःश्वस्योष्णं पुनः पुनः ॥ ६७ ॥
यां न वायुर्न चादित्यो नेन्दुर्न च पृथग्जनः ।
दृष्टवन्तः पुरा पत्नीं सेयं दासीत्वमागता ॥ ६८ ॥
सूर्य्यवंशप्रसूतोऽयं सुकुमारकराङ्गुलिः ।
संप्राप्तो विक्रयं बालो धिङ्मामस्तु सुदुर्म्मतिं ॥ ६९ ॥
हा प्रिये हा शिशो वत्स ममानार्य्यस्य दुर्नयैः ।
दैवाधीनां दशां प्राप्तो न मृतोऽस्मि तथापि धिक् ॥ ७० ॥

पक्षिण ऊचुः ॥

एवं विलपतो राज्ञः स विप्रोऽन्तरधीयत ।
वृक्षगेहादिभिस्तुङ्गैस्तावादाय त्वरान्वितः ॥ ७१ ॥
विश्वामित्रस्ततः प्राप्तो नृपं वित्तमयाचत ।
तस्मै समर्पयामास हरिश्चन्द्रोऽपि तद्धनं ॥ ७२ ॥
तद्वित्तं स्तोकमालोक्य दारविक्रयसम्भवं ।
शोकाभिभूतं राजानं कुपितः कौशिकोऽब्रवीत् ॥ ७३ ॥
क्षत्रबन्धो ममेमां त्वं सदृशीं यज्ञदक्षिणां ।
मन्यसे यदि तत् क्षिप्रं पश्य त्वं मे बलं परं ॥ ७४ ॥
तपसोऽत्र सुतप्तस्य ब्राह्मण्यस्यामलस्य च ।
मत्प्रभावस्य चोग्रस्य शुद्धस्याध्ययनस्य च ॥ ७५ ॥

हरिश्चन्द्र उवाच ॥

अन्यां दास्यामि भगवन् कालः कश्चित् प्रतीच्यतां ।
साम्प्रतं नास्ति विक्रीना पत्नी पुत्रश्च बालकः ॥ ७६ ॥

विश्वामित्र उवाच ॥

चतुर्भागः स्थितो योऽयं दिवसस्य नराधिप ।
एष एव प्रतीच्यो मे वक्तव्यं नोत्तरं त्वया ॥ ७७ ॥

पक्षिण ऊचुः ॥

तमेवमुक्त्वा राजेन्द्रं निष्ठुरं निर्घृणं वचः ।
तदादाय धनं तूर्णं कुपितः कौशिको ययौ ॥ ७८ ॥
विश्वामित्रे गते राजा भयशोकाब्धिमध्यगः ।
सर्व्वाकारं विनिश्चित्य प्रोवाचोच्चैरधोमुखः ॥ ७९ ॥
वित्तक्रीतेन यो ह्यर्थी मया प्रेष्येण मानवः ।
स ब्रवीतु त्वरायुक्तो यावत्तपति भास्करः ॥ ८० ॥
अथाजगाम त्वरितो धर्मश्चण्डालरूपधृक् ।
दुर्गन्धो विकृतो रूक्षः श्मश्रुलो दन्तुरो घृणी ॥ ८१ ॥
कृष्णो लम्बोदरः पिङ्गरूक्षाक्षः परुषाक्षरः ।
गृहीतपक्षिपुञ्जश्च शवमाल्यैरलङ्कृतः ॥ ८२ ॥
कपालहस्तो दीर्घास्यो भैरवोऽतिवदन् मुहुः ।
श्वगणाभिवृतो घोरो यष्टिहस्तो निराकृतिः ॥ ८३ ॥

चण्डाल उवाच ॥

अहमर्थी त्वया शीघ्रं कथयस्वात्मवेतनं ।
स्तोकेन बहुना वापि येन वै लभ्यते भवान् ॥ ८४ ॥

पक्षिण ऊचुः ॥

तं तादृशमथालक्ष्य क्रूरदृष्टिं सुनिष्ठुरं ।
वदन्तमतिदुःशीलं कस्त्वमित्याह पार्थिवः ॥ ८५ ॥

चण्डाल उवाच ॥

चण्डालोऽहमिहाख्यातः प्रवीरेति पुरोत्तमे ।
विख्यातो बध्यबधको मृतकम्बलहारकः ॥ ८६ ॥

हरिश्चन्द्र उवाच ॥

नाहं चण्डालदासत्वमिच्छेयं सुविगर्हितं ।
वरं शापाग्निना दग्धो न चण्डालवशं गतः ॥ ८७ ॥

पक्षिण ऊचुः ॥

तस्यैवं वदतः प्राप्तो विश्वामित्रस्तपोनिधिः ।
कोपामर्षविवृत्ताक्षः प्राह चेदं नराधिपं ॥ ८८ ॥

विश्वामित्र उवाच ॥

चण्डालोऽयमनल्पं ते दातुं वित्तमुपस्थितः ।
कस्मान्न दीयते मह्यमशेषा यज्ञदक्षिणा ॥ ८९ ॥

हरिश्चन्द्र उवाच ॥

भगवन् सूर्य्यवंशोत्थमात्मानं वेद्मि कौशिक ।
कथं चण्डालदासत्वं गमिष्ये वित्तकामुकः ॥ ९० ॥

विश्वामित्र उवाच ॥

यदि चण्डालवित्तं त्वमात्मविक्रयजं मम ।
न प्रदास्यसि कालेन शप्स्यामि त्वामसंशयं ॥ ९१ ॥

पक्षिण ऊचुः ॥

हरिश्चन्द्रस्ततो राजा चिन्तावस्थितजीवितः ।
प्रसीदेति वदन् पादादृषेर्जग्राह विह्वलः ॥ ९२ ॥
दासोऽस्म्यार्त्तोऽस्मि भीतोऽस्मि त्वद्भक्तश्च विशेषतः ।
कुरु प्रसादं विप्रर्षे कष्टश्चण्डालसङ्करः ॥ ९३ ॥
भवेयं वित्तशेषेण सर्व्वकर्मकरो वशः ।
तवैव मुनिशार्द्दूल प्रेष्यश्चित्तानुवर्त्तकः ॥ ९४ ॥

विश्वामित्र उवाच ॥

यदि प्रेष्यो मम भवान् चण्डालाय ततो मया ।
दासभावमनुप्राप्तो दत्तो वित्तार्व्वुदेन वै ॥ ९५ ॥

पक्षिण ऊचुः ॥

एवमुक्ते तदा तेन श्वपाको हृष्टमानसः ।
विश्वामित्राय तद्द्रव्यं दत्वा बद्धा नरेश्वरं ॥ ९६ ॥
दण्डप्रहारसंभ्रान्तमतीवव्याकुलेन्द्रियं ।
इष्टबन्धुवियोगार्त्तमनयन्निजपत्तनं ॥ ९७ ॥
हरिश्चन्द्रस्ततो राजा वसंश्चण्डालपत्तने ।
प्रातर्मध्याह्नसमये सायञ्चैतदगायत ॥ ९८ ॥
बाला दीनमुखी दृष्ट्वा बालं दीनमुखं पुरः ।
मां स्मरत्यसुखाविष्टा मोचयिष्यति नौ नृपः ॥ ९९ ॥
उपात्तवित्तो विप्राय दत्वा वित्तमतोऽधिकं ।
न सा मां मृगशावाक्षी वेत्ति पापतरं कृतं ॥ १०० ॥

राज्यनाशः सुहृत्त्यागो भार्य्यातनयविक्रयः।
प्राप्ता चण्डालता चेयमहो दुःखपरम्परा ॥ १०१ ॥
एवं स निवसन्नित्यं सस्मार दयितं सुतं।
भार्य्याञ्चात्मसमाविष्टां हृतसर्व्वस्व आतुरः ॥ १०२ ॥
कस्य चित्त्वथ कालस्य मृतचेलापहारकः।
हरिश्चन्द्रोऽभवद्राजा श्मशाने तद्वशानुगः ॥ १०३ ॥
चण्डालेनानुशिष्टश्च मृतचेलापहारिणा।
शवागमनमन्विच्छन्निह तिष्ठ दिवानिशं ॥ १०४ ॥
इदं राज्ञेऽपि देयञ्च षड्भागन्तु शवं प्रति।
चयस्तु मम भागाः स्युर्द्वौ भागौ तव वेतनं ॥ १०५ ॥
इति प्रतिसमादिष्टो जगाम शवमन्दिरं।
दिशं तु दक्षिणां यच वाराणस्यां स्थितं तदा ॥ १०६ ॥
श्मशानं घोरसंनादं शिवाशतसमाकुलं।
शवमौलिसमाकीर्णं दुर्गन्धं बहुधूमकं ॥ १०७ ॥
पिशाचभूतवेतालडाकिनीयक्षसंकुलं।
गृध्रगोमायुसंकीर्णं श्ववृन्दपरिवारितं ॥ १०८ ॥
अस्थिसंघातसंकीर्णं महादुर्गन्धसंकुलं।
नानामृतसुहृन्नादरौद्रकोलाहलायुतं ॥ १०९ ॥
हा पुच मिच हा बन्धो भ्रातर्वत्स प्रियाद्य मे।
हा पते भगिनि मातर्हा मातुल पितामह ॥ ११० ॥
मातामह पितः पौच्च क्व गतोऽस्येहि बान्धव।
इत्येवं वदतां यच ध्वनिः संश्रूयते महान् ॥ १११ ॥

ज्वलन्मांसवसामेदच्छमच्छमितसंकुलं ॥ ११२ ॥
अर्द्धदग्धाः शवाः श्यामाविकसद्दन्तपंक्तयः ।
हसन्तीवाग्निमध्यस्थाः कायस्येयं दशा त्विति ॥ ११३ ॥
अग्नेश्चटचटाशब्दो वयसामस्थिपंक्तिषु ।
बान्धवाक्रन्दशब्दश्च पुक्कसेषु प्रहर्षजः ॥ ११४ ॥
गायतां भूतवेतालपिशाचगणरक्षसां ।
श्रूयते सुमहान् घोरः कल्पान्त इव निःस्वनः ॥ ११५ ॥
महामहिषकारीषगोशकृद्राशिसंकुलं ॥
तदुत्थभस्मकूटैश्च वृतं सास्थिभिरुन्नतैः ॥ ११६ ॥
नानोपहारस्रग्दीपकाकविच्छेपकालिकं ।
अनेकशब्दबहुलं श्मशानं नरकायते ॥ ११७ ॥
सवह्निगर्भैरशिवैः शिवारुतैर्निनादितं भीषणरावगह्वरं ।
भयं भयस्याप्युपसञ्जनैर्भृशं श्मशानमाक्रन्दविरावदारुणं ।
स राजा तत्र संप्राप्तो दुःखितः शोचनोद्यतः ॥ [११८॥]
हा भृत्या मन्त्रिणो विप्राः क्व तद्राज्यं विधे गतं ॥ ११९ ॥
हा शैव्ये पुत्र हा बाल मां त्यक्त्वा मन्दभाग्यकं ।
विश्वामित्रस्य दोषेण गताः कुत्रापि ते मम ॥ १२० ॥
इत्येवं चिन्तयंस्तत्र चण्डालोक्तं पुनः पुनः ।
मलिनो रूक्षसर्वाङ्गः केशवान् गन्धवान् ध्वजी ॥ १२१ ॥
लकुटी कालकल्पश्च धावंश्चापि ततस्ततः ।
अस्मिन् शव इदं मूल्यं प्राप्तं प्राप्स्यामि चाप्युत ॥ १२२ ॥
इदं मम इदं राज्ञे मुख्यचण्डालके त्विदं ।

इति धावन् दिशो राजा जीवन् योन्यन्तरं गतः ॥१२३॥
जीर्णकर्पटसुग्रन्थिकृतकन्थापरिग्रहः ।
चिताभस्मरजोलिप्तमुखबाहूदराङ्घ्रिकः ॥ १२४ ॥
नानामेदोवसामज्जालिप्तपाण्यङ्गुलिः श्वसन् ।
नानाशवौदनकृताहारतृप्तिपरायणः ॥ १२५ ॥
तदीयमाल्यसंश्लेषकृतमस्तकमण्डनः ।
न रात्रौ न दिवा शेते हा हेति प्रवदन् मुहुः ॥ १२६ ॥
एवं द्वादशमासास्तु नीताः शतसमोपमाः ।
स कदाचिन्नृपश्रेष्ठः श्रान्तो बन्धुवियोगवान् ॥ १२७ ॥
निद्राभिभूतो रूक्षाङ्गो निश्चेष्टः सुप्त एव च ।
तत्रापि शयनीये स दृष्टवानद्भुतं महत् ॥ १२८ ॥
श्मशानाभ्यासयोगेन दैवस्य बलवत्तया ।
अन्यदेहेन दत्वा तु गुरवे गुरुदक्षिणां ॥ १२९ ॥
तदा द्वादश वर्षाणि दुःखदानात्तु निष्कृतिः ।
आत्मानं स ददर्शाथ पुक्कसीगर्भसम्भवं ॥ १३० ॥
तत्रस्थश्चाप्यसौ राजा सोऽचिन्तयदिदं तदा ।
इतो निष्क्रान्तमात्रो हि दानधर्मं करोम्यहम् ॥ १३१ ॥
अनन्तरं स जातस्तु तदा पुक्कसबालकः ।
श्मशानमृतसंस्कारकरणेषु सदोद्यतः ॥ १३२ ॥
प्राप्ते तु सप्तमे वर्षे श्मशानेऽथ मृतो द्विजः ।
आनीतो बन्धुभिर्दृष्टस्तेन तत्राधनो गुणी ॥ १३३ ॥
मूल्यार्थिना तु तेनापि परिभूतास्तु ब्राह्मणाः ।

ऊचुस्ते ब्राह्मणास्तच विश्वामिचस्य चेष्टितम् ॥ १३४ ॥
पापिष्ठमशुभं कर्म्म कुरु त्वं पापकारक ।
हरिश्चन्द्रः पुरा राजा विश्वामिचेण पुक्कसः ॥ १३५ ॥
कृतः पुण्यविनाशेन ब्राह्मणस्वापनाशनात् ।
यदा न क्षमते तेषां तैः स शप्तो रुषा तदा ॥ १३६ ॥
गच्छ त्वं नरकं घोरमधुनैव नराधम ।
इत्युक्तमाचे वचने स्वप्नस्थः स नृपस्तदा ॥ १३७ ॥
अपश्यद्यमदूतान् वै पाशहस्तान् भयावहान् ।
तैः सङ्गृहीतमात्मानं नीयमानं तदा बलात् ॥ १३८ ॥
पश्यति स्म भृशं खिन्नो हा मातः पितरश्च मे ।
एवं वादी स नरके तैलद्रोण्यां निपातितः ॥ १३९ ॥
क्रकचैः पाद्यमानस्तु क्षुरधाराभिरप्यधः ।
अन्धे तमसि दुःखार्त्तः पूयशोणितभोजनः ॥ १४० ॥
सप्तवर्षं मृतात्मानं पुक्कसत्वे ददर्श ह ।
दिनं दिनं तु नरके दह्यते पच्यतेऽन्यतः ॥ १४१ ॥
खिद्यते क्षोभ्यतेऽन्यच मार्यते पाद्यतेऽन्यतः ।
क्षार्यते दीप्यतेऽन्यच शीतवाताहतोऽन्यतः ॥ १४२ ॥
एकं दिनं वर्षशतप्रमाणं नरकेऽभवत् ।
तथा वर्षशतं तच श्रावितं नरके भटैः ॥ १४३ ॥
ततो निपातितो भूमौ विष्ठाशी श्वा व्यजायत ।
वान्ताशी शीतदग्धश्च मासमाचे मृतोऽपि सः ॥ १४४ ॥
अथापश्यत् खरं देहं हस्तिनं वानरं पशुं ।

छागं विडालं कङ्कं च गामविं पक्षिणां कृमिम् ॥ १४५ ॥
मत्स्यं कूर्मं वराहञ्च श्वाविधं कुक्कुटं शुकं ।
शारिकां स्थावरांश्चैव सर्पमन्यांश्च देहिनः ॥ १४६ ॥
दिवसे दिवसे जन्म प्राणिनः प्राणिनस्तदा ।
अपश्यद्दुःखसन्तप्तो दिनं वर्षशतं तथा ॥ १४७ ॥
एवं वर्षशतं पूर्णं गतं तत्र कुयोनिषु ।
अपश्यच्च कदाचित् स राजा तत् स्वकुलोद्भवम् ॥ १४८ ॥
तत्र स्थितस्य तस्यापि राज्यं द्यूतेन हारितम् ।
भार्या हृता च पुत्रश्च स चैकाकी वनं गतः ॥ १४९ ॥
तत्रापश्यत् स सिंहं वै व्यादितास्यं भयावहम् ।
बिभक्षयिषुमायातं शरभेण समन्वितम् ॥ १५० ॥
पुनश्च भक्षितः सोऽपि भार्य्यां शोचितुमुद्यतः ।
हा शैब्ये क्व गतास्यद्य मामिहापास्य दुःखितं ॥ १५१ ॥
अपश्यत् पुनरेवापि भार्य्यां स्वां सहपुत्रकां ।
त्रायस्व त्वं हरिश्चन्द्र किं द्यूतेन तव प्रभो ॥ १५२ ॥
पुत्रस्ते शोच्यतां प्राप्तो भार्य्यया शैब्यया सह ।
स नापश्यत् पुनरपि धावमानः पुनः पुनः ॥ १५३ ॥
अथापश्यत् पुनरपि स्वर्गस्थः स नराधिपः ।
नीयते मुक्तकेशी सा दीना विवसना बलात् ॥ १५४ ॥
हाहावाक्यं प्रमुञ्चन्ती त्रायस्वेत्यसकृत्स्वना ।
अथापश्यत् पुनस्तत्र धर्म्मराजस्य शासनात् ॥ १५५ ॥
आक्रन्दन्त्यन्तरिक्षस्था आगच्छेह नराधिप ।

विश्वामित्रेण विप्राप्तो यमो राजंस्तवार्थतः ॥ १५६ ॥
इत्युक्त्वा सर्पपाशैस्तु नीयते बलवद्भिभुः ।
श्राद्धदेवेन कथितं विश्वामित्रस्य चेष्टितं ॥ १५७ ॥
तत्रापि तस्य विकृतिर्नाधर्म्मोत्था व्यवर्द्धत ।
एताः सर्व्वा दशास्तस्य याः स्वप्ने सम्प्रदर्शिताः ॥ १५८ ॥
सर्व्वास्तास्तेन सम्भुक्ता यावद्वर्षाणि द्वादश ।
अतीते द्वादशे वर्षे नीयमानो भटैर्बलात् ॥ १५९ ॥
यमं सोऽपश्यदाकारादुवाच च नराधिपम् ।
विश्वामित्रस्य कोपोऽयं दुर्निवार्य्यो महात्मनः ॥ १६० ॥
पुत्रस्य ते मृत्युमपि प्रदास्यति स कौशिकः ।
गच्छ त्वं मानुषं लोकं दुःखशेषं च भुंच्व वै ॥
गतस्य तत्र राजेन्द्र श्रेयस्तव भविष्यति ॥ १६१ ॥
व्यतीते द्वादशे वर्षे दुःखस्यान्ते नराधिपः ।
अन्तरिक्षाच्च पतितो यमदूतैः प्रणोदितः ॥ १६२ ॥
पतितो यमलोकाच्च विबुद्धो भयसम्भ्रमात् ।
अहो कष्टमिति ध्यात्वा क्षते क्षारावसेवनं ॥ १६३ ॥
स्वप्ने दुःखं महद्दृष्टं यस्यान्तो नोपलभ्यते ।
स्वप्ने दृष्टं मया यत्तु किन्तु मे द्वादशाः समाः ॥ १६४ ॥
गतेत्यपृच्छत्तत्रस्थान् पुक्कसांस्तु स सम्भ्रमात् ।
नेत्युचुः केचित्तत्रस्था एवमेवापरेऽब्रवन् ॥ १६५ ॥
श्रुत्वा दुःखी तदा राजा देवान् शरणमोयिवान् ।
स्वस्ति कुर्व्वन्तु मे देवाः शैव्याया बालकस्य च ॥ १६६ ॥

नमो धर्म्माय महते नमः कृष्णाय वेधसे ।
परावराय शुद्धाय पुराणायाव्ययाय च ॥ १६७ ॥
नमो बृहस्पते तुभ्यं नमस्ते वासवाय च ।
एवमुक्त्वा स राजा तु युक्तः पुक्कसकर्म्मणि ॥ १६८ ॥
शवानां मूल्यकरणे पुनर्नष्टस्मृतिर्यथा ।
मलिनो जटिलः कृष्णो लकुटी विह्वलो नृपः ॥ १६९ ॥
नैव पुत्रो न भार्य्या तु तस्य वै स्मृतिगोचरे ।
नष्टोत्साहो राज्यनाशाच्छ्मशाने निवसंस्तदा ॥ १७० ॥
अथाजगाम स्वसुतं मृतमादाय लापिनी ।
भार्य्या तस्य नरेन्द्रस्य सर्पदष्टं हि बालकं ॥ १७१ ॥
हा वत्स हा पुत्र शिशो इत्येवं वदती मुहुः ।
कृशा विवर्णा विमनाः पांशुध्वस्तशिरोरुहा ॥ १७२ ॥

राजपत्नुवाच ॥

हा राजन्नाद्य बालं त्वं पश्यसीमं महीतले ।
रममाणं पुरा दृष्टं दष्टं पुष्टाहिना मृतं ॥ १७३ ॥
तस्या विलापशब्दन्तमाकर्ण्य स नराधिपः ।
जगाम त्वरितोऽचेति भविता मृतकम्बलः ॥ १७४ ॥
स तां रोरुदतीं भार्य्यां नाभ्यजानात्तु पार्थिवः ।
चिरप्रवाससन्तप्तां पुनर्जातामिवाबलां ॥ १७५ ॥
सापि तं चारुकेशान्तं पुरा दृष्ट्वा जटालकं ।
नाभ्यजानान्नृपसुता शुष्कवृक्षोपमं नृपं ॥ १७६ ॥
सोऽपि कृष्णपटे बालं दृष्ट्वाशीविषपीडितं ।

नरेन्द्रलक्षणोपेतं चिन्तामाप नरेश्वरः ॥ १७७ ॥
अहो कष्टं नरेन्द्रस्य कस्याप्येष कुले शिशुः ।
जातो नीतः कृतान्तेन कामप्यांशां दुरात्मना ॥ १७८ ॥
एवं दृष्ट्वा हि मे बालं मातुरुत्सङ्गशायिनं ।
स्मृतिमभ्यागतो बालो रोहितास्योऽब्जलोचनः ॥ १७९ ॥
सोऽप्येतामेव मे वत्सो वयोऽवस्थामुपागतः ।
नीतो यदि न घोरेण कृतान्तेनात्मनो वशं ॥ १८० ॥

राजपत्नुवाच ॥

हा वत्स कस्य पापस्य अपध्यानादिदं महत् ।
दुःखमापतितं घोरं यस्यान्तो नोपलभ्यते ॥ १८१ ॥
हा नाथ राजन् भवता मामनाश्वास्य दुःखितां ।
क्वापि सन्तिष्ठता स्थाने विश्रब्धं स्थीयते कथं ॥ १८२ ॥
राज्यनाशः सुहृत्त्यागो भार्य्यातनयविक्रयः ।
हरिश्चन्द्रस्य राजर्षेः किं विधे न कृतं त्वया ॥ १८३ ॥
इति तस्या वचः श्रुत्वा राजा स्वस्थानतश्च्युतः ।
प्रत्यभिज्ञाय दयितां पुत्रञ्च निधनं गतं ॥ १८४ ॥
कष्टं शैब्येयमेषा हि स बालोऽयमितीरयन् ।
रुरोद दुःखसन्तप्तो मूर्च्छामभिजगाम च ॥ १८५ ॥
सा च तं प्रत्यभिज्ञाय तामवस्थामुपागतं ।
मूर्च्छिता निपपातार्त्ता निश्चेष्टा धरणीतले ॥ १८६ ॥
चेतः संप्राप्य राजेन्द्रो राजपत्नी च तौ समं ।
विलेपतुः सुसन्तप्तौ शोकभारावपीडितौ ॥ १८७ ॥

राजोवाच ॥

हा वत्स सुकुमारं ते स्वक्षिभ्रूनासिकालकं ।
पश्यतो मे मुखं दीनं हृदयं किं न दीर्य्यते ॥ १८८ ॥
तात तातेति मधुरं ब्रुवाणं स्वयमागतं ।
उपगुह्य वदिष्ये कं वत्स वत्सेति सौहृदात् ॥ १८९ ॥
कस्य जानुप्रणीतेन पिङ्गेन क्षितिरेणुना ।
ममोत्तरीयमुत्सङ्गं तथाङ्गं मलमेष्यति ॥ १९० ॥
अङ्गप्रत्यङ्गसम्भूतो मनोहृदयनन्दनः ।
मया कुपित्रा हा वत्स विक्रीतो येन वस्तुवत् ॥ १९१ ॥
हृत्वा राज्यमशेषं मे ससाधनधनं महत् ।
दैवाहिना नृशंसेन दष्टो मे तनयस्ततः ॥ १९२ ॥
अहं दैवाहिदष्टस्य पुत्त्रस्याननपङ्कजं ।
निरीक्षन्नपि घोरेण विषेणान्धीकृतोऽधुना ॥ १९३ ॥
एवमुक्त्वा तमादाय बालकं बाष्पगद्गदः ।
परिष्वज्य च निश्चेष्टो मूर्च्छया निपपात ह ॥ १९४ ॥

राजपत्न्युवाच ॥

अयं स पुरुषव्याघ्रः स्वरेणैवोपलक्ष्यते ।
विद्वज्जनमनश्चन्द्रो हरिश्चन्द्रो न संशयः ॥ १९५ ॥
तथास्य नासिका तुङ्गा अग्रतोऽधोमुखं गता ।
दन्ताश्च मुकुलप्रख्याः ख्यातकीर्त्तेर्म्महात्मनः ॥ १९६ ॥
श्मशानमागतः कस्मादद्यैष स नरेश्वरः ।
अपहाय पुत्त्रशोकं साऽपश्यत् पतितं पतिं ॥ १९७ ॥

प्रकृष्टा विस्मिता दीना भर्त्तृपुत्राधिपीडिता।
वीक्षन्ती सा ततोऽपश्यत् भर्त्तृदण्डं जुगुप्सितं॥ १९८॥
श्वपाकार्हमतो मोहं जगामायतलोचना।
प्राप्य चेतश्च शनकैः सगद्गदमभाषत॥ १९९॥
धिक् त्वां दैवातिकरुणं निर्म्मर्य्यादं जुगुप्सितं।
येनायममरप्रख्यो नीतो राजा श्वपाकतां॥ २००॥
राज्यनाशं सुहृत्त्यागं भार्य्यातनयविक्रयं।
प्रापयित्वापि नो मुक्तश्चण्डालोऽयं कृतो नृपः॥ २०१॥
हा राजन् जातसन्तापामित्थं मां धरणीतलात्।
उत्थाप्य नाद्य पर्य्यङ्कमारोहेति किमुच्यते॥॥ २०२॥
नाद्य पश्यामि ते छत्रं भृङ्गारमथवा पुनः।
चामरं व्यजनञ्चापि कोऽयं विधिविपर्य्ययः॥ २०३॥
यस्याग्रे व्रजतः पूर्व्वं राजानो भृत्यतां गताः।
स्वोत्तरीयैरकुर्व्वन्त नीरजस्कं महीतलं॥ २०४॥
सोऽयं कपालसंलग्नघटीघटनिरन्तरे।
मृतनिर्म्माल्यसूत्रान्तर्गूढकेशे सुदारुणे॥ २०५॥
वसानिस्यन्दसंशुष्कमहीपुटकमण्डिते।
भस्माङ्गारार्द्धदग्धास्थिमज्जसंघट्टभीषणे॥ २०६॥
गृध्रगोमायुनादार्त्तनष्टक्षुद्रविहङ्गमे।
चिताधूमाततिरुचा नीलीकृतदिगन्तरे॥ २०७॥
कुणपास्वादनमुदा संप्रहृष्टनिशाचरे।
चरत्यमेध्ये राजेन्द्रः श्मशाने दुःखपीडितः॥ २०८॥

एवमुक्त्वा समाश्लिष्य कण्ठं राज्ञो नृपात्मजा ।
कष्टशोकशताधारा विललापार्त्तया गिरा ॥ २०९ ॥

राजपत्न्युवाच ॥

राजन् स्वप्नोऽथ तथ्यं वा यदेतन्मन्यते भवान् ।
तत् कथ्यतां महाभाग मनो वै मुह्यते मम ॥ २१० ॥
यद्येतदेवं धर्म्मञ्च नास्ति धर्म्मे सहायता ।
तथैव विप्रदेवादिपूजने पालने भुवः ॥ २११ ॥
नास्ति धर्म्मः कुतः सत्यमार्जवं चानृशंसता ।
यत्र त्वं धर्म्मपरमः स्वराज्यादवरोपितः ॥ २१२ ॥
इति तस्या वचः श्रुत्वा निःश्वस्योष्णं सगद्गदं ।
कथयामास तन्वङ्ग्या यथा प्राप्ता श्वपाकता ॥ २१३ ॥
रुदित्वा सापि सुचिरं निःश्वस्योष्णञ्च दुःखिता ।
स्वपुत्रमरणं भीरुर्यथा वृत्तं न्यवेदयत् ॥ २१४ ॥

राजोवाच ॥

प्रिये न रोचये दीर्घं कालं क्लेशमुपासितुम् ।
नात्मायत्तश्च तन्वङ्गि पश्य मे मन्दभाग्यतां ॥ २१५ ॥
चण्डालेनाननुज्ञातः प्रवेक्ष्ये ज्वलनं यदि ।
चण्डालदासतां यास्ये पुनरप्यन्यजन्मनि ॥ २१६ ॥
नरके च पतिष्यामि कीटकः कृमिभोजनः ।
वैतरण्यां महापूयवसासृक्स्नायुपिच्छिले ॥ २१७ ॥
असिपत्रवने प्राप्य च्छेदं प्राप्स्यामि दारुणं ।
तापं प्राप्स्यामि वा प्राप्य महारौरवरौरवौ ॥ २१८ ॥

मग्नस्य दुःखजलधौ पारः प्राणवियोजनं ।
एकोऽपि बालको योऽयमासीद्वंशकरः सुतः ॥ २१९ ॥
मम दैवाम्बुवेगेन मग्नः सोऽपि बलीयसा ।
कथं प्राणान् विमुञ्चामि परायत्तोऽस्मि दुर्गतः ॥ २२० ॥
अथवा नार्त्तिना क्लिष्टो नरः पापमवेक्षते ।
तिर्य्यक्त्वे नास्ति तद्दुःखं नासिपत्रवने तथा ॥ २२१ ॥
वैतरण्यां कुतस्तादृग् यादृशं पुत्रविप्लवे ।
सोऽहं सुतशरीरेण दीप्यमाने हुताशने ॥ २२२ ॥
निपतिष्यामि तन्वङ्गि क्षन्तव्यं कुकृतं मम ।
अनुज्ञाता च गच्छ त्वं विप्रवेश्म शुचिस्मिते ॥ २२३ ॥
मम वाक्यञ्च तन्वङ्गि निबोधादृतमानसा ।
यदि दत्तं यदि हुतं गुरवो यदि तोषिताः ॥ २२४ ॥
परत्र सङ्गमो भूयात् पुत्रेण सह च त्वया ।
इह लोके कुतस्त्वेतद्भविष्यति ममेङ्गितम् ॥ २२५ ॥
त्वया सह मम श्रेयो गमनं पुत्रमार्गणे ।
यन्मया हसता किञ्चिद्रहस्ये वा शुचिस्मिते ॥ २२६ ॥
अश्लीलमुक्तं तत् सर्वं क्षन्तव्यं मम याचतः ।
राजपत्नीति गर्व्वेण नावज्ञेयः स ते द्विजः ॥
सर्व्वयत्नेन ते तोष्यः स्वामिदैवतवच्छुभे ॥ २२७ ॥

राजपत्न्युवाच ॥

अहमप्यत्र राजर्षे दीप्यमाने हुताशने ।
दुःखभारासहाद्यैव सह यास्यामि वै त्वया ॥ २२८ ॥

पक्षिण ऊचुः ॥

ततः कृत्वा चितां राजा आरोप्य तनयं स्वकं ।
भार्य्यया सहितश्चासौ बद्धाञ्जलिपुटस्तदा ॥ २२९ ॥
चिन्तयन् परमात्मानमीशं नारायणं हरिं ।
हृत्कोटरगुहासीनं वासुदेवं सुरेश्वरं ॥
अनादिनिधनं ब्रह्म कृष्णं पीताम्बरं शुभं ॥ २३० ॥
तस्य चिन्तयमानस्य सर्वे देवाः सवासवाः ।
धर्म्मं प्रमुखतः कृत्वा समाजग्मुस्त्वरान्विताः ॥ २३१ ॥
आगत्य सर्व्वे प्रोचुस्ते भो भो राजन् शृणु प्रभो ।
अयं पितामहः साक्षाद्धर्म्मश्च भगवान् स्वयं ॥ २३२ ॥
साध्याश्च विश्वे मरुतो लोकपालाः सवाहनाः ।
नागाः सिद्धाः सगन्धर्व्वा रुद्राश्चैव तथाश्विनौ ॥ २३३ ॥
एते चान्ये च बहवो विश्वामित्रस्तथैव च ।
विश्वत्रयेण यो मित्रं कर्त्तुं न शकितः पुरा ॥ २३४ ॥
विश्वामित्रस्तु ते मैत्रीमिष्टञ्चाहर्त्तुमिच्छति ।
आरुरोह ततः प्राप्तो धर्म्मः शक्रोऽथ गाधिजः ॥ २३५ ॥

धर्म्म उवाच ॥

मा राजन् साहसं कार्षीर्धर्म्मोऽहं त्वामुपागतः ।
तितिक्षादमसत्याद्यैः स्वगुणैः परितोषितः ॥ २३६ ॥

इन्द्र उवाच ॥

हरिश्चन्द्र महाभाग प्राप्तः शक्रोऽस्मि तेऽन्तिकं ।
त्वया सभार्य्यपुत्रेण जिता लोकाः सनातनाः ॥ २३७ ॥

आरोह त्रिदिवं राजन् भार्य्यापुत्त्रसमन्वितः ।
सुदुष्प्रापं नरैरन्यैर्जितमात्मीयकर्म्मभिः ॥ २३८ ॥

पक्षिण ऊचुः ॥

ततोऽमृतमयं वर्षमपमृत्युविनाशनं ।
इन्द्रः प्राक्सृजदाकाशाच्चितास्थानगतः प्रभुः ॥ २३९ ॥
पुष्पवर्षञ्च सुमहद्देवदुन्दुभिनिस्वनं ।
ततस्ततो वर्त्तमाने समाजे देवसंकुले ॥ २४० ॥
समुत्तस्थौ ततः पुत्त्रो राज्ञस्तस्य महात्मनः ।
सुकुमारतनुः सुस्थः प्रसन्नेन्द्रियमानसः ॥ २४१ ॥
ततो राजा हरिश्चन्द्रः परिष्वज्य सुतं क्षणात् ।
सभार्य्यः स्वश्रिया युक्तो दिव्यमाल्याम्बरान्वितः ॥ २४२ ॥
सुस्थः सम्पूर्णहृदयो मुदा परमया युतः ।
बभूव तत्क्षणादिन्द्रो भूयश्चैनमभाषत ॥ २४३ ॥
सभार्य्यस्त्वं सपुत्त्रश्च प्राप्स्यसे सद्गतिं परां ।
समारोह महाभाग निजानां कर्म्मणां फलैः ॥ २४४ ॥

हरिश्चन्द्र उवाच ॥

देवराजाननुज्ञातः स्वामिना श्वपचेन वै ।
अगत्वा निष्कृतिं तस्य नारोक्ष्येऽहं सुरालयं ॥ २४५ ॥

धर्म्म उवाच ।

तवैनं भाविनं क्लेशमवगम्यात्ममायया ।
आत्मा श्वपाकतां नीतो दर्शितं तच्च चापलं ॥ २४६ ॥

इन्द्र उवाच ॥

प्रार्थ्यते यत् परं स्थानं समस्तैर्मनुजैर्भुवि ।
तदारोह हरिश्चन्द्र स्थानं पुण्यकृतां नृणां ॥ २४७ ॥

हरिश्चन्द्र उवाच ॥

देवराज नमस्तुभ्यं वाक्यञ्चैतन्निबोध मे ।
प्रसादसुमुखं यत्त्वां ब्रवीमि प्रश्रयान्वितः ॥ २४८ ॥
मच्छोकमग्नमनसः कोशलानगरे जनाः ।
तिष्ठन्ति तानपोह्याद्य कथं यास्याम्यहं दिवं ॥ २४९ ॥
ब्रह्महत्या गुरोर्घातो गोबधः स्त्रीबधस्तथा ।
तुल्यमेभिर्महापापं भक्तत्यागेऽप्युदाहृतं ॥ २५० ॥
भजन्तं भक्तमत्याज्यमदुष्टं त्यजतः सुखं ।
नेह नामुत्र पश्यामि तस्माच्छक्र दिवं ब्रज ॥ २५१ ॥
यदि ते सहिताः स्वर्गं मया यान्ति सुरेश्वर ।
ततोऽहमपि यास्यामि नरकं वापि तैः सह ॥ २५२ ॥

इन्द्र उवाच ॥

बहूनि पुण्यपापानि तेषां भिन्नानि वै पृथक् ।
कथं संघातभोग्यं त्वं भूयः स्वर्गमवाप्स्यसि ॥ २५३ ॥

हरिश्चन्द्र उवाच ॥

शक्र भुङ्क्ते नृपो राज्यं प्रभावेण कुटुम्बिनां ।
यजते च महायज्ञैः कर्म्म पौर्त्तं करोति च ॥ २५४ ॥
तच्च तेषां प्रभावेण मया सर्व्वमनुष्ठितं

उपकर्त्तॄन् न सन्त्यक्ष्ये तानहं स्वर्गलिप्सया ॥ २५५ ॥
तस्माद्यन्मम देवेश किञ्चिदस्ति सुचेष्टितं ।
दत्तमिष्टमथो जप्तं सामान्यं तैस्तदस्तु नः ॥ २५६ ॥
बहुकालोपभोग्यं हि फलं यन्मम कर्म्मणः ।
तदस्तु दिनमप्येकं तैः समं त्वत्प्रसादतः ॥ २५७ ॥

पक्षिण ऊचुः ॥

एवं भविष्यतीत्युक्का शक्रस्त्रिभुवनेश्वरः ।
प्रसन्नचेता धर्म्मश्च विश्वामित्रश्च गाधिजः ॥ २५८ ॥
विमानकोटिसम्बद्धं स्वर्गलोकान्महीतलं ।
गत्वायोध्याजनं प्राह दिवमरुह्यतामिति ॥ २५९ ॥
तदिन्द्रस्य वचः श्रुत्वा प्रीत्या तस्य च भूपतेः ।
आनीय रोहिताश्वञ्च विश्वामित्रो महातपाः ॥ २६० ॥
अयोध्याख्ये पुरे रम्ये सोऽभ्यसिञ्चन्नृपात्मजं ।
देवैश्च मुनिभिः सिद्धैरभिषिच्य नराधिपं ॥ २६१ ॥
राज्ञा सह तदा सर्व्वे हृष्टपुष्टसुहृज्जनाः ।
सपुत्रभृत्यदारास्ते दिवमारुरुहुर्जनाः ॥ २६२ ॥
पदे पदे विमानात्ते विमानमगमन्नराः ।
तदा सम्भूतहर्षोऽसौ हरिश्चन्द्रश्च पार्थिवः ॥ २६३ ॥
सम्प्राप्य भूतिमतुलां विमानैः स महीपतिः ।
आसाञ्चक्रे पुराकारे वप्रप्राकारसंवृते ॥ २६४ ॥
ततस्तस्यर्द्धिमालोक्य श्लोकं तत्रोशना जगौ ।
दैत्याचार्य्यो महाभागः सर्व्वशास्त्रार्थतत्त्ववित् ॥ २६५ ॥

शुक्र उवाच ॥

हरिश्चन्द्रसमो राजा न भूतो न भविष्यति ।
यः शृणोति स्वदुःखार्त्तः स सुखं महदाप्नुयात् ॥ २६६ ॥
स्वर्गार्थी प्राप्नुयात् स्वर्गं पुत्त्रार्थी पुत्त्रमाप्नुयात् ।
भार्य्यार्थी प्राप्नुयाद्भार्य्यां राज्यार्थी राज्यमाप्नुयात् ॥ २६७ ॥
अहो तितिक्षामाहात्म्यमहो दानफलं महत् ।
यदागतो हरिश्चन्द्रः पुरीञ्चेन्द्रत्वमाप्तवान् ॥ २६८ ॥

पक्षिण ऊचुः ॥

एतत्ते सर्व्वमाख्यातं हरिश्चन्द्रविचेष्टितं ।
अतःपरं कथाशेषः श्रूयतां मुनिसत्तम ॥ २६९ ॥
विपाको राजसूयस्य पृथिवीक्षयकारणं ।
तद्विपाकनिमित्तञ्च युद्धमाडिवकं महत् ॥ २७० ॥

इति मार्कण्डेयपुराणे हरिश्चन्द्रोपाख्यानं ॥ ८ ॥

नवमोऽध्यायः ॥

पक्षिण ऊचुः ॥

राज्यच्युते हरिश्चन्द्रे गते च त्रिदशालयं ।
निश्चक्राम महातेजा जलवासात् पुरोहितः ॥ १ ॥
वशिष्ठो द्वादशाब्दान्ते गङ्गापर्य्युषितो मुनिः ।
शुश्राव च समस्तन्तु विश्वामित्रविचेष्टितं ॥ २ ॥

हरिश्चन्द्रस्य नाशञ्च राज्ञश्चोदारकर्म्मणः ।
चण्डालसंप्रयोगञ्च भार्य्यातनयविक्रयं ॥ ३ ॥
स श्रुत्वा सुमहाभागः प्रीतिमानवनीपतौ ।
चकार कोपं तेजस्वी विश्वामित्रमृषिम्प्रति ॥ ४ ॥

वशिष्ठ उवाच ॥

मम पुत्त्रशतं तेन विश्वामित्रेण घातितं ।
तत्रापि नाभवत्क्रोधस्तादृशो यादृशोऽद्य मे ॥ ५ ॥
श्रुत्वा नराधिपमिमं स्वराज्यादवरोपितं ।
महात्मानं महाभागं देवब्राह्मणपूजकं ॥ ६ ॥
यस्मात् स सत्यवाक् शान्तः शत्रावपि विमत्सरः ।
अनागाश्चैव धर्म्मात्मा अप्रमत्तो मदाश्रयः ॥ ७ ॥
सपत्नीभृत्यपुत्त्रस्तु प्रापितोऽन्त्यां दशां नृपः ।
स राज्याच्च्यावितोऽनेन बहुशश्च खिलीकृतः ॥ ८ ॥
तस्माद्दुरात्मा ब्रह्मद्विट् प्राज्ञानामवरोपितः ।
मच्छापोपहतो मूढः स वकत्वमवाप्स्यति ॥ ९ ॥

पक्षिण ऊचुः ॥

श्रुत्वा शापं महातेजा विश्वामित्रोऽपि कौशिकः ।
त्वमप्याडिर्भवस्वेति प्रतिशापमयच्छत ॥ १० ॥
अन्योन्यशापात्तौ प्राप्तौ तिर्य्यक्त्वं परमद्युती ।
वशिष्ठः स महातेजा विश्वामित्रश्च कौशिकः ॥ ११ ॥
अन्यजातिसमायोगं गतावप्यमितौजसौ ।
युयुधातेऽतिसंरब्धौ महाबलपराक्रमौ ॥ १२ ॥

योजनानां सहस्रे द्वे प्रमाणेनाडिरुच्छ्रितः ।
यन्नवत्यधिकं ब्रह्मन् सहस्रचितयं वकः ॥ १३ ॥
तौ तु पक्षप्रहाराभ्यामन्योन्यस्योरुविक्रमौ ।
प्रहरन्तौ भयं तीव्रं प्रजानाञ्चक्रतुस्तदा ॥ १४ ॥
विधूय पक्षाणि वको रक्तोद्वृत्ताच्छिराहनत् ।
आडिं सोऽप्युन्नतग्रीवो वकं पद्भ्यामताडयत् ॥ १५ ॥
तयोः पक्षानिलापास्ताः प्रपेतुर्गिरयो भुवि ।
गिरिप्रपाताभिहता चकम्पे च वसुन्धरा ॥ १६ ॥
क्ष्मा कम्पमाना जलधीनुद्वृत्ताम्बूंश्चकार च ।
ननाम चैकपार्श्वेन पातालगमनोन्मुखी ॥ १७ ॥
केचिद्गिरिनिपातेन केचिदम्भोधिवारिणा ।
केचिन्महीसञ्चलनात् प्रययुः प्राणिनः क्षयं ॥ १८ ॥
इति सर्व्वं परित्रस्तं हाहाभूतमचेतनं ।
जगदासीत्सुसम्भ्रान्तं पर्य्यस्तक्षितिमण्डलं ॥ १९ ॥
हा वत्स हा कान्त शिशो प्रयाह्येषोऽस्मि संस्थितः ।
हा प्रिये कान्त शैलोऽयं पतत्याशु पलायतां ॥ २० ॥
इत्याकुलीकृते लोके सन्त्रासविमुखे तदा ।
सुरैः परिवृतः सर्व्वैराजगाम पितामहः ॥ २१ ॥
प्रत्युवाच च विश्वेशस्तावुभावतिकोपितौ ।
युद्धं वां विरमत्वेतल्लोकाः स्वास्थ्यं व्रजन्तु च ॥ २२ ॥
शृण्वन्तावपि तौ वाक्यं ब्रह्मणोऽव्यक्तजन्मनः ।
कोपामर्षसमाविष्टौ युयुधाते न तस्थतुः ॥ २३ ॥

ततः पितामहो देवस्तं दृष्ट्वा लोकसंक्षयं ।
तयोश्च हितमन्विच्छन् तिर्य्यग्भावमपानुदत् ॥ २४ ॥
ततस्तौ पूर्व्वदेहस्थौ प्राह देवः प्रजापतिः ।
व्युदस्ते तामसे भावे वशिष्ठकौशिकर्षभौ ॥ २५ ॥
जहि वत्स वशिष्ठ त्वं त्वञ्च कौशिक सत्तम ।
तामसं भावमाश्रित्य ईदृग्युद्धं चिकीर्षितं ॥ २६ ॥
राजसूयविपाकोऽयं हरिश्चन्द्रस्य भूपतेः ।
युवयोर्विग्रहश्चायं पृथिवीक्षयकारकः ॥ २७ ॥
नचापि कौशिकश्रेष्ठस्तस्य राज्ञोऽपराध्यते ।
स्वर्गप्राप्तिकरो ब्रह्मन्नुपकारपदे स्थितः ॥ २८ ॥
तपोविघ्नस्य कर्त्तारौ कामक्रोधवशं गतौ ।
परित्यजत भद्रं वो ब्रह्म हि प्रचुरं बलं ॥ २९ ॥
एवमुक्तौ ततस्तेन लज्जितौ तावुभावपि ।
क्षमयामासतुः प्रीत्या परिष्वज्य परस्परं ॥ ३० ॥
ततः सुरैर्वन्द्यमानो ब्रह्मा लोकं निजं ययौ ।
वशिष्ठोऽप्यात्मनः स्थानं कौशिकोऽपि स्वमाश्रमं ॥ ३१ ॥
एतदाडिवकं युद्धं हरिश्चन्द्रकथान्तथा ।
कथयिष्यन्ति ये मर्त्याः सम्यक् श्रोष्यन्ति चैव ये ॥ ३२ ॥
तेषां पापापनोदन्तु श्रुतं ह्येव करिष्यति ।
नचैव विघ्नकार्य्याणि भविष्यन्ति कदाचन ॥ ३३ ॥

इति मार्कण्डेयपुराणे आडिवकयुद्धं ॥ ९ ॥

दशमोऽध्यायः ॥

जैमिनिरुवाच ॥

संशयं द्विजशार्दूलाः प्रब्रूत मम पृच्छतः।
आविर्भावतिरोभावौ भूतानां यत्र संस्थितौ ॥ १ ॥
कथं सञ्जायते जन्तुः कथं वा स विवर्द्धते।
कथं वोदरमध्यस्थस्तिष्ठत्यङ्गनिपीडितः ॥ २ ॥
निष्क्रान्तिमुदरात् प्राप्य कथं वा वृद्धिमृच्छति।
उत्क्रान्तिकाले च कथं चिद्भावेन वियुज्यते ॥ ३ ॥
कृत्स्नो मृतस्तथाश्नाति उभे सुकृतदुष्कृते।
कथन्ते च तथा तस्य फलं सम्पादयन्त्युत ॥ ४ ॥
कथं न जीर्य्यते तत्र पिण्डीकृत इवाशये।
स्त्रीकोष्ठे यत्र जीर्य्यन्ते भुक्तानि सुगुरूण्यपि ॥
भक्ष्याणि तत्र नो जन्तुर्जीर्य्यते कथमल्पकः ॥ ५ ॥
एतन्मे ब्रूत सकलं सन्देहोक्तिविवर्जितं।
तदेतत् परमं गुह्यं यत्र मुह्यन्ति जन्तवः ॥ ६ ॥

पक्षिण ऊचुः ॥

प्रश्नभारोऽयमतुलस्त्वयास्मासु निवेशितः।
दुर्भाव्यः सर्व्वभूतानां भावाभावसमाश्रितः ॥ ७ ॥
तं शृणुष्व महाभाग यथा प्राह पितुः पुरा।
पुत्त्रः परमधर्म्मात्मा सुमतिर्नाम नामतः ॥ ८ ॥
ब्राह्मणो भार्गवः कश्चित् सुतमाह महामतिः।

कृतोपनयनं शान्तं सुमतिं जडरूपिणं ॥ ९ ॥
वेदानधीस्व सुमते यथानुक्रममादितः ।
गुरुशुश्रूषणे व्यग्रो भैक्षान्नकृतभोजनः ॥ १० ॥
ततो गार्हस्थ्यमास्थाय चेष्ट्वा यज्ञाननुत्तमान् ।
इष्टमुत्पादयापत्यमाश्रयेथा वनन्ततः ॥ ११ ॥
वनस्थश्च ततो वत्स परिव्राट निष्परिग्रहः ।
एवमाप्स्यसि तद्ब्रह्म यत्र गत्वा न शोचसि ॥ १२ ॥

पक्षिण ऊचुः ॥

इत्येवमुक्तो बहुशो जडत्वान्नाह किञ्चन ।
पितापि तं सुबहुशः प्राह प्रीत्या पुनः पुनः ॥ १३ ॥
इति पित्रा सुतस्नेहात् प्रलोभि मधुराक्षरं ।
स चोद्यमानो बहुशः प्रहस्येदमथाब्रवीत् ॥ १४ ॥
तातैतत् बहुशोऽभ्यस्तं यत्त्वयाद्योपदिश्यते ।
तथैवान्यानि शास्त्राणि शिल्पानि विविधानि च ॥ १५ ॥
जन्मनामयुतं साग्रं मम स्मृतिपथं गतं ।
निर्वेदाः परितोषाश्च क्षयबुद्ध्युदये रताः ॥ १६ ॥
शत्रुमित्रकलत्राणां वियोगाः सङ्गमास्तथा ।
मातरो विविधा दृष्टाः पितरो विविधास्तथा ॥ १७ ॥
अनुभूतानि सौख्यानि दुःखानि च सहस्रशः ।
बान्धवा बहवः प्राप्ताः पितरश्च पृथग्विधाः । १८ ॥
विण्मूत्रपिच्छिले स्त्रीणां तथा कोष्ठे मयोषितं ।
पीडाश्च सुभृशं प्राप्ता रोगाणाञ्च सहस्रशः ॥ १९ ॥

गर्भदुःखान्यनेकानि बालत्वे यौवने तथा ।
वृद्धतायां तथाप्तानि तानि सर्व्वाणि संस्मरे ॥ २० ॥
ब्राह्मणक्षत्रियविशां शूद्राणाञ्चापि योनिषु ।
पुनश्च पशुकीटानां मृगाणामथ पक्षिणां ॥ २१ ॥
तथैव राजभृत्यानां राज्ञाञ्चाहवशालिनाम् ।
समुत्पन्नोऽस्मि गेहेषु तथैव तव वेश्मनि ॥ २२ ॥
भृत्यतां दासताञ्चैव गतोऽस्मि बहुशो नृणां ।
स्वामित्वमीश्वरत्वञ्च दरिद्रत्वं तथा गतः ॥ २३ ॥
हतं मया हतश्चान्यैर्हतं मे घातितं तथा ।
दत्तं ममान्यैरन्येभ्यो मया दत्तमनेकशः ॥ २४ ॥
पितृमातृसुहृद्भ्रातृकलत्रादिकृतेन च ।
तुष्टोऽसकृत्तथा दैन्यमश्रुधौताननो गतः ॥ २५ ॥
एवं संसारचक्रेऽस्मिन् भ्रमता तात सङ्कटे ।
ज्ञानमेतन्मया प्राप्तं मोक्षसम्प्राप्तिकारकं ॥ २६ ॥
विज्ञाते यत्र सर्व्वोऽयमृग्यजुःसामसंज्ञितः ।
क्रियाकलापो विगुणो न सम्यक् प्रतिभाति मे ॥ २७ ॥
तस्मादुत्पन्नबोधस्य वेदैः किं मे प्रयोजनं ।
गुरुविज्ञानतृप्तस्य निरीहस्य सदात्मनः ॥ २८ ॥
षट्प्रकारक्रियादुःखसुखहर्षरसैश्च यत् ।
गुणैश्च वर्ज्जितं ब्रह्म तत्प्राप्स्यामि परं पदं ॥ २९ ॥
रसहर्षभयोद्वेगक्रोधामर्षजरातुरां ।
विज्ञातां स्वमृगग्राहिसङ्कुपाशशताकुलां ॥ ३० ॥

तस्मात् यास्याम्यहं तात त्यक्त्वेमां दुःखसन्ततिं ।
त्रयीधर्म्ममधर्म्माढ्यं किम्पाकफलसन्निभं ॥ ३१ ॥

पक्षिण ऊचुः ॥

तस्य तद्वचनं श्रुत्वा हर्षविस्मयगद्गदं ।
पिता प्राह महाभागः स्वसुतं हृष्टमानसः ॥ ३२ ॥

पितोवाच ॥

किमेतद्वदसे वत्स कुतस्ते ज्ञानसम्भवः ।
केन ते जडता पूर्व्वमिदानीञ्च प्रबुद्धता ॥ ३३ ॥
किन्नु शापविकारोऽयं मुनिदेवकृतस्तव ।
यत्ते ज्ञानं तिरोभूतमाविर्भावमुपागतं ॥ ३४ ॥

पुत्र उवाच ॥

शृणु तात यथा वृत्तं ममेदं सुखदुःखदं ।
यश्चाहमासमन्यस्मिन् जन्मन्यस्मात्परन्तु यत् ॥ ३५ ॥
अहमासं पुरा विप्रो न्यस्तात्मा परमात्मनि ।
आत्मविद्याविचारेषु परां निष्ठामुपागतः ॥ ३६ ॥
सततं योगयुक्तस्य सतताभ्याससङ्गमात् ।
सत्संयोगात् स्वस्वभावाद् विचारविधिशोधनात् ॥ ३७ ॥
तस्मिन्नेव परा प्रीतिर्ममासीत् युञ्जतः सदा ।
आचार्य्यताञ्च सम्प्राप्तः शिष्यसन्देहहृत्तमः ॥ ३८ ॥
ततः कालेन महता ऐकान्तिकमुपागतः ।
अज्ञानात्कष्टसद्भावो विपन्नश्च प्रमादतः ॥ ३९ ॥

उत्क्रान्तिकालादारभ्य स्मृतिलोपो न मेऽभवत् ।
यावदब्दङ्गतश्चैव जन्मनां स्मृतिमागतं ॥ ४० ॥
पूर्व्वाभ्यासेन तेनैव सोऽहं तात जितेन्द्रियः ।
यतिष्यामि तथा कर्त्तुं न भविष्ये यथा पुनः ॥ ४१ ॥
ज्ञानदानफलं ह्येतद्यज्जातिस्मरणं मम ।
नह्येतत्प्राप्यते तात त्रयीधर्म्माश्रितैर्नरैः ॥ ४२ ॥
सोऽहं पूर्व्वाश्रमादेव निष्ठाधर्म्ममुपाश्रितः ।
एकान्तित्वमुपागम्य यतिष्याम्यात्ममोक्षणे ॥ ४३ ॥
तद्ब्रूहि त्वं महाभाग यत्ते सांशयिकं हृदि ।
एतावतापि ते प्रीतिमुत्पाद्यानृण्यमाप्नुयां ॥ ४४ ॥

पक्षिण ऊचुः ॥

पिता प्राह ततः पुत्रं श्रद्दधत्तस्य तद्वचः ।
भवता यद्यं पृष्टाः संसारग्रहणाश्रयं ॥ ४५ ॥

पुत्र उवाच ॥

शृणु तात यथा तत्त्वमनुभूतं मयाऽसकृत् ।
संसारचक्रमजरं स्थितिर्यस्य न विद्यते ॥ ४६ ॥
सोऽहं वदामि ते सर्व्वं तवैवानुज्ञया पितः ।
उत्क्रान्तिकालादारभ्य यथा नान्यो वदिष्यति ॥ ४७ ॥
उष्मा प्रकुपितः काये तीव्रवायुसमीरितः ।
भिनत्ति मर्म्मस्थानानि दीप्यमानो निरिन्धनः ॥ ४८ ॥
उदानो नाम पवनस्ततश्चोर्द्ध्वं प्रवर्त्तते ।
भुक्तानामम्बुभक्ष्याणामधोगतिनिरोधकृत् ॥ ४९ ॥

ततो येनाम्बुदानानि कृतान्यन्नरसास्तथा ।
दत्ताः स तस्य आह्लादमापदि प्रतिपद्यते ॥ ५० ॥
अन्नानि येन दत्तानि श्रद्धापूतेन चेतसा ।
सोऽपि तृप्तिमवाप्नोति विनाप्यन्नेन वै तदा ॥ ५१ ॥
येनानृतानि नोक्तानि प्रीतिभेदः कृतो न च ।
आस्तिकः श्रद्दधानश्च स सुखं मृत्युमृच्छति ॥ ५२ ॥
देवब्राह्मणपूजायां ये रता नानुसूयवः ।
शुक्ला वदान्या ह्रीमन्तस्ते नराः सुखमृत्यवः ॥ ५३ ॥
यो न कामान्न संरम्भान्न द्वेषाद्धर्म्ममुत्सृजेत् ।
यथोक्तकारी सौम्यश्च स सुखं मृत्युमृच्छति ॥ ५४ ॥
अवारिदायिनो दाहं क्षुधाञ्चानन्नदायिनः ।
प्राप्नुवन्ति नराः काले तस्मिन्मृत्यावुपस्थिते ॥ ५५ ॥
शीतं जयन्तीन्धनदास्तापं चन्दनदायिनः ।
प्राणघ्नीं वेदनां कष्टां ये चानुद्वेगकारिणः ॥ ५६ ॥
मोहाज्ञानप्रदातारः प्राप्नुवन्ति महद्भयं ।
वेदनाभिरुदग्राभिः प्रपीड्यन्तेऽधमा नराः ५७ ॥
कूटसाक्षी मृषावादी यश्चासदनुशास्ति वै ।
ते मोहमृत्यवः सर्व्वे तथा वेदविनिन्दकाः ॥ ५८ ॥
विभीषणाः पूतिगन्धाः कूटमुद्गरपाणयः ।
आगच्छन्ति दुरात्मानो यमस्य पुरुषास्तदा ॥ ५९ ॥
प्राप्तेषु दृक्पथं तेषु जायते तस्य वेपथुः ।
क्रन्दत्यविरतं सोऽथ भ्रातृमातृसुतानथ ॥ ६० ॥

सास्य वागस्फुटा तात एकवर्णा विभाव्यते ।
दृष्टिश्च भ्राम्यते चासाच्छ्वासाच्छुष्यत्यथाननं ॥ ६१ ॥
ऊर्द्ध्वश्वासान्वितः सोऽथ दृष्टिभङ्गसमन्वितः ।
ततः स वेदनाविष्टस्तच्छरीरं विमुञ्चति ॥ ६२ ॥
वाय्वग्रसारी तद्रूपं देहमन्यत् प्रपद्यते ।
तत्कर्म्मजं यातनार्थं न मातृपितृसम्भवं ॥
तत्प्रमाणवयोवस्थासंस्थानैः प्राग्भवं यथा ॥ ६३ ॥
ततो दूतो यमस्याशु पाशैर्बध्नाति दारुणैः ।
दण्डप्रहारसम्भ्रान्तं कर्षते दक्षिणां दिशं ॥ ६४ ॥
कुशकण्टकवल्मीकशङ्कुपाषाणकर्कशे ।
तथा प्रदीप्तज्वलने क्वचिच्छ्वभ्रशतोत्कटे ॥ ६५ ॥
प्रदीप्तादित्यतप्ते च दह्यमाने तदंशुभिः ।
कृष्यते यमदूतैश्चाशिवसन्नादभीषणैः ॥ ६६ ॥
विकृष्यमाणस्तैर्घोरैर्भक्ष्यमाणः शिवाशतैः ।
प्रयाति दारुणे मार्गे पापकर्म्मा यमक्षयं ॥ ६७ ॥
छत्रोपानत्प्रदातारो ये च वस्त्रप्रदा नराः ।
ते यान्ति मनुजा मार्गं तं सुखेन तथान्नदाः ॥ ६८ ॥
एवं क्लेशाननुभवन्नवशः पापपीडितः ।
नीयते द्वादशाहेन धर्म्मराजपुरं नरः ॥ ६९ ॥
कलेवरे दह्यमाने महान्तं दाहमृच्छति ।
ताड्यमाने तथैवार्त्तिं छिद्यमाने च दारुणां ॥ ७० ॥
क्लिद्यमाने चिरतरं जन्तुर्दुःखमवाप्नुते ।

स्वेन कर्म्मविपाकेन देहान्तरगतोऽपि सन् ॥ ७१ ॥
तत्र यद्बान्धवास्तोयं प्रयच्छन्ति तिलैः सह ।
यच्च पिण्डं प्रयच्छन्ति नीयमानस्तदश्नुते ॥ ७२ ॥
तैलाभ्यङ्गो बान्धवानामङ्गसंवाहनञ्च यत् ।
तेन चाप्याय्यते जन्तुर्यच्चाश्नन्ति स बान्धवाः ॥ ७३ ॥
भूमौ स्वपद्भिर्नात्यन्तं क्लेशमाप्नोति बान्धवैः ।
दानं ददद्भिश्च तथा जन्तुराप्याय्यते मृतः ॥ ७४ ॥
नीयमानः स्वकं गेहं द्वादशाहं स पश्यति ।
उपभुङ्क्ते तथा दत्तं तोयपिण्डादिकं भुवि ॥ ७५ ॥
द्वादशाहात्परं घोरमायसं भीषणाकृतिं ।
याम्यं पश्यत्यथो जन्तुः कृष्यमाणः पुरं ततः ॥ ७६ ॥
गतमात्रोऽतिरक्ताक्षं भिन्नाञ्जनचयप्रभं ।
मृत्युकालान्तकादीनां मध्ये पश्यति वै यमं ॥ ७७ ॥
दंष्ट्राकरालवदनं भ्रुकुटीदारुणाकृतिं ।
विरूपैर्भीषणैर्व्वक्रैर्वृतं व्याधिशतैः प्रभुं ॥ ७८ ॥
दण्डासक्तं महाबाहुं पाशहस्तं सुभैरवं ।
तन्निर्दिष्टां ततो याति गतिं जन्तुः शुभाशुभां ॥ ७९ ॥
रौरवे कूटसाक्षी तु याति यश्चानृतो नरः ।
तस्य स्वरूपं गदतो रौरवस्य निशामय ॥ ८० ॥
योजनानां सहस्रे द्वे रौरवो हि प्रमाणतः ।
जानुमात्रप्रमाणश्च ततः श्वभ्रः सुदुस्तरः ॥ ८१ ॥
तत्राङ्गारचयोपेतं कृतञ्च धरणीसमं ।

जाज्वल्यमानस्तीव्रेण तापिताङ्गारभूमिना ॥ ८२ ॥
तन्मध्ये पापकर्म्माणं विमुञ्चन्ति यमानुगाः ।
स दह्यमानस्तीव्रेण वह्निना तत्र धावति ॥ ८३ ॥
पदे पदे च पादोऽस्य शीर्य्यते जीर्य्यते पुनः ।
अहोरात्रेणोद्धरणं पादन्यासं च गच्छति ॥ ८४ ॥
एवं सहस्रमुत्तीर्णो योजनानां विमुच्यते ।
ततोऽन्यं पापशुद्ध्यर्थं तादृङ्निरयमृच्छति ॥ ८५ ॥
ततः सर्व्वेषु निस्तीर्णः पापी तिर्य्यक्त्वमश्नुते ।
कृमिकीटपतङ्गेषु श्वापदे मशकादिषु ॥ ८६ ॥
गत्वा गजद्रुमाद्येषु गोष्वश्वेषु तथैव च ।
अन्यासु चैव पापासु दुःखदासु च योनिषु ॥ ८७ ॥
मानुषं प्राप्य कुब्जो वा कुत्सितो वामनोऽपिवा ।
चण्डालपुक्कषाद्यासु नरो योनिषु जायते ॥ ८८ ॥
अवशिष्टेन पापेन पुण्येन च समन्वितः ।
ततश्चारोहणीं जातिं शूद्रवैश्यन्टपादिकां ॥ ८९ ॥
विप्रदेवेन्द्रताञ्चापि कदाचिदवरोहणीं ।
एवन्तु पापकर्म्माणो नरकेषु पतन्त्यधः ॥ ९० ॥
यथा पुण्यकृतो यान्ति तन्मे निगदतः शृणु ।
ते यमेन विनिर्दिष्टां यान्ति पुण्यां गतिं नराः ॥ ९१ ॥
प्रगीतगन्धर्व्वगणाः प्रन्टत्ताप्सरसां गणाः ।
हारनूपुरमाधुर्य्यशोभितान्युत्तमानि च ॥ ९२ ॥
प्रयान्त्याशु विमानानि नानादिव्यस्रगुज्ज्वलाः ।

तस्माच्च प्रच्युता राज्ञामन्येषाञ्च महात्मनां ॥ ९३ ॥
जायन्ते च कुले तच सद्वृत्तपरिपालकाः ।
भोगान् सम्प्राप्नुवन्त्युग्रांस्ततो यान्त्यूर्द्ध्वमन्यथा ॥ ९४ ॥
अवरोहणीञ्च सम्प्राप्य पूर्व्ववद्यान्ति मानवाः ।
एतत्ते सर्व्वमाख्यातं यथा जन्तुर्विपद्यते ॥
अतः शृणुष्व विप्रर्षे यथा गर्भं प्रपद्यते ॥ ९५ ॥

इति मार्कण्डेयपुराणे पितापुत्त्रसंवादे ॥ १० ॥

एकादशोऽध्यायः ॥

पुत्त्र उवाच ॥

निषेकं मानवं स्त्रीणां वीजं प्रोक्तं रजस्यथ ।
विमुक्तमात्रो नरकात् स्वर्गाद्वापि प्रपद्यते ॥ १ ॥
तेनाभिभूतं तत् स्थैर्य्यं याति वीजद्वयं पितः ।
कललत्वं बुद्बुदत्वं ततः पेषित्वमेव च ॥ २ ॥
पेष्यां यथाणुवीजं स्यादङ्कुरस्तद्वदुच्यते ।
अङ्गानाञ्च तथोत्पत्तिः पञ्चानामनुभागशः ॥ ३ ॥
उपाङ्गान्यङ्गुलीनेत्रनासास्यश्रवणानि च ।
प्ररोहं यान्ति चाङ्गेभ्यस्तद्वत्तेभ्यो नखादिकं ॥ ४ ॥
त्वचि रोमाणि जायन्ते केशाश्चैव ततः परं ।
समं सम्वृद्धिमायाति तेनैवोद्भवकोषकं ॥ ५ ॥

नारिकेलफलं यद्वत् सकोषं वृद्धिमृच्छति ।
तद्वत् प्रयात्यसौ वृद्धिं स कोषोऽधोमुखः स्थितः ॥ ६ ॥
तले तु जानुपार्श्वाभ्यां करौ न्यस्य स वर्द्धते ।
अङ्गुष्ठौ चोपरि न्यस्तौ जान्वोरग्रे तथाङ्गुली ॥ ७ ॥
जानुपृष्ठे तथा नेत्रे जानुमध्ये च नासिका ।
स्फिचौ पार्ष्णिद्वयस्थे च बाहुजङ्घे बहिःस्थिते ॥ ८ ॥
एवं वृद्धिं क्रमाद्याति जन्तुः स्त्रीगर्ब्भसंस्थितः ।
अन्यसत्वोदरे जन्तोर्यथा रूपं तथा स्थितिः ॥ ९ ॥
काठिन्यमग्निना याति भुक्तपीतेन जीवति ।
पुण्या पुण्याश्रयमयी स्थितिर्जन्तोस्तथोदरे ॥ १० ॥
नाडी चाप्यायनी नाम नाभ्यां तस्य निबध्यते ।
स्त्रीणां तथान्त्रशुषिरे सा निबद्धोपजायते ॥ ११ ॥
क्रामन्ति भुक्तपीतानि स्त्रीणां गर्ब्भोदरे यथा ।
तैराप्यायितदेहोऽसौ जन्तुर्वृद्धिमुपैति वै ॥ १२ ॥
स्मृतीस्तस्य प्रयान्त्यस्य बह्वयः संसारभूमयः ।
ततो निर्वेदमायाति पीड्यमान इतस्ततः ॥ १३ ॥
पुनर्न्नैवं करिष्यामि मुक्तमात्र इहोदरात् ।
तथा तथा यतिष्यामि गर्ब्भं नाप्स्याम्यहं यथा ॥ १४ ॥
इति चिन्तयते स्मृत्वा जन्मदुःखशतानि वै ।
यानि पूर्व्वानुभूतानि दैवभूतानि यानि वै ॥ १५ ॥
ततः कालक्रमाज्जन्तुः परिवर्त्तत्यधोमुखः ।
नवमे दशमे वापि मासि सञ्जायते यतः ॥ १६ ॥

निष्क्राम्यमाणो वातेन प्राजापत्येन पीड्यते।
निष्क्राम्यते च विलपन् हृदि दुःखनिपीडितः ॥ १७ ॥
निष्क्रान्तश्चोदरान्मूर्च्छामसह्यां प्रतिपद्यते।
प्राप्नोति चेतनां चासौ वायुस्पर्शसमन्वितः ॥ १८ ॥
ततस्तं वैष्णवी माया समास्कन्दति मोहिनी।
तया विमोहितात्मासौ ज्ञानभ्रंशमवाप्नुते ॥ १९ ॥
भ्रष्टज्ञानो बालभावं ततो जन्तुः प्रपद्यते।
ततः कौमारकावस्थां यौवनं वृद्धतामपि ॥ २० ॥
पुनश्च मरणं तद्वज्जन्म चाप्नोति मानवः।
ततः संसारचक्रेऽस्मिन् भ्राम्यते घटियन्त्रवत् ॥ २१ ॥
कदाचित्स्वर्गमाप्नोति कदाचिन्निरयं नरः।
नरकञ्चैव स्वर्गञ्च कदाचिच्च मृतोऽश्नुते ॥ २२ ॥
कदाचिदत्रैव पुनर्जातः स्वं कर्म्म सोऽश्नुते।
कदाचिद्भुक्तकर्म्मा च मृतः स्वल्पेन गच्छति ॥ २३ ॥
कदाचिदल्पैश्च ततो जायतेऽत्र शुभाशुभैः।
स्वर्लोके नरके चैव भुक्तप्रायो द्विजोत्तम ॥ २४ ॥
नरकेषु महद्दुःखमेतद्यत् स्वर्गवासिनः।
दृश्यन्ते तात मोदन्ते पात्यमानाश्च नारकाः ॥ २५ ॥
स्वर्गेऽपि दुःखमतुलं यदारोहणकालतः।
प्रभृत्यहं पतिष्यामीत्येतन्मनसि वर्त्तते ॥ २६ ॥
नारकांश्चैव संप्रेक्ष्य महद्दुःखमवाप्यते।
एतां गतिमहं गन्तेत्यहर्निशमनिर्वृतः ॥ २७ ॥

गर्ब्भवासे महद्दुःखं जायमानस्य योनितः ।
जातस्य बालभावे च वृद्धत्वे दुःखमेव च ॥ २८ ॥
कामेर्ष्याक्रोधसम्बन्धं यौवने चातिदुःसहं ।
दुःखप्राया वृद्धता च मरणे दुःखमुत्तमं ॥ २९ ॥
कृष्यमाणस्य याम्यैश्च नरकेषु च पात्यतः ।
पुनश्च गर्ब्भो जन्माथ मरणं नरकस्तथा ॥ ३० ॥
एवं संसारचक्रेऽस्मिन् जन्तवो घटियन्त्रवत् ।
भ्राम्यन्ते प्राकृतैर्बन्धैर्बद्धा बध्यन्ति चासकृत् ॥ ३१ ॥
नास्ति तात सुखं किञ्चिदत्र दुःखशताकुले ।
तस्मान्मोक्षाय यतता कथं सेव्या मया त्रयी ॥ ३२ ॥

इति मार्कण्डेयपुराणे पितापुत्रसंवादे ॥ ११ ॥

द्वादशोऽध्यायः ॥

पितोवाच ॥

साधु वत्स त्वयाख्यातं संसारगहनं परं ।
ज्ञानप्रदानसम्भूतं समाश्रित्य महाफलं ॥ १ ॥
तत्र ते नरकाः सर्व्वे यथा वै रौरवस्तथा ।
वर्णितास्तान् समाचक्ष्व विस्तरेण महामते ॥ २ ॥

पुत्र उवाच ॥

रौरवस्ते समाख्यातः प्रथमं नरको मया ।
महारौरवसञ्ज्ञन्तु शृणुष्व नरकं पितः ॥ ३ ॥
योजनानां सहस्राणि सप्त पञ्च समन्ततः ।
तत्र ताम्रमयी भूमिरधस्तस्य हुताशनः ॥ ४ ॥
तत्तापतप्ता सर्व्वाशा प्रोद्यदिन्दुसमप्रभा ।
विभात्यतिमहारौद्रा दर्शनस्पर्शनादिषु ॥ ५ ॥
तस्यां बद्धः कराभ्याञ्च पद्भ्याञ्चैव यमानुगैः ।
मुच्यते पापकृन्मध्ये लुठमानः स गच्छति ॥ ६ ॥
काकैर्वकैर्वृकोलूकैर्वृश्चिकैर्म्मशकैस्तथा ।
भक्ष्यमाणस्तथा गृध्रैर्द्रुतं मार्गं विकृष्यते ॥ ७ ॥
दह्यमानः पितर्मातर्भ्रातस्तातेति चाकुलः ।
वदत्यसकृदुद्विग्नो न शान्तिमधिगच्छति ॥ ८ ॥
एवं तस्मान्नरैर्म्मोक्षो ह्यतिक्रान्तैरवाप्यते ।
वर्षायुतायुतैः पापं यैः कृतं दुष्टबुद्धिभिः ॥ ९ ॥
तथान्यस्तु तमो नाम सोऽतिशीतः स्वभावतः ।
महारौरववद्दीर्घस्तथा स तमसा वृतः ॥ १० ॥
शीतार्त्तास्तत्र धावन्तो नरास्तमसि दारुणे ।
परस्परं समासाद्य परिरभ्याश्रयन्ति च ॥ ११ ॥
दन्तास्तेषाञ्च भज्यन्ते शीतार्त्तिपरिकम्पिताः ।
क्षुत्तृष्णाप्रबलास्तत्र तथैवान्येऽप्युपद्रवाः ॥ १२ ॥
हिमखण्डवहो वायुर्भिनत्त्यस्थीनि दारुणः ।

मज्जास्रुग्गलितन्तस्मादश्नुवन्ति क्षुधान्विताः ॥ १३ ॥
लेलिह्यमाना भ्राम्यन्ते परस्परसमागमे ।
एवं तत्रापि सुमहान् क्लेशस्तमसि मानवैः ॥ १४ ॥
प्राप्यते ब्राह्मणश्रेष्ठ यावद्दुष्कृतसंक्षयः ।
निकृन्तन इति ख्यातस्ततोऽन्यो नरकोत्तमः ॥ १५ ॥
तस्मिन् कुलालचक्राणि भ्राम्यन्त्यविरतं पितः ।
तेष्वारोप्य निकृत्यन्ते कालसूत्रेण मानवाः ॥ १६ ॥
यमानुगाङ्गुलिस्थेन आपादतलमस्तकम् ।
नचैषां जीवितभ्रंशो जायते द्विजसत्तम ॥ १७ ॥
छिन्नानि तेषां शतशः खण्डान्यैक्यं व्रजन्ति च ।
एवं वर्षसहस्राणि छिद्यन्ते पापकर्म्मिणः ॥ १८ ॥
तावद्यावदशेषं वै तत्पापं हि क्षयं गतं ।
अप्रतिष्ठञ्च नरकं शृणुष्व गदतो मम ॥ १९ ॥
यत्रस्थैर्न्नारकैः दुःखमसह्यमनुभूयते ।
तान्येव तत्र चक्राणि घटीयन्त्राणि चान्यतः ॥ २० ॥
दुःखस्य हेतुभूतानि पापकर्म्मकृतां न्हणां ।
चक्रेष्वारोपिताः केचिद्भ्राम्यन्ते तत्र मानवाः ॥ २१ ॥
यावद्वर्षसहस्राणि न तेषां स्थितिरन्तरा ।
घटीयन्त्रेषु चैवान्यो बद्धस्तोये यथा घटी ॥ २२ ॥
भ्राम्यन्ते मानवा रक्तमुद्गिरन्तः पुनः पुनः ।
अन्त्रैर्मुखविनिष्क्रान्तैर्न्नेत्रैरन्त्रविलम्बिभिः ॥ २३ ॥
दुःखानि ते प्राप्नुवन्ति यान्यसह्यानि जन्तुभिः ।

असिपत्रवनं नाम नरकं शृणु चापरं ॥ २४ ॥
योजनानां सहस्रं यो ज्वलदग्न्यास्तृतावनिः ।
तप्ताः सूर्य्यकरैश्चण्डैर्यत्रातीव सुदारुणैः ॥ २५ ॥
प्रपतन्ति सदा तत्र प्राणिनो नरकौकसः ।
तन्मध्ये च वनं रम्यं स्निग्धपत्रं विभाव्यते ॥ २६ ॥
पत्राणि तत्र खड्गानां फलानि द्विजसत्तम ।
श्वानश्च तत्र सबलाः स्वनन्त्ययुतशोभिताः ॥ २७ ॥
महावक्त्रा महादंष्ट्रा व्याघ्रा इव भयानकाः ।
ततस्तद्वनमालोक्य शिशिरच्छायमग्रतः ॥ २८ ॥
प्रयान्ति प्राणिनस्तत्र तीव्रतृट्परिपीडिताः ।
हा मातर्हा तात इति क्रन्दन्तोऽतीव दुःखिताः ॥ २९ ॥
दह्यमानाङ्घ्रियुगला धरणीस्थेन वह्निना ।
तेषां गतानां तत्रासिपत्रपाती समीरणः ॥ ३० ॥
प्रवाति तेन पात्यन्ते तेषां खड्गान्यथोपरि ।
ततः पतन्ति ते भूमौ ज्वलत्पावकसञ्चये ॥ ३१ ॥
लेलिह्यमाने चान्यत्र व्याप्ताशेषमहीतले ।
सारमेयास्ततः शीघ्रं शातयन्ति शरीरतः ॥ ३२ ॥
तेषामङ्गानि रुदतामनेकान्यतिभीषणाः ।
असिपत्रवनं तात मयैतत् कीर्त्तितं तव ॥ ३३ ॥
अतः परं भीमतरं तप्तकुम्भं निबोध मे ।
समन्ततस्तप्तकुम्भा वह्निज्वालासमावृताः ॥ ३४ ॥
ज्वलदग्निचयोद्वृत्ततैलायश्चूर्णपूरिताः ।

तेषु दुष्कृतकर्म्माणो याम्यः क्षिप्ता ह्यधोमुखाः ॥ ३५ ॥
क्वाथ्यन्ते विस्फुटद्गात्रगलन्मज्जजलाविलाः ।
स्फुटत्कपालनेत्रास्थिच्छिद्यमाना विभीषणैः ॥ ३६ ॥
गृध्रैरुत्पाट्य मुच्यन्ते पुनस्तेष्वेव वेगितैः ।
पुनःसिमसिमायन्ते तैलेनैक्यं व्रजन्ति च ॥ ३७ ॥
द्रवीभूतैः शिरोगात्रस्नायुमांसत्वगस्थिभिः ।
ततो याम्यैर्नरैराशु दर्व्या घट्टनघट्टिताः ॥ ३८ ॥
कृतावर्त्ते महातैले मथ्यन्ते पापकर्म्मिणः ।
एष ते विस्तरेणोक्तस्तप्तकुम्भो मया पितः ॥ ३९ ॥

इति मार्कण्डेयपुराणे पितापुत्रसंवादे महारौरवादिनरकाख्यानं ॥ १२ ॥

त्रयोदशोऽध्यायः ॥

पुत्र उवाच ॥

अहं वैश्यकुले जातो जन्मन्यस्मात्तु सप्तमे ।
समतीते गवां रोधं निपाने कृतवान् पुरा ॥ १ ॥
विपाकात् कर्म्मणस्तस्य नरकं भृशदारुणं ।
संप्राप्तोऽग्निशिखाघोरमयोमुखखगाकुलं ॥ २ ॥
यन्त्रपीडनगात्रास्टक्प्रवाहोद्भूतकर्दमं ।
विशस्यमानदुष्कर्म्मितन्निपातरवाकुलं ॥ ३ ॥
पात्यमानस्य मे तत्र साग्रं वर्षशतं गतं ।
महातापार्त्तितप्तस्य तृष्णादाहान्वितस्य च ॥ ४ ॥

तथाह्लादकरः सद्यः पवनः सुखशीतलः ।
कुम्भबालुकाकुम्भमध्यस्थो मे समागतः ॥ ५ ॥
तत्सम्पर्कादशेषाणां नाभवद्यातना नृणां ।
मम चापि यथा स्वर्गे स्वर्गिणां निर्वृतिः परा ॥ ६ ॥
किमेतदिति चाह्लादविस्तारस्तिमितेक्षणैः ।
दृष्टमस्माभिरासन्नं नररत्नमनुत्तमं ॥ ७ ॥
याम्यश्च पुरुषो घोरो दण्डहस्तोऽशनिप्रभः ।
पुरतो दर्शयन्मार्गमितएहीति वागथ ॥ ८ ॥
पुरुषः स तदा दृष्ट्वा यातनाशतसङ्कुलं ।
नरकं प्राह तं याम्यं किङ्करं कृपयान्वितः ॥ ९ ॥

पुरुष उवाच ॥

भो याम्य पुरुषाचक्ष्व किं मया दुष्कृतं कृतं ।
येनेदं यातनाभीमं प्राप्तोऽस्मि नरकं परं ॥ १० ॥
विपश्चिदिति विख्यातो जनकानामहं कुले ।
जातो विदेहविषये सम्यङ्मनुजपालकः ॥ ११ ॥
यज्ञैर्मयेष्टं बहुभिर्धर्म्मतः पालिता मही ।
नोत्सृष्टश्चैव संग्रामो नातिथिर्विमुखो गतः ॥ १२ ॥
पितृदेवर्षिभृत्याश्च न चापचरिता मया ।
कृता स्पृहा च न मया परस्त्रीविभवादिषु ॥ १३ ॥
पर्व्वकालेषु पितरस्तिथिकालेषु देवताः ।
पुरुषं स्वयमायान्ति निपानमिव धेनवः ॥ १४ ॥
यतस्ते विमुखा यान्ति निश्वस्य गृहमेधिनः ।

तस्मादिष्टस्य पूर्त्तस्य धर्म्मौ द्वावपि नश्यतः ॥ १५ ॥
पितृनिश्वासविध्वस्तं सप्तजन्मार्जितं शुभं ।
त्रिजन्मप्रभवं दैवं निश्वासो हन्त्यसंशयं ॥ १६ ॥
तस्माद्दैवे च पित्र्ये च नित्यमेव हितोऽभवं ।
सोऽहं कथमिमं प्राप्तो नरकं भृशदारुणं ॥ १७ ॥

इति मार्कण्डेयपुराणे पितापुत्त्रसंवादे ॥ १३ ॥

चतुर्द्दशोऽध्यायः ॥

पुत्त्र उवाच ॥

इति पृष्टस्तदा तेन शृण्वतां नो महात्मना ।
उवाच पुरुषो याम्यो घोरोऽपि प्रश्रितं वचः ॥ १ ॥

यमकिङ्कर उवाच ॥

महाराज यथात्थ त्वं तथैतन्नात्र संशयः ।
किन्तु स्वल्पं कृतं पापं भवता स्मारयामि तत् ॥ २ ॥
वैदर्भी तव या पत्नी पीवरी नाम नामतः ।
ऋतुमत्या ऋतुर्वन्ध्यस्त्वया तस्याः कृतः पुरा ॥ ३ ॥
सुशोभनायां कैकेय्यामासक्तेन ततो भवान् ।
ऋतुव्यतिक्रमात् प्राप्तो नरकं घोरमीदृशं ॥ ४ ॥
होमकाले यथा वह्निराज्यपातमवेक्षते ।
ऋतौ प्रजापतिस्तद्वद्बीजपातमवेक्षते ॥ ५ ॥

यस्तमुल्लङ्घ्य धर्म्मात्मा कामेष्वासक्तिमान् भवेत् ।
स तु पित्र्यादृणात् पापमवाप्य नरकं पतेत् ॥ ६ ॥
एतावदेव ते पापं नान्यत् किञ्चन विद्यते ।
तदेहि गच्छ पुण्यानामुपभोगाय पार्थिव ॥ ७ ॥

राजोवाच ॥

यास्यामि देवानुचर यत्र त्वं मां नयिष्यसि ।
किञ्चित् पृच्छामि तन्मे त्वं यथावद्वक्तुमर्हसि ॥ ८ ॥
वज्रतुण्डास्त्वमी काकाः पुंसां नयनहारिणः ।
पुनः पुनश्च नेत्राणि तद्वदेषां भवन्ति हि ॥ ९ ॥
किं कर्म्म कृतवन्तश्च कथयैतज्जुगुप्सितं ।
हरन्त्येषां तथा जिह्वां जायमानां पनर्नवां ॥ १० ॥
करपत्रेण पाट्यन्ते कस्मादेतेऽतिदुःखिताः ।
करम्भवालुकास्वेते पच्यन्ते तैलगोचराः ॥ ११ ॥
अयोमुखैः खगैश्चैते कृष्यन्ते किंविधा वद ।
विश्लिष्टदेहबन्धार्त्तिमहारावविराविणः ॥ १२ ॥
अयश्चञ्चुनिपातेन सर्व्वाङ्गक्षतदुःखिताः ।
किमेतेऽनिष्टकर्त्तारस्तुद्यन्तेऽहर्निशं नराः ॥ १३ ॥
एताश्चान्याश्च दृश्यन्ते यातनाः पापकर्म्मिणां ।
येन कर्म्मविपाकेन तन्ममाशेषतो वद ॥ १४ ॥

यमकिङ्कर उवाच ॥

यन्मां पृच्छसि भूपाल पापकर्म्मफलोदयं ।
तत्तेऽहं संप्रवक्ष्यामि संक्षेपेण यथातथं ॥ १५ ॥

पुण्यापुण्ये हि पुरुषः पर्य्यायेण समश्नुते ।
भुञ्जतश्च क्षयं याति पापं पुण्यमथापि वा ॥ १६ ॥
नतु भोगादृते पुण्यं किञ्चिद्वा कर्म्म मानवं ।
पापकं वा पुनात्याशु च्चयो भोगात् प्रजायते ॥ १७ ॥
परित्यजति भोगाच्च पुण्यापुण्ये निबोध मे ।
दुर्भिक्षादेव दुर्भिक्षं क्लेशात् क्लेशं भयाद्भयं ॥ १८ ॥
मृतेभ्यः प्रमृता यान्ति दरिद्राः पापकर्म्मिणः ।
गतिं नानाविधां यान्ति जन्तवः कर्म्मबन्धनात् ॥ १९ ॥
उत्सवादुत्सवं यान्ति स्वर्गात् स्वर्गं सुखात् सुखं ।
श्रद्दधानाश्च शान्ताश्च धनदाः शुभकारिणः ॥ २० ॥
व्यालकुञ्जरदुर्गाणि सर्पचौरभयानि तु ।
हताः पापेन गच्छन्ति पापिनः किमतःपरं ॥ २१ ॥
सुगन्धिमाल्यसद्वस्त्रसाधुयानासनाशनाः ।
स्तूयमानाः सदा यान्ति पुण्यैः पुण्याटवीष्वपि ॥ २२ ॥
अनेकशतसाहस्रजन्मसञ्चयसञ्चितं ।
पुण्यापुण्यं नृणां तद्वत् सुखदुःखाङ्कुरोद्भवं ॥ २३ ॥
यथा वीजं हि भूपाल पयांसि समवेक्षते ।
पुण्यापुण्ये तथा कालदेशान्यकर्म्मकारकं ॥ २४ ॥
स्वल्पं पापं कृतं पुंसा देशकालोपपादितं ।
पादन्यासकृतं दुःखं कण्टकोत्थं प्रयच्छति ॥ २५ ॥
तत् प्रभूततरं स्थूलं शूलकीलकसम्भवं ।
दुःखं यच्छति तद्वच्च शिरोरोगादि दुःसहं ॥ २६ ॥

अपथ्याशनशीतोष्णश्रमतापादिकारकं ।
तथान्योन्यमपेक्षन्ते पापानि फलसङ्गमे ॥ २७ ॥
एवं महान्ति पापानि-दीर्घरोगादिविक्रियां ।
तद्वच्छस्त्राग्निकृच्छ्रार्त्तिबन्धनादिफलाय वै ॥ २८ ॥
स्वल्पं पुण्यं शुभं गन्धं हेलया सम्प्रयच्छति ।
स्पर्शं वाप्यथवा शब्दं रसं रूपमथापि वा ॥ २९ ॥
चिराद्गुरुतरं तद्वन्महान्तमपि कालजं ।
एवञ्च सुखदुःखानि पुण्यापुण्योद्भवानि वै ॥ ३० ॥
भुञ्जानोऽनेकसंसारसम्भवानीह तिष्ठति ।
जातिदेशावरुद्धानि ज्ञानाज्ञानफलानि च ॥ ३१ ॥
तिष्ठन्ति तत्र युक्तानि लिङ्गमात्रेण चात्मनि ।
वपुषा मनसा वाचा न कदाचित् क्वचिन्नरः ॥ ३२ ॥
अकुर्व्वन् पापकं कर्म्म पुण्यं वाप्यवतिष्ठते ।
यद्यत्प्राप्नोति पुरुषो दुःखं सुखमथापि वा ॥ ३३ ॥
प्रभूतमथवा स्वल्पं विक्रियाकारि चेतसः ।
तावता तस्य पुण्यं वा पापं वाप्यथ चेतरत् ॥ ३४ ॥
उपभोगात् क्षयं याति भुज्यमानमिवाशनं ।
एवमेते महापापं यातनाभिरहर्न्निशं ॥ ३५ ॥
क्षपयन्ति नरा घोरं नरकान्तर्व्विवर्त्तिनः ।
तथैव राजन् पुण्यानि स्वर्गलोकेऽमरैः सह ॥ ३६ ॥
गन्धर्व्वसिद्धाप्सरसां गीताद्यैरुपभुञ्जते ।
देवत्वे मानुषत्वे च तिर्य्यक्त्वे च शुभाशुभं ॥ ३७ ॥

पुण्यपापोद्भवं भुङ्क्ते सुखदुःखोपलक्षणं ।
यत्त्वं पृच्छसि मां राजन् यातनाः पापकर्म्मिणां ॥
केन केनेति पापेन तत्ते वक्ष्याम्यशेषतः ॥ ३८ ॥
दुष्टेन चक्षुषा दृष्टाः परदारा नराधमैः ।
मानसेन च दुष्टेन परद्रव्यञ्च सस्पृहैः ॥ ३९ ॥
वज्रतुण्डाः खगास्तेषां हरन्त्येते त्रिलोचने ।
पुनःपुनश्च सम्भूतिरक्ष्णोरेषां भवत्यथ ॥ ४० ॥
यावतोऽक्षिनिमेषांस्तु पापमेभिर्नृभिः कृतं ।
तावद्वर्षसहस्राणि नेत्रार्त्तिं प्राप्नुवन्त्युत ॥ ४१ ॥
असच्छास्त्रोपदेशास्तु यैर्दत्ता यैश्च मन्त्रिताः ।
सम्यग्दृष्टेर्विनाशाय रिपूणामपि मानवैः ॥ ४२ ॥
यैः शास्त्रमन्यथा प्रोक्तं यैरसद्वागुदाहृता ।
वेददेवद्विजातीनां गुरोर्निन्दा च यैः कृता ॥ ४३ ॥
हरन्ति तेषां जिह्वाश्च जायमानाः पुनःपुनः ।
तावतो वत्सरानेते वज्रतुण्डाः सुदारुणाः ॥ ४४ ॥
मित्रभेदन्तथा पित्रा पुत्रस्य स्वजनस्य च ।
याज्योपाध्याययोर्म्मात्रा सुतस्य सहचारिणः ॥ ४५ ॥
भार्य्यापत्योश्च ये केचिद्भेदं चक्रुर्नराधमाः ।
त इमे पश्य पाट्यन्ते करपत्रेण पार्थिव ॥ ४६ ॥
परोपतापका ये च ये चाह्लादनिषेधकाः ।
तालवृन्तानिलस्थानचन्दनोशीरहारिणः ॥ ४७ ॥
प्राणान्तिकं ददुस्तापमदुष्टानाञ्च येऽधमाः ।

करम्भबालुकासंस्थास्तइमे पापभागिनः ॥ ४८ ॥
भुङ्क्ते श्राद्धं तु योऽन्यस्य नरोऽन्येन निमन्त्रितः ।
दैवे वाप्यथवा पित्र्ये स द्विधा कृष्यते खगैः ॥ ४९ ॥
मर्म्माणि यस्तु साधूनामसद्वाग्भिर्निकृन्तति ।
तमिमे तुदमानास्तु खगास्तिष्ठन्त्यवारिताः ॥ ५० ॥
यः करोति च पैशुन्यमन्यवागन्यथामतिः ।
पाट्यते हि द्विधा जिह्वा तस्येत्थं निशितैः क्षुरैः ॥ ५१ ॥
मातापित्रोर्गुरूणाञ्च येऽवज्ञां चक्रुरुद्धताः ।
त इमे पूयविण्मूत्रगर्त्ते मज्जन्त्यधोमुखाः ॥ ५२ ॥
देवतातिथिभूतेषु भृत्येष्वभ्यागतेषु च ।
अभुक्तवत्सु येऽश्नन्ति तद्वत् पित्रग्निपक्षिषु ॥ ५३ ॥
दुष्टास्ते पूयनिर्यासभुजः सूचीमुखास्तु ते ।
जायन्ते गिरिवर्ष्माणः पश्यैते यादृशा नराः ॥ ५४ ॥
एकपङ्क्त्या तु ये विप्रमथवेतरवर्णजं ।
विषमं भोजयन्तीह विड्भुजस्त इमे यथा ॥ ५५ ॥
एकसार्थप्रयातं ये निःस्वमर्थार्थिनं नरं ।
अपास्य स्वान्नमश्नन्ति त इमे श्लेष्मभोजिनः ॥ ५६ ॥
गोब्राह्मणाग्नयः स्पृष्टा यैरुच्छिष्टैर्नरेश्वर ।
तेषामेतेऽग्निकुम्भेषु लेलिह्यन्त्याहिताः कराः ॥ ५७ ॥
सूर्य्येन्दुतारका दृष्टा यैरुच्छिष्टैस्तु कामतः ।
तेषां याम्यैर्नरैर्नेत्रे न्यस्तो वह्निः समेध्यते ॥ ५८ ॥
गावोऽग्निर्जननी विप्रो ज्येष्ठभ्राता पिता स्वसा ।

यामयो गुरवो वृद्धा यैः स्पृष्टास्तु पदा नृभिः ॥ ५९ ॥
बद्धाङ्घ्रयस्ते निगडैर्लौहैरग्निप्रतापितैः ।
अङ्गारराशिमध्यस्थास्तिष्ठन्त्याजानुदाहिनः ॥ ६० ॥
पायसं कृशरं छागो देवान्नानि च यानि वै ।
भुक्तानि यैरसंस्कृत्य तेषां नेत्राणि पापिनां ॥ ६१ ॥
निपातितानां भूपृष्ठे उद्वृत्ताक्षि निरीक्षतां ।
सन्दंशैः पश्य कृष्यन्ते नरैर्याम्यैर्मुखात्ततः ॥ ६२ ॥
गुरुदेवद्विजातीनां वेदानाञ्च नराधमैः ।
निन्दा निशामिता यैश्च पापानामभिनन्दतां ॥ ६३ ॥
तेषामयोमयान् कीलानग्निवर्णान् पुनःपुनः ।
कर्णेषु प्रेरयन्त्येते याम्या विलपतामपि ॥ ६४ ॥
यैः प्रपादेवविप्रौको देवालयसभाः शुभाः ।
भङ्क्त्वा विध्वंसमानीताः क्रोधलोभानुवर्त्तिभिः ॥ ६५ ॥
तेषामेतैः शितैः शस्त्रैर्मुहुर्विलपतां त्वचः ।
पृथक् कुर्व्वन्ति वै याम्याः शरीरादतिदारुणाः ॥ ६६ ॥
गोब्राह्मणार्कमार्गांस्तु येऽवमेहन्ति मानवाः ।
तेषामेतानि कृष्यन्ते गुदेनान्त्राणि वायसैः ॥ ६७ ॥
दत्वा कन्यां यच कस्मै द्वितीयाय प्रयच्छति ।
स त्वेवं नैकधा छिन्नः क्षारनद्यां प्रवाह्यते ॥ ६८ ॥
स्वपोषणपरो यस्तु परित्यजति मानवः ।
पुत्त्रभृत्यकलत्रादिबन्धुवर्गमकिञ्चनं ॥ ६९ ॥
दुर्भिक्षे सम्भ्रमे वापि सोऽप्येवं यमकिङ्करैः ।

उत्कृत्य दत्तानि मुखे स्वमांसान्यश्नुते क्षुधा ॥ ७० ॥
शरणागतान् यस्त्यजति लोभाद्वृत्त्युपजीविनः ।
सोऽप्येवं यन्त्रपीडाभिः पीड्यते यमकिङ्करैः ॥ ७१ ॥
सुकृतं ये प्रयच्छन्ति यावज्जन्म कृतं नराः ।
ते पिष्यन्ते शिलापेषैर्यथैते पापकर्म्मिणः ॥ ७२ ॥
न्यासापहारिणो बद्धाः सर्व्वगात्रेषु बन्धनैः ।
कृमिवृश्चिककाकोलैर्भुज्यन्तेऽहर्न्निशं नराः ॥ ७३ ॥
क्षुत्क्षामास्तृट्पतज्जिह्वातालवो वेदनातुराः ।
दिवामैथुनिनः पापाः परदारभुजश्च ये ॥ ७४ ॥
तथैव कण्टकैर्दीर्घैरायसैः पश्य शाल्मलिं ।
आरोपिता विभिन्नाङ्गाः प्रभूतासृक्स्रवाविलाः ॥ ७५ ॥
मूषायामपि पश्यैतान् नाश्यमानान् यमानुगैः ।
पुरुषैः पुरुषव्याघ्र परदारावमर्षिणः ॥ ७६ ॥
उपाध्यायमधःकृत्वा स्तब्धो योऽध्ययनं नरः ।
गृह्णाति शिल्पमथवा सोऽप्येवं शिरसा शिलां ॥ ७७ ॥
बिभ्रत् क्लेशमवाप्नोति जनमार्गेऽतिपीडितः ।
क्षुत्क्षामोऽहर्न्निशं भारपीडाव्यथितमस्तकः ॥ ७८ ॥
मूत्रश्लेष्मपुरीषाणि यैरुत्सृष्टानि वारिणि ।
त इमे श्लेष्मविण्मूत्रदुर्गन्धं नरकं गताः ॥ ७९ ॥
परस्परञ्च मांसानि भक्षयन्ति क्षुधान्विताः ।
भुक्तं नातिथ्यविधिना पूर्व्वमेभिः परस्परं ॥ ८० ॥
अपविद्धास्तु यैर्वेदा वह्नयश्चाहिताग्निभिः ।

तद्रूमे शैलशृङ्गाग्रात् पात्यन्तेऽधः पुनःपुनः ॥ ८१ ॥
पुनर्भूपतयो जीर्णा यावज्जीवन्ति ये नराः ।
द्रुमे कृमित्वमापन्ना भक्ष्यन्तेऽच पिपीलिकैः ॥ ८२ ॥
पतितप्रतिग्रहादानाद्याजनान्नित्यसेवनात् ।
पाषाणमध्यकीटत्वं नरः सततमश्नुते ॥ ८३ ॥
पश्यतो भृत्यवर्गस्य मित्राणामतिथेस्तथा ।
एको मिष्टान्नभुग्भुङ्क्ते ज्वलदङ्गारसञ्चयं ॥ ८४ ॥
वृकैर्भयङ्करैः पृष्ठन्नित्यमस्योपभुज्यते ।
पृष्ठमांसं नृपैतेन यतो लोकस्य भक्षितं ॥ ८५ ॥
अन्धोऽथ बधिरो मूको भ्राम्यतेऽयं क्षुधातुरः ।
अकृतज्ञोऽधमः पुंसामुपकारेषु वर्त्तताम् ॥ ८६ ॥
अयं कृतघ्नो मित्राणामपकारी सुदुर्म्मतिः ।
तप्तकुम्भे निपतति ततो यास्यति पेषणं ॥ ८७ ॥
करम्भबालुकां तस्मात्ततो यन्त्रावपीडनं ।
असिपत्रवनं तस्मात् करपत्रेण पाटनं ॥ ८८ ॥
कालसूत्रे तथा छेदमनेकाश्चैव यातनाः ।
प्राप्य निष्कृतिमेतस्मान्न वेद्मि कथमेष्यति ॥ ८९ ॥
श्राद्धसङ्गतिनो विप्राः समुत्पत्य परस्परं ।
दृष्टा हि निःसृतं फेनं सर्व्वाङ्गेभ्यः पिबन्ति वै ॥ ९० ॥
सुवर्णस्तेयी विप्रघ्नः सुरापो गुरुतल्पगः ।
अधश्चोर्द्ध्वञ्च दीप्ताग्नौ दह्यमानाः समन्ततः ॥ ९१ ॥
तिष्ठन्त्यब्दसहस्राणि सुबहूनि ततः पुनः ।

जायन्ते मानवाः कुष्ठक्षयरोगादिचिह्निताः ॥ ९२ ॥
मृताः पुनश्च नरकं पुनर्जातास्च तादृशं ।
व्याधिमृच्छन्ति कल्पान्तपरिमाणं नराधिप ॥ ९३ ॥
गोघ्नो न्यूनतरं याति नरकेऽथ त्रिजन्मनि ।
तथोपपातकानाञ्च सर्व्वेषामिति निश्चयः ॥ ९४ ॥
नरकप्रच्युता यान्ति यैर्यैर्विहितपातकैः ।
प्रयान्ति योनिजातानि तन्मे निगदतः शृणु ॥ ९५ ॥

इति श्रीमार्कण्डेयपुराणे जडोपाख्याने यमकिङ्करसंवादे ॥ १४ ॥

पञ्चदशोऽध्यायः ॥

यमकिङ्कर उवाच ॥

पतितात्प्रतिगृह्यार्थं खरयोनिं व्रजेद्द्विजः ।
नरकात् प्रतिमुक्तस्तु कृमिः पतितयाजकः ॥ १ ॥
उपाध्यायव्यलीकन्तु कृत्वा श्वा भवति द्विजः ।
तज्जायां मनसा वाञ्छन् तद्द्रव्यं चाप्यसंशयं ॥ २ ॥
गर्द्दभो जायते जन्तुः पित्रोश्चाप्यवमानकः ।
मातापितरावाक्रुश्य शारिका सम्प्रजायते ॥ ३ ॥
भ्रातुः पत्नवमन्ता च कपोतत्वं प्रपद्यते ।
तामेव पीडयित्वा तु कच्छपत्वं प्रपद्यते ॥ ४ ॥
भर्तृपिण्डमुपाश्नन् यस्तदिष्टं न निषेवते ।

सोऽपि मोहसमापन्नो जायते वानरो मृतः ॥ ५ ॥
न्यासापहर्त्ता नरकाद्विमुक्तो जायते कृमिः ।
असूयकश्च नरकान्मुक्तो भवति राक्षसः ॥ ६ ॥
विश्वासहन्ता च नरो मीनयोनौ प्रजायते ।
धान्यं यवांस्तिलान्माषान् कुलत्थान् सर्षपांश्चणान् ॥ ७ ॥
कलायान् कलमान्मुद्गान् गोधूमानतसीस्तथा ।
सस्यान्यन्यानि वा हृत्वा मोहाज्जन्तुरचेतनः ॥ ८ ॥
सञ्जायते महावक्त्रो मूषिको बभ्रुसन्निभः ।
परदाराभिमर्षात्तु वृको घोरोऽभिजायते ॥ ९ ॥
श्वा शृगालो वको गृध्रो व्याडः कङ्कस्तथा क्रमात् ।
भ्रातृभार्य्याञ्च दुर्बुद्धिर्यो धर्षयति पापकृत् ॥ १० ॥
पुंस्कोकिलत्वमाप्नोति स चापि नरकाच्चुग्रतः ।
सखिभार्य्यां गुरोर्भार्य्यां राजभार्य्याञ्च पापकृत् ॥ ११ ॥
प्रधर्षयित्वा कामात्मा शूकरो जायते नरः ।
यज्ञदानविवाहानां विघ्नकर्त्ता भवेत् कृमिः ॥ १२ ॥
पुनर्द्दाता च कन्यायाः कृमिरेवोपजायते ।
देवतापितृविप्राणामदत्वा योऽन्नमश्नुते ॥ १३ ॥
प्रमुक्तो नरकात् सोऽपि वायसः सम्प्रजायते ।
ज्येष्ठं पितृसमं वापि भ्रातरं योऽवमन्यते ॥ १४ ॥
नरकात् सोऽपि विभ्रष्टः क्रौञ्चयोनौ प्रजायते ।
शूद्रश्च ब्राह्मणीं गत्वा कृमियोनौ प्रजायते ॥ १५ ॥
तस्यामपत्यमुत्पाद्य काष्ठान्तःकीटको भवेत् ।

शूकरः कृमिको मद्गुश्चण्डालश्च प्रजायते ॥ १६ ॥
अकृतज्ञोऽधमः पुंसां विमुक्तो नरकान्नरः ।
कृतघ्नः कृमिकः कीटः पतङ्गो वृश्चिकस्तथा ॥ १७ ॥
मत्स्यस्तु वायसः कूर्म्मः पुक्कशो जायते ततः ।
अशस्त्रं पुरुषं हत्वा नरः संजायते खरः ॥ १८ ॥
कृमिः स्त्रीबधकर्त्ता च बालहन्ता च जायते ।
भोजनं चोरयित्वा तु मक्षिका जायते नरः ॥ १९ ॥
तत्राप्यस्ति विशेषो वै भोजनस्य शृणुष्व तत् ।
हृत्वान्नन्तु स मार्जारो जायते नरकाच्चुत्यतः ॥ २० ॥
तिलपिण्याकसंमिश्रमन्नं हृत्वा तु मूषिकः ।
घृतं हृत्वा च नकुलः काको मद्गुरजामिषं ॥ २१ ॥
मत्स्यमांसापहृत् काकः श्येनो मार्गामिषापहृत् ।
वीचीकाकस्त्वपहृते लवणे दधनि कृमिः ॥ २२ ॥
चोरयित्वा पयश्चापि बलाका सम्प्रजायते ।
यस्तु चोरयते तैलं तैलपायी स जायते ॥ २३ ॥
मधु हृत्वा नरो दंशः पूपं हृत्वा पिपीलिकः ।
चोरयित्वा तु निष्पावान् जायते गृहगोलकः ॥ २४ ॥
आसवञ्चोरयित्वा तु तित्तिरित्वमवाप्नुयात् ।
अयो हृत्वा तु पापात्मा वायसः सम्प्रजायते ॥ २५ ॥
हृते कांस्ये च हारीतः कपोतो रूप्यभाजने ।
हृत्वा तु काञ्चनं भाण्डं कृमियोनौ प्रजायते ॥ २६ ॥
पत्रोर्णं चोरयित्वा तु क्रकरत्वञ्च गच्छति ।

कोषकारश्च कौषेये हृते वस्त्रेऽभिजायते ॥ २७ ॥
दुकूले शार्ङ्गिके पापो हृते चैवांशुके शुकः ।
तथैवाजाविकं हृत्वा वस्त्रं क्षौमञ्च जायते ॥ २८ ॥
कार्पासिके हृते क्रौञ्चो वाल्कहर्त्ता बकस्तथा ।
मयूरो वर्णकान् हृत्वा शाकपत्रञ्च जायते ॥ २९ ॥
जीवञ्जीवकतां याति रक्तवस्त्रापहृन्नरः ।
छुछुन्दरिः शुभान् गन्धान् वासो हृत्वा शशो भवेत् ॥३०॥
शण्डः फलापहरणात् काष्ठस्य घुणकीटकः ।
पुष्पापहृद्दरिद्रस्य पङ्गुर्यानापहृन्नरः ॥ ३१ ॥
शाकहर्त्ता च हारीतस्तोयहर्त्ता च चातकः ।
भूहर्त्ता नरकान् गत्वा रौरवादीन् सुदारुणान् ॥ ३२ ॥
तृणगुल्मलतावल्लित्वक्सारतरुतां क्रमात् ।
प्राप्य क्षीणाल्पपापस्तु नरो भवति वै ततः ॥ ३३ ॥
कृमिः कीटः पतङ्गोऽथ पक्षी तोयचरो मृगः ।
गोत्वं प्राप्य च चण्डालपुक्कशादि जुगुप्सितं ॥ ३४ ॥
पङ्ग्वन्धो बधिरः कुष्ठी यक्ष्मणा च प्रपीडितः ।
मुखरोगाक्षिरोगैश्च गुदरोगैश्च बाध्यते ॥ ३५ ॥
अपस्मारी च भवति शूद्रत्वं च स गच्छति ।
एष एव क्रमो दृष्टो गोसुवर्णापहारिणां ॥ ३६ ॥
विद्यापहारिणश्चोग्रा निष्क्रयभ्रंसिनो गुरोः ।
जायामन्यस्य पुरुषः पारक्यां प्रतिपादयन् ॥ ३७ ॥
प्राप्नोति शण्ढतां मूढो यातनाभ्यः परिच्युतः ।

यः करोति नरो होममसमिद्धे विभावसौ॥ ३८॥
सोऽजीर्णव्याधिदुःखार्त्तो मन्दाग्निः संप्रजायते।
परनिन्दा कृतघ्नत्वं परमर्म्मविघट्टनं॥ ३९॥
नैष्ठुर्य्यं निर्घृणत्वञ्च परदारोपसेवनं।
परस्वहरणाशौचं देवतानाञ्च कुत्सनं॥ ४०॥
निकृत्या वञ्चनं नृणां कार्पण्यञ्च नृणां बधः।
यानि च प्रतिषिद्धानि तत्प्रवृत्तिश्च सन्तता॥ ४१॥
उपलक्ष्याणि जानीयान्मुक्तानां नरकादनु।
दया भूतेषु संवादः परलोकप्रतिक्रिया॥ ४२॥
सत्यं भूतहितार्थोक्तिर्वेदप्रामाण्यदर्शनं।
गुरुदेवर्षिसिद्धर्षिपूजनं साधुसङ्गमः॥ ४३॥
सत्क्रियाभ्यसनं मैत्रीमिति बुध्येत पण्डितः।
अन्यानि चैव सद्धर्म्मक्रियाभूतानि यानि च॥ ४४॥
स्वर्गच्युतानां लिङ्गानि पुरुषाणामपापिनां।
एतदुद्देशतो राजन् भवतः कथितं मया॥ ४५॥
स्वकर्म्मफलभोक्तॄणां पुण्यानां पापिनान्तथा।
तदेह्यन्यत्र गच्छामो दृष्टं सर्व्वं त्वयाधुना॥
त्वया दृष्टो हि नरकस्तदेह्यन्यत्र गम्यतां॥ ४६॥

पुत्र उवाच॥

ततस्तमग्रतः कृत्वा स राजा गन्तुमुद्यतः।
ततश्च सर्व्वैरुत्कुष्टं यातनास्थायिभिर्नृभिः॥ ४७॥
प्रसादं कुरु भूपेति तिष्ठ तावन्मुहूर्त्तकं।

त्वदङ्गसङ्गी पवनो मनो ह्लादयते हि नः ॥ ४८ ॥
परितापश्च गात्रेभ्यः पीडाबाधाश्च कृत्स्नशः ।
अपहन्ति नरव्याघ्र दयां कुरु महीपते ॥ ४९ ॥
एतच्छ्रुत्वा वचस्तेषां तं याम्यपुरुषं नृपः ।
पप्रच्छ कथमेतेषामाह्लादो मयि तिष्ठति ॥ ५० ॥
किं मया कर्म्म तत् पुण्यं मर्त्यलोके महत् कृतं ।
आह्लाददायिनी दृष्टिर्येनेयं तदुदीरय ॥ ५१ ॥

यमपुरुष उवाच ॥

पितृदेवातिथिप्रेष्यशिष्टेनान्नेन ते तनुः ।
पुष्टिमभ्यागता यस्मात्तद्गतञ्च मनो यतः ॥ ५२ ॥
ततस्त्वद्गात्रसंसर्गी पवनो ह्लाददायकः ।
पापकर्म्मकृतो राजन् यातना न प्रबाधते ॥ ५३ ॥
अश्वमेधादयो यज्ञास्त्वयेष्टा विधिवद्यतः ।
ततस्त्वद्दर्शनाद्याम्या यन्त्रशस्त्राग्निवायसाः ॥ ५४ ॥
पीडनच्छेददाहादिमहादुःखस्य हेतवः ।
मृदुत्वमागता राजन् तेजसापहतास्तव ॥ ५५ ॥

राजोवाच ॥

न स्वर्गे ब्रह्मलोके वा तत्सुखं प्राप्यते नरैः ।
यदार्त्तजन्तुनिर्व्वाणदानोत्थमिति मे मतिः ॥ ५६ ॥
यदि मत्सन्निधावेतान् यातना न प्रबाधते ।
ततो भद्रमुखात्राहं स्थास्ये स्थाणुरिवाचलः ॥ ५७ ॥

यमपुरुष उवाच ॥

एहि राजन् प्रगच्छामो निजपुण्यसमर्जितान् ।
भुङ्क्ष्व भोगानपास्येह यातनाः पापकर्म्मणां ॥ ५८ ॥

राजोवाच ॥

तस्मान्न तावद्यास्यामि यावदेते सुदुःखिताः ।
मत्सन्निधानात् सुखिनो भवन्ति नरकौकसः ॥ ५९ ॥
धिक् तस्य जीवनं पुंसः शरणार्थिनमातुरं ।
यो नार्त्तमनुगृह्णाति वैरिपक्षमपि ध्रुवं ॥ ६० ॥
यज्ञदानतपांसीह परत्र च न भूतये ।
भवन्ति तस्य यस्यार्त्तपरित्राणे न मानसं ॥ ६१ ॥
नरस्य यस्य कठिनं मनो बालातुरादिषु ।
वृद्धेषु च न तं मन्ये मानुषं राक्षसो हि सः ॥ ६२ ॥
एतेषां सन्निकर्षात्तु यद्यग्निपरितापजं ।
तथोग्रगन्धजं वापि दुःखं नरकसम्भवं ॥ ६३ ॥
क्षुत्पिपासाभवं दुःखं यच्च मूर्च्छाप्रदं महत् ।
एतेषां त्राणदानन्तु मन्ये स्वर्गसुखात् परं ॥ ६४ ॥
प्राप्स्यन्त्यार्त्ता यदि सुखं बहवो दुःखिते मयि ।
किन्नु प्राप्तं मया न स्यात्तस्मात्त्वं व्रज मा चिरं ॥ ६५ ॥

यमपुरुष उवाच ॥

एष धर्म्मश्च शक्रश्च त्वां नेतुं समुपागतौ ।
अवश्यन्तस्माद्गन्तव्यं तस्मात् पार्थिव गम्यतां ॥ ६६ ॥

धर्म्म उवाच ॥

नयामि त्वामहं स्वर्गं त्वया सम्यगुपासितः ।
विमानमेतदारुह्य मा विलम्बस्व गम्यतां ॥ ६७ ॥

राजोवाच ॥

नरके मानवा धर्म्म पीड्यन्तेऽत्र सहस्रशः ।
त्राहीति चार्त्ताः क्रन्दन्ति मामतो न व्रजाम्यहं ॥ ६८ ॥

इन्द्र उवाच ॥

कर्म्मणा नरकप्राप्तिरेतेषां पापकर्म्मिणां ।
स्वर्गस्त्वयापि गन्तव्यो नृप पुण्येन कर्म्मणा ॥ ६९ ॥

राजोवाच ॥

यदि जानासि धर्म्म त्वं त्वं वा शक्र शचीपते ।
मम यावत्प्रमाणन्तु शुभं तद्वक्तुमर्हथः ॥ ७० ॥

धर्म्म उवाच ॥

अब्बिन्दवो यथाम्भोधौ यथा वा दिवि तारकाः ।
यथा वा वर्षतो धारा गङ्गायां सिकता यथा ॥ ७१ ॥
असंख्येया महाराज यथा विन्द्वादयो ह्यपां ।
तथा तवापि पुण्यस्य संख्या नैवोपपद्यते ॥ ७२ ॥
अनुकम्यामिमामद्य नारकेष्विह कुर्व्वतः ।
तदेव शतसाहस्रं संख्यामुपगतं तव ॥ ७३ ॥
तद्गच्छ त्वं नृपश्रेष्ठ तद्भोक्तुममरालयं ।
एतेऽपि पापन्नरके क्षपयन्तु स्वकर्म्मजं ॥ ७४ ॥

राजोवाच ॥

कथं स्पृहां करिष्यन्ति मत्सम्पर्केषु मानवाः ।
यदि मत्सन्निधावेषामुत्कर्षो नोपजायते ॥ ७५ ॥
तस्मात् यत् सुकृतं किञ्चिन्ममास्ति त्रिदशाधिप ।
तेन मुच्यन्तु नरकात् पापिनो यातनां गताः ॥ ७६ ॥

इन्द्र उवाच ॥

एवमूर्द्ध्वतरं स्थानं त्वयावाप्तं महीपते ।
एतांश्च नरकात् पश्य विमुक्तान् पापकारिणः ॥ ७७ ॥

पुत्र उवाच ॥

ततोऽपतत् पुष्पवृष्टिस्तस्योपरि महीपतेः ।
विमानञ्चाधिरोप्यैनं स्वर्लोकमनयद्धरिः ॥ ७८ ॥
अहञ्चान्ये च ये तत्र यातनाभ्यः परिच्युताः ।
स्वकर्म्मफलनिर्दिष्टं ततो जात्यन्तरं गताः ॥ ७९ ॥
एवमेते समाख्याता नरका द्विजसत्तम ।
येन येन च पापेन यां यां योनिमुपैति वै ॥ ८० ॥
तत्तत् सर्व्वं समाख्यातं यथा दृष्टं मया पुरा ।
पुरानुभवजं ज्ञानमवाप्यावितथं तव ॥
अतःपरं महाभाग किमन्यत् कथयामि ते ॥ ८१ ॥

इति श्री मार्कण्डेयपुराणे पितापुत्रसंवादे ॥ १५ ॥

षोडशोऽध्यायः ॥

पितोवाच ॥

कथितं मे त्वया वत्स संसारस्य व्यवस्थितं ।
स्वरूपमतिहेयस्य घटीयन्त्रवदव्ययं ॥ १ ॥
तदेवमेतदखिलं मयावगतमीदृशं ।
किम्मया वद कर्त्तव्यमेवमस्मिन् व्यवस्थिते ॥ २ ॥

पुत्र उवाच ॥

यदि मद्वचनं तात श्रद्दधास्यविशङ्कितः ।
तत्परित्यज्य गार्हस्थ्यं वानप्रस्थपरो भव ॥ ३ ॥
तमनुष्ठाय विधिवद् विहायाग्निपरिग्रहं ।
आत्मन्यात्मानमाधाय निर्द्वन्द्वो निष्परिग्रहः ॥ ४ ॥
एकान्तराशी वश्यात्मा भव भिक्षुरतन्द्रितः ।
तत्र योगपरो भूत्वा बाह्यस्पर्शविवर्जितः ॥ ५ ॥
ततः प्राप्स्यसि तं योगं दुःखसंयोगभेषजं ।
मुक्तिहेतुमनौपम्यमनाख्येयमसङ्गिनं ॥
यत्संयोगान्न ते योगो भूयो भूतैर्भविष्यति ॥ ६ ॥

पितोवाच ॥

वत्स योगं ममाचक्ष्व मुक्तिहेतुमतःपरं ।
येन भूतैः पुनर्भूतो नेदृग्दुःखमवाप्नुयां ॥ ७ ॥
यत्रासक्तिपरस्यात्मा मम संसारबन्धनैः ।
नैति योगमयोगोऽपि तं योगमधुना वद ॥ ८ ॥

संसारादित्यतापार्त्तिविशुष्यद्देहमानसं ।
ब्रह्मज्ञानाम्बुशीतेन सिञ्च मां वाक्यवारिणा ॥ ९ ॥
अविद्याकृष्णसर्पेण दष्टं तद्विषपीडितं ।
स्ववाक्यामृतपानेन मां जीवय पुनर्मृतं ॥ १० ॥
पुत्रदारगृहक्षेत्रममत्वनिगडार्द्दितं ।
मां मोचयेष्टसद्भावविज्ञानोद्घाटनैस्त्वरन् ॥ ११ ॥

पुत्र उवाच ॥

शृणु तात यथा योगो दत्तात्रेयेण धीमता ।
अलर्काय पुरा प्रोक्तः सम्यक् पृष्टेन विस्तरात् ॥ १२ ॥

पितोवाच ॥

दत्तात्रेयः सुतः कस्य कथं वा योगमुक्तवान् ।
कश्चालर्को महाभागो यो योगं परिपृष्टवान् ॥ १३ ॥

पुत्र उवाच ॥

कौशिको ब्राह्मणः कश्चित् प्रतिष्ठानेऽभवत्पुरे ।
सोऽन्यजन्मकृतैः पापैः कुष्ठरोगातुरोऽभवत् ॥ १४ ॥
तं तथा व्याधितं भार्य्या पतिं देवमिवार्च्चयत् ।
पादाभ्यङ्गाङ्गसंवाहस्नानाच्छादनभोजनैः ॥ १५ ॥
श्लेष्ममूत्रपुरीषासृक्प्रवाहक्षालनेन च ।
रहस्यैवोपचारेण प्रियसम्भाषणेन च ॥ १६ ॥
स तया पूज्यमानोऽपि सदातीव विनीतया ।
अतीवतीव्रकोपत्वान्निर्भर्त्सयति निष्ठुरः ॥ १७

तथापि प्रणता भार्य्या तममन्यत दैवतं।
तं तथाप्यतिबीभत्सं सर्व्वश्रेष्ठममन्यत ॥ १८ ॥
अचंक्रमणशीलोऽपि स कदाचिद्द्विजोत्तमः।
प्राह भार्य्यां नयस्वेति त्वं मां तस्या निवेशनं ॥ १९ ॥
या सा वेश्या मया दृष्टा राजमार्गे गृहोषिता।
तां मां प्रापय धर्म्मज्ञे सैव मे हृदि वर्त्तते ॥ २० ॥
दृष्टा सूर्य्योदये बाला रात्रिश्चेयमुपागता।
दर्शनानन्तरं सा मे हृदयान्नापसर्पति ॥ २१ ॥
यदि सा चारुसर्व्वाङ्गी पीनश्रोणिपयोधरा।
नोपगूहति तन्वङ्गी तन्मां द्रक्ष्यसि वै मृतं ॥ २२ ॥
वामः कामो मनुष्याणां बहुभिः प्रार्थ्यते च सा।
ममाशक्तिश्च गमने संकुलं प्रतिभाति मे ॥ २३ ॥
तत्तदा वचनं श्रुत्वा भर्त्तुः कामातुरस्य सा।
तत्पत्नी सत्कुलोत्पन्ना महाभागा पतिव्रता ॥ २४ ॥
गाढं परिकरं बद्ध्वा शुल्कमादाय चाधिकं।
स्कन्धे भर्त्तारमादाय जगाम मृदुगामिनी ॥ २५ ॥
निशि मेघास्तृते व्योम्नि चलद्विद्युत्प्रदर्शिते।
राजमार्गे प्रियं भर्त्तुश्चिकीर्षन्ती द्विजाङ्गना ॥ २६ ॥
पथि शूले तथा प्रोतमचौरं चौरशङ्कया।
माण्डव्यमतिदुःखार्त्तमन्धकारेऽथ स द्विजः ॥ २७ ॥
पत्नीस्कन्धे समारूढश्चालयामास कौशिकः।
पादावमर्षणात् क्रुद्धो माण्डव्यस्तमुवाच ह ॥ २८ ॥

येनाहमेवमत्यर्थं दुःखितश्चालितः पदा।
दशां कष्टामनुप्राप्तः स पापात्मा नराधमः ॥ २९ ॥
सूर्य्योदयेऽवशः प्राणैर्विमोक्ष्यति न संशयः।
भास्करालोकनादेव स विनाशमवाप्स्यति ॥ ३० ॥
तस्य भार्य्या ततः श्रुत्वा तं शापमतिदारुणं।
प्रोवाच व्यथिता सूर्य्यो नैवोदयमुपैष्यति ॥ ३१ ॥
ततः सूर्य्योदयाभावादभवत् सन्तता निशा।
बह्वन्यहःप्रमाणानि ततो देवा भयं ययुः ॥ ३२ ॥
निःस्वाध्यायवषट्कारस्वधास्वाहाविवर्जितं।
कथं नु खल्विदं सर्व्वं न गच्छेत् संक्षयं जगत् ॥ ३३ ॥
अहोरात्रव्यवस्थाया विना मासर्त्तुसंक्षयः।
तत्संक्षयान्नत्वयने ज्ञायेते दक्षिणोत्तरे ॥ ३४ ॥
विना चायनविज्ञानात् कालः संवत्सरः कुतः।
संवत्सरं विना नान्यत् कालज्ञानं प्रवर्त्तते ॥ ३५ ॥
पतिव्रताया वचसा नोद्गच्छति दिवाकरः।
सूर्य्योदयं विना नैव स्नानदानादिकाः क्रियाः ॥ ३६ ॥
नाग्नेर्विहरणञ्चैव क्रत्वभावश्च लक्ष्यते।
नैवाप्यायनमस्माकं विना होमेन जायते ॥ ३७ ॥
वयमाप्यायिता मर्त्यैर्यज्ञभागैर्यथोचितैः।
वृष्ट्याताननुगृह्णीमो मर्त्त्यान् सस्यादिसिद्धये ॥ ३८ ॥
निष्पादितास्वोषधीषु मर्त्या यज्ञैर्यजन्ति नः।
तेषां वयं प्रयच्छामः कामान् यज्ञादिपूजिताः ॥ ३९ ॥

अधो हि वर्षाम वयं मर्त्त्याश्चोर्द्ध्वप्रवर्षिणः ।
तोयवर्षेण हि वयं हविर्वर्षेण मानवाः ॥ ४० ॥
ये नास्माकं प्रयच्छन्ति नित्यनैमित्तिकीः क्रियाः ।
क्रतुभागं दुरात्मानः स्वयं चाश्नन्ति लोलुपाः ॥ ४१ ॥
विनाशाय वयं तेषां तोयसूर्य्याग्निमारुतान् ।
क्षितिञ्च सन्दूषयामः पापानामपकारिणां ॥ ४२ ॥
दुष्टतोयादिभोगेन तेषां दुष्कृतकर्म्मिणां ।
उपसर्गाः प्रवर्त्तन्ते मरणाय सुदारुणाः ॥ ४३ ॥
ये त्वस्मान् प्रीणयित्वा तु भुञ्जते शेषमात्मना ।
तेषां पुण्यान् वयं लोकान् विदधाम महात्मनां ॥४४ ॥
तन्नास्ति सर्व्वमेवैतद् विनैषां व्युष्टिसंस्थितिं ।
कथन्नु दिनसर्गः स्यादन्योन्यमवदन् सुराः ॥ ४५ ॥
तेषामेव समेतानां यज्ञव्युच्छित्तिशङ्किनां ।
देवानां वचनं श्रुत्वा प्राह देवः प्रजापतिः ॥ ४६ ॥
तेजः परं तेजसैव तपसा च तपस्तथा ।
प्रशाम्यतेऽमरास्तस्माच्छृणुध्वं वचनं मम ॥ ४७ ॥
पतिव्रताया माहात्म्यान्नोद्गच्छति दिवाकरः ।
तस्य चानुदयाद्धानिर्मर्त्त्यानां भवतां तथा ॥ ४८ ॥
तस्मात् पतिव्रतामत्रेरनसूयां तपस्विनीं ।
प्रसादयत वै पत्नीं भानोरुदयकाम्यया ॥ ४९ ॥

पुत्र उवाच ॥

तैः सा प्रसादिता गत्वा प्राहेष्टं व्रियतामिति ।

अयाचन्त दिनं देवा भवत्विति यथा पुरा ॥ ५० ॥

अनसूयोवाच ॥

पतिव्रताया माहात्म्यं न हीयेत कथन्त्विति ।
सम्मान्य तस्मात्तां साध्वीमहः स्रक्ष्याम्यहं सुराः ॥ ५१ ॥
यथा पुनरहोरात्रसंस्थानमुपजायते ।
यथा च तस्याः स्वपतिर्न्न साध्व्या नाशमेष्यति ॥ ५२ ॥

पुत्र उवाच ॥

एवमुक्त्वा सुरांस्तस्या गत्वा सा मन्दिरं शुभा ।
उवाच कुशलं पृष्टा धर्म्मं भर्त्तुस्तथात्मनः ॥ ५३ ॥

अनसूयोवाच ॥

कच्चिन्नन्दसि कल्याणि स्वभर्त्तुर्मुखदर्शनात् ।
कच्चिच्चाखिलदेवेभ्यो मन्यसेऽभ्यधिकं पतिं ॥ ५४ ॥
भर्तृशुश्रूषणादेव मया प्राप्तं महत् फलं ।
सर्व्वकामफलावाप्त्या प्रत्यूहाः परिवर्त्तिताः ॥ ५५ ॥
पञ्चर्णानि मनुष्येण साध्वि देयानि सर्व्वदा ।
तथात्मवर्णधर्म्मेण कर्त्तव्यो धनसञ्चयः ॥ ५६ ॥
प्राप्तश्चार्थस्ततः पात्रे विनियोज्यो विधानतः ।
सत्यार्जवतपोदानैर्दयायुक्तो भवेत् सदा ॥ ५७ ॥
क्रियाश्च शास्त्रनिर्दिष्टा रागद्वेषविवर्जिताः ।
कर्त्तव्या अन्वहं श्रद्धापुरस्कारेण शक्तितः ॥ ५८ ॥
स्वजातिविहितानेव लोकानाप्नोति मानवः ।
क्लेशेन महता साध्वि प्राजापत्यादिकान् क्रमात् ॥ ५९ ॥

स्त्रियस्त्वेवं समस्तस्य नरैर्दुःखार्जितस्य वै ।
पुण्यस्यार्द्धोपहारिण्यः पतिशुश्रूषयैव हि ॥ ६० ॥
नास्ति स्त्रीणां पृथग्यज्ञो न श्राद्धं नाप्युपोषितं ।
भर्तृशुश्रूषयैवैतान् लोकानिष्टान् व्रजन्ति हि ॥ ६१ ॥
तस्मात् साध्वि महाभागे पतिशुश्रूषणं प्रति ।
त्वया मतिः सदा कार्य्या यतो भर्त्ता परा गतिः ॥ ६२ ॥
यद्देवेभ्यो यच्च पित्रागतेभ्यः
कुर्य्याद्भर्त्ताभ्यर्च्चनं सत्क्रियातः ।
तस्याप्यर्द्धं केवलानन्यचित्ता
नारी भुङ्क्ते भर्तृशुश्रूषयैव ॥ ६३ ॥

पुत्र उवाच ॥

तस्यास्तद्वचनं श्रुत्वा प्रतिपूज्य तथादरात् ।
प्रत्युवाचात्रिपत्नीं तामनसूयामिदं वचः ॥ ६४ ॥
धन्यास्म्यनुगृहीतास्मि देवैश्चाप्यवलोकिता ।
यन्मे प्रकृतिकल्याणि श्रद्धां वर्द्धयसे पुनः ॥ ६५ ॥
जानाम्येतन्न नारीणां काचित् पतिसमागतिः ।
तत्प्रीतिश्चोपकाराय इह लोके परत्र च ॥ ६६ ॥
पतिप्रसादादिह च प्रेत्य चैव यशस्विनि ।
नारी सुखमवाप्नोति नार्य्या भर्त्ता हि देवता ॥ ६७ ॥
सा त्वं ब्रूहि महाभागे प्राप्तया मम मन्दिरं ।
आर्य्याया यन्मया कार्य्यन्तथार्य्येणापि वा शुभे ॥ ६८ ॥

अनसूयोवाच ॥

एते देवाः सहेन्द्रेण मामुपागम्य दुःखिताः ।
त्वद्वाक्यापास्तसत्कर्म्मदिननक्तनिरूपणाः ॥ ६९ ॥
याचन्तेऽहर्न्निशासंस्थां यथावदविखण्डितां ।
अहं तदर्थमायाता शृणु चैतद्वचो मम ॥ ७० ॥
दिनाभावात् समस्तानामभावो यागकर्म्मणां ।
तदभावात् सुराः पुष्टिं नोपयान्ति तपस्विनि ॥ ७१ ॥
अह्नश्चैव समुच्छेदादुच्छेदः सर्व्वकर्म्मणां ।
तदुच्छेदादनावृष्ट्या जगदुच्छेदमेष्यति ॥ ७२ ॥
तत्त्वमिच्छसि चेदेतत् जगदुद्धर्त्तुमापदः ।
प्रसीद साध्वि लोकानां पूर्व्ववद्वर्त्ततां रविः ॥ ७३ ॥

ब्राह्मण्युवाच ॥

माण्डव्येन महाभागे शप्तो भर्त्ता ममेश्वरः ।
सूर्य्योदये विनाशं त्वं प्राप्स्यसीत्यतिमन्युना ॥ ७४ ॥

अनसूयोवाच ॥

यदि वा रोचते भद्रे ततस्त्वद्वचनादहं ।
करोमि पूर्व्ववद्देहं भर्त्तारञ्च नवं तव ॥ ७५ ॥
मया हि सर्व्वथा स्त्रीणां माहात्म्यं वरवर्ण्णिनि ।
पतिव्रतानामाराध्यमिति सम्मानयामि ते ॥ ७६ ॥

पुत्र उवाच ॥

तथेत्युक्ते तया सूर्य्यमाजुहाव तपस्विनी ।
अनसूयार्घ्यमुद्यम्य दशरात्रे तदा निशि ॥ ७७ ॥

ततो विवस्वान् भगवान् फुल्लपद्मारुणाकृतिः ।
शैलराजानमुदयमारुरोहोरुमण्डलः ॥ ७८ ॥
समनन्तरमेवास्या भर्त्ता प्राणैर्व्ययुज्यत ।
पपात च महीपृष्ठे पतन्तं जगृहे च सा ॥ ७९ ॥

अनसूयोवाच ॥

न विषादस्त्वया भद्रे कर्त्तव्यः पश्य मे बलं ।
पतिशुश्रूषयावाप्तं तपसः किञ्चिरेण ते ॥ ८० ॥
यथा भर्तृसमं नान्यमपश्यं पुरुषं क्वचित् ।
रूपतः शीलतो बुद्ध्या वाङ्माधुर्य्यादिभूषणैः ॥ ८१ ॥
तेन सत्येन विप्रोऽयं व्याधिमुक्तः पुनर्युवा ।
प्राप्नोतु जीवितं भार्य्यासहायः शरदां शतं ॥ ८२ ॥
यथा भर्तृसमं नान्यमहं पश्यामि दैवतं ।
तेन सत्येन विप्रोऽयं पुनर्जीवत्वनामयः ॥ ८३ ॥
कर्म्मणा मनसा वाचा भर्त्तुराराधनं प्रति ।
यथा ममोद्यमो नित्यं तथायं जीवतां द्विजः ॥ ८४ ॥

पुत्र उवाच ॥

ततो विप्रः समुत्तस्थौ व्याधिमुक्तः पुनर्युवा ।
स्वभाभिर्भासयन् वेश्म वृन्दारक इवाजरः ॥ ८५ ॥
ततोऽपतत् पुष्पवृष्टिर्दैववाद्यादिनिस्वनः ;
लेभिरे च मुदं देवा अनसूयामथाब्रुवन् ॥ ८६ ॥

देवा ऊचुः ॥

वरं वृणीष्व कल्याणि देवकार्य्यं महत् कृतं ।

त्वया यस्मात्ततो देवा वरदास्ते तपस्विनि ॥ ८७ ॥

अनसूयोवाच ॥

यदि देवाः प्रसन्ना मे पितामहपुरोगमाः ।
वरदा वरयोग्या च यद्यहं भवतां मता ॥ ८८ ॥
तद्यान्तु मम पुत्रत्वं ब्रह्मविष्णुमहेश्वराः ।
योगञ्च प्राप्नुयां भर्तृसहिता क्लेशमुक्तये ॥ ८९ ॥
एवमस्त्विति तां देवा ब्रह्मविष्णुशिवादयः ।
प्रोक्ता जग्मुर्यथान्यायमनुमान्य तपस्विनीं ॥ ९० ॥

इति मार्कण्डेयपुराणे पितापुत्रसंवादे अनसूयावरप्राप्तिः ॥ १६ ॥

सप्तदशोऽध्यायः ॥

पुत्र उवाच ॥

ततः काले बहुतिथे द्वितीयो ब्रह्मणः सुतः ।
स्वभार्य्यां भगवानत्रिरनसूयामपश्यत ॥ १ ॥
ऋतुस्नातां सुचार्व्वङ्गीं लोभनीयोत्तमाकृतिं ।
सकामो मनसा भेजे स मुनिस्तामनिन्दितां ॥ २ ॥
तस्याभिध्यायतस्तान्तु विकारो योऽन्वजायत ।
तमेवोवाह पवनस्तिरश्चोर्द्ध्वञ्च वेगवान् ॥ ३ ॥
ब्रह्मरूपञ्च शुक्लाभं पतमानं समन्ततः ।
सोमरूपं रजोपेतं दिशस्तं जगृहुर्दश ॥ ४ ॥

स सोमो मानसो जज्ञे तस्यामत्रेः प्रजापतेः ।
पुत्त्रः समस्तसत्वानामायुराधार एवच ॥ ५ ॥
तुष्टेन विष्णुना जज्ञे दत्तात्रेयो महात्मना ।
स्वशरीरात् समुत्पाद्य सत्वोद्रिक्तो द्विजोत्तमः ॥ ६ ॥
दत्तात्रेय इति ख्यातः सोऽनुसूयास्तनं पपौ ।
विष्णुरेवावतीर्णोऽसौ द्वितीयोऽत्रेः सुतोऽभवत् ॥ ७ ॥
सप्ताहात् प्रच्युतो मातुरुदरात् कुपितो यतः ।
हैहयेन्द्रमुपावृत्तमपराध्यन्तमुद्धतं ॥ ८ ॥
दृष्ट्वात्रौ कुपितः सद्यो दग्धुकामः स हैहयं ।
गर्भवासमहायासदुःखामर्षसमन्वितः ॥ ९ ॥
दुर्व्वासास्तमसोद्रिक्तो रुद्रांशः समजायत ।
इति पुत्त्रत्रयं तस्या जज्ञे ब्रह्मेशवैष्णवं ॥ १० ॥
सोमो ब्रह्माभवद्विष्णुर्दत्तात्रेयो व्यजायत ।
दुर्व्वासाः शङ्करो जज्ञे वरदानाद्दिवौकसां ॥ ११ ॥
सोमः स्वरश्मिभिः शीतैर्वीरुधौषधिमानवान् ।
आप्याययन् सदा स्वर्गे वर्त्तते स प्रजापतिः ॥ १२ ॥
दत्तात्रेयः प्रजां पाति दुष्टदैत्यनिबर्हनात् ।
शिष्टानुग्रहकृच्चेति ज्ञेयस्त्वांशः स वैष्णवः ॥ १३ ॥
निर्दहत्यवमन्तारं दुर्व्वासा भगवानजः ।
रौद्रं समाश्रित्य वपुर्दृङ्मनोवाग्भिरुद्धतः ॥ १४ ॥
सोमत्वं भगवानत्रिः पुनश्चक्रे प्रजापतिः ।
दत्तात्रेयोऽपि विषयान् योगस्थो बुभुजे हरिः ॥ १५ ॥

दुर्व्वासाः पितरं हित्वा मातरं चोत्तमं व्रतं ।
उन्मत्ताख्यं समाश्रित्य परिबभ्राम मेदिनीं ॥ १६ ॥
मुनिपुत्त्रैस्ततो योगी दत्तात्रेयोऽप्यसङ्गितां ।
अभीप्सुमानः सरसि निममज्ज चिरं प्रभुः ॥ १७ ॥
तथापि तं महात्मानमतीव प्रियदर्शनं ।
तत्यजुर्न्न कुमारास्ते सरसस्तीरमाश्रिताः ॥ १८ ॥
दिव्ये वर्षशते पूर्णे यदा ते न त्यजन्ति तं ।
तत्प्रीत्या सरसस्तीरं सर्व्वे मुनिकुमारकाः ॥ १९ ॥
ततो दिव्याम्बरधरां चारुपीननितम्बिनीं ।
नारीमादाय कल्याणीमुत्ततार जलान्मुनिः ॥ २० ॥
स्त्रीसन्निकर्षाद्यद्येते परित्यक्ष्यन्ति मामिति ।
मुनिपुत्त्रास्ततोऽसङ्गी स्थास्यामीति विचिन्तयन् ॥ २१ ॥
तथापि तं मुनिसुता न त्यजन्ति यदा मुनिं ।
ततः सह तया नार्य्या मद्यपानमथापिवत् ॥ २२ ॥
सुरापानरतं ते न सभार्य्यं तत्यजुस्ततः ।
गीतवाद्यादिवनिताभोगसंसर्गदूषितं ॥ २३ ॥
मन्यमाना महात्मानं तया सह वहिष्क्रियं ।
नावाप दोषं योगीशो वारुणीं स पिवन्नपि ॥ २४ ॥
अन्तावसायिवेश्मान्तर्मातरिश्वा वसन्निव ।
सुरां पिवन् सपत्नीकस्तपस्तेपे स योगवित् ॥
योगीश्वरश्चिन्त्यमानो योगिभिर्मुक्तिकाङ्क्षिभिः ॥ २५ ॥

इति श्रीमार्कण्डेयपुराणे दत्तात्रेयोत्पत्तिः ॥ १७ ॥

अष्टादशोऽध्यायः॥

पुत्र उवाच॥

कस्यचित्त्वथ कालस्य कृतवीर्य्यात्मजोऽर्जुनः।
कृतवीर्य्ये दिवं याते मन्त्रिभिः सपुरोहितैः॥ १॥
पौरैश्चात्माभिषेकार्थं समाहूतोऽब्रवीदिदं।
नाहं राज्यं करिष्यामि मन्त्रिणो नरकोत्तरं॥ २॥
यदर्थं गृह्यते शुल्कं तदनिष्पादयन् वृथा।
पण्यानां द्वादशं भागं भूपालाय वणिग्जनः॥ ३॥
दत्वार्थरक्षिभिर्म्मार्गे रक्षितो याति दस्युतः।
गोपाश्च घृततक्रादेः षड्भागञ्च कृषीबलाः॥ ४॥
दत्वान्यद्भूभुजे दद्युर्यदि भागं ततोऽधिकं।
पण्यादीनामशेषाणां बणिजो गृह्णतस्ततः॥ ५॥
इष्टापूर्त्तविनाशाय तद्राज्ञश्चौरधर्म्मिणः।
यद्यन्यैः पाल्यते लोकस्तद्वृत्त्यन्तरसंश्रितः॥ ६॥
गृह्णतो बलिषड्भागं नृपतेर्नरको ध्रुवं।
निरूपितमिदं राज्ञः पूर्व्वैरक्षणवेतनं॥ ७॥
अरक्षंश्चौरतश्चौर्य्यन्तदेनो नृपतेर्भवत्।
तस्माद्यदि तपस्तप्त्वा प्राप्तो योगित्वमीप्सितं॥ ८॥
भुवः पालनसामर्थ्ययुक्त एको महीपतिः।
पृथिव्यां शस्त्रधृङ्मान्यस्त्वहमेवर्द्धिसंयुतः॥
ततो भविष्ये नात्मानं करिष्ये पापभागिनं॥ ९॥

पुत्र उवाच ॥

तस्य तन्निश्चयं ज्ञात्वा मन्त्रिमध्ये स्थितोऽब्रवीत् ।
गर्गो नाम महाबुद्धिर्मुनिश्रेष्ठो वयोऽतिगः ॥ १० ॥
यद्येवं कर्त्तुकामस्त्वं राज्यं सम्यक् प्रशासितुं ।
ततः शृणुष्व मे वाक्यं कुरुष्व च नृपात्मज ॥ ११ ॥
दत्तात्रेयं महाभागं सह्यद्रोणीकृताश्रयं ।
तमाराधय भूपाल पाति यो भुवनत्रयं ॥ १२ ॥
योगयुक्तं महाभागं सर्व्वत्र समदर्शिनं ।
विष्णोरंशं जगद्धातुरवतीर्णं महीतले ॥ १३ ॥
यमाराध्य सहस्राक्षः प्राप्तवान् पदमात्मनः ।
हृतं दुरात्मभिर्दैत्यैर्जघान च दितेः सुतान् ॥ १४ ॥

अर्जुन उवाच ॥

कथमाराधितो देवैर्दत्तात्रेयः प्रतापवान् ।
कथञ्चापहृतं दैत्यैरिन्द्रत्वं प्राप वासवः ॥ १५ ॥

गर्ग उवाच ॥

देवानां दानवानाञ्च युद्धमासीत् सदारुणं ।
दैत्यानामीश्वरो जम्भो देवानाञ्च शचीपतिः ॥ १६ ॥
तेषाञ्च युद्ध्यमानानान्दिव्यः संवत्सरो गतः ।
ततो देवाः पराभूता दैत्या विजयिनोऽभवन् ॥ १७ ॥
विप्रचित्तिमुखैर्देवा दानवैस्ते पराजिताः ।
पलायनकृतोत्साहा निरुत्साहां द्विषज्जये ॥ १८ ॥

बृहस्पतिमुपागम्य दैत्यसैन्यबधेप्सवः ।
अमन्त्रयन्त सहिता बालिखिल्यैस्तथर्षिभिः ॥ १९ ॥

बृहस्पतिरुवाच ॥

दत्तात्रेयं महात्मानमत्रेः पुत्रं तपोधनं ।
विकृताचरणं भक्त्या सन्तोषयितुमर्हथ ॥ २० ॥
स वो दैत्यविनाशाय वरदो दास्यते वरं ।
ततो हनिष्यथ सुरा सहिता दैत्यदानवान् ॥ २१ ॥

गर्ग उवाच ॥

इत्युक्तास्ते तदा जग्मुर्दत्तात्रेयाश्रमं सुराः ।
ददृशुश्च महात्मानं तं ते लक्ष्म्या समन्वितं ॥ २२ ॥
उद्गीयमानं गन्धर्वैः सुरापानरतं मुनिं ।
ते तस्य गत्वा प्रणतिमवदन् साध्यसाधनं ॥ २३ ॥
चक्रुः स्तवं चोपजह्रुर्भक्ष्यभोज्यस्रगादिकं ।
तिष्ठन्तमनुतिष्ठन्ति यान्तं यान्ति दिवौकसः ॥ २४ ॥
आराधयामासुरधः स्थितास्तिष्ठन्तमासने ।
स प्राह प्रणतान्देवान्दत्तात्रेयः किमिष्यते ॥
मत्तो भवद्भिर्येनेयं शुश्रूषा क्रियते मम ॥ २५ ॥

देवा ऊचुः ॥

दानवैर्मुनिशार्दूल जम्भाद्यैर्भूर्भुवादिकं ।
हृतं त्रैलोक्यमाक्रम्य क्रतुभागाश्च कृत्स्नशः ॥ २६ ॥
तद्वधे कुरु बुद्धिं त्वं परित्राणाय नोऽनघ ।
त्वत्प्रसादादभीप्सामः पुनः प्राप्तं त्रिपिष्टपं ॥ २७ ॥

दत्तात्रेय उवाच ॥

मद्यासक्तोऽहमुच्छिष्टो नचैवाहं जितेन्द्रियः ।
कथमिच्छथ मत्तोऽपि देवाः शत्रुपराभवं ॥ २८ ॥

देवा ऊचुः ॥

अनघस्त्वं जगन्नाथ न लेपस्तव विद्यते ।
विद्याक्षालनशुद्धान्तर्न्निविष्टज्ञानदीधिते ॥ २९ ॥

दत्तात्रेय उवाच ॥

सत्यमेतत् सुरा विद्या ममास्ति समदर्शिनः ।
अस्यास्तु योषितः सङ्गादहमुच्छिष्टतां गतः ॥ ३० ॥
स्त्रीसम्भोगो हि दोषाय सातत्येनोपसेवितः ।
एवमुक्तास्ततो देवाः पुनर्व्वचनमब्रुवन् ॥ ३१ ॥

देवा ऊचुः ॥

अनघेयं द्विजश्रेष्ठ जगन्माता न दुष्यते ।
यथांशुमाला सूर्य्यस्य द्विजचण्डालसङ्गिनी ॥ ३२ ॥

गर्ग उवाच ॥

एवमुक्तस्ततो देवैर्द्दत्तात्रेयोऽब्रवीदिदं ।
प्रहस्य त्रिदशान् सर्व्वान् यद्येतद्भवतां मतं ॥ ३३ ॥
तदाहूयासुरान् सर्व्वान् युद्धाय सुरसत्तमाः ।
इहानयत मद्दृष्टिगोचरं मा विलम्बत ॥ ३४ ॥
मद्दृष्टिपातहुतभुक्प्रक्षीणबलतेजसः ।
येन नाशमशेषास्ते प्रयान्ति मम दर्शनात् ॥ ३५ ॥

गर्ग उवाच॥

तस्य तद्वचनं श्रुत्वा देवैर्दैत्या महाबलाः।
आहवाय समाहूता जग्मुर्देवगणान् रुषा॥ ३६॥
ते हन्यमाना दैतेयैर्देवाः शीघ्रं भयातुराः।
दत्तात्रेयाश्रमं जग्मुः समेताः शरणार्थिनः॥ ३७॥
तमेव विविशुर्दैत्याः कालयन्तो दिवौकसः।
ददृशुश्च महात्मानं दत्तात्रेयं महाबलं॥ ३८॥
वामपार्श्वस्थितामिष्टामशेषजगतां शुभां।
भार्य्याञ्चास्य सुचार्व्वङ्गीं लक्ष्मीमिन्दुनिभाननां॥ ३९॥
नीलोत्पलाभनयनां पीनश्रोणिपयोधरां।
गदन्तीं मधुरां भाषां सर्व्वैर्योषिद्गुणैर्युतां॥ ४०॥
ते तां दृष्ट्वाग्रतो दैत्याः साभिलाषा मनोभवं।
न शेकुरुद्गतं धैर्य्यान्मनसा वोढुमातुराः॥ ४१॥
त्यक्त्वा देवान् स्त्रियं तान्तु हर्त्तुकामा हतौजसः।
तेन पापेन मुह्यन्तः संसक्तास्ते ततोऽब्रुवन्॥ ४२॥
स्त्रीरत्नमेतत् त्रैलोक्ये सारं नो यदि वै भवेत्।
कृतकृत्यास्ततः सर्व्वे इति नो भावितं मनः॥ ४३॥
तस्मात् सर्व्वे समुत्क्षिप्य शिविकायां सुरार्द्दनाः।
आरोप्य स्वमधिष्ठानं नयाम इति निश्चिताः॥ ४४॥

गर्ग उवाच॥

सानुरागास्ततस्ते तु प्रोक्ताश्चेत्थं परस्परं।
तस्य तां योषितं साध्वीं समुत्क्षिप्य स्मरार्द्दिताः॥ ४५॥

शिविकायां समारोप्य सहिता दैत्यदानवाः ।
शिरःसु शिविकां कृत्वा स्वस्थानाभिमुखं ययुः ॥ ४६ ॥
दत्तात्रेयस्ततो देवान् विहस्येदमथाब्रवीत् ।
दिष्ट्या वर्द्धथ दैत्यानामेषा लक्ष्मीः शिरोगता ॥
सप्त स्थानान्यतिक्रान्ता नवमन्यमुपैष्यति ॥ ४७ ॥

देवा ऊचुः ॥

कथयस्व जगन्नाथ केषु स्थानेष्ववस्थिता ।
पुरुषस्य फलं किं वा प्रयच्छत्यथ नश्यति ॥ ४८ ॥

दत्तात्रेय उवाच ॥

नृणां पदे स्थिता लक्ष्मीर्निलयं संप्रयच्छति ।
सक्थ्नोश्च संस्थिता वस्त्रं तथा नानाविधं वसु ॥ ४९ ॥
कलत्रञ्च गुह्यसंस्था क्रोडस्थापत्यदायिनी ।
मनोरथान् पूरयति पुरुषाणां हृदि स्थिता ॥ ५० ॥
लक्ष्मीर्लक्ष्मीवतां श्रेष्ठा कण्ठस्था कण्ठभूषणं ।
अभीष्टबन्धुदारैश्च तथाश्लेषं प्रवासिभिः ॥ ५१ ॥
मृष्टानुवाक्यलावण्यमाज्ञामवितथां तथा ।
मुखसंस्था कवित्वञ्च यच्छत्युदधिसम्भवा ॥ ५२ ॥
शिरोगता सन्त्यजति ततोऽन्यं याति चाश्रयं ।
सेयं शिरोगता चैतान् परित्यक्ष्यति साम्प्रतं ॥ ५३ ॥
प्रगृह्यास्त्राणि बध्यन्तां तस्मादेते सुरारयः ।
न भेतव्यं भृशं चैते मया निस्तेजसः कृताः ॥
परदारावमर्षाच्च दग्धपुण्या हतौजसः ॥ ५४ ॥

गर्ग उवाच ॥

ततस्ते विविधैरस्त्रैर्बध्यमानाः सुरारयः ।
मूर्द्ध्नि लक्ष्म्या समाक्रान्ता विनेशुरिति नः श्रुतं ॥ ५५ ॥
लक्ष्मीश्चोत्पत्य संप्राप्ता दत्तात्रेयं महामुनिं ।
स्तूयमाना सुरैः सर्व्वैर्दैत्यनाशान्मुदान्वितैः ॥ ५६ ॥
प्रणिपत्य ततो देवा दत्तात्रेयं मनीषिणं ।
नाकपृष्ठमनुप्राप्ता यथापूर्व्वं गतज्वराः ॥ ५७ ॥
तथा त्वमपि राजेन्द्र यदीच्छसि यथेप्सितं ।
प्राप्तुमैश्वर्य्यमतुलं तूर्णमाराधयस्व तं ॥ ५८ ॥

इति श्रीमार्कण्डेयपुराणे गर्गवाक्यं ॥ १८ ॥

ऊनविंशोऽध्यायः ॥

पुत्र उवाच ॥

इत्यृषेर्व्वचनं श्रुत्वा कार्त्तवीर्य्यो नरेश्वरः ।
दत्तात्रेयाश्रमं गत्वा तं भक्त्या समपूजयत् ॥ १ ॥
पादसंवाहनाद्येन मध्वाद्याहरणेन च ।
स्रक्चन्दनादिगन्धाम्बुफलाद्यानयनेन च ॥ २ ॥
तथान्नसाधनैस्तस्य उच्छिष्टापोहनेन च ।
परितुष्टो मुनिर्भूपं तमुवाच तथैव सः ॥ ३ ॥
यथैवोक्ताः पुरा देवा मद्यभोगादिकुत्सनं ।

स्त्री चेयं मम पार्श्वस्थेत्येतद्भोगाच्च कुत्सितं ॥ ४ ॥
सदैवाहं न मामेवमुपरोद्धुं त्वमर्हसि ।
अशक्तमुपकाराय शक्तमाराधयस्व भोः ॥ ५ ॥

जड उवाच ॥

तेनैवमुक्तो मुनिना स्मृत्वा गर्गवचश्च तत् ।
प्रत्युवाच प्रणम्यैनं कार्त्तवीर्य्यार्जुनस्तदा ॥ ६ ॥

अर्जुन उवाच ॥

किं मां मोहयसे देव स्वां मायां समुपाश्रितः ।
अनघस्त्वं तथैवेयं देवी सर्व्वभवारणिः ॥ ७ ॥
इत्युक्तः प्रीतिमान् देवस्ततस्तं प्रत्युवाच ह ।
कार्त्तवीर्य्यं महाभागं वशीकृतमहीतलं ॥ ८ ॥
वरं वृणीष्व गुह्यं मे यत् त्वया समुदीरितं ।
तेन तुष्टिः परा जाता त्वय्यद्य मम पार्थिव ॥ ९ ॥
ये च मां पूजयिष्यन्ति गन्धमाल्यादिभिर्न्नराः ।
मांसमद्योपहारैश्च मिष्टान्नैश्चाज्यसंयुतैः ॥ १० ॥
लक्ष्मीसमेतं गीतैश्च ब्राह्मणानान्तथार्च्चनैः ।
वाद्यैर्मनोरमैर्व्वीणावेणुशङ्खादिभिस्तथा ॥ ११ ॥
तेषामहं परां तुष्टिं पुत्त्रदारधनादिकं ।
प्रदास्याम्यवघातञ्च हनिष्याम्यव मन्यतां ॥ १२ ॥
स त्वं वरय भद्रं ते वरं यन्मनसेप्सितं ।
प्रसादसुमुखस्तेऽहं गुह्यनामप्रकीर्त्तनात् ॥ १३ ॥

कार्त्तवीर्य्य उवाच ॥

यदि देव प्रसन्नस्त्वं तत्प्रयच्छर्द्धिमुत्तमां ।
यया प्रजाः पालयेऽहं नचाधर्म्ममवाप्नुयां ॥ १४ ॥
परानुसरणे ज्ञानमप्रतिद्वन्द्वतां रणे ।
सहस्रमाप्तुमिच्छामि बाहूनां लघुतागुणं ॥ १५ ॥
असङ्गा गतयः सन्तु शैलाकाशाम्बुभूमिषु ।
पातालेषु च सर्व्वेषु बधश्चाप्यधिकान्नरात् ॥ १६ ॥
तथोन्मार्गप्रवृत्तस्य चास्तु सन्मार्गदेशकः ।
सन्तु मेऽतिथयः श्लाघ्या वित्तदाने तथाक्षये ॥ १७ ॥
अनष्टद्रव्यता राष्ट्रे ममानुस्मरणेन च ।
त्वयि भक्तिर्म्ममैवास्तु नित्यमव्यभिचारिणी ॥ १८ ॥

दत्तात्रेय उवाच ॥

यच ते कीर्त्तिताः सर्व्वं तान् वरान् समवाप्स्यसि ।
मत्प्रसादाच्च भविता चक्रवर्त्ती त्वमीश्वरः ॥ १९ ॥

जड उवाच ॥

प्रणिपत्य ततस्तस्मै दत्तात्रेयाय सोऽर्जुनः ।
आनाय्य प्रकृतीः सम्यगभिषेकमगृह्लत ॥ २० ॥
आघोषयामास तदा स्थितो राज्ये स हैहयः ।
दत्तात्रेयात् परामृद्धिमवाप्यातिबलान्वितः ॥ २१ ॥
अद्य प्रभृति यः शस्त्रं मामृतेऽन्यो ग्रहीष्यति ।
हन्तव्यः स मया दस्युः परहिंसारतोऽपि वा ॥ २२ ॥
इत्याज्ञप्ते न तद्राष्ट्रे कश्चिदायुधधृङ्नरः ।

तस्मिते पुरुषव्याघ्रं बभूवोरुपराक्रमं ॥ २३ ॥
सएव ग्रामपालोऽभूत् पशुपालः स एव च ।
क्षेत्रपालः स एवासीद्द्विजातीनाञ्च रक्षिता ॥ २४ ॥
तपस्विनां पालयिता सार्थपालस्तु सोऽभवत् ।
दस्युव्यालाग्निशस्त्रादिभयेष्वब्धौ निमज्जतां ॥ २५ ॥
अन्यासु चैव मग्नानामापत्सु परवीरहा ।
स एव संस्मृतः सद्यः समुद्धर्त्ताभवन्नृणां ॥ २६ ॥
अनष्टद्रव्यता चासीत्तस्मिन् शासति पार्थिवे ।
तेनेष्टं बहुभिर्यज्ञैः समाप्तवरदक्षिणैः ॥ २७ ॥
तेनैव च तपस्तप्तं संग्रामेष्वभिचेष्टितं ।
तस्यर्द्धिमतिमानञ्च दृष्ट्वा प्राहाङ्गिरा मुनिः ॥ २८ ॥
न नूनं कार्त्तवीर्य्यस्य गतिं यास्यन्ति पार्थिवाः ।
यज्ञैर्दानैस्तपोभिर्व्वा संग्रामे चातिचेष्टितैः ॥ २९ ॥
दत्तात्रेयाद्दिने यस्मिन् स प्रापर्द्धिं नरेश्वरः ।
तस्मिंस्तस्मिन् दिने यागं दत्तात्रेयस्य सोऽकरोत् ॥ ३० ॥
तत्रैव च प्रजाः सर्व्वास्तस्मिन्नहनि भूपतेः ।
तस्यर्द्धिं परमां दृष्ट्वा यागञ्चक्रुः समाधिना ॥ ३१ ॥
इत्येतत्तस्य माहात्म्यं दत्तात्रेयस्य धीमतः ।
विष्णोश्चराचरगुरोरनन्तस्य महात्मनः ॥ ३२ ॥
प्रादुर्भावाः पुराणेषु कथ्यन्ते शार्ङ्गधन्विनः ।
अनन्तस्याप्रमेयस्य शंखचक्रगदाभृतः ॥ ३३ ॥
एतस्य परमं रूपं यश्चिन्तयति मानवः ।

स सुखी स च संसारात् समुत्तीर्णोऽचिराद्भवेत् ॥ ३४ ॥
सदैव वैष्णवानाञ्च भक्त्याहं सुलभोऽस्मि भोः ।
इत्येवं यस्य वै वाचस्तं कथं नाश्रयेज्जनः ॥ ३५ ॥
अधर्म्मस्य विनाशाय धर्म्माचारार्थमेव च ।
अनादिनिधनो देवः करोति स्थितिपालनं ॥ ३६ ॥
तथैव जन्म चाख्यातमनर्कं कथयामि ते ।
तथा च योगः कथितो दत्तात्रेयेण तस्य वै ॥
पितृभक्तस्य राजर्षेरनर्कस्य महात्मनः ॥ ३७ ॥

इति श्रीमार्कण्डेयपुराणे दत्तात्रेयीयं समाप्तं ॥ १९ ॥

विंशोऽध्यायः ॥

जड उवाच ॥

प्राग्बभूव महावीर्य्यः शत्रुजिन्नाम पार्थिवः ।
तुतोष यस्य यज्ञेषु सोमावाप्त्या पुरन्दरः ॥ १ ॥
तस्यात्मजो महावीर्य्यो बभूवारिविदारणः ।
बुद्धिविक्रमलावण्यैर्गुरुशक्राश्विभिः समः ॥ २ ॥
स समानवयोबुद्धिसत्त्वविक्रमचेष्टितैः ।
नृपपुत्रो नृपसुतैर्नित्यमास्ते समावृतः ॥ ३ ॥
कदाचिच्छास्त्रसम्भारविवेककृतनिश्चयः ।
कदाचित् काव्यसंलापगीतनाटकसम्भवैः ॥ ४ ॥
तथैवाक्षविनोदैश्च शस्त्रास्त्रविनयेषु च ।

योग्यानि युद्धनागाश्वस्यन्दनाभ्यासतत्परः ॥ ५ ॥
रेमे नरेन्द्रपुत्रोऽसौ नरेन्द्रतनयैः सह ।
यथैव हि दिवा तद्वद्रात्रावपि मुदा युतः ॥ ६ ॥
तेषान्तु क्रीडतां तत्र द्विजभूपविशां सुताः ।
समानवयसः प्रीत्या रन्तुमायान्त्यनेकशः ॥ ७ ॥
कस्यचित्त्वथ कालस्य नागलोकान्महीतलं ।
कुमारावागतौ नागौ पुत्रावश्वतरस्य तु ॥ ८ ॥
ब्रह्मरूपप्रतिच्छन्नौ तरुणौ प्रियदर्शनौ ।
तौ तैर्नृपसुतैः सार्द्धं तथैवान्यैर्द्विजन्मभिः ॥ ९ ॥
विनोदैर्व्विविधैस्तत्र तस्थतुः प्रीतिसंयुतौ ।
सर्व्वे च ते नृपसुतास्ते च ब्रह्मविशां सुताः ॥ १० ॥
नागराजात्मजौ तौ च स्नानसंवाहनादिकं ।
वस्त्रगन्धानुसंयुक्तांश्चक्रुर्भोगभुजिक्रियां ॥ ११ ॥
अहन्यहन्यनुप्राप्ते तौ च नागकुमारकौ ।
आजग्मतुर्मुदा युक्तौ प्रीत्या सूनोर्महीपतेः ॥ १२ ॥
स च ताभ्यां नृपसुतः परं निर्व्वाणमाप्तवान् ।
विनोदैर्विविधैर्हास्यसंलापादिभिरेव च ॥ १३ ॥
विना ताभ्यां न बुभुजे न सस्नौ न पपौ मधु ।
न रराम न जग्राह शास्त्राण्यात्मगुणर्द्धये ॥ १४ ॥
रसातले च तौ रात्रिं विना तेन महात्मना ।
निश्वासपरमौ नीत्वा जग्मतुस्तं दिने दिने ॥ १५ ॥
मर्त्यलोके परा प्रीतिर्भवतोः केन पुत्रकौ ।

सहेति पप्रच्छ पिता तावुभौ नागदारकौ ॥ १६ ॥
दृष्टयोरत्र पाताले बहूनि दिवसानि मे ।
दिवा रजन्यामेवोभौ पश्यामि प्रियदर्शनौ ॥ १७ ॥

जड उवाच ॥

इति पित्रा स्वयं पृष्टौ प्रणिपत्य कृताञ्जली ।
प्रत्यूचतुर्म्महाभागावुरगाधिपतेः सुतौ ॥ १८ ॥

पुत्त्रावूचतुः ॥

पुत्त्रः शत्रुजितस्तात नाम्ना ख्यात ऋतध्वजः ।
रूपवानार्जवोपेतः शूरो मानी प्रियम्वदः ॥ १९ ॥
अनापृष्टकथो वाग्मी विद्वान् मैत्रो गुणाकरः ।
मान्यमानयिता धीमान् ह्रीमान् विनयभूषणः ॥ २० ॥
तस्योपचारसंप्रीतिसम्भोगापहृतं मनः ।
नागलोके भुवो लोके न रतिं विन्दते पितः ॥ २१ ॥
तद्वियोगेन नस्तात न पातालञ्च शीतलं ।
परितापाय तत्सङ्गादाह्लादाय रविर्दिवा ॥ २२ ॥

पितोवाच ॥

पुत्त्रः पुण्यवतो धन्यः स यस्यैवं भवद्विधैः ।
परोक्षस्यापि गुणिभिः क्रियते गुणकीर्त्तनं ॥ २३ ॥
सन्ति शास्त्रविदोऽशीलाः सन्ति मूर्खाः सुशीलिनः ।
शास्त्रशीलसमं मन्ये पुत्त्रौ धन्यतरं तु तं ॥ २४ ॥
यस्य मित्त्रंगुणान् मित्त्रागण्यमित्त्राश्च पराक्रमं ।
कथयन्ति सदा सत्सु पुत्त्रवांस्तेन वै पिता ॥ २५ ॥

तस्योपकारिणः कश्चिद्भवद्भ्राममभिवाञ्छितं ।
किञ्चिन्निष्पादितं वत्सौ परितोषाय चेतसः ॥ २६ ॥
स धन्यो जीवितं तस्य तस्य जन्म सुजन्मनः ।
यस्यार्थिनो न विमुखा मित्रार्थो न च दुर्ब्बलः ॥ २७ ॥
मद्गृहे यत्सुवर्णादि रत्नं वाहनमासनं ।
यच्चान्यत्प्रीतये तस्य तद्देयमविशङ्कया २८ ॥
धिक् तस्य जीवितं पुंसो मित्राणामुपकारिणां ।
प्रतिरूपमकुर्व्वन् यो जीवामीत्यवगच्छति ॥ २९ ॥
उपकारं सुहृद्वर्गे योऽपकारञ्च शत्रुषु ।
न्नमेघो वर्षति प्राज्ञस्तस्येच्छन्ति सदोन्नतिं ॥ ३० ॥

पुत्त्रावूचतुः ॥

किन्तस्य कृतकृत्यस्य कर्त्तुं शक्येत केनचित् ।
यस्य सर्व्वार्थिनो गेहे सर्व्वकामैः सदार्च्चिताः ॥ ३१ ॥
यानि रत्नानि तद्गेहे पाताले तानि नः कुतः ।
वाहनासनयानानि भूषणान्यम्बराणि च ॥ ३२ ॥
विज्ञानं तत्र यच्चास्ति तदन्यत्र न विद्यते ।
प्राज्ञानामप्यसौ तात सर्व्वसन्देहहृत्तमः ॥ ३३ ॥
एकं तस्यास्ति कर्त्तव्यमसाध्यं तत्र नौ मतं ।
हिरण्यगर्भगोविन्दशर्व्वादीनीश्वरादृते ॥ ३४ ॥

पितोवाच ॥

तथापि श्रोतुमिच्छामि तस्य यत्कार्य्यमुत्तमं ।
असाध्यमथवा साध्यं किं वासाध्यं विपश्चितां ॥ ३५ ॥

देवत्वममरेशत्वं तत्पूज्यत्वञ्च मानवाः ।
प्रयान्ति वाञ्छितं वान्यद्दृढं ये व्यवसायिनः ॥ ३६ ॥
नाविज्ञातं नचागम्यं नाप्राप्यं दिवि चेह वा ।
उद्यतानां मनुष्याणां यतचित्तेन्द्रियात्मनां ॥ ३७ ॥
योजनानां सहस्राणि व्रजन् याति पिपीलिकः ।
अगच्छन् वैनतेयोऽपि पादमेकं न गच्छति ॥ ३८ ॥
क्व भूतलं क्वच ध्रौवं स्थानं यत्प्राप्तवान् ध्रुवः ।
उत्तानपादनृपतेः पुत्रः सन् भूमिगोचरः ॥ ३९ ॥
तत्कथ्यतां महाभाग कार्य्यवान् येन पुत्रकौ ।
स भूपालसुतः साधुर्येनानृण्यं भवेत वां ॥ ४० ॥

पुत्रावूचतुः ॥

तेनाख्यातमिदं तात पूर्व्ववृत्तं महात्मना ।
कौमारके यथा तस्य वृत्तं सद्वृत्तशालिनः ॥ ४१ ॥
तन्तु शत्रुजितं तात पूर्व्वं कश्चिद्द्विजोत्तमः ।
गालवोऽभ्यागमद्धीमान् गृहीत्वा तुरगोत्तमं ॥ ४२ ॥
प्रत्युवाच च राजानं समुत्पेत्याश्रमं मम ।
कोऽपि दैत्याधमो राजन् विध्वंसयति पापकृत् ॥ ४३ ॥
तत्तद्रूपं समास्थाय सिंहेभवनचारिणां ।
अन्येषाञ्चाल्पकायानामहर्न्निशमकारणात् ॥ ४४ ॥
समाधिध्यानयुक्तस्य मौनव्रतरतस्य च ।
तथा करोति विघ्नानि यथा चलति मे मनः ॥ ४५ ॥

दग्धुं कोपाग्निना सद्यः समर्थस्त्वं वयं न तु ।
दुःखार्जितस्य तपसो व्ययमिच्छामि पार्थिव ॥ ४६ ॥
एकदा तु मया राजन्नतिनिर्व्विसचेतसा ।
तत्क्लेशितेन निश्वासो निरीच्यासुरमुज्झितः ॥ ४७ ॥
ततोऽम्बरतलात् सद्यः पतितोऽयं तुरङ्गमः ।
वाक् चाशरीरिणी प्राह नरनाथ शृणुष्व तां ॥ ४८ ॥
अश्रान्तः सकलं भूमेर्बलयं तुरगोत्तमः ।
समर्थः क्रान्तुमर्केण तवायं प्रतिपादितः ॥ ४९ ॥
पातालाम्बरतोयेषु न चास्य विहता गतिः ।
समस्तदिक्षु व्रजतो न भङ्गः पर्व्वतेष्वपि ॥ ५० ॥
यतो भूबलयं सर्व्वमश्रान्तोऽयं चरिष्यति ।
अतः कुबलयो नाम्ना ख्यातिं लोके प्रयास्यति ॥ ५१ ॥
क्लिश्यत्यहर्न्निशं पापी यश्च त्वां दानवाधमः ।
तमप्येनं समारुह्य द्विजश्रेष्ठ हनिष्यति ॥ ५२ ॥
शत्रुजिन्नाम भूपालस्तस्य पुत्र ऋतध्वजः ।
प्राप्यैतदश्वरत्नञ्च ख्यातिमेतेन यास्यति ॥ ५३ ॥
सोऽहं त्वां समनुप्राप्तस्तपसो विघ्नकारिणं ।
तं निवारय भूपाल भागभाङ्न्नृपतिर्यतः ५४ ॥
तदेतदश्वरत्नं ते मया भूप निवेदितं ।
पुत्रमाज्ञापय तथा यथा धर्म्मो न लुप्यते ॥ ५५ ॥
स तस्य वचनाद्राजा तं वै पुत्रमृतध्वजं ।
तमश्वरत्नमारोप्य कृतकौतुकमङ्गलं ॥ ५६ ॥

अप्रेषयत धर्म्मात्मा गालवेन समं तदा ।
स्वमाश्रमपदं सोऽपि तमादाय ययौ मुनिः ॥ ५७ ॥

इति श्रीमार्कण्डेयपुराणे कुवलाश्वीये ॥ २० ॥

एकविंशोऽध्यायः ॥

पितोवाच ॥

गालवेन समं गत्वा नृपपुत्त्रेण तेन यत् ।
कृतं तत्कथ्यतां पुत्त्रौ विचित्रा युवयोः कथा ॥ १ ॥

पुत्त्रावूचतुः ॥

स गालवाश्रमे रम्ये तिष्ठन् भूपालनन्दनः ।
सर्व्वविघ्नोपशमनञ्चकार ब्रह्मवादिनां ॥ २ ॥
वीरं कुवलयाश्वं तं वसन्तं गालवाश्रमे ।
मदावलेपोपहतो नाजानाद्दानवाधमः ॥ ३ ॥
ततस्तं गालवं विप्रं सन्ध्योपासनतत्परं ।
शौकरं रूपमास्थाय प्रधर्षयितुमागमत् ॥ ४ ॥
मुनिशिष्यैरथोत्क्रुष्टे शीघ्रमारुह्य तं हयं ।
अन्वधावद्वराहं तं नृपपुत्त्रः शरासनी ॥ ५ ॥
आजघान च बाणेन चन्द्रार्द्धाकारवर्च्चसा ।
आकृष्य बलवच्चापञ्चारुचित्रोपशोभितं ॥ ६ ॥
नाराचाभिहतः शीघ्रमात्मत्राणपरो मृगः ।
गिरिपादपसम्बाधां सोऽन्वक्रामन्महाटवीं ॥ ७ ॥

तमन्वधावद्वेगेन तुरगोऽसौ मनोजवः ।
चोदितो राजपुत्रेण पितुरादेशकारिणा ॥ ८ ॥
अतिक्रम्याथ वेगेन योजनानि सहस्रशः ।
धरण्यां विवृते गर्त्ते निपपात लघुक्रमः ॥ ९ ॥
तस्यानन्तरमेवाशु सोऽप्यश्वी नृपतेः सुतः ।
निपपात महागर्त्ते तिमिरौघसमावृते ॥ १० ॥
ततो नादृश्यत मृगः स तस्मिन्राजसूनुना ।
प्रकाशञ्च स पातालमपश्यत्तच नापि तं ॥ ११ ॥
ततोऽपश्यत् स सौवर्णप्रासादशतसंकुलं ।
पुरन्दरपुरप्रख्यं पुरं प्राकारशोभितं ॥ १२ ॥
तत्प्रविश्य स नापश्यत्तच कञ्चिन्नरं पुरे ।
भ्रमता च ततो दृष्टा तत्र योषित्त्वरान्विता ॥ १३ ॥
सा पृष्टा तेन तन्वङ्गी प्रस्थिता केन कस्य वा ।
नोवाच किञ्चित् प्रासादमारुरोह च भाविनी ॥ १४ ॥
सोऽप्यश्वमेकतो बद्ध्वा तामेवानुससार वै ।
विस्मयोत्फुल्लनयनो निःशङ्को नृपतेः सुतः ॥ १५ ॥
ततोऽपश्यत् सुविस्तीर्णे पर्य्यङ्के सर्व्वकाञ्चने ।
निषण्णां कन्यकामेकां कामयुक्तां रतीमिव ॥ १६ ॥
विस्पष्टेन्दुमुखीं सुभ्रूं पीनश्रोणिपयोधरां ।
विम्बाधरौष्ठीं तन्वङ्गीं नीलोत्पलविलोचनां ॥ १७ ॥
रक्ततुङ्गनखीं श्यामां मृद्वीं ताम्रकराङ्घ्रिकां ।
करभोरूं सुदशनां नीलसूक्ष्मस्थिरालकां ॥ १८ ॥

तां दृष्ट्वा चारुसर्व्वाङ्गीमनङ्गाङ्गलतामिव ।
सोऽमन्यत्पार्थिवसुतस्तां रसातलदेवतां ॥ १९ ॥
सा च दृष्ट्वैव तं बाला नीलकुञ्चितमूर्द्धजं ।
पीनोरुस्कन्धबाहुं तममंस्त मदनं शुभा ॥ २० ॥
उत्तस्थौ च महाभागा चित्तक्षोभमवाप्य सा ।
लज्जाविस्मयदैन्यानां सद्यस्तन्वी वशं गता ॥ २१ ॥
कोऽयं देवो नु यक्षो वा गन्धर्व्वो वोरगोऽपिवा ।
विद्याधरो वा संप्राप्तः कृतपुण्यरतिर्नरः ॥ २२ ॥
एवं विचिन्त्य बहुधा निश्वस्य च महीतले ।
उपविश्य ततो भेजे सा मूर्च्छां मदिरेक्षणा ॥ २३ ॥
सोऽपि कामशराघातमवाप्य नृपतेः सुतः ।
तां समाश्वासयामास न भेतव्यमिति ब्रुवन् ॥ २४ ॥
सा च स्त्री या तदा दृष्टा पूर्व्वं तेन महात्मना ।
तालवृन्तमुपादाय पर्य्यवीजयदाकुला ॥ २५ ॥
समाश्वास्य तदा पृष्टा तेन सम्मोहकारणं ।
किञ्चिल्लज्जान्विता बाला तस्याः सख्युर्न्यवेदयत् ॥ २६ ॥
सा चास्मै कथयामास नृपपुत्राय विस्तरात् ।
मोहस्य कारणं सर्व्वं तद्दर्शनसमुद्भवं ॥
यथा तया समाख्यातं तद्वृत्तान्तञ्च भाविनी ॥ २७ ॥

स्त्र्युवाच ॥

विश्वावसुरिति ख्यातो दिवि गन्धर्व्वराट् प्रभो ।
तस्येयमात्मजा सुभ्रूर्नाम्ना ख्याता मदालसा ॥ २८ ॥

वज्रकेतोः सुतश्चोग्रो दानवोऽरिविदारणः ।
पातालकेतुर्व्विख्यातः पातालान्तरसंश्रयः ॥ २९ ॥
तेनेयमुद्यानगता कृत्वा मायां तमोमयीं ।
अपहृत्य मया हीना बालानीता दुरात्मना ॥ ३० ॥
आगामिन्यां त्रयोदश्यामुद्वक्ष्यति किलासुरः ।
स तु नार्हति चार्व्वङ्गीं शूद्रो वेदश्रुतीमिव ॥ ३१ ॥
अतीते च दिने बालामात्मव्यापादनोद्यतां ।
सुरभिः प्राह नायं त्वां प्राप्स्यते दानवाधमः ॥ ३२ ॥
मर्त्यलोकमनुप्राप्तं य एनं छेत्स्यते शरैः ।
स ते भर्त्ता महाभागे अचिरेण भविष्यति ॥ ३३ ॥
अहञ्चास्याः सखी नाम्ना कुण्डलेति मनस्विनी ।
सुता बिन्ध्यवतः पत्नी वीर पुष्करमालिनः ॥ ३४ ॥
हते भर्त्तरि शुम्भेन तीर्थात्तीर्थमनुव्रता ।
चरामि दिव्यया गत्या परलोकार्थमुद्यता ॥ ३५ ॥
पातालकेतुर्दुष्टात्मा वाराहं वपुरास्थितः ।
केनापि विद्धो बाणेन मुनीनां त्राणकारणात् ॥ ३६ ॥
तच्चाहं तत्त्वतोऽन्विष्य त्वरिता समुपागता ।
सत्यमेव स केनापि ताडितो दानवाधमः ॥ ३७ ॥
इयञ्च मूर्च्छामगमत् कारणं यत् शृणुष्व तत् ।
त्वयि प्रीतिमती बाला दर्शनादेव मानद ॥ ३८ ॥
देवपुत्त्रोपमे चारुवाक्यादिगुणशालिनि ।
भार्य्या चान्यस्य विहिता येन विद्धः स दानवः ॥ ३९ ॥

एतस्मात् कारणान्मोहं महान्तमियमागता ।
यावज्जीवञ्च तन्वङ्गी दुःखमेवोपभोच्यते ॥ ४० ॥
त्वय्यस्या हृदयं रागि भर्त्ता चान्यो भविष्यति ।
यावज्जीवमतो दुःखं सुरभ्या नान्यथा वचः ॥ ४१ ॥
अहं त्वस्याः प्रभो प्रीत्या दुःखिताच समागता ।
यतो विशेषो नैवास्ति स्वसखीनिजदेहयोः ॥ ४२ ॥
यद्येषाभिमतं वीरं पतिमाप्नोति शोभना ।
ततस्तपस्त्वहं कुर्य्यां निर्व्यलीकेन चेतसा ॥ ४३ ॥
त्वन्तु को वा किमर्थं वा संप्राप्तोऽत्र महामते ।
देवो दैत्यो नु गन्धर्व्वः पन्नगः किन्नरोऽपिवा ॥ ४४ ॥
नह्यत्र मानुषगतिर्नचेदृङ्मानुषं वपुः ।
तत्त्वमाख्याहि कथितं यथैवावितथं मया ॥ ४५ ॥

कुवलयाश्व उवाच ॥

यन्मां पृच्छसि धर्म्मज्ञे कस्त्वं किं वा समागतः ।
तच्छृणुष्वामलप्रज्ञे कथयाम्यादितस्तव ॥ ४६ ॥
राज्ञः शत्रुजितः पुत्रः पित्रा संप्रेषितः शुभे ।
मुनिरक्षणमुद्दिश्य गालवाश्रममागतः ॥ ४७ ॥
कुर्व्वतो मम रक्षाञ्च मुनीनां धर्म्मचारिणां ।
विघ्नार्थमागतः कोऽपि शौकरं रूपमास्थितः ॥ ४८ ॥
मया स विद्धो बाणेन चन्द्रार्द्धाकारवर्च्चसा ।
अपक्रान्तोऽतिवेगेन तमस्म्यनुगतो हयी ॥ ४९ ॥
पपात सहसा गर्त्ते सक्रोडोऽश्वश्च मामकः ।

सोऽहमश्वं समारूढस्तमस्येकः परिभ्रमन् ॥ ५० ॥
प्रकाश्यमासादितवान् दृष्टा च भवती मया ।
पृष्टया च न मे किञ्चिद्भवत्या दत्तमुत्तरं ॥ ५१ ॥
त्वाञ्चैवानुप्रविष्टोऽहमिमं प्रासादमुत्तमं ।
इत्येतत् कथितं सत्यं न देवोऽहं न दानवः ॥ ५२ ॥
न पन्नगो न गन्धर्व्वः किन्नरो वा शुचिस्मिते ।
समस्ताः पूज्यपक्षा वै देवाद्या मम कुण्डले ॥
मनुष्योऽस्मि विशङ्का ते न कर्त्तव्याच कर्हिचित् ॥ ५३ ॥

पुत्रावूचतुः ॥

ततः प्रहृष्टा सा कन्या सखीवदनमुत्तमं ।
लज्जाजडं वीक्षमाणा किञ्चिन्नोवाच भाविनी ॥ ५४ ॥
सा सखी पुनरप्येनं प्रहृष्टा प्रत्युवाच ह ।
यथावत् कथितं तेन सुरभ्या वचनानुगे ॥ ५५ ॥

कुण्डलोवाच ॥

वीर सत्यमसन्दिग्धं भवताभिहितं वचः ।
नान्यत्र हृदयं त्वस्या दृष्ट्वा स्थैर्य्यं प्रयास्यति ॥ ५६ ॥
चन्द्रमेवाधिका कान्तिः समुपैति रविं प्रभा ।
भूतिर्धन्यं धृतिर्धीरं क्षान्तिरभ्येति चोत्तमं ॥ ५७ ॥
त्वयैव विद्धोऽसंदिग्धं स पापो दानवाधमः ।
सुरभिः सा गवां माता कथं मिथ्या वदिष्यति ॥ ५८ ॥
तद्धन्येयं सभाग्या च त्वत्सम्बन्धं समेत्य वै ।
कुरुष्व वीर यत्कार्य्यं विधिनैव समाहितं ॥ ५९ ॥

पुत्रावूचतुः ॥

परवानहमित्याह राजपुत्रः स तां पितः ।
सा च तं चिन्तयामास तुम्बूरुं तत्कुले गुरुं ॥ ६० ॥
स चापि तत्क्षणात्प्राप्तः प्रगृहीतसमित्कुशः ।
मदालसायाः संप्रीत्या कुण्डलागौरवेण च ॥ ६१ ॥
प्रज्वाल्य पावकं हुत्वा मन्त्रवित् कृतमङ्गलां ।
वैवाहिकविधिं कन्यां प्रतिपाद्य यथागतं ॥ ६२ ॥
जगाम तपसे धीमान् स्वमाश्रमपदं तदा ।
सा चाह तां सखीं बालां कृतार्थास्मि वरानने ॥ ६३ ॥
संयुक्ताममुना दृष्ट्वा त्वामहं रूपशालिनीं ।
तपस्तप्स्येऽहमतुलं निर्व्व्यलीकेन चेतसा ॥ ६४ ॥
तीर्थाम्बुधूतपापा च भविची नेदृशी यथा ।
तं चाह राजपुत्रं सा प्रश्रयावनता तदा ॥
गन्तुकामा निजसखीस्नेहविक्लवभाषिणी ॥ ६५ ॥

कुण्डलोवाच ॥

पुंभिरप्यमितप्रज्ञ नोपदेश्यो भवद्विधे ।
दातव्यः किमुत स्त्रीभिरतो नोपदिशामि ते ॥ ६६ ॥
किं त्वस्यास्तनुमध्यायाः स्नेहाकृष्टेन चेतसा ।
त्वया विश्रम्भिता चास्मि स्मारयाम्यरिसूदन ॥ ६७ ॥
भर्त्तव्या रक्षितव्या च भार्य्या हि पतिना सदा ।
धर्म्मार्थकामसंसिद्धौ भार्य्या भर्तृसहायिनी ॥ ६८ ॥
यदा भार्य्या च भर्त्ता च परस्परवशानुगौ ।

तदा धर्म्मार्थकामानां त्रयाणामपि संगतं ॥ ६९ ॥
कथं भार्य्यामृते धर्म्ममर्थं वा पुरुषः प्रभो ।
प्राप्नोति काममथवा तस्यां त्रितयमाहितं ॥ ७० ॥
तथैव भर्त्तारमृते भार्य्या धर्म्मादिसाधने ।
न समर्था त्रिवर्गोऽयं दाम्पत्यं समुपाश्रितः ॥ ७१ ॥
देवतापितृभृत्यानामतिथीनाञ्च पूजनं ।
न पुंभिः शक्यते कर्त्तुमृते भार्य्यां नृपात्मज ॥ ७२ ॥
प्राप्तोऽपि चार्थो मनुजैरानीतोऽपि निजं गृहं ।
क्षयमेति विना भार्य्यां कुभार्य्यासंश्रयेऽपि वा ॥ ७३ ॥
कामस्तु तस्य नैवास्ति प्रत्यक्षेणोपलक्ष्यते ।
दम्पत्योः सहधर्म्मेण त्रयीधर्म्ममवाप्नुयात् ॥ ७४ ॥
पितॄन् पुत्रैस्तथैवान्नसाधनैरतिथीन्नरः ।
पूजाभिरमरांस्तद्वत् साध्वीं भार्य्यां नरोऽवति ॥ ७५ ॥
स्त्रियाश्चापि विना भर्त्रा धर्म्मकामार्थसन्ततिः ।
नैव तस्मात्त्रिवर्गोऽयं दाम्पत्यमधिगच्छति ॥ ७६ ॥
एतन्मयोक्तं युवयोर्गच्छामि च यथेप्सितं ।
वर्द्ध त्वमनया सार्द्धं धनपुत्रसुखायुषा ॥ ७७ ॥

पुत्रावूचतुः ॥

इत्युक्त्वा सा परिष्वज्य स्वसखीं तं नमस्य च ।
जगाम दिव्यया गत्या यथाभिप्रेतमात्मनः ॥ ७८ ॥
सोऽपि शत्रुजितः पुत्रस्तामारोप्य तुरङ्गमं ।
निर्गन्तुकामः पातालाद्विज्ञातो दनुसंभवैः ॥ ७९ ॥

ततस्तैःसहसोत्क्रुष्टं ह्रियते ह्रियतेऽति वै ।
कन्यारत्नं यदानीतं दिवः पातालकेतुना ॥ ८० ॥
ततः परिघनिस्त्रिंशगदाशूलशरायुधं ।
दानवानां बलं प्राप्तं सह पातालकेतुना ॥ ८१ ॥
तिष्ठ तिष्ठेति जल्पन्तस्ते तदा दानवोत्तमाः ।
शरवर्षैस्तथा शूलैर्व्ववर्षुर्नृपनन्दनं ॥ ८२ ॥
स च शत्रुजितः पुत्त्रस्तदस्त्राण्यतिवीर्य्यवान् ।
चिच्छेद शरजालेन प्रहसन्निव लीलया ॥ ८३ ॥
क्षणेन पातालतलमसिशक्त्यृष्टिशायकैः ।
छिन्नैः संछन्नमभवत्तच्छ्रजशरोत्करैः ॥ ८४ ॥
ततोऽस्त्रं त्वाष्ट्रमादाय चिक्षेप प्रति दानवान् ।
तेन ते दानवाः सर्व्वे सह पातालकेतुना ॥ ८५ ॥
ज्वालामालातितीव्रेण स्फुटदस्थिचयाः कृताः ।
निर्द्दग्धाः कापिलं तेजः समासाद्येव सागराः ॥ ८६ ॥
ततः स राजपुत्त्रोऽश्वी निहत्यासुरसत्तमान् ।
स्त्रीरत्नेन समं तेन समागच्छत् पितुः पुरं ॥ ८७ ॥
प्रणिपत्य च तत्सर्व्वं स तु पित्रे न्यवेदयत् ।
पातालगमनञ्चैव कुण्डलायाश्च दर्शनं ॥ ८८ ॥
तद्वन्मदालसाप्राप्तिं दानवैश्चापि सङ्गरं ।
बधञ्च तेषामस्त्रेण पुनरागमनं तथा ॥ ८९ ॥
इति श्रुत्वा पिता तस्य चरितं चारुचेतसः ।
प्रीतिमानभवच्चेदं परिष्वज्याह चात्मजं ॥ ९० ॥

सत्पात्रेण त्वया पुत्र तारितोऽहं महात्मना ।
भयेभ्यो मुनयस्त्राता येन सद्धर्म्मचारिणः ॥ ९१ ॥
मत्पूर्व्वैः ख्यातमानीतं मया विस्तारितं पुनः ।
पराक्रमवता वीर त्वया तद्बहुलीकृतं ॥ ९२ ॥
यदुपात्तं यशः पित्रा धनं वीर्य्यमथापि वा ।
तन्न ह्रापयते यस्तु स नरो मध्यमः स्मृतः ॥ ९३ ॥
तद्वीर्य्यादधिकं यस्तु पुनरन्यत् स्वशक्तितः ।
निष्पादयति तं प्राज्ञाः प्रवदन्ति नरोत्तमं ॥ ९४ ॥
यः पित्रा समुपात्तानि धनवीर्य्ययशांसि वै ।
न्यूनतां नयति प्राज्ञास्तमाहुः पुरुषाधमं ॥ ९५ ॥
तन्मया ब्राह्मणत्राणं कृतमासीद्यथा त्वया ।
पातालगमनं यच्च यच्चासुरविनाशनं ॥ ९६ ॥
एतदप्यधिकं वत्स तेन त्वं पुरुषोत्तमः ।
तद्धन्योऽस्यथ वाल त्वमहमेव गुणाधिकं ॥ ९७ ॥
त्वां पुत्रमीदृशं प्राप्य श्लाघ्यः पुण्यवतामपि ।
न स पुत्रकृतां प्रीतिं मन्ये प्राप्नोति मानवः ॥ ९८ ॥
पुत्रेण नातिशयितो यः प्रज्ञादानविक्रमैः ।
धिग्जन्म तस्य यः पित्रा लोके विज्ञायते नरः ॥ ९९ ॥
यः पुत्रात् ख्यातिमभ्येति तस्य जन्म सुजन्मनः ।
आत्मना ज्ञायते धन्यो मध्यः पितृपितामहैः ॥ १०० ॥
मातृपक्षेण मात्रा च ख्यातिमेति नराधमः ।
तत् पुत्र धनवीर्य्यैस्त्वं विवर्द्धस्व सुखेन च ॥ १०१ ॥

गन्धर्व्वतनया चेयं मा त्वया वै वियुज्यतां।
इति पित्रा बहुविधं प्रियमुक्तः पुनः पुनः॥ १०२॥
परिष्वज्य स्वमावासं सभार्य्यः स विसर्जितः।
स तया भार्य्यया सार्द्धं रेमे तत्र पितुःपुरे॥ १०३॥
अन्येषु च तथोद्यानवनपर्व्वतसानुषु।
श्वश्रूश्वशुरयोः पादौ प्रणिपत्य च सा शुभा॥
प्रातः प्रातस्ततस्तेन सह रेमे सुमध्यमा॥ १०४॥

इति श्रीमार्कण्डेयपुराणे कुवलयाश्वीये मदालसापरिणयनं॥ २१॥

द्वाविंशोऽध्यायः॥

पुत्त्रावूचतुः॥

ततःकाले बहुतिथे गते राजा पुनः सुतं।
प्राह गच्छाशु विप्राणां त्राणाय चर मेदिनीं॥ १॥
अश्वमेनं समारुह्य प्रातः प्रातर्दिने दिने।
अबाधा द्विजमुख्यानामन्वेष्टव्या सदैव हि॥ २॥
दुर्वृत्ताः सन्ति शतशो दानवाः पापयोनयः।
तेभ्यो न स्याद्यथा बाधा मुनीनां त्वं तथा कुरु॥ ३॥
स यथोक्तस्ततः पित्रा तथा चक्रे नृपात्मजः।
परिक्रम्य महीं सर्व्वां ववन्दे चरणौ पितुः॥ ४॥
अहन्यहन्यनुप्राप्ते पूर्व्वाह्णे नृपनन्दनः।
ततश्च शेषं दिवसं तया रेमे सुमध्यया॥ ५॥

एकदा तु चरन् सोऽथ ददर्श यमुनातटे।
पातालकेतोरनुजं तालकेतुं कृताश्रमं॥ ६॥
मायावी दानवः सोऽय मुनिरूपं समास्थितः।
स प्राह राजपुत्त्रं तं पूर्व्ववैरमनुस्मरन्॥ ७॥
राजपुत्त्र ब्रवीमि त्वां तत्कुरुष्व यदीच्छसि।
न च ते प्रार्थनाभङ्गः कार्य्यः सत्यप्रतिश्रव॥ ८॥
यक्ष्ये यज्ञेन धर्म्माय कर्त्तव्याश्च तथेष्टयः।
चितयस्तत्र कर्त्तव्या नान्तरिक्षगता यतः॥ ९॥
अतः प्रयच्छ मे वीर हिरण्यार्थं स्वभूषणं।
यदेतत् कण्ठलग्नं ते रक्ष चेमं ममाश्रमं॥ १०॥
यावदन्तर्जले देवं वरुणं यादसां पतिं।
वैदिकैर्व्वारुणैर्म्मन्त्रैः प्रजानां पुष्टिहेतुकैः॥ ११॥
अभिष्टूय त्वरायुक्तः समभ्येमीति वादिनं।
तं प्रणम्य ततःप्रादात् स तस्मै कण्ठभूषणं॥ १२॥
प्राह चैनं भवान् यातु निर्व्यलीकेन चेतसा।
स्थास्यामि तावदत्रैव तवाश्रमसमीपतः॥ १३॥
तवादेशान्महाभाग यावदागमनं तव।
न तेऽत्र कश्चिदाबाधां करिष्यति मयि स्थिते॥
विस्रब्धश्चात्वरन् ब्रह्मन् कुरुष्व त्वं मनोगतं॥ १४॥

पुत्त्रावूचतुः॥

एवमुक्तस्ततस्तेन स ममज्ज नदीजले।
ररक्ष सोऽपि तस्यैव मायाविहितमाश्रमं॥ १५॥

गत्वा जलाशयात्तस्मात्तालकेतुश्च तत्परं ।
मदालसायाः प्रत्यक्षमन्येषाञ्चैतदुक्तवान् ॥ १६ ॥

तालकेतुरुवाच ॥

वीरः कुवलयाश्वोऽसौ ममाश्रमसमीपतः ।
केनापि दुष्टदैत्येन कुर्व्वन्रक्षां तपस्विनां ॥ १७ ॥
युद्ध्यमानो यथाशक्ति निघ्नन् ब्रह्मद्विषो युधि ।
मायामाश्रित्य पापेन भिन्नः शूलेन वक्षसि ॥ १८ ॥
म्रियमाणेन तेनेदं दत्तं मे कण्ठभूषणं ।
प्रापितश्चाग्निसंयोगं स वने शूद्रतापसैः ॥ १९ ॥
कृतार्त्तहेषाशब्दो वै त्रस्तः साश्रुविलोचनः ।
नीतः सोऽश्वश्च तेनैव दानवेन दुरात्मना ॥ २० ॥
एतन्मया नृशंसेन दृष्टं दुष्कृतकारिणा ।
यदत्रानन्तरं कृत्यं क्रियतां तदकालिकं ॥ २१ ॥
हृदयाश्वासनञ्चैतद्गृह्यतां कण्ठभूषणं ।
नास्माकं हि सुवर्णेन कृत्यमस्ति तपस्विनां ॥ २२ ॥

पुत्त्रावूचतुः ॥

इत्युक्त्वोत्सृज्य तद्भूमौ स जगाम यथागतं ।
निपपात जनः सोऽथ शोकार्त्तो मूर्च्छयातुरः ॥ २३ ॥
तत्क्षणात् चेतनां प्राप्य सर्व्वास्ता नृपयोषितः ।
राजपत्न्यश्च राजा च विलेपुरतिदुःखिताः ॥ २४ ॥
मदालसा तु तद्दृष्ट्वा तदीयं कण्ठभूषणं ।
तत्याजाशु प्रियान् प्राणान् श्रुत्वा च निहतं पतिं ॥ २५ ॥

ततस्तथा महा क्रन्दः पौराणां भवनेष्वभूत्।
यथैव तस्य नृपतेः स्वगेहे समवर्त्तत॥ २६॥
राजा च तां मृतां दृष्ट्वा विना भर्त्त्रा मदालसां।
प्रत्युवाच जनं सर्व्वं विमृष्य सुस्थमानसः॥ २७॥
न रोदितव्यं पश्यामि भवतामात्मनस्तथा।
सर्व्वेषामेव संचिन्त्य सम्बन्धानामनित्यतां॥ २८॥
किन्नु शोचामि तनयं किन्नु शोचाम्यहं स्नुषां।
विमृष्य कृतकृत्यत्वान्मन्येऽशोच्यावुभावपि॥ २९॥
मच्छुश्रूषुर्म्मद्वचनाद्द्विजरक्षणतत्परः।
प्राप्तो मे यः सुतो मृत्युं कथं शोच्यः स धीमतां॥ ३०॥
अवश्यं याति यद्देहं तद्द्विजानां कृते यदि।
मम पुत्त्रेण संत्यक्तं नन्वभ्युदयकारि तत्॥ ३१॥
इयञ्च सत्कुलोत्पन्ना भर्त्तर्य्येवमनुव्रता।
कथन्नु शोच्या नारीणां भर्त्तुरन्यन्न दैवतं॥ ३२॥
अस्माकं बान्धवानाञ्च तथान्येषां दयावतां।
शोच्या ह्येषा भवेदेवं यदि भर्त्त्रा वियोगिनी॥ ३३॥
या तु भर्त्तुर्व्वधं श्रुत्वा तत्क्षणादेव भाविनी।
भर्त्तारमनुयातेयं न शोच्यातो विपश्चितां॥ ३४॥
ताः शोच्या या वियोगिन्यो न शोच्या या मृताः सह।
भर्त्त्रा वियोगस्त्वनया नानुभूतः कृतज्ञया॥ ३५॥
दातारं सर्व्वसौख्यानामिह चामुत्र चोभयोः।
लोकयोः का हि भर्त्तारं नारी मन्येत मानुषं॥ ३६॥

नासौ शोच्यो नचैवेयं नाहं तज्जननी न च ।
त्यजता ब्राह्मणार्थाय प्राणान् सर्व्वे स्म तारिताः ॥ ३७ ॥
विप्राणां मम धर्म्मस्य गतः स हि महामतिः ।
आनृण्यमद्यभुक्तस्य त्यागाद्देहस्य मे सुतः ॥ ३८ ॥
मातुः सतीत्वं मद्वंशवैमल्यं शौर्य्यमात्मनः ।
संग्रामे संत्यजन् प्राणान् नात्यजद्द्विजरक्षणे ॥ ३९ ॥

पुत्त्रावूचतुः ॥

ततः कुवलयाश्वस्य माता भर्त्तुरनन्तरं ।
श्रुत्वा पुत्त्रबधं तादृक् प्राह दृष्ट्वा तु तं पतिं ॥ ४० ॥

मातोवाच ॥

न मे मात्रा न मे स्वस्रा प्राप्ता प्रीतिर्नृपेदृशी ।
श्रुत्वा मुनिपरित्राणे हतं पुत्त्रं यथा मया ॥ ४१ ॥
शोचतां बान्धवानां ये निःश्वसन्तोऽतिदुःखिताः ।
म्रियन्ते व्याधिना क्लिष्टास्तेषां माता वृथाप्रजा ॥ ४२ ॥
संग्रामे युद्ध्यमाना येऽभीता गोद्विजरक्षणे ।
क्षुण्णाः शस्त्रैर्विपद्यन्ते तएव भुवि मानवाः ॥ ४३ ॥
अर्थिनां मित्त्रवर्गस्य विद्विषाञ्च पराङ्मुखः ।
यो न याति पिता तेन पुत्त्री माता च वीरसूः ॥ ४४ ॥
गर्भक्लेशः स्त्रियो मन्ये साफल्यं भजते तदा ।
यदारिविजयी वास्यात् संग्रामे वा हतः सुतः ॥ ४५ ॥

पुत्त्रावूचतुः ॥

ततः स राजा संस्कारं पुत्त्रपत्नीमलम्भयत् ।

निर्गम्य च वहिः स्नातो ददौ पुत्राय चोदकं ॥ ४६ ॥
तालकेतुश्च निर्गम्य तथैव यमुनाजलात् ।
राजपुत्रमुवाचेदं प्रणयान्मधुरं वचः ॥ ४७ ॥
गच्छ भूपालपुत्र त्वं कृतार्थोऽहं कृतस्त्वया ।
कार्य्यं चिराभिलषितं त्वय्यत्राविचले स्थिते ॥ ४८ ॥
वारुणं यज्ञकार्य्यञ्च जलेशस्य महात्मनः ।
तन्मया साधितं सर्व्वं यन्ममासीदभीप्सितं ॥ ४९ ॥
प्रणिपत्य स तं प्रायाद्राजपुत्रः पुरं पितुः ।
समारुह्य तमेवाश्वं सुपर्णानिलविक्रमं ॥ ५० ॥

इति श्रीमार्कण्डेयपुराणे कुवलयाश्वीये मदालसावियोगः॥ २२ ॥

त्रयोविंशोऽध्यायः ॥

पुत्रावूचतुः ॥

स राजपुत्रः संप्राप्य वेगादात्मपुरं ततः ।
पित्रोर्व्विवन्दिषुः पादौ दिदृक्षुश्च मदालसां ॥ १ ॥
ददर्श जनमुद्विग्नमप्रहृष्टमुखं पुरः ।
पुनश्च विस्मिताकारं प्रहृष्टवदनं ततः ॥ २ ॥
अन्यमुत्फुल्लनयनं दिष्ट्या दिष्ट्येति वादिनं ।
परिष्वजन्तमन्योन्यमतिकौतूहलान्वितं ॥ ३ ॥
चिर जीवोरुकल्याण हतास्ते परिपन्थिनः ।
पित्रोः प्रह्लादय मनस्तथास्माकमकण्टकं ॥ ४ ॥

पुत्रावूचतुः ॥

इत्येवं वादिभिः पौरैः पुरः पृष्ठे च संवृतः ।
तत्क्षणप्रभवानन्दः प्रविवेश पितुर्गृहं ॥ ५ ॥
पिता च तं परिष्वज्य माता चान्ये च बान्धवाः ।
चिरं जीवेति कल्याणीर्ददुस्तस्मै तदाशिषः ॥ ६ ॥
प्रणिपत्य ततः सोऽथ किमेतदिति विस्मितः ।
पप्रच्छ पितरं तात सोऽस्मै सम्यक् तदुक्तवान् ॥ ७ ॥
स भार्य्यां तां मृतां श्रुत्वा हृदयेष्टां मदालसां ।
पितरौ च पुरो दृष्ट्वा लज्जाशोकाब्धिमध्यगः ॥ ८ ॥
चिन्तयामास सा बाला मां श्रुत्वा निधनं गतं ।
तत्याज जीवितं साध्वी धिङ्मां निष्ठुरमानसं ॥ ९ ॥
नृशंसोऽहमनार्य्योऽहं विना तां मृगलोचनां ।
मत्कृते निधनं प्राप्तां यज्जीवाम्यतिनिर्घृणः ॥ १० ॥
पुनः स चिन्तयामास परिसंस्तभ्य मानसं ।
मोहोद्गममपास्याशु निःश्वस्योच्छ्वस्य चातुरः ॥ ११ ॥
मृतेति सा मन्निमित्तं त्यजामि यदि जीवितं ।
किं मयोपकृतं तस्याः श्लाघ्यमेतत्तु योषितां ॥ १२ ॥
यदि रोदिमि वा दीनो हा प्रियेति वदन्मुहुः ।
तथाप्यश्लाघ्यमेतन्नो वयं हि पुरुषाः किल ॥ १३ ॥
अथ शोकजडो दीनो स्रजा हीनो मलान्वितः ।
विपक्षस्य भविष्यामि ततः परिभवास्पदं ॥ १४ ॥
मयारिशातनं कार्य्यं राज्ञः शुश्रूषणं पितुः ।

जीवितं तस्य चायत्तं सन्त्यज्यं तत्कथं मया ॥ १५ ॥
किन्त्वच मन्ये कर्त्तव्यस्त्यागो भोगस्य योषितः ।
स चापि नोपकाराय तन्वङ्ग्याः किन्तु सर्व्वथा ॥ १६ ॥
मयात्मनृशंस्यं कर्त्तव्यं नोपकार्य्यपकारि च ।
या मदर्थेऽत्यजत् प्राणांस्तदर्थेऽल्पमिदं मम ॥ १७ ॥

पुत्रावूचतुः ॥

इति कृत्वा मतिं सोऽथ निष्पाद्योदकदानिकं ।
क्रियाश्चानन्तरं कृत्वा प्रत्युवाच ऋतध्वजः ॥ १८ ॥

ऋतध्वज उवाच ॥

यदि सा मम तन्वङ्गी न स्याद्भार्य्या मदालसा ।
अस्मिन् जन्मनि नान्या मे भवित्री सहचारिणी ॥ १९ ॥
तामृते मृगशावाक्षीं गन्धर्व्वतनयामहं ।
न भोक्ष्ये योषितं काञ्चिदिति सत्यं मयोदितं ॥ २० ॥
सद्धर्म्मचारिणीं पत्नीं तां मुक्त्वा गजगामिनीं ।
काञ्चिन्नाङ्गीकरिष्यामीत्येतत् सत्यं मयोदितं ॥ २१ ॥

पुत्रावूचतुः ॥

परित्यज्य च स्त्रीभोगान् तात सर्व्वांस्तया विना ।
क्रीडन्नास्ते समं तुल्यैर्वयस्यैः शीलसम्पदा ॥ २२ ॥
एतत्तस्य परं कार्य्यं तात तत् केन शक्यते ।
कर्त्तुमत्यर्थं दुष्प्राप्यमीश्वरैः किमुतेतरैः ॥ २३ ॥

जड उवाच ॥

इति वाक्यं तयोः श्रुत्वा विमर्षमगमत्पिता ।

विमृष्य चाह तौ पुत्रौ नागराट् प्रहसन्निव ॥ २४ ॥

नागराडश्वतर उवाच ॥

यद्यशक्यमिति ज्ञात्वा न करिष्यन्ति मानवाः ।
कर्म्मण्युद्यममुद्योगहान्या हानिस्ततः परं ॥ २५ ॥
आरभेत नरः कर्म्म स्वपौरुषमहापयन् ।
निष्पत्तिः कर्म्मणो दैवे पौरुषे च व्यवस्थिता ॥ २६ ॥
तस्मादहं तथा यत्नं करिष्ये पुत्रकावितः ।
तपश्चर्य्यां समास्थाय यथैतत् साध्यते चिरात् ॥ २७ ॥

जड उवाच ॥

एवमुक्त्वा स नागेन्द्रः प्लक्षावतरणं गिरेः ।
तीर्थं हिमवतो गत्वा तपस्तेपे सुदुश्चरं ॥ २८ ॥
तुष्टाव गीर्भिश्च ततस्तत्र देवीं सरस्वतीं ।
तन्मना नियताहारो भूत्वा त्रिसवनाप्लुतः ॥ २९ ॥

अश्वतर उवाच ॥

जगद्धात्रीमहं देवीमारिराधयिषुः शुभां ।
स्तोष्ये प्रणम्य शिरसा ब्रह्मयोनिं सरस्वतीं ॥ ३० ॥
सदसद्देवि यत्किञ्चिन्मोक्षवच्चार्थवत्पदं ।
तत्सर्व्वं त्वय्यसंयोगं योगवद्देवि संस्थितं ॥ ३१ ॥
त्वमक्षरं परं देवि यत्र सर्व्वं प्रतिष्ठितं ।
अक्षरं परमं देवि संस्थितं परमाणुवत् ॥ ३२ ॥
अक्षरं परमं ब्रह्म विश्वञ्चैतत् क्षरात्मकं ।
दारुण्यवस्थितो वह्निर्भौमाश्च परमाणवः ॥ ३३ ॥

तथा त्वयि स्थितं ब्रह्म जगच्चेदमशेषतः ।
ओँकाराक्षरसंस्थानं यत्तु देवि स्थिरास्थिरं ॥ ३४ ॥
तत्र मात्रात्रयं सर्व्वमस्ति यद्देवि नास्ति च ।
त्रयो लोकास्त्रयो वेदास्त्रैविद्यं पावकत्रयं ॥ ३५ ॥
त्रीणि ज्योतींषि वर्णाश्च त्रयो धर्म्मागमास्तथा ।
त्रयो गुणास्त्रयः शब्दास्त्रयो वेदास्तथाश्र ॥ ३६ ॥
त्रयः कालास्तथावस्थाः पितरोऽहर्न्निशादयः ।
एतन्मात्रात्रयं देवि तव रूपं सरस्वति ॥ ३७ ॥
विभिन्नदर्शिनामाद्या ब्रह्मणो हि सनातनाः ।
सोमसंस्था हविःसंस्थाः पाकसंस्थाश्च सप्त याः ॥ ३८ ॥
तास्त्वदुच्चारणाद्देवि क्रियन्ते ब्रह्मवादिभिः ।
अनिर्द्देश्यं तथा चान्यदर्द्धमात्रान्वितं परं ॥ ३९ ॥
अविकार्य्यक्षयं दिव्यं परिणामविवर्जितं ।
तवैतत्परमं रूपं यन्न शक्यं मयोदितुं ॥ ४० ॥
न चास्येन च तज्जिह्वा ताम्रोष्ठादिभिरुच्यते ।
इन्द्रोऽपि वसवो ब्रह्मा चन्द्रार्कौ ज्योतिरेव च ॥ ४१ ॥
विश्वावासं विश्वरूपं विश्वेशं परमेश्वरं ।
सांख्यवेदान्तवादोक्तं बहुशाखास्थिरीकृतं ॥ ४२ ॥
अनादिमध्यनिधनं सदसन्न सदेव यत् ।
एकन्त्वनेकं नाप्येकं भवभेदसमाश्रितं ॥ ४३ ॥
अनाख्यं षड्गुणाख्यञ्च वर्गाख्यं त्रिगुणाश्रयं ।
नानाशक्तिमतामेकं शक्तिवैभविकं परं ॥ ४४ ॥

सुखासुखं महासौख्यरूपं त्वयि विभाव्यते ।
एवं देवि त्वया व्याप्तं सकलं निष्कलञ्च यत् ॥
अद्वैतावस्थितं ब्रह्म यच्च द्वैते व्यवस्थितं ॥ ४५ ॥

येऽर्था नित्या ये विनश्यन्ति चान्ये
ये वा स्थूला ये च सूक्ष्मातिसूक्ष्माः ।
ये वा भूमौ येऽन्तरीक्षेऽन्यतो वा
तेषां तेषां त्वत्त एवोपलब्धिः ॥ ४६ ॥

यच्चामूर्त्तं यच्च मूर्त्तं समस्तं
यद्वा भूतेष्वेकमेकञ्च किञ्चित् ।
यद्दिव्यस्ति क्ष्मातले खेऽन्यतो वा
त्वत्सम्बन्धं त्वत्स्वरैर्व्यञ्जनैश्च ॥ ४७ ॥

जड उवाच ॥

एवं स्तुता तदा देवी विष्णोर्जिह्वा सरस्वती ।
प्रत्युवाच महात्मानं नागमश्वतरं ततः ॥ ४८ ॥

सरस्वत्युवाच ॥

वरं ते कम्बलभ्रातः प्रयच्छाम्युरगाधिप ।
तदुच्यतां प्रदास्यामि यत्ते मनसि वर्त्तते ॥ ४९ ॥

अश्वतर उवाच ॥

सहायं देहि देवि त्वं पूर्व्वं कम्बलमेव मे ।
समस्तस्वरसम्बन्धमुभयोः संप्रयच्छ च ॥ ५० ॥

सरस्वत्युवाच ॥

सप्त स्वरा ग्रामरागाः सप्त पन्नगसत्तम ।

गीतकानि च सप्तैव तावतीश्चापि मूर्च्छनाः ॥ ५१ ॥
तालाश्चैकोनपञ्चाशत्तथा ग्रामचयञ्च यत् ।
एतत्सर्व्वं भवान् गाता कम्बलश्च तथानघ ॥ ५२ ॥
ज्ञास्यसे मत्प्रसादेन भुजगेन्द्रापरं तथा ।
चतुर्व्विधं पदं तालं त्रिःप्रकारं लयत्रयं ॥ ५३ ॥
यतित्रयं तथा तोद्यं मया दत्तं चतुर्व्विधं ।
एतद्भवान् मत्प्रसादात् पन्नगेन्द्रापरञ्च यत् ॥ ५४ ॥
अस्यान्तर्गतमायत्तं स्वरव्यञ्जनसम्मितं ।
तदशेषं मया दत्तं भवतः कम्बलस्य च ॥ ५५ ॥
तथा नान्यस्य भूर्लोके पाताले चापि पन्नग ।
प्रणेतारौ भवन्तौ च सर्व्वस्यास्य भविष्यतः ।
पाताले देवलोके च भूर्लोके चैव पन्नगौ ॥ ५६ ॥

जड उवाच ॥

इत्युक्ता सा तदा देवी सर्व्वजिह्वा सरस्वती ।
जगामादर्शनं सद्यो नागस्य कमलेक्षणा ॥ ५७ ॥
तयोश्च तद्यथा वृत्तं भ्रात्रोः सर्व्वमजायत ।
विज्ञानमुभयोरग्र्यं पदतालस्वरादिकं ॥ ५८ ॥
ततः कैलासशैलेन्द्रशिखरस्थितमीश्वरं ।
गीतकैः सप्तभिर्नागौ तन्त्रीलयसमन्वितौ ॥ ५९ ॥
आरिराधयिषू देवमनङ्गाङ्गहरं हरं ।
प्रचक्रतुः परं यत्नमुभौ संहतवाक्कलौ ॥ ६० ॥
प्रातर्निशायां मध्याह्ने सन्ध्ययोश्चापि तत्परौ ।

तयोः कालेन महता स्तूयमानो वृषध्वजः ॥ ६१ ॥
तुतोष गीतकैस्तौ च प्राहेशो गृह्यतां वरः ।
ततः प्रणम्याश्वतरः कम्बलेन समं तदा ॥ ६२ ॥
व्यज्ञापयन्महादेवं शितिकण्ठमुमापतिं ।
यदि नौ भगवान् प्रीतो देवदेवस्त्रिलोचनः ॥ ६३ ॥
ततो यथाऽभिलषितं वरमेनं प्रयच्छ नौ ।
मृता कुवलयाश्वस्य पत्नी देव मदालसा ॥ ६४ ॥
तेनैव वयसा सद्यो दुहितृत्वं प्रयातु मे ।
जातिस्मरा यथा पूर्व्वं तद्वत्कान्तिसमन्विता ॥
योगिनी योगमाता च मद्गेहे जायतां भव ॥ ६५ ॥

महादेव उवाच ॥

यथोक्तं पन्नगश्रेष्ठ सर्व्वमेतद्भविष्यति ।
मत्प्रसादादसन्दिग्धं शृणु चेदं भुजङ्गम ॥ ६६ ॥
श्राद्धे तु समनुप्राप्ते मध्यमं पिण्डमात्मना ।
भक्षयेथाः फणिश्रेष्ठ शुचिः प्रयतमानसः ॥ ६७ ॥
भक्षिते तु ततस्तस्मिन् भवतो मध्यमात् फणात् ।
समुत्पत्स्यति कल्याणी तथारूपा यथा मृता ॥ ६८ ॥
कामञ्चेममभिध्याय कुरु त्वं पितृतर्पणं ।
तत्क्षणादेव सा सुभ्रूः श्वसतो मध्यमात् फणात् ॥ ६९ ॥
समुत्पत्स्यति कल्याणी तथारूपा यथा मृता ।
एतच्छ्रुत्वा ततस्तौ तु प्रणिपत्य महेश्वरं ॥ ७० ॥
रसातलं पुनः प्राप्तौ परितोषसमन्वितौ ।

तथाच कृतवान् श्राद्धं स नागः कम्बलानुजः ॥ ७१ ॥
पिण्डञ्च मध्यमं तद्वद्यथावदुपभुक्तवान् ।
तञ्चापि ध्यायतः कामं ततः सा तनुमध्यमा ॥ ७२ ॥
यज्ञे निश्वसतः सद्यस्तद्रूपा मध्यमात् फणात् ।
न चापि कथयामास कस्यचित् स भुजङ्गमः ॥ ७३ ॥
अन्तर्गृहे तां सुदतीं स्त्रीभिर्गुप्तामधारयत् ।
तौ चानुदिनमागम्य पुत्रौ नागपतेः सुखं ॥ ७४ ॥
ऋतध्वजेन सहितौ चिक्रीडातेऽमराविव ।
एकदा तु सुतौ प्राह नागराजो मुदान्वितः ॥ ७५ ॥
यन्मया पूर्व्वमुक्तन्तु क्रियते किं न तत्तथा ।
स राजपुत्रो युवयोरुपकारी ममान्तिकं ॥ ७६ ॥
कस्मान्नानीयते वत्सावुपकाराय मानदः ।
एवमुक्तौ ततस्तेन पित्रा स्नेहवता तु तौ ॥ ७७ ॥
गत्वा तस्य पुरं सख्यू रेमाते तेन धीमता ।
ततः कुबलयाश्वं तौ कृत्वा किञ्चित्कथान्तरं ॥ ७८ ॥
अब्रूतां प्रणयोपेतं स्वगेहगमनं प्रति ।
तावाह नृपपुत्रोऽसौ नन्विदं भवतोर्गृहं ॥ ७९ ॥
धनवाहनवस्त्रादि यन्मदीयं तदेव वां ।
यत्तु वां वाञ्छितं दातुं धनं रत्नमथापि वा ॥ ८० ॥
तद्दीयतां द्विजसुतौ यदि वां प्रणयो मयि ।
एतावताहं दैवेन वञ्चितोऽस्मि दुरात्मना ॥ ८१ ॥
यद्भवद्भ्यां ममत्वं नो मदीये क्रियते गृहे ।

यदि वां मत्प्रियं कार्य्यमनुग्राह्योऽस्मि वां यदि ॥ ८२ ॥
तद्धने मम गेहे च ममत्वमनुकल्प्यतां ।
युवयोर्यन्मदीयं तन्मामकं युवयोः स्वकं ॥ ८३ ॥
एतत् सत्यं विजानीतं युवां प्राणा बहिश्चराः ।
पुनर्नैवं विभिन्नार्थं वक्तव्यं द्विजसत्तमौ ॥ ८४ ॥
मत्प्रसादपरौ प्रीत्या शापितौ हृदयेन मे ।
ततः स्नेहार्द्रवदनौ तावुभौ नागनन्दनौ ॥ ८५ ॥
ऊचतुर्नृपतेः पुत्रं किञ्चित् प्रणयकोपितौ ।
ऋतध्वज न सन्देहो यथैवाह भवानिदं ॥ ८६ ॥
तथैव चास्मन्मनसि नाच चिन्त्यमतोऽन्यथा ।
किन्त्वावयोः स्वयं पिचा प्रोक्तमेतन्महात्मना ॥ ८७ ॥
द्रष्टुं कुवलयाश्वं तमिच्छामीति पुनः पुनः ।
ततः कुवलयाश्वोऽसौ समुत्थाय वरासनात् ॥
यथाह तातेति वदन् प्रणाममकरोद्भुवि ॥ ८८ ॥

कुवलयाश्व उवाच ॥

धन्योऽहमतिपुण्योऽहं कोऽन्योऽस्ति सदृशो मया ।
यत्तातो मामभिद्रष्टुं करोति प्रवणं मनः ॥ ८९ ॥
तदुत्तिष्ठत गच्छामस्तामाज्ञां क्षणमप्यहं ।
नातिक्रान्तुमिहेच्छामि पद्भ्यां तस्य शपाम्यहं ॥ ९० ॥

जड उवाच ॥

एवमुक्का ययौ सोऽथ सह ताभ्यां नृपात्मजः ।
प्राप्तश्च गोमतीं पुण्यां निर्गम्य नगराद्बहिः ॥ ९१ ॥

तन्मध्येन ययुस्ते वै नागेन्द्रन्टपनन्दनाः ।
मेने च राजपुत्रोऽसौ पारे तस्यास्तयोर्गृहं ॥ ९२ ॥
ततश्चाकृष्य पातालं ताभ्यां नीतो न्टपात्मजः ।
पाताले ददृशे चोभौ स पन्नगकुमारकौ ॥ ९३ ॥
फणामणिकृतोद्योतौ व्यक्तस्वस्तिकलक्षणौ ।
विलोक्य तौ सुरूपाङ्गौ विस्मयोत्फुल्ललोचनः ॥ ९४ ॥
विहस्य चाब्रवीत् प्रेम्णा साधु भो द्विजसत्तमौ ।
कथयामासतुस्तौ च पितरं पन्नगेश्वरं ॥ ९५ ॥
शान्तमश्वतरं नाम माननीयं दिवौकसां ।
रमणीयं ततोऽपश्यत् पातालं स न्टपात्मजः ॥ ९६ ॥
कुमारैस्तरुणैर्वृद्धैरुरगैरुपशोभितं ।
तथैव नागकन्याभिः क्रीडन्तीभिरितस्ततः ॥ ९७ ॥
चारुकुण्डलहाराभिस्ताराभिर्गगणं यथा ।
गीतशब्दैस्तथान्यच वीणावेणुस्वनानुगैः ॥ ९८ ॥
म्टदङ्गपणवातोद्यं हारिवेश्मशताकुलं ।
वीक्षमाणः स पातालं ययौ शत्रुजितः सुतः ॥ ९९ ॥
सह ताभ्यामभीष्टाभ्यां पन्नगाभ्यामरिन्दमः ।
ततः प्रविश्य ते सर्व्वे नागराजनिवेशनं ॥ १०० ॥
ददृशुस्ते महात्मानमुरगाधिपतिं स्थितं ।
दिव्यमाल्याम्बरधरं मणिकुण्डलभूषणं ॥ १०१ ॥
स्वच्छमुक्ताफललताहारिहारोपशोभितं ।
केयूरिणं महाभागमासने सर्व्वकाञ्चने ॥ १०२ ॥

मणिविद्रुमवैदूर्य्यजालान्तरितरूपके ।
स ताभ्यां दर्शितस्तस्य तातोऽस्माकमसाविति ॥ १०३ ॥
वीरः कुवलयाश्वोऽयं पित्रे चासौ निवेदितः ।
ततो ननाम चरणौ नागेन्द्रस्य कृतध्वजः ॥ १०४ ॥
तमुत्थाप्य बलाद्गाढं नागेन्द्रः परिषस्वजे ।
मूर्द्धि चैनमुपाघ्राय चिरं जीवेत्युवाच सः ॥ १०५ ॥
निहतामित्रवर्गश्च पित्रोः शुश्रूषणं कुरु ।
वत्स धन्यस्य कथ्यन्ते परोक्षस्यापि ते गुणाः ॥ १०६ ॥
भवतो मम पुत्राभ्यामसामान्या निवेदिताः ।
त्वमेवानेन वर्द्धथा मनोवाक्कायचेष्टितैः ॥ १०७ ॥
जीवितं गुणिनः श्लाघ्यं जीवन्नेव मृतोऽगुणः ।
गुणवान्निर्वृतिं पित्रोः शत्रूणां हृदयज्वरं ॥ १०८ ॥
करोत्यात्महितं कुर्व्वन् विश्वासञ्च महाजने ।
देवताः पितरो विप्रा मित्रार्थिविकलादयः ॥ १०९ ॥
बान्धवाश्च तथेच्छन्ति जीवितं गुणिनश्चिरं ।
परिवादनिवृत्तानां दुर्गतेषु दयावतां ॥
गुणिनां सफलं जन्म संश्रितानां विपन्नतैः ॥ ११० ॥

जड उवाच ॥

एवमुक्त्वा स तं वीरं पुत्राविदमथाब्रवीत् ।
पूजां कुवलयाश्वस्य कर्त्तुंकामो भुजङ्गमः ॥ १११ ॥
स्नानादिकक्रमं कृत्वा सर्व्वमेव यथाक्रमं ।
मधुपानादिसम्भोगमाहारञ्च यथेप्सितं ॥ ११२ ॥

ततः कुवलयाश्वेन हृदयोत्सवभूतया ।
कथया स्वल्पकं कालं स्थास्यामो हृष्टचेतसः ॥ ११३ ॥
अनुमेने च तन्मौनी वचः शत्रुजितः सुतः ।
तथा चकार नृपतिः पन्नगानामुदारधीः ॥ ११४ ॥

समेत्य तैरात्मजभूपनन्दनै
र्महोरगाणामधिपः स सत्यवाक् ।
मुदान्वितोऽन्नानि मधूनि चात्मवान्
यथोपयोगं बुभुजे स भोगभुक् ॥ ११५ ॥

इति श्रीमार्कण्डेयपुराणे मदालसोपाख्याने कुवलयाश्वपाताल-
गमनं ॥ २३ ॥

चतुर्विंशोऽध्यायः ॥

जड उवाच ॥

कृताहारं महात्मानमधिपं पवनाशिनां ।
उपासाञ्चक्रिरे पुत्रौ भूपालतनयस्तथा ॥ १ ॥
कथाभिरनुरूपाभिः स महात्मा भुजङ्गमः ।
प्रीतिं सञ्जनयामास पुत्रसख्युरुवाच च ॥ २ ॥
तव भद्र सुखं ब्रूहि गेहमभ्यागतस्य यत् ।
कर्त्तव्यमुत्सृजाशङ्कां पितरीव सुतो मयि ॥ ३ ॥
रजतं वा सुवर्णं वा वस्त्रं वाहनमासनं ।
यद्वाभिमतमत्यर्थं दुर्लभं तद्वृणुष्व मां ॥ ४ ॥

कुवलयाश्व उवाच ॥

तव प्रसादाद्भगवन् सुवर्णादि गृहे मम ।
पितुरस्ति ममाद्यापि न किञ्चित् कार्य्यमीदृशं ॥ ५ ॥
ताते वर्षसहस्राणि शासतीमां वसुन्धरां ।
तथैव त्वयि पातालं न मे याचञोन्मुखं मनः ॥ ६ ॥
ते स्वर्ग्याश्च सुपुण्याश्च येषां पितरि जीवति ।
तृणकोटिसमं वित्तं तारुण्याद्वित्तकोटिषु ॥ ७ ॥
मित्राणि तुल्यशिष्टानि तद्वद्देहमनामयं ।
जनिता भ्रियते वित्तं यौवनं किन्नु नास्ति मे ॥ ८ ॥
असत्यर्थे नृणां याचञा प्रवणं जायते मनः ।
सत्यशेषे कथं याचञां मम जिह्वा करिष्यति ॥ ९ ॥
यैर्न चिन्त्यं धनं किञ्चिन्मम गेहेऽस्ति नास्ति वा ।
पितृबाहुतरुच्छायां संश्रिताः सुखिनो हि ते ॥ १० ॥
ये तु बाल्यात् प्रभृत्येव विना पित्रा कुटुम्बिनः ।
ते सुखास्वादविभ्रंसान्मन्ये धात्रैव वञ्चिताः ॥ ११ ॥
तद्वयं त्वत्प्रसादेन धनरत्नादिसञ्चयान् ।
पितृमुक्तान् प्रयच्छामः कामतो नित्यमर्थिनां ॥ १२ ॥
तत्सर्व्वमिह संप्राप्तं यदङ्घ्रियुगलं तव ।
मच्चूडामणिना स्पृष्टं यच्चाङ्गस्पर्शमाप्तवान् ॥ १३ ॥

जड उवाच ॥

इत्येवं प्रश्रितं वाक्यमुक्तः पन्नगसत्तमः ।
प्राह राजसुतं प्रीत्या पुत्रयोरुपकारिणं ॥ १४ ॥

नाग उवाच ॥

यदि रत्नसुवर्णादि मत्तोऽवाप्तुं न ते मनः ।
यदन्यन्मनसः प्रीत्यै तद्ब्रूहि त्वं ददाम्यहं ॥ १५ ॥

कुवलयाश्व उवाच ॥

भगवंस्त्वत्प्रसादेन प्रार्थितस्य गृहे मम ।
सर्व्वमस्ति विशेषेण संप्राप्तं तव दर्शनात् ॥ १६ ॥
कृतकृत्योऽस्मि चैतेन सफलं जीवितञ्च मे ।
यदङ्गसंश्लेषमितस्तव देवस्य मानुषः ॥ १७ ॥
ममोत्तमाङ्गे त्वत्पादरजसा यदिहास्पदं ।
कृतं तेनैव न प्राप्तं किं मया पन्नगेश्वर ॥ १८ ॥
यदि त्ववश्यं दातव्यो वरो मम यथेप्सितः ।
तत्पुण्यकर्म्मसंस्कारो हृदयान्मा व्यपैतु मे ॥ १९ ॥
सुवर्णमणिरत्नादि वाहनं गृहमासनं ।
स्त्रियोऽन्नपानं पुत्राश्च चारुमाल्यानुलेपनं ॥ २० ॥
एते च विविधाः कामा गीतवाद्यादिकञ्च यत् ।
सर्व्वमेतन्मम मतं फलं पुण्यवनस्पतेः ॥ २१ ॥
तस्मान्नरेण तन्मूलः कार्य्यो यत्नः कृतात्मना ।
कर्त्तव्यः पुण्यसक्तानां नकिञ्चिद्भुवि दुर्ल्लभं ॥ २२ ॥

अश्वतर उवाच ॥

एवं भविष्यति प्राज्ञ तव धर्म्माश्रिता मतिः ।
सत्यञ्चैतत्फलं सर्व्वं धर्म्मस्योक्तं यथा त्वया ॥ २३ ॥
तथाप्यवश्यं मद्गेहमागतेन त्वयाधुना ।

ग्राह्यं यन्मानुषे लोके दुष्प्रापं भवतो मतं ॥ २४ ॥

जड उवाच ॥

तस्यैतद्वचनं श्रुत्वा स तदा नृपनन्दनः ।
मुखावलोकनञ्चक्रे पन्नगेश्वरपुत्रयोः ॥ २५ ॥
ततस्तौ प्रणिपत्योभौ राजपुत्रस्य यन्मतं ।
तत् पितुः सकलं वीरौ कथयामासतुः स्फुटं ॥ २६ ॥

पुत्रावूचतुः ॥

ततोऽस्य पत्नी दयिता श्रुत्वेमं विनिपातितं ।
अत्यजद्दयितान् प्राणान् विप्रलब्धा दुरात्मना ॥ २७ ॥
केनापि कृतवैरेण दानवेन कुबुद्धिना ।
गन्धर्व्वराजस्य सुता नाम्ना ख्याता मदालसा ॥ २८ ॥
कृतज्ञोऽयं ततस्तात प्रतिज्ञां कृतवानिमां ।
नान्या भार्य्या भवित्रीति वर्जयित्वा मदालसां ॥ २९ ॥
द्रष्टुं तां चारुसर्व्वाङ्गीमयं वीर ऋतध्वजः ।
तात वाञ्छति यद्येतत् क्रियते तत्कृतं भवेत् ॥ ३० ॥

अश्वतर उवाच ॥

भूतैर्वियोगिनो योगस्तादृशैरेव तादृशः ।
कथमेतद्विना स्वप्नं मायां वा शम्बरोदितां ॥ ३१ ॥

जड उवाच ॥

प्रणिपत्य भुजङ्गेशं पुत्रः शत्रुजितस्ततः ।
प्रत्युवाच महात्मानं प्रेमलज्जासमन्वितः ॥ ३२ ॥
मायामयीमप्यधुना मम तात मदालसां ।

यदि दर्शय ते मन्ये परं कृतमनुग्रहं ॥ ३३ ॥

अश्वतर उवाच ॥

तस्मात् पश्येह वत्स त्वं मायाञ्चेद् द्रष्टुमिच्छसि।
अनुयाह्यो भवान् गेहं बालोऽप्यभ्यागतो गुरुः ॥ ३४ ॥

जड उवाच ॥

आनयामास नागेन्द्रो गृहगुप्तां मदालसां।
तेषां सम्मोहनार्थाय जजल्प च ततः स्फुटं ॥ ३५ ॥
दर्शयामास च तदा राजपुत्राय तां शुभां।
सेयं न वेति ते भार्य्या राजपुत्र मदालसा ॥ ३६ ॥

जड उवाच ॥

स दृष्ट्वा तां तदा तन्वीं तत्क्षणात् विगतत्रपः।
प्रियेति तामभिमुखं ययौ वाचमुदीरयन् ॥
निवारयामास च तं नागः सोऽश्वतरस्त्वरन् ॥ ३७ ॥

अश्वतर उवाच ॥

मायेयं पुत्र मास्प्राक्षीः प्रागेव कथितं तव।
अन्तर्द्धानमुपैत्याशु माया संस्पर्शनादिभिः ॥ ३८ ॥
ततः पपात मेदिन्यां स तु मूर्च्छापरिप्लुतः।
हा प्रियेति वदन् सोऽथ चिन्तयामास भाविनीं ॥ ३९ ॥
अहो स्नेहोऽस्य नृपतेर्म्ममोपर्य्यचलं मनः।
येनायं पातनोऽरीणां विना शस्त्रेण पातितः ॥ ४० ॥
मायेति दर्शिता तेन मिथ्या मायेति यत् स्फुटं।
वाय्वम्बुतेजसां भूमेराकाशस्य च चेष्टया ॥ ४१ ॥

जड उवाच ॥

ततः कुवलयाश्वं तं समाश्वास्य भुजङ्गमः ।
कथयामास तत्सर्व्वं मृतसञ्जीवनादिकं ॥ ४२ ॥

ततः प्रहृष्टः प्रतिलभ्य कान्तां
प्रणम्य नागं निजगाम सोऽथ ।
सुशोभमानः स्वपुरं तमश्व-
मारुह्य संचिन्तितमभ्युपेतं ॥ ४३ ॥

इति श्रीमार्कण्डेयपुराणे मदालसा प्राप्तिः ॥ २४ ॥

पञ्चविंशोऽध्यायः ॥

जड उवाच ॥

आगम्य स्वपुरं सोऽथ पित्रोः सर्व्वमशेषतः ।
कथयामास तन्वङ्गी यथा प्राप्ता पुनर्मृता ॥ १ ॥
ननाम सा च चरणौ श्वश्रूश्वशुरयोः शुभा ।
स्वजनञ्च यथापूर्व्वं वन्दनाश्लेषणादिभिः ॥ २ ॥
पूजयामास तन्वङ्गी यथान्यायं यथावयः ।
ततो महोत्सवो जज्ञे पौराणां तत्र वै पुरे ॥ ३ ॥
ऋतध्वजश्च सुचिरं तया रेमे सुमध्यया ।
निर्झरेषु च शैलानां निम्नगापुलिनेषु च ॥ ४ ॥
काननेषु च रम्येषु तथैवोपवनेषु च ।
पुण्यक्षयं वाञ्छमाना सापि कामोपभोगतः ॥ ५ ॥

सह तेनातिकान्तेन रेमे रम्यासु भूमिषु।
ततः कालेन महता शत्रुजित् स नराधिपः ॥ ६ ॥
सम्यक् प्रशास्य वसुधां कालधर्म्ममुपेयिवान्।
ततः पौरा महात्मानं पुत्रं तस्य ऋतध्वजं ॥ ७ ॥
अभ्यषिञ्चन्त राजानमुदाराचारचेष्टितं।
सम्यक् पालयतस्तस्य प्रजाः पुत्रानिवौरसान् ॥ ८ ॥
मदालसायाः सञ्जज्ञे पुत्रः प्रथमजस्ततः।
तस्य चक्रे पिता नाम विक्रान्त इति धीमतः ॥ ९ ॥
तुतुषुस्तेन वै भृत्या जहास च मदालसा।
सा वै मदालसा पुत्रं बालमुत्तानशायिनं ॥
उल्लापनच्छलेनाह रुदमानमविस्वरं ॥ १० ॥

शुद्धोऽसि रे तात न तेऽस्ति नाम
कृतं हि ते कल्पनयाधुनैव।
पञ्चात्मकं देहमिदं तवैत-
न्नैवास्य त्वं रोदिषि कस्य हेतोः ॥ ११ ॥
न वा भवान्रोदिति वै स्वजन्मा
शब्दोऽयमासाद्य महीशसूनुं।
विकल्प्यमाना विविधा गुणास्ते
ऽगुणाश्च भौताः सकलेन्द्रियेषु ॥ १२ ॥
भूतानि भूतैः परिदुर्ब्बलानि
वृद्धिं समायान्ति यथेह पुंसः।
अन्नाम्बुदानादिभिरेव कस्य

न तेऽस्ति वृद्धिर्न च तेऽस्ति हानिः ॥ १३ ॥
त्वं कञ्चुके शीर्य्यमाणे निजेऽस्मिं-
स्तस्मिंश्च देहे मूढतां मा व्रजेथाः ।
शुभाशुभैः कर्म्मभिर्देहमेत-
न्मदादिमूढैः कञ्चुकस्तेपि नद्धः ॥ १४ ॥
तातेति किञ्चित्तनयेति किञ्चि-
दम्बेति किञ्चिद्दयितेति किञ्चित् ।
ममेति किञ्चिन्न ममेति किञ्चित्
त्वं भूतसङ्घं बहु मानयेथाः ॥ १५ ॥
दुःखानि दुःखोपशमाय भोगान्
सुखाय जानाति विमूढचेताः ।
तान्येव दुःखानि पुनः सुखानि
जानात्यविद्वान् सुविमूढचेताः ॥ १६ ॥
हासोऽस्थिसन्दर्शनमक्षियुग्म-
मत्युज्ज्वलं तर्जनमङ्गनायाः ।
कुचादि पीनं पिशितं घनं तत्
स्थानं रतेः किं नरकं न योषित् ॥ १७ ॥
यानं क्षितौ यानगतञ्च देहं
देहेऽपि चान्यः पुरुषो निविष्टः ।
ममत्वबुद्धिर्न तथा यथा स्वे
देहेऽतिमात्रं वत मूढतैषा ॥ १८ ॥

इति श्रीमार्कण्डेयपुराणे मदालसोपाख्याने ॥ २५ ॥

षड्विंशोऽध्यायः ॥

जड उवाच ॥

वर्द्धमानं सुतं सा तु राजपत्नी दिने दिने ।
तमुल्लापादिना बोधमनयन्निर्ममात्मकं ॥ १ ॥
यथायथं बलं लेभे यथा लेभे मतिं पितुः ।
तथा तथात्मबोधञ्च सोऽवाप मातृभाषितैः ॥ २ ॥
इत्थं तया स तनयो जन्मप्रभृति बोधितः ।
चकार न मतिं प्राज्ञो गार्हस्थ्यं प्रति निर्म्ममः ॥ ३ ॥
द्वितीयोऽस्याः सुतो जज्ञे तस्य नामाकरोत्पिता ।
सुबाहुरयमित्युक्ते सा जहास मदालसा ॥ ४ ॥
तमप्येवं यथापूर्व्वं बालमुल्लापनादिना ।
प्राह बाल्यात् स च प्राप तथा बोधं महामतिः ॥ ५ ॥
तृतीयं तनयं जातं स राजा शत्रुमर्द्दनं ।
यदाह तेन सा सुभ्रूर्जहासातिचिरं पुनः ॥ ६ ॥
तथैव सोऽपि तन्वङ्ग्या बालत्वादवबोधितः ।
क्रियाश्चकार निष्कामो न किञ्चिदुपकारकं ॥ ७ ॥
चतुर्थस्य सुतस्याथ चिकीर्षुर्न्नाम भूमिपः ।
ददर्श तां शुभाचारामीषद्धासां मदालसां ॥
तामाह राजा हसतीं किञ्चित् कौतूहलान्वितः ॥ ८ ॥

राजोवाच ॥

क्रियमाणे सकृन्नाम्नि कथ्यतां हास्यकारणं ।

विक्रान्तश्च सुबाहुश्च तथान्यः शत्रुमर्द्दनः ॥ ९ ॥
शोभनानीति नामानि मया मन्ये कृतानि वै ।
योग्यानि क्षत्त्रबन्धूनां शौर्य्याटोपयुतानि च ॥ १० ॥
असन्त्येतानि चेद्भद्रे यदि ते मनसि स्थितं ।
तदस्य क्रियतां नाम चतुर्थस्य सुतस्य मे ॥ ११ ॥

मदालसोवाच ॥

मयाज्ञा भवतः कार्य्या महाराज यथात्थ मां ।
तथा नाम करिष्यामि चतुर्थस्य सुतस्य ते ॥ १२ ॥
अलर्क इति धर्म्मज्ञः ख्यातिं लोके प्रयास्यति ।
कनीयानेष ते पुत्त्रो मतिमांश्च भविष्यति ॥ १३ ॥
तच्छ्रुत्वा नाम पुत्त्रस्य कृतं मात्रा महीपतिः ।
अलर्क इत्यसम्बद्धं प्रहस्येदमथाब्रवीत् ॥ १४ ॥

राजोवाच ॥

भवत्या यदिदं नाम मत्पुत्त्रस्य कृतं शुभे ।
किमीदृशमसम्बद्धमर्थः कोऽस्य मदालसे ॥ १५ ॥

मदालसोवाच ॥

कल्पनेयं महाराज कृता सा व्यवहारिकी ।
त्वत्कृतानां तथा नाम्नां शृणु भूप निरर्थतां ॥ १६ ॥
वदन्ति पुरुषाः प्राज्ञा व्यापिनं पुरुषं यतः ।
क्रान्तिश्च गतिरुद्दिष्टा देशाद्देशान्तरन्तु या ॥ १७ ॥
सर्व्वगो न प्रयातीति व्यापी देहेश्वरो यतः ।
ततो विक्रान्तसंज्ञेयं मता मम निरर्थका ॥ १८ ॥

सुबाहुरिति या संज्ञा कृतान्यस्य सुतस्य ते ।
निरर्था साप्यमूर्त्तत्वात् पुरुषस्य महीपते ॥ १९ ॥
पुत्रस्य यत्कृतं नाम तृतीयस्यारिमर्द्दनः ।
मन्ये तदप्यसम्बद्धं शृणु चाप्यत्र कारणं ॥ २० ॥
एक एव शरीरेषु सर्व्वेषु पुरुषो यदा ।
तदास्य राजन् कः शत्रुः को वा मित्रमिहेष्यते ॥ २१ ॥
भूतैर्भूतानि मृद्यन्ते अमूर्त्तो मृद्यते कथं ।
क्रोधादीनां पृथग्भावात् कल्पनेयं निरर्थका ॥ २२ ॥
यदि संव्यवहारार्थमसन्नाम प्रकल्प्यते ।
नाम्नि कस्मादलर्काख्ये नैरर्थ्यं भवतो मतं ॥ २३ ॥

जड उवाच ॥

एवमुक्तस्तया साधु महिष्या स महीपतिः ।
तथेत्याह महाबुद्धिर्दयितां तथ्यवादिनीं ॥ २४ ॥
तञ्चापि सा सुतं सुभ्रूर्यथापूर्व्वसुतांस्तथा ।
प्रोवाच बोधजननं तामुवाच स पार्थिवः ॥ २५ ॥
करोषि किमिदं मूढे मम भावाय सन्ततेः ।
दुष्टावबोधदानेन यथापूर्व्वं सुतेषु मे ॥ २६ ॥
यदि ते मत्प्रियं कार्य्यं यदि ग्राह्यं वचो मम ।
तदेनं तनयं मार्गे प्रवृत्तेः सन्नियोजय ॥ २७ ॥
कर्म्ममार्गः समुच्छेदं नैवं देवि गमिष्यति ।
पितृपिण्डनिवृत्तिश्च नैवं साध्वि भविष्यति ॥ २८ ॥
पितरो देवलोकस्थास्तथा तिर्य्यक्त्वमागताः ।

तद्वन्मनुष्यतां याता भूतवर्गे च संस्थिताः ॥ २९ ॥
सपुण्यानसपुण्यांश्च क्षुत्क्षामान् तृट्परिप्लुतान् ।
पिण्डोदकप्रदानेन नरः कर्म्मण्यवस्थितः ॥ ३० ॥
सदाप्यायते सुभ्रु तद्वद्देवातिथीनपि ।
देवैर्मनुष्यैः पितृभिः प्रेतैर्भूतैः सगुह्यकैः ॥ ३१ ॥
वयोभिः कृमिकीटैश्च नर एवोपजीव्यते ।
तस्मात्तन्वङ्गि पुत्रं मे यत्कार्य्यं क्षत्रयोनिभिः ॥ ३२ ॥
ऐहिकामुष्मिकफलं तत्सम्यक् प्रतिपादय ।
तेनैवमुक्ता सा भर्त्रा वरनारी मदालसा ॥ ३३ ॥
अलर्कं नाम तनयमुवाचोल्लापवादिनी ।
पुत्र बर्द्धस्व मद्भर्त्तुर्मनो नन्दय कर्म्मभिः ॥
मित्राणामुपकाराय दुर्हृदां नाशनाय च ॥ ३४ ॥

धन्योऽसि रे यो वसुधामशत्रु-
रेकश्चिरं पालयितासि पुत्र ।
तत्पालनादस्तु सुखोपभोगो
धर्म्मात्फलं प्राप्स्यसि चामरत्वं ॥ ३५ ॥
धरामरान् पर्व्वसु तर्पयेथाः
समीहितं बन्धुषु पूरयेथाः ।
हितं परस्मै हृदि चिन्तयेथाः
मनः परस्त्रीषु निवर्त्तयेथाः ॥ ३६ ॥
यज्ञैरनेकैर्विबुधानजस्र-
मर्थैर्द्विजान् प्रीणय संश्रितांश्च ।

स्त्रियश्च कामैरतुलैश्चिराय
युद्धैश्चारींस्तोषयितासि वीर ॥ ३७ ॥
बालो मनो नन्दय बान्धवानां
गुरोस्तथाज्ञाकरणैः कुमारः ।
स्त्रीणां युवा सत्कुलभूषणानां
वृद्धो वने वत्स वनेचराणां ॥ ३८ ॥
राज्यं कुर्व्वन् सुहृदो नन्दयेथाः
साधून्रक्षंस्तात यज्ञैर्यजेथाः ।
दुष्टान्निघ्नन् वैरिणश्चाजिमध्ये
गोविप्रार्थे वत्स मृत्युं व्रजेथाः ॥ ३९ ॥

इति श्रीमार्कंण्डेयपुराणे पुत्रानुशासनं ॥ २६ ॥

सप्तविंशोऽध्यायः ॥

जड उवाच ॥

एवमुल्लाप्यमानस्तु स तु मात्रा दिने दिने ।
ववृधे वयसा बालो बुद्ध्या चालर्कसंज्ञितः ॥ १ ॥
स कौमारकमासाद्य ऋतध्वजसुतस्ततः ।
कृतोपनयनः प्राज्ञः प्रणिपत्याह मातरं ॥ २ ॥
मया यदत्र कर्त्तव्यमैहिकामुष्मिकाय वै ।
सुखाय वद तत्सर्व्वं प्रश्रयावनतस्य मे ॥ ३ ॥

मदालसोवाच ॥

वत्स राज्येऽभिषिक्तेन प्रजारञ्जनमादितः।
कर्त्तव्यमविरोधेन स्वधर्म्मस्य महीभृता ॥ ४ ॥
व्यसनानि परित्यज्य सप्त मूलहराणि वै।
आत्मा रिपुभ्यः संरक्ष्यो वहिर्म्मन्त्रविनिर्गमात् ॥ ५ ॥
अष्टधा नाशमाप्नोति सुचक्रात् स्यन्दनाद्यथा।
तथा राजाप्यसन्दिग्धं वहिर्म्मन्त्रविनिर्गमात् ॥ ६ ॥
दुष्टादुष्टांश्च जानीयादमात्यानरिदोषतः।
चरैश्चरास्तथा शत्रोरन्वेष्टव्याः प्रयत्नतः ॥ ७ ॥
विश्वासो न तु कर्त्तव्यो राज्ञा मित्राप्तबन्धुषु।
कार्य्ययोगादमित्रेऽपि विश्वसीत नराधिपः ॥ ८ ॥
स्थानवृद्धिक्षयज्ञेन षाड्गुण्यगुणिनात्मना।
भवितव्यं नरेन्द्रेण न कामवशवर्त्तिना ॥ ९ ॥
प्रागात्मा मन्त्रिणश्चैव ततो भृत्या महीभृता।
जेयाश्चानन्तरं पौरा विरुध्येत ततोऽरिभिः ॥ १० ॥
यस्त्वेतानविजित्यैव वैरिणो विजिगीषते।
सोऽजितात्मा जितामात्यः शत्रुवर्गेण बाध्यते ॥ ११ ॥
तस्मात् कामादयः पूर्व्वं जेयाः पुत्र महीभुजा।
तज्जये हि जयोऽवश्यं राजा नश्यति तैर्जितः ॥ १२ ॥
कामः क्रोधश्च लोभश्च मदो मानस्तथैव च।
हर्षश्च शत्रवो ह्येते विनाशाय महीभृतां ॥ १३ ॥
कामप्रसक्तमात्मानं स्मृत्वा पाण्डुं निपातितं।

निवर्त्तयेत्तथा क्रोधादनुह्रादं हतात्मजं ॥ १४ ॥
हतमैलं तथा लोभान्मदाद्वेनं द्विजैर्हतं ।
मानादनायुषा पुत्त्रं बलिं हर्षात् पुरञ्जयं ॥ १५ ॥
एभिर्जितैर्जितं सर्व्वं मरुत्तेन महात्मना ।
स्मृत्वा विवर्जयेदेतान् दोषान् स्वीयान्महीपतिः ॥ १६ ॥
काककोकिलभृङ्गाणां मृगव्यालशिखण्डिनां ।
हंसकुक्कुटलोहानां शिक्षेत चरितं नृपः ॥ १७ ॥
कौटकस्य क्रियां कुर्य्यात् विपक्षे मनुजेश्वरः ।
चेष्टां पिपीलिकानाञ्च काले भूपः प्रदर्शयेत् ॥ १८ ॥
ज्ञेयाग्निविस्फुलिङ्गानां वीजचेष्टा च शाल्मलेः ।
चन्द्रसूर्य्यस्वरूपेण नीत्यर्थं पृथिवीक्षिता ॥ १९ ॥
बन्धकीपद्मशरभशूलिकागुर्व्विणीस्तनात् ।
प्रज्ञा नृपेण चादेया तथा गोपालयोषितः ॥ २० ॥
शक्रार्कयमसोमानां तद्वद्वायोर्महीपतिः ।
रूपाणि पञ्च कुर्व्वीत महीपालनकर्म्मणि ॥ २१ ॥
यथेन्द्रश्चतुरो मासान् तोयोत्सर्गेण भूगतं ।
आप्याययेत्तथा लोकं परिहारैर्म्महीपतिः ॥ २२ ॥
मासानष्टौ यथा सूर्य्यस्तोयं हरति रश्मिभिः ।
सूक्ष्मेणैवाभ्युपायेन तथा शुल्कादिकं नृपः ॥ २३ ॥
यथा यमः प्रियद्वेष्ये प्राप्तकाले नियच्छति ।
तथा प्रियाप्रिये राजा दुष्टादुष्टे समो भवेत् ॥ २४ ॥
पूर्णेन्दुमालोक्य यथा प्रीतिमान् जायते नरः ।

एवं यत्र प्रजाः सर्व्वा निर्वृत्तास्तच्छशिव्रतं ॥ २५ ॥
मारुतः सर्व्वभूतेषु निगूढश्चरते यथा ।
एवं नृपश्चरेच्चारैः पौरामात्यादिबन्धुषु ॥ २६ ॥
न लोभाद्वा न कामाद्वा नार्थाद्वा यस्य मानसं ।
यथान्यैः कृष्यते वत्स स राजा स्वर्गमृच्छति ॥ २७ ॥
उत्पथग्राहिणो मूढान् स्वधर्म्माच्चलतो नरान् ।
यः करोति निजे धर्म्मे स राजा स्वर्गमृच्छति ॥ २८ ॥
वर्णधर्म्मा न सीदन्ति यस्य राज्ये तथाश्रमाः ।
वत्स तस्य सुखं प्रेत्य परत्रेह च शास्वतं ॥ २९ ॥
एतद्राज्ञः परं कृत्यं तथैतत् सिद्धिकारकं ।
स्वधर्म्मस्थापनं नृणां चाल्यते यत्कुबुद्धिभिः ॥ ३० ॥
पालनेनैव भूतानां कृतकृत्यो महीपतिः ।
सम्यक् पालयिता भागं धर्म्मस्याप्नोति यत्नतः ॥ ३१ ॥

इति श्रीमार्कण्डेयपुराणे पुत्रानुशासनं ॥ २७ ॥

अष्टाविंशोऽध्यायः ॥

जड उवाच ॥

तन्मातुर्व्वचनं श्रुत्वा सोऽलर्को मातरं पुनः ।
पप्रच्छ वर्णधर्म्मांश्च धर्म्मा ये चाश्रमेषु च ॥ १ ॥

अलर्क उवाच ॥

कथितोऽयं महाभागे राज्यतन्त्राश्रितस्त्वया ।
धर्म्मं तमहमिच्छामि श्रोतुं वर्णाश्रमात्मकं ॥ २ ॥

मदालसोवाच ॥

दानमध्ययनं यज्ञो ब्राह्मणस्य त्रिधा मतः ।
नान्यश्चतुर्थो धर्म्मोऽस्ति धर्म्मस्तस्य पदं विना ॥ ३ ॥
याजनाध्यापने शुद्धे तथा पूतप्रतिग्रहः ।
एषा सम्यक् समाख्याता त्रिविधा चास्य जीविका ॥ ४ ॥
दानमध्ययनं यज्ञः क्षत्रियस्याप्ययं त्रिधा ।
धर्म्मः प्रोक्तः क्षितेरक्षा शस्त्राजीवश्च जीविका ॥ ५ ॥
दानमध्ययनं यज्ञो वैश्यस्यापि त्रिधैव सः ।
वाणिज्यं पाशुपाल्यञ्च कृषिश्चैवास्य जीविका ॥ ६ ॥
दानं यज्ञोऽथ शुश्रूषा द्विजातीनां त्रिधा मया ।
व्याख्यातः शूद्रधर्म्मोऽपि जीविका कारुकर्म्म च ॥ ७ ॥
तद्वद्द्विजातिशुश्रूषा पोषणं क्रयविक्रयौ ।
वर्णधर्म्मास्त्विमे प्रोक्ताः श्रूयन्तां चाश्रमाश्रयाः ॥ ८ ॥
स्ववर्णधर्म्मात् संसिद्धिं नरः प्राप्नोति न च्युतः ।
प्रयाति नरकं प्रेत्य प्रतिषिद्धनिषेवनात् ॥ ९ ॥
यावत्तु नोपनयनं क्रियते वै द्विजन्मनः ।
कामचेष्टोक्तिभक्ष्यश्च तावद्भवति पुत्रक ॥ १० ॥
कृतोपनयनः सम्यक् ब्रह्मचारी गुरोर्गृहे ।
वसेत्तत्र च धर्म्मोऽस्य कथ्यते तं निबोध मे ॥ ११ ॥

स्वाध्यायोऽथाग्निशुश्रूषा स्नानं भिक्षाटनं तथा ।
गुरोर्निवेद्य तच्चान्नमनुज्ञातेन सर्व्वदा ॥ १२ ॥
गुरोः कर्म्मणि सोद्योगः सम्यक् प्रीत्युपपादनं ।
तेनाहूतः पठेच्चैव तत्परो नान्यमानसः ॥ १३ ॥
एकं द्वौ सकलान् वापि वेदान् प्राप्य गुरोर्मुखात् ।
अनुज्ञातोऽथ वन्दित्वा दक्षिणां गुरवे ततः ॥ १४ ॥
गार्हस्थ्याश्रमकामस्तु गृहस्थाश्रममावसेत् ।
वानप्रस्थाश्रमं वापि चतुर्थं चेच्छयात्मनः ॥ १५ ॥
तत्रैव वा गुरोर्गेहे द्विजो निष्ठामवाप्नुयात् ।
गुरोरभावे तत्पुत्रे तच्छिष्ये तत्सतं विना ॥ १६ ॥
शुश्रूषुर्निरभीमानो ब्रह्मचर्य्याश्रमं वसेत् ।
उपावृत्तस्ततस्तस्मात् गृहस्थाश्रमकाम्यया ॥ १७ ॥
ततोऽसमानर्षिकुलां तुल्यां भार्य्यामरोगिणीं ।
उद्वहेन्न्यायतोऽव्यङ्गां गृहस्थाश्रमकारणात् ॥ १८ ॥
स्वकर्म्मणा धनं लब्ध्वा पितृदेवातिथींस्तथा ।
सम्यक् सम्प्रीणयन् भक्त्या पोषयेच्चाश्रितांस्तथा ॥ १९ ॥
भृत्यात्मजान् जामयोऽथ दीनान्धपतितानपि ।
यथाशक्त्यान्नदानेन वयांसि पशवस्तथा ॥ २० ॥
एष धर्म्मो गृहस्थस्य ऋतावभिगमस्तथा ।
पञ्चयज्ञविधानन्तु यथाशक्त्या न हापयेत् ॥ २१ ॥
पितृदेवातिथिज्ञातिभुक्तशेषं स्वयं नरः ।
भुञ्जीत च समं भृत्यैर्यथाविभवमादृतः ॥ २२ ॥

एष तूद्देशतः प्रोक्तो गृहस्थस्याश्रमो मया ।
वानप्रस्थस्य धर्म्मन्ते कथयाम्यवधार्य्यतां ॥ २३ ॥
अपत्यसन्ततिं दृष्ट्वा प्राज्ञो देहस्य चाननतिं ।
वानप्रस्थाश्रमं गच्छेदात्मनः शुद्धिकारणात् ॥ २४ ॥
तचारण्योपभोगश्च तपोभिश्चानुकर्षणं ।
भूमौ शय्या ब्रह्मचर्य्यं पितृदेवातिथिक्रिया ॥ २५ ॥
होमस्त्रिषवणस्नानं जटावल्कलधारणं ।
योगाभ्यासः सदा चैव वन्यस्नेहनिषेवनं ॥ २६ ॥
इत्येष पापशुद्ध्यर्थमात्मनश्चोपकारकः ।
वानप्रस्थाश्रमस्तस्माद्भिक्षोस्तु चरमोऽपरः ॥ २७ ॥
चतुर्थस्य स्वरूपन्तु श्रूयतामाश्रमस्य मे ।
यः स्वधर्म्मोऽस्य धर्म्मज्ञैः प्रोक्तस्तात महात्मभिः ॥ २८ ॥
सर्व्वसङ्गपरित्यागो ब्रह्मचर्य्यमकोपिता ।
यतेन्द्रियत्वमावासे नैकस्मिन् वसतिश्चिरं ॥ २९ ॥
अनारम्भस्तथाहारो भैक्षान्नेनैककालिना ।
आत्मज्ञानावबोधेच्छा तथा चात्मावलोकनं ॥ ३० ॥
चतुर्थे त्वाश्रमे धर्म्मो मयायं ते निवेदितः ।
सामान्यमन्यवर्णानामाश्रमाणाञ्च मे शृणु ॥ ३१ ॥
सत्यं शौचमहिंसा च अनसूया तथा क्षमा ।
आनृशंस्यमकार्पण्यं सन्तोषश्चाष्टमो गुणः ॥ ३२ ॥
एते सङ्क्षेपतः प्रोक्ता धर्म्मा वर्णाश्रमेषु ते ।
एतेषु च स्वधर्म्मेषु स्वेषु तिष्ठेत् समन्ततः ॥ ३३ ॥

यश्चोल्लङ्घ्य स्वकं धर्म्मं स्ववर्णाश्रमसंज्ञितं ।
नरोऽन्यथा प्रवर्त्तेत स दण्ड्यो भूभृतो भवेत् ॥ ३४ ॥
ये च स्वधर्म्मसन्त्यागात् पापं कुर्व्वन्ति मानवाः ।
उपेक्षतस्तान्नृपतेरिष्टापूर्त्तं प्रणश्यति ॥ ३५ ॥
तस्माद्राज्ञा प्रयत्नेन सर्व्वे वर्णाः स्वधर्म्मतः ।
प्रवर्त्तन्तोऽन्यथा दण्ड्याः स्थाप्याश्चैव स्वकर्म्मसु ॥ ३६ ॥

इति श्रीमार्कण्डेयपुराणे पुत्त्रानुशासने मदालसावाक्यं ॥ २८ ॥

ऊनत्रिंशोऽध्यायः ॥

अलर्क उवाच ॥

यत्कार्य्यं पुरुषाणाञ्च गार्हस्थ्यमनुवर्त्ततां ।
बन्धश्च स्यादकरणे क्रियाया यस्य चोज्झितिः ॥ १ ॥
उपकाराय यन्नृणां यच्च वर्ज्यं गृहे सता ।
यथा च क्रियते तन्मे यथावत् पृच्छतो वद ॥ २ ॥

मदालसोवाच ॥

वत्स गार्हस्थ्यमादाय नरः सर्व्वमिदं जगत् ।
पुष्णाति तेन लोकांश्च स जयत्यभिवाञ्छितान् ॥ ३ ॥
पितरो मुनयो देवा भूतानि मनुजास्तथा ।
कृमिकीटपतङ्गाश्च वयांसि पशवोऽसुराः ॥ ४ ॥
गृहस्थमुपजीवन्ति ततस्तृप्तिं प्रयान्ति च ।

मुखं चास्य निरीक्षन्ते अपि नो दास्यतीति वै ॥ ५ ॥
सर्व्वस्याधारभूतेयं वत्स धेनुस्त्रयीमयी ।
यस्यां प्रतिष्ठितं विश्वं विश्वहेतुश्च या मता ॥ ६ ॥
ऋक्पृष्ठासौ यजुर्मध्या सामवक्त्रशिरोधरा ।
इष्टापूर्त्तविषाणा च साधुसूक्ततनूरुहा ॥ ७ ॥
शान्तिपुष्टिशकृन्मूत्रा वर्णपादप्रतिष्ठिता ।
आजीव्यमाना जगतां साक्षया नापचीयते ॥ ८ ॥
स्वाहाकारस्वधाकारौ वषटकारश्च पुत्रक ।
हन्तकारस्तथा चान्यस्तस्यास्तनचतुष्टयं ॥ ९ ॥
स्वाहाकारं स्तनं देवाः पितरश्च स्वधामयं ।
मुनयश्च वषट्कारं देवभूतसुरेतराः ॥ १० ॥
हन्तकारं मनुष्याश्च पिवन्ति सततं स्तनं ।
एवमाप्याययत्येषा वत्स धेनुस्त्रयीमयी ॥ ११ ॥
तेषामुच्छेदकर्त्ता च यो नरोऽत्यन्तपापकृत् ।
स तमस्यन्धतामिस्रे तामिस्रे च निमज्जति ॥ १२ ॥
यश्चेमां मानवो धेनुं स्वैर्वत्सैरमरादिभिः ।
पाययत्युचिते काले स स्वर्गायोपपद्यते ॥ १३ ॥
तस्मात् पुत्र मनुष्येण देवर्षिपितृमानवाः ।
भूतानि चानुदिवसं पोष्याणि स्वतनुर्यथा ॥ १४ ॥
तस्मात् स्नातः शुचिर्भूत्वा देवर्षिपितृतर्पणं ।
प्रजापतेस्तथैवाद्भिः काले कुर्य्यात् समाहितः ॥ १५ ॥
सुमनोगन्धपुष्पैश्च देवानभ्यर्च्च मानवाः ।

ततोऽग्नेस्तर्पणं कुर्य्याद्देयाश्च बलयस्तथा ॥ १६ ॥
ब्रह्मणे गृहमध्ये तु विश्वेदेवेभ्य एव च ।
धन्वन्तरिं समुद्दिश्य प्रागुदीच्यां बलिं क्षिपेत् ॥ १७ ॥
प्राच्यां शक्राय याम्यायां यमाय बलिमाहरेत् ।
प्रतीच्यां वरुणायाथ सोमायोत्तरतो बलिं ॥ १८ ॥
दद्याद्धात्रे विधात्रे च बलिं द्वारे गृहस्य तु ।
अर्य्यम्णोऽथ वहिर्दद्याद्गृहेभ्यश्च समन्ततः ॥ १९ ॥
नक्तञ्चरेभ्यो भूतेभ्यो बलिमाकाशतो हरेत् ।
पितॄणां निर्व्वपेच्चैव दक्षिणाभिमुखस्थितः ॥ २० ॥
गृहस्थस्तत्परो भूत्वा सुसमाहितमानसः ।
ततस्तोयमुपादाय तेष्वेवाचमनाय वै ॥ २१ ॥
स्थानेषु निक्षिपेत् प्राज्ञस्तास्ता उद्दिश्य देवताः ।
एवं गृहबलिं कृत्वा गृहे गृहपतिः शुचिः ॥ २२ ॥
आप्यायनाय भूतानां कुर्य्यादुत्सर्गमादरात् ।
श्वभ्यश्च श्वपचेभ्यश्च वयोभ्यश्चावपेद्भुवि ॥ २३ ॥
वैश्वदेवं हि नामैतत् सायं प्रातरुदाहृतं ।
आचम्य च ततः कुर्य्यात् प्राज्ञो द्वारावलोकनं ॥ २४ ॥
मुहूर्त्तस्याष्टमं भागमुदीक्ष्योऽप्यतिथिर्भवेत् ।
अतिथिं तत्र सम्प्राप्तमन्नाद्येनोदकेन च ॥ २५ ॥
सम्पूजयेद्यथा शक्ति गन्धपुष्पादिभिस्तथा ।
न मित्रमतिथिं कुर्य्यान्नैकग्रामनिवासिनं ॥ २६ ॥
अज्ञातकुलनामानं तत्कालसमुपस्थितं ।

बुभुक्षुमागतं श्रान्तं याचमानमकिञ्चनं ॥ २७ ॥
ब्राह्मणं प्राहुरतिथिं स पूज्यः शक्तितो बुधैः ।
न पृच्छेद्गोत्रचरणं स्वाध्यायञ्चापि पण्डितः ॥ २८ ॥
शोभनाशोभनाकारं तं मन्येत प्रजापतिं ।
अनित्यं हि स्थितो यस्मात्तस्मादतिथिरुच्यते ॥ २९ ॥
तस्मिंस्तृप्ते न्ययज्ञोत्थादृणान्मुच्येद् गृहाश्रमी ।
तस्मा अदत्वा यो भुङ्क्ते स्वयं किल्विषभुङ्नरः ॥ ३० ॥
स पापं केवलं भुङ्क्ते पुरीषञ्चान्यजन्मनि ।
अतिथिर्यस्य भग्नाशो गृहात् प्रतिनिवर्त्तते ॥ ३१ ॥
स दत्त्वा दुष्कृतं तस्मै पुण्यमादाय गच्छति ।
अप्यम्बुशाकदानेन यद्वाप्यश्नाति स स्वयं ॥ ३२ ॥
पूजयेत्तु नरः शक्त्या तेनैवातिथिमादरात् ।
कुर्य्याच्चाहरहः श्राद्धमन्नाद्येनोदकेन च ॥ ३३ ॥
पितॄनुद्दिश्य विप्रांश्च भोजयेद्विप्रमेव वा ।
अन्नस्याग्रं तदुद्धृत्य ब्राह्मणायोपपादयेत् ॥ ३४ ॥
भिक्षाञ्च याचतां दद्यात् परिव्राड्ब्रह्मचारिणां ।
ग्रासप्रमाणा भिक्षा स्यादग्रं ग्रासचतुष्टयं ॥ ३५ ॥
अग्रं चतुर्गुणं प्राहुर्हन्तकारं द्विजोत्तमाः ।
भोजनं हन्तकारं वा अग्रं भिक्षामथापि वा ॥ ३६ ॥
अदत्त्वा तु न भोक्तव्यं यथाविभवमात्मनः ।
पूजयित्वातिथीनिष्टान् ज्ञातीन् बन्धूंस्तथार्थिनः ॥ ३७ ॥
विकलान् बालवृद्धांश्च भोजयेच्चातुरांस्तथा ।

वाञ्छते चुत्परीतात्मा यच्चान्योऽन्नमकिञ्चनः ॥ ३८ ॥
कुटुम्बिना भोजनीयः समर्थो विभवे सति ।
श्रीमन्तं ज्ञातिमासाद्य यो ज्ञातिरवसीदति ॥ ३९ ॥
सीदता यत्कृतं तेन तत्पापं स समश्नुते ।
सायं चैव विधिः कार्य्यः सूर्य्योढं तत्र चातिथिं ॥ ४० ॥
पूजयीत यथाशक्ति शयनासनभोजनैः ।
एवमुद्वहतस्तात गार्हस्थ्यं भारमाहितं ॥ ४१ ॥
स्कन्धे विधाता देवाश्च पितरश्च महर्षयः ।
श्रेयोभिवर्षिणः सर्व्वे तथैवातिथिबान्धवाः ॥ ४२ ॥
पशुपक्षिगणास्तृप्ता ये चान्ये सूक्ष्मकीटकाः ।
गाथाश्चात्र महाभाग स्वयमत्रिरगायत ॥ ४३ ॥
ताः शृणुष्व महाभाग गृहस्थाश्रमसंस्थिताः ।
देवान् पितॄंश्चातिथींश्च तद्वत् सम्पूज्य बान्धवान् ॥ ४४ ॥
जामयश्च गुरूंश्चैव गृहस्थो विभवे सति ।
श्वभ्यश्च श्वपचेभ्यश्च वयोभ्यश्चावपेद्भुवि ॥ ४५ ॥
वैश्वदेवं हि नामैतत् कुर्य्यात् सायं तथा दिने ।
मांसमन्नं तथा शाकं गृहे यच्चोपसाधितं ॥
न च तत् स्वयमश्नीयाद्विधिवद्यन्न निर्व्वपेत् ॥ ४६ ॥

इति श्रीमार्कण्डेयपुराणे मदालसोपदेशः ॥ २९ ॥

त्रिंशोऽध्यायः ॥

मदालसोवाच ॥

नित्यं नैमित्तिकञ्चैव नित्यनैमित्तिकं तथा ।
गृहस्थस्य तु यत् कर्म्म तन्निशामय पुत्रक ॥ १ ॥
पञ्चयज्ञाश्रितं नित्यं यदेतत् कथितं तव ।
नैमित्तिकं तथैवान्यत् पुत्रजन्मक्रियादिकं ॥ २ ॥
नित्यनैमित्तिक ज्ञेयं पर्व्वश्राद्धादि पण्डितैः।
तत्र नैमित्तिकं वक्ष्ये श्राद्धमभ्युदयं तव ॥ ३ ॥
पुत्रजन्मनि यत्कार्य्यं जातकर्म्म समं नरैः ।
विवाहादौ च कर्त्तव्यं सर्व्वं सम्यक् क्रमोदितं ॥ ४ ॥
पितरश्चात्र सम्पूज्याः ख्याता नान्दीमुखास्तु ये ।
पिण्डांश्च दधिसंमिश्रान्दद्याद्यवसमन्वितान् ॥ ५ ॥
उदङ्मुखः प्राङ्मुखो वा यजमानः समाहितः ।
वैश्वदेवविहीनन्तत् केचिदिच्छन्ति मानवाः ॥ ६ ॥
युग्माश्चात्र द्विजाः कार्य्यास्ते च पूज्याः प्रदक्षिणं ।
एतन्नैमित्तिकं वृद्धौ तथान्यच्चौर्द्ध्वदेहिकं ॥ ७ ॥
मृताहनि च कर्त्तव्यमेकोद्दिष्टं शृणुष्व तत् ।
दैवहीनं तथा कार्य्यं तथैवैकपवित्रकं ॥ ८ ॥
आवाहनं न कर्त्तव्यमग्नौ करणवर्ज्जितं ।
प्रेतस्य पिण्डमेकञ्च दद्यादुच्छिष्टसन्निधौ ॥ ९ ॥
तिलोदकं चापसव्यं तन्नामस्मरणान्वितं ।

अक्षय्यममुकस्येति स्थाने विप्रविसर्जने ॥ १० ॥
अभिरम्यतामिति ब्रूयाद्ब्रूयुस्तेऽभिरताः स्म ह ।
प्रतिमासं भवेदेतत् कार्य्यमावत्सरं नरैः ॥ ११ ॥
अथ संवत्सरे पूर्णे यदा वा क्रियते नरैः ।
सपिण्डीकरणं कार्य्यं तस्यापि विधिरुच्यते ॥ १२ ॥
तत्रापि दैवरहितमेकार्घैकपवित्रकं ।
नैवाग्नौ करणं तत्र तत्रावाहनवर्ज्जितं ॥ १३ ॥
अपसव्यञ्च तत्रापि भोजयेदयुजो द्विजान् ।
विशेषस्तत्र चान्योऽस्ति प्रतिमासं क्रियाधिकः ॥ १४ ॥
तं कथ्यमानमेकाग्रो वदन्त्या मे निशामय ।
तिलगन्धोदकैर्युक्तं तत्र पात्रचतुष्टयं ॥ १५ ॥
कुर्य्यात् पितॄणां त्रितयमेकं प्रेतस्य पुत्रक ।
पात्रत्रये प्रेतपात्रमर्घ्यञ्चैव प्रसेचयेत् ॥ १६ ॥
ये समाना इति जपन् पूर्व्ववच्छेषमाचरेत् ।
स्त्रीणामप्येवमेवैतदेकोद्दिष्टमुदाहृतं ॥ १७ ॥
सपिण्डीकरणं तासां पुत्राभावे न विद्यते ।
प्रतिसंवत्सरं कार्य्यमेकोद्दिष्टं नरैः स्त्रियाः ॥ १८ ॥
मृताहनि यथान्यायं नृणां यद्वदिहोदितं ।
पुत्राभावे सपिण्डास्तु तदभावे सहोदकाः ॥ १९ ॥
मातुः सपिण्डा ये च स्युर्ये च मातुः सहोदकाः ।
कुर्य्युरेनं विधिं सम्यगपुत्रस्य सुतासुतः ॥ २० ॥
कुर्य्युर्मातामहायैवं पुत्रिकास्तनयास्तथा ।

द्यामुष्यायणसंज्ञास्तु मातामहपितामहान् ॥ २१ ॥
पूजयेयुर्यथान्यायं श्राद्धैर्नैमित्तिकैरपि ।
सर्व्वाभावे स्त्रियः कुर्य्युः स्वभर्तॄणाममन्त्रकं ॥ २२ ॥
तदभावे च नृपतिः कारयेत् स्वकुटुम्बिना ।
तज्जातीयैर्नरैः सम्यक् दाहाद्याः सकलाः क्रियाः ॥ २३ ॥
सर्व्वेषामेव वर्णानां बान्धवो नृपतिर्यतः ।
एतास्ते कथिता वत्स नित्यनैमित्तिकास्तथा ॥ २४ ॥
क्रियां श्राद्धाश्रयामन्यां नित्यनैमित्तिकीं शृणु ।
दर्शस्तत्र निमित्तं वै कालश्चन्द्रक्षयात्मकः ॥
नित्यतां नियतः कालस्तस्याः संसूचयत्यथ ॥ २५ ॥

इति श्रीमार्कण्डेयपुराणेऽलर्कानुशासने नैमित्तिकादिश्राद्धकल्पः ॥ ३० ॥

एकत्रिंशोऽध्यायः ॥

मदालसोवाच ॥

सपिण्डीकरणादूर्द्ध्वं पितुर्यः प्रपितामहः ।
स तु लेपभुजो याति प्रलुप्तः पितृपिण्डतः ॥ १ ॥
तेषामन्यश्चतुर्थो यः पुत्त्रलेपभुजान्नभुक् ।
सोऽपि सम्बन्धतो हीनमुपभोगं प्रपद्यते ॥ २ ॥
पिता पितामहश्चैव तथैव प्रपितामहः ।
पिण्डसम्बन्धिनो ह्येते विज्ञेयाः पुरुषास्त्रयः ॥ ३ ॥

लेपसम्बन्धिनश्चान्ये पितामहपितामहात्।
प्रभृत्युक्तास्त्रयस्तेषां यजमानश्च सप्तमः ॥ ४ ॥
इत्येष मुनिभिः प्रोक्तः सम्बन्धः साप्तपौरुषः।
यजमानात् प्रभृत्यूर्द्धमनुलेपभुजस्तथा ॥ ५ ॥
ततोऽन्ये पूर्व्वजाः सर्व्वे ये चान्ये नरकौकसः।
ये च तिर्य्यक्त्वमापन्ना ये च भूतादिसंस्थिताः ॥ ६ ॥
तान् सर्व्वान् यजमानो वै श्राद्धं कुर्व्वन् यथाविधि।
समाप्याययते वत्स येन येन शृणुष्व तत् ॥ ७ ॥
अन्नप्रकिरणं यत्तु मनुष्यैः क्रियते भुवि।
तेन तृप्तिमुपायान्ति ये पिशाचत्वमागताः ॥ ८ ॥
यदम्बु स्नानवस्त्रोत्थं भूमौ पतति पुत्रक।
तेन ते तरुतां प्राप्तास्तेषां तृप्तिः प्रजायते ॥ ९ ॥
यास्तु गात्राम्बुकणिकाः पतन्ति धरणीतले।
ताभिराप्यायनं तेषां ये देवत्वं कुले गताः ॥ १० ॥
उद्धृतेष्वथ पिण्डेषु यांश्चान्नकणिका भुवि।
ताभिराप्यायनं प्राप्ता ये तिर्य्यक्त्वं कुले गताः ॥ ११ ॥
ये वा दग्धाः कुले बालाः क्रियायोग्या ह्यसंस्कृताः।
विपन्नास्तेऽन्नविकिरसम्मार्जनजलाशिनः ॥ १२ ॥
भुक्त्वा चाचामतां यच्च जलं यच्चाङ्घ्रिसेचने।
ब्राह्मणानां तथैवान्ये तेन तृप्तिं प्रयान्ति वै ॥ १३ ॥
एवं यो यजमानस्य यश्च तेषां द्विजन्मनां।
कश्चिज्जलान्नविक्षेपः शुचिरुच्छिष्ट एव वा ॥ १४ ॥

तेनान्ये तत्कुले तत्र तत्तद्योन्यन्तरं गताः ।
प्रयान्त्याप्यायनं वत्स सम्यक् श्राद्धक्रियावतां ॥ १५ ॥
अन्यायोपार्जितैरर्थैर्यच्छ्राद्धं क्रियते नरैः ।
तृप्यन्ते तेन चाण्डालपुक्कशाद्यासु योनिषु ॥ १६ ॥
एवमाप्यायनं वत्स बहूनामिह बान्धवैः ।
श्राद्धं कुर्व्वद्भिरन्नाम्बुविन्दुक्षेपेण जायते ॥ १७ ॥
तस्माच्छ्राद्धं नरो भक्त्या शाकैरपि यथा विधि ।
कुर्व्वीत कुर्व्वतः श्राद्धं कुले कश्चिन्न सीदति ॥ १८ ॥
तस्य कालानहं वक्ष्ये नित्यनैमित्तिकात्मकान् ।
विधिना येन च नरैः क्रियते तन्निबोध मे ॥ १९ ॥
कार्य्यं श्राद्धममावास्यां मासि मास्युडुपक्षये ।
तथाष्टकास्वप्यवश्यमिच्छाकालं निबोध मे ॥ २० ॥
विशिष्टब्राह्मणप्राप्तौ सूर्य्येन्दुग्रहणेऽयने ।
विषुवे रविसंक्रान्तौ व्यतिपाते च पुत्रक ॥ २१ ॥
श्राद्धार्हद्रव्यसम्प्राप्तौ तथा दुःस्वप्नदर्शने ।
जन्मर्क्षग्रहपीडासु श्राद्धं कुर्व्वीत चेच्छया ॥ २२ ॥
विशिष्टः श्रोत्रियो योगी वेदविज्ज्येष्ठसामगः ।
त्रिणाचिकेतस्त्रिमधुस्त्रिसुपर्णः षडङ्गवित् ॥ २३ ॥
दौहित्र ऋत्विग्जामातृस्वस्रीयाः श्वशुरस्तथा ।
पञ्चाग्निकर्म्मनिष्ठश्च तपोनिष्ठोऽथ मातुलः ॥ २४ ॥
मातापितृपरश्चैव शिष्यसम्बन्धिबान्धवाः ।
एते द्विजोत्तमाः श्राद्धे समस्ता केतनक्षमाः ॥ २५ ॥

अवकीर्णी तथा रोगी न्यूने चाङ्गे तथाधिके।
पौनर्भवस्तथा काणः कुण्डो गोलोऽथ पुत्त्रक ॥ २६ ॥
मित्त्रध्रुक् कुनखी क्लीवः श्यावदन्तो-निराकृतिः।
अभिशस्तस्तु तातेन पिशुनः सोमविक्रयी ॥ २७ ॥
कन्यादूषयिता वैद्यो गुरुपित्त्रोस्तथोज्झकः।
भृतकाध्यापको मित्त्रः परपूर्व्वापतिस्तथा ॥ २८ ॥
वेदोज्झोऽथाग्निसन्त्यागी वृषलीपतिदूषितः।
तथान्ये च विकर्म्मस्था वर्ज्याः पित्त्र्येषु वै द्विजाः ॥ २९ ॥
निमन्त्रयेत पूर्व्वेद्युः पूर्व्वोक्तान् द्विजसत्तमान्।
दैवे नियोगे पित्त्र्ये च तांस्तथैवोपकल्पयेत् ॥ ३० ॥
तैश्च संयतिभिर्भाव्यं यश्च श्राद्धं करिष्यति।
श्राद्धं दत्वा च भुक्त्वा च मैथुनं योऽनुगच्छति ॥ ३१ ॥
पितरस्तु तयोर्म्मासं तस्मिन्रेतसि शेरते।
गत्वा च योषितं श्राद्धे यो भुङ्क्ते यश्च गच्छति ॥ ३२ ॥
रेतोमूत्रकृताहारास्तन्मासं पितरस्तयोः।
तस्मात्तु प्रथमं कार्य्यं प्राज्ञेनोपनिमन्त्रणं ॥ ३३ ॥
अप्राप्तौ तद्दिने चापि वर्ज्या योषित्प्रसङ्गिनः।
भिक्षार्थमागतान् वापि काले संयमिनो यतीन् ॥ ३४ ॥
भोजयेत् प्रणिपाताद्यैः प्रसाद्य यतमानसः।
यथैव शुक्लपक्षाद्वै पितॄणामसितः प्रियः ॥ ३५ ॥
तथापराह्णः पूर्व्वाह्णात् पितॄणामतिरिच्यते।
संपूज्य स्वागतेनैतानभ्युपेतान् गृहे द्विजान् ॥ ३६ ॥

पवित्रपाणिराचान्तानासनेषूपवेशयेत् ।
पितृणामयुजः कामं युग्मान् दैवे द्विजोत्तमान् ॥ ३७ ॥
एकैकं वा पितृणाञ्च देवानाञ्च स्वशक्तितः ।
तथा मातामहानाञ्च तुल्यं वा वैश्वदेविकं ॥ ३८ ॥
पृथक् तयोस्तथा चान्ये केचिदिच्छन्ति मानवाः ।
प्राङ्मुखान्दैवसंकल्पान् पैत्र्यान् कुर्य्यादुदङ्मुखान् ॥ ३९ ॥
तथैव मातामहानां विधिरुक्तो मनीषिभिः ।
विष्टरार्थं कुशान् दत्वापूज्य चार्घ्यादिना बुधः ॥ ४० ॥
पवित्रकादि वै दत्वा तेभ्योऽनुज्ञामवाप्य च ।
कुर्य्यादावाहनं प्राज्ञो देवानां मन्त्रतो द्विजः ॥ ४१ ॥
यवाम्भोभिस्तथा चार्घ्यं दत्वा वै वैश्वदेविकं ।
गन्धमाल्याम्बुधूपञ्च दत्वा सम्यक् सदीपकं ॥ ४२ ॥
अपसव्यं पितृणाञ्च सर्व्वमेवोपकल्पयेत् ।
दर्भांश्च द्विगुणान्दत्वा तेभ्योऽनुज्ञामवाप्य च ॥ ४३ ॥
मन्त्रपूर्व्वं पितृणाञ्च कुर्य्यादावाहनं बुधः ।
अपसव्यं तथा चार्घ्यं यवार्थञ्च तथा तिलैः ॥ ४४ ॥
निष्पादयेन्महाभाग पितृणां प्रीणने रतः ।
अग्नौ कार्य्यमनुज्ञातः कुरुष्वेति ततो द्विजैः ॥ ४५ ॥
जुहुयाद्व्यञ्जनंक्षारवर्ज्यमन्नं यथाविधि ।
अग्नये कव्यवाहाय स्वाहेति प्रथमाहुतिः ॥ ४६ ॥
सोमाय वै पितृमते स्वाहेत्यन्या तथा भवेत् ।
यमाय प्रेतपतये स्वाहेति त्रितयाहुतिः ॥ ४७ ॥

हुतावशिष्टं दद्याच्च भाजनेषु द्विजन्मनां ।
भाजनालम्भनं कृत्वा दद्याच्चान्नं यथाविधि ॥ ४८ ॥
यथा सुखं जुषध्वं भोयितिवाच्यमनिष्ठुरं ।
भुञ्जीरंश्च ततस्तेऽपि तच्चित्ता मौनिनः सुखं ॥ ४९ ॥
यद्यदिष्टतमं तेषां तत्तदन्नमसत्वरं ।
अक्रुध्यंश्च नरो दद्यात् सम्भवेन प्रलोभयन् ॥ ५० ॥
रक्षोघ्नांश्च जपेन्मन्त्रांस्तिलैश्च विकिरेन्महीं ।
सिद्धार्थकैश्च रक्षार्थं श्राद्धं हि प्रचुरच्छलं ॥ ५१ ॥
पुष्टैस्तृप्तैश्च तृप्ताः स्थ तृप्ताः स्म इति वादिभिः ।
अनुज्ञातो नरस्त्वन्नं प्रकिरेत् भुवि सर्व्वतः ॥ ५२ ॥
तद्वदाचमनार्थाय दद्यादापः सकृत् सकृत् ।
अनुज्ञाश्च ततः प्राप्य यतवाक्कायमानसः ॥ ५३ ॥
सतिलेन ततोऽन्नेन पिण्डान् सव्येन पुत्रक ।
पितॄनुद्दिश्य दर्भेषु दद्यादुच्छिष्टसन्निधौ ॥ ५४ ॥
पितृतीर्थेन तोयञ्च दद्यात्तेभ्यः समाहितः ।
पितॄनुद्दिश्य यद्भक्त्या यजमानो नृपात्मज ॥ ५५ ॥
तद्वन्मातामहानाञ्च दत्वा पिण्डान् यथाविधि ।
गन्धमाल्यादिसंयुक्तं दद्यादाचमनं ततः ॥ ५६ ॥
दत्वा च दक्षिणां शक्त्या सुस्वधास्त्विति तान् वदेत् ।
तैश्च तुष्टैस्तथेत्युक्ता वाचयेद्वैश्वदेविकान् ॥ ५७ ॥
प्रीयन्तामिति भद्रं वो विश्वे देवा इतीरयेन् ।
तथेति चोक्ते तैर्विप्रैः प्रार्थनीयास्तदाशिषः ॥ ५८ ॥

विसर्जयेत् प्रियाण्युक्त्वा प्रणिपत्य च भक्तितः ।
आद्वारमनुगच्छेत्तागच्छेच्चानुप्रमोदितः ॥ ५९ ॥
ततो नित्यक्रियां कुर्य्याद्भोजयेच्च तथातिथीन् ।
नित्यक्रियां पितॄणाञ्च केचिदिच्छन्ति सत्तमाः ॥ ६० ॥
न पितॄणान्तथैवान्ये शेषं पूर्व्ववदाचरेत् ।
पृथक् पाकेन नेत्यन्ये केचित् पूर्व्वञ्च पूर्व्ववत् ॥ ६१ ॥
ततस्तदन्नं भुञ्जीत सह भृत्यादिभिर्न्नरः ।
एवं कुर्व्वीत धर्म्मज्ञः श्राद्धं पित्र्यं समाहितः ॥ ६२ ॥
यथा वा द्विजमुख्यानां परितोषोऽभिजायते ।
त्रीणि श्राद्धे पवित्राणि दौहित्रं कुतपस्तिलाः ॥ ६३ ॥
वर्ज्ज्यानि चाहुर्विप्रेन्द्र कोपोऽध्वगमनं त्वरा ।
राजतञ्च तथा पात्रं शस्तं श्राद्धेषु पुत्रक ॥ ६४ ॥
रजतस्य तथा कार्य्यं दर्शनं दानमेव वा ।
राजते हि स्वधा दुग्धा पितृभिः श्रूयते मही ॥
तस्मात् पितॄणां रजतमभीष्टं प्रीतिवर्द्धनं ॥ ६५ ॥

इति श्रीमार्कण्डेयपुराणेऽलर्कानुशासने पार्व्वणश्राद्धकल्पः ॥ ३१ ॥

द्वात्रिंशोऽध्यायः ॥

मदालसोवाच ॥

अतः परं शृणुष्वेमं पुत्र भक्त्या यदाहृतं ।
पितॄणां प्रीतये यद्वा वर्ज्ज्यं वा प्रीतिकारकं ॥ १ ॥

मासं पितॄणां तृप्तिश्च हविष्यान्नेन जायते ।
मासद्वयं मत्स्यमांसैस्तृप्तिं यान्ति पितामहाः ॥ २ ॥
त्रीन्मासान् हारिणं मांसं विज्ञेयं पितृतृप्तये ।
चतुर्म्मासांस्तु पुष्णाति शशस्य पिशितं पितॄन् ॥ ३ ॥
शाकुनं पञ्च वै मासान् षण्मासान् शूकरामिषं ।
छागलं सप्त वै मासानैणेयञ्चाष्टमासिकीं ॥ ४ ॥
करोति तृप्तिं नव वै रुरोर्म्मांसं न संशयः ।
गवयस्यामिषं तृप्तिं करोति दशमासिकीं ॥ ५ ॥
तथैकादशमासांस्तु औरभ्रं पितृतृप्तिदं ।
संवत्सरं तथा गव्यं पयः पायसमेव वा ॥ ६ ॥
वाध्रीणसामिषं लौहं कालशाकन्तथा मधु ।
दौहित्रामिषमन्यच्च यच्चान्यत् स्वकुलोद्भवैः ॥ ७ ॥
अनन्तां वै प्रयच्छन्ति तृप्तिं गौरी सुतस्तथा ।
पितॄणां नात्र सन्देहो गयाश्राद्धञ्च पुत्रक ॥ ८ ॥
श्यामाकराजश्यामाकौ तद्वच्चैव प्रसातिकाः ।
नीवाराः पौष्कलाश्चैव धान्यानां पितृतृप्तये ॥ ९ ॥
यवव्रीहिसगोधूमतिला मुद्गाः ससर्षपाः ।
प्रियङ्गवः कोविदारा निष्पावाश्चातिशोभनाः ॥ १० ॥
वर्ज्या मर्कटकाः श्राद्धे राजमाषास्तथाणवः ।
विप्रुषिका मसूराश्च श्राद्धकर्म्मणि गर्हिताः ॥ ११ ॥
लशुनं गृञ्जनञ्चैव पलाण्डुं पिण्डमूलकं ।
करम्भं यानि चान्यानि हीनानि रसवर्णतः ॥ १२ ॥

गान्धारिकामलाबूनि लवणान्यूषराणि च ।
आरक्ता ये च निर्य्यासाः प्रत्यक्षलवणानि च ॥ १३ ॥
वर्ज्यान्येतानि वै श्राद्धे यच्च वाचा न शस्यते ।
यच्चोत्कोचादिना प्राप्तं पतिताद्यदुपार्जितं ॥ १४ ॥
अन्यायकन्याशुल्कोत्थं द्रव्यञ्चात्र विगर्हितं ।
दुर्गन्धि फेणिलञ्चाम्बु तथैवाल्पतरोदकं ॥ १५ ॥
न लभेद्यच गौस्तृप्तिं नक्तं यच्चाप्युपाहृतं ।
यन्न सर्व्वापचोत्सृष्टं यच्चाभोज्यं निपानजं ॥ १६ ॥
तद्वर्ज्यं सलिलं तात सदैव पितृकर्म्मणि ।
मार्गमाविकमौष्ट्रञ्च सर्व्वमैकशफञ्च यत् ॥ १७ ॥
माहिषञ्चामरञ्चैव धेन्वा गोश्चाप्यनिर्द्दशं ।
पित्रर्थं मे प्रयच्छस्वेत्युक्ता यच्चाप्युपाहृतं ॥ १८ ॥
वर्ज्जनीयं सदा सद्भिस्तत्पयः श्राद्धकर्म्मणि ।
वर्ज्या जन्तुमती रूक्षा क्षितिः प्लुष्टा तथाग्निना ॥ १९ ॥
अनिष्टदुष्टशब्दोग्रैर्दुर्गन्धा चात्र कर्म्मणि ।
कुलापमानकाः श्राद्धे व्यायुज्य कुलहिंसकाः ॥ २० ॥
नग्नाः पातकिनश्चैव हन्युर्दृष्ट्या पितृक्रियां ।
अपुमानपविद्धश्च कुक्कुटो ग्रामशूकरः ॥ २१ ॥
श्वा चैव हन्ति श्राद्धानि यातुधानाश्च दर्शनात् ।
तस्मात्सुसंवृतो दद्यात्तिलैश्चावकिरन्महीं ॥ २२ ॥
एवं रक्षा भवेच्छ्राद्धे कृता तातोभयोरपि ।
शावसूतकसंस्पृष्टं दीर्घरोगिभिरेव च ॥ २३ ॥

पतितैर्म्मलिनैश्चैव न पुष्णाति पितामहान् ।
वर्जनीयं तथा श्राद्धे तथोदक्याश्च दर्शनं ॥ २४ ॥
मुण्डशौण्डसमाभ्यासो यजमानेन चादरात् ।
केशकीटावपन्नञ्च तथाश्वभिरवेक्षितं ॥ २५ ॥
पूति पर्य्युषितञ्चैव वार्त्ताक्यभिषवांस्तथा ।
वर्जनीयानि वै श्राद्धे यच्च वस्त्रानिलाहतं ॥ २६ ॥
श्रद्धया परया दत्तं पितृणां नामगोत्रतः ।
यदाहारास्तु ते जातास्तदाहारत्वमेति तत् ॥ २७ ॥
तस्मात् श्रद्धावता पात्रे यच्छस्तं पितृकर्म्मणि ।
यथावच्चैव दातव्यं पितृणां तृप्तिमिच्छता ॥ २८ ॥
योगिनश्च सदा श्राद्धे भोजनीया विपश्चिता ।
योगाधारा हि पितरस्तस्मात्तान् पूजयेत् सदा ॥ २९ ॥
ब्राह्मणानां सहस्रेभ्यो योगी त्वग्राशनो यदि ।
यजमानञ्च भोक्तृंश्च नौरिवाम्भसि तारयेत् ॥ ३० ॥
पितृगाथास्तथैवात्र गीयन्ते ब्रह्मवादिभिः ।
या गीताः पितृभिः पूर्व्वमैलस्यासीन्महीपतेः ॥ ३१ ॥
कदा नः सन्ततावग्र्यः कस्यचिद्भविता सुतः ।
यो योगिभुक्तशेषान्नो भुवि पिण्डं प्रदास्यति ॥ ३२ ॥
गयायामथवा पिण्डं खड्गमांसं महाहविः ।
कालशाकं तिलाढ्यं वा कृसरं मासतृप्तये ॥ ३३ ॥
वैश्वदेवञ्च सौम्यञ्च खड्गमांसं परं हविः ।
विषाणवर्ज्ज्यं खड्गाप्या आसूर्य्यञ्चाश्नुवामहे ॥ ३४ ॥

दद्यात् श्राद्धं त्रयोदश्यां मघासु च यथाविधि ।
मधुसर्प्पिःसमायुक्तं पायसं दक्षिणायने ॥ ३५ ॥
तस्मात् सम्पूजयेत् भक्त्या स्वपितॄन् पुत्र मानवः ।
कामानभीप्सन् सकलान् पापाच्चात्मविमोचनं ॥ ३६ ॥
वसून् रुद्रांस्तथादित्यान्नक्षत्रग्रहतारकाः ।
प्रीणयन्ति मनुष्याणां पितरः श्राद्धतर्पिताः ॥ ३७ ॥
आयुः प्रज्ञां धनं विद्यां स्वर्गं मोक्षं सुखानि च ।
प्रयच्छन्ति तथा राज्यं पितरः श्राद्धतर्पिताः ॥ ३८ ॥
एतत्ते पुत्र कथितं श्राद्धकर्म्म यथोदितं ।
काम्यानां श्रूयतां वत्स श्राद्धानां तिथिकीर्त्तनं ॥ ३९ ॥

इति श्रीमार्कण्डेयपुराणे श्राद्धकल्पः ॥ ३२ ॥

त्रयस्त्रिंशोऽध्यायः ॥

सदालसोवाच ॥

प्रतिपद्धनलाभाय द्वितीया द्विपदप्रदा ।
वरार्थिनी तृतीया तु चतुर्थी शत्रुनाशिनी ॥ १ ॥
श्रियं प्राप्नोति पञ्चम्यां षष्ठ्यां पूज्यो भवेन्नरः ।
गाणाधिपत्यं सप्तम्यामष्टम्यां वृद्धिमुत्तमां ॥ २ ॥
स्त्रियो नवम्यां प्राप्नोति दशम्यां पूर्णकामतां ।
वेदांस्तथाप्नुयात् सर्व्वानेकादश्यां क्रियापरः ॥ ३ ॥

द्वादश्यां जयलाभञ्च प्राप्नोति पितृपूजकः ।
प्रजां मेधां पशुं वृद्धिं स्वातन्त्र्यं पुष्टिमुत्तमां ॥ ४ ॥
दीर्घमायुरथैश्वर्य्यं कुर्व्वाणस्तु त्रयोदशीं ।
अवाप्नोति न सन्देहः श्राद्धं श्रद्धापरो नरः ॥ ५ ॥
यथा संभावितान्नेन श्राद्धसम्पत्समन्वितः ।
युवानः पितरो यस्य मृताः शस्त्रेण वा हताः ॥ ६ ॥
तेन कार्य्यं चतुर्द्दश्यां तेषां प्रीतिमभीप्सता ।
श्राद्धं कुर्व्वन्नमावस्यां यत्नेन पुरुषः शुचिः ॥ ७ ॥
सर्व्वान् कामानवाप्नोति स्वर्गञ्चानन्तमश्नुते ।
कृत्तिकासु पितॄनर्च्च्य स्वर्गमाप्नोति मानवः ॥ ८ ॥
अपत्यकामो रोहिण्यां सौम्ये चौजस्वितां लभेत् ।
शौर्य्यमार्द्रासु चाप्नोति क्षेत्रादि च पुनर्व्वसौ ॥ ९ ॥
पुष्टिं पुष्ये सदाभ्यर्च्च्य अश्लेषासु वरान् सुतान् ।
मघासु स्वजनश्रैष्ठ्यं सौभाग्यं फल्गुणीषु च ॥ १० ॥
प्रदानशीलो भवति सापत्यश्चोत्तरासु च ।
प्रयाति श्रेष्ठतां सत्यं हस्ते श्राद्धप्रदो नरः ॥ ११ ॥
रूपयुक्तश्च चित्रासु तथापत्यान्यवाप्नुयात् ।
वाणिज्यलाभदा स्वातिर्व्विशाखा पुत्रकामदा ॥ १२ ॥
कुर्व्वन्तश्चानुराधासु लभन्ते चक्रवर्त्तितां ।
आधिपत्यञ्च ज्येष्ठासु मूले चारोग्यमुत्तमं ॥ १३ ॥
आषाढासु यशःप्राप्तिरुत्तरासु विशोकता ।
श्रवणे च शुभान् लोकान् धनिष्ठासु धनं महत् ॥ १४ ॥

वेदविस्त्वमभिजिति भिषक्सिद्धिन्तु वारुणे ।
अजाविकं प्रौष्ठपदे विन्देद्गावांस्तथोत्तरे ॥ १५ ॥
रेवतीषु तथा कुप्यमश्विनीषु तुरङ्गमान् ।
श्राद्धं कुर्व्वंस्तथाप्नोति भरणीष्वायुरुत्तमं ॥
तस्मात् काम्यानि कुर्व्वीत ऋक्षेष्वेतेषु तत्त्ववित् ॥ १६ ॥

इति श्रीमार्कण्डेयपुराणे काम्यश्राद्धफलकथनं ॥ ३३ ॥

चतुस्त्रिंशोऽध्यायः ॥

मदालसोवाच ॥

एवं पुत्र गृहस्थेन देवताः पितरस्तथा ।
संपूज्या हव्यकव्याभ्यामन्नेनातिथिबान्धवाः ॥ १ ॥
भूतानि भृत्याः सकलाः पशुपक्षिपिपीलिकाः ।
भिक्षवो याचमानाश्च ये चान्ये वसता गृहे ॥ २ ॥
सदाचारवता तात साधुना गृहमेधिना ।
पापं भुङ्क्ते समुल्लङ्घ्य नित्यनैमित्तिकीः क्रियाः ॥ ३ ॥

अलर्क उवाच ॥

कथितं मे त्वया मातर्नित्यं नैमित्तिकञ्च यत् ।
नित्यनैमित्तिकञ्चैव त्रिविधं कर्म्म पौरुषं ॥ ४ ॥
सदाचारमहं श्रोतुमिच्छामि कुलनन्दिनि ।
यत् कुर्व्वन् सुखमाप्नोति परत्रेह च मानवः ॥ ५ ॥

मदालसोवाच ॥

गृहस्थेन सदा कार्य्यमाचारपरिपालनं ।
न ह्याचारविहीनस्य सुखमत्र परत्र वा ॥ ६ ॥
यज्ञदानतपांसीह पुरुषस्य न भूतये ।
भवन्ति यः सदाचारं समुल्लङ्घ्य प्रवर्त्तते ॥ ७ ॥
दुराचारो हि पुरुषो नेहायुर्विन्दते महत् ।
कार्य्यो यत्नः सदाचारे आचारो हन्त्यलक्षणं ॥ ८ ॥
तस्य स्वरूपं वक्ष्यामि सदाचारस्य पुत्रक ।
तन्ममैकमनाः श्रुत्वा तथैव परिपालय ॥ ९ ॥
त्रिवर्गसाधने यत्नः कर्त्तव्यो गृहमेधिना ।
तत्संसिद्धौ गृहस्थस्य सिद्धिरत्र परत्र च ॥ १० ॥
पादेनार्थस्य पारत्र्यं कुर्य्यात् सञ्चयमात्मवान् ।
अर्द्धेन चात्मभरणन्नित्यनैमित्तिकान्वितं ॥ ११ ॥
पादञ्चात्मार्थमायस्य मूलभूतं विवर्द्धयेत् ।
एवमाचरतः पुत्र अर्थः साफल्यमर्हति ॥ १२ ॥
तद्वत् पापनिषेधार्थं धर्म्मः कार्य्यो विपश्चिता ।
परत्रार्थं तथैवान्यः काम्योऽत्रैव फलप्रदः ॥ १३ ॥
प्रत्यवायभयात् काम्यस्तथान्यश्चाविरोधवान् ।
द्विधा कामोऽपि गदितस्त्रिवर्गस्याविरोधतः ॥ १४ ॥
परम्परानुबन्धांश्च सर्व्वानेतान् विचिन्तयेत् ।
विपरीतानुबन्धांश्च धर्म्मादींस्तान् शृणुष्व मे ॥ १५ ॥
धर्म्मो धर्म्मानुबन्धार्थो धर्म्मो नात्मार्थबाधकः ।

उभाभ्याञ्च द्विधा कामस्तेन तौ च द्विधा पुनः ॥ १६ ॥
ब्राह्मे मुहूर्त्ते बुध्येत धर्म्मार्थौ चापि चिन्तयेत् ।
समुत्थाय तथाचम्य प्राङ्मुखो नियतः शुचिः ॥ १७ ॥
पूर्व्वां सन्ध्यां सनक्षत्रां पश्चिमां सदिवाकरां ।
उपासीत यथान्यायं नैनां जह्यादनापदि ॥ १८ ॥
असत्प्रलापमनृतं वाक्पारुष्यञ्च वर्जयेत् ।
असच्छास्त्रमसद्वादमसत्सेवाञ्च पुत्रक ॥ १९ ॥
सायं प्रातस्तथा होमं कुर्व्वीत नियतात्मवान् ।
नोदयास्तमने विम्बमुदीक्षेत विवस्वतः ॥ २० ॥
केशप्रसाधनादर्शदर्शनं दन्तधावनं ।
पूर्व्वाह्न एव कार्य्याणि देवतानाञ्च तर्पणं ॥ २१ ॥
ग्रामावसथतीर्थानां क्षेत्राणाञ्चैव वर्त्मनि ।
विण्मूत्रं नानुतिष्ठेत न कृष्टे न च गोव्रजे ॥ २२ ॥
नग्नां परस्त्रियं नेक्षेन्न पश्येदात्मनः शकृत् ।
उदक्या दर्शनं स्पर्शो वर्ज्यं संभाषणन्तथा ॥ २३ ॥
नाप्सु मूत्रं पुरीषं वा मैथुनं वा समाचरेत् ।
नाधितिष्ठेच्छकृन्मूत्रकेशभस्मकपालिकाः ॥ २४ ॥
तुषाङ्गारास्थिशीर्णानि रज्जुवस्त्रादिकानि च ।
नाधितिष्ठेत्तथा प्राज्ञः पथि चैवन्तथा भुवि ॥ २५ ॥
पितृदेवमनुष्याणां भूतानाञ्च तथार्च्चनं ।
कृत्वा विभवतः पश्चाद्गृहस्थो भोक्तुमर्हति ॥ २६ ॥
प्राङ्मुखोदङ्मुखोवापि स्वाचान्तो वाग्यतः शुचिः ।

भुञ्जीतान्नञ्च तच्चित्तो ह्यन्तर्जानुः सदा नरः ॥ २७ ॥
उपघाताद्दृते दोषं नान्यस्योदीरयेद्बुधः ।
प्रत्यक्षलवणं वर्ज्यमन्नमत्युष्णमेव च ॥ २८ ॥
न गच्छन्न च तिष्ठन् वै विण्मूत्रोत्सर्गमात्मवान् ।
कुर्व्वीत नैव चाचामन् यत् किञ्चिदपि भक्षयेत् ॥ २९ ॥
उच्छिष्टो नालपेत् किञ्चित् स्वाध्यायञ्च विवर्जयेत् ।
गां ब्राह्मणं तथा चाग्निं स्वमूर्द्धानञ्च न स्पृशेत् ॥ ३० ॥
न च पश्येद्रविं नेन्दुं न नक्षत्राणि कामतः ।
भिन्नासनं तथा शय्यां भाजनञ्च विवर्जयेत् ॥ ३१ ॥
गुरूणामासनं देयमभ्युत्थानादिसत्कृतं ।
अनुकूलं तथालापमभिवादनपूर्व्वकं ॥ ३२ ॥
तथानुगमनं कुर्य्यात् प्रतिकूलं न संजपेत् ।
नैकवस्त्रश्च भुञ्जीत न कुर्य्याद्देवतार्च्चनं ॥ ३३ ॥
न वाहयेद्द्विजान्नाग्नौ मेहं कुर्व्वीत बुद्धिमान् ।
स्नायीत न नरो नग्नो न शयीत कदाचन ॥ ३४ ॥
न पाणिभ्यामुभाभ्याञ्च कण्डूयेत शिरस्तथा ।
न चाभीक्ष्णं शिरःस्नानं कार्य्यं निष्कारणं नरैः ॥ ३५ ॥
शिरःस्नातश्च तैलेन नाङ्गं किञ्चिदपि स्पृशेत् ।
अनध्यायेषु सर्व्वेषु स्वाध्यायञ्च विवर्ज्जयेत् ॥ ३६ ॥
ब्राह्मणानिलगोसूर्य्यान्न मेहेत कदाचन ।
उदङ्मुखो दिवा रात्रावुत्सर्गं दक्षिणामुखः ॥ ३७ ॥
आबाधासु यथाकामं कुर्य्यान्मूत्रपुरीषयोः ।

दुष्कृतं न गुरोर्ब्रूयात् क्रुद्धं चैनं प्रसादयेत् ॥ ३८ ॥
परिवादं न शृणुयादन्येषामपि कुर्व्वतां ।
पन्था देयो ब्राह्मणानां राज्ञो दुःखातुरस्य च ॥ ३९ ॥
विद्याधिकस्य गुर्व्विण्या भारार्त्तस्य यवीयसः ।
मूकान्धबधिराणाञ्च मत्तस्योन्मत्तकस्य च ॥ ४० ॥
पुंश्चल्याः कृतवैरस्य बालस्य पतितस्य च ।
देवालयं चैत्यतरुं तथैव च चतुष्पथं ॥ ४१ ॥
विद्याधिकं गुरुं देवं बुधः कुर्य्यात् प्रदक्षिणं ।
उपानद्वस्त्रमाल्यादि धृतमन्यैर्न धारयेत् ॥ ४२ ॥
उपवीतमलङ्कारं करकञ्चैव वर्जयेत् ।
चतुर्द्दश्यान्तथाष्टम्यां पञ्चदश्याञ्च पर्व्वसु ॥ ४३ ॥
तैलाभ्यङ्गं तथा भोगं योषितश्च विवर्जयेत् ।
न क्षिप्तपादजङ्घश्च प्राज्ञस्तिष्ठेत् कदाचन ॥ ४४ ॥
न चापि विक्षिपेत् पादौ पादं पादेन नाक्रमेत् ।
मर्म्माभिघातमाक्रोशं पैशुन्यञ्च विवर्जयेत् ॥ ४५ ॥
दम्भाभिमानतीक्ष्णानि न कुर्व्वीत विचक्षणः ।
मूर्खोन्मत्तव्यसनिनो विरूपान्मायिनस्तथा ॥ ४६ ॥
न्यूनाङ्गांश्चाधिकाङ्गांश्च नोपहासैर्व्विदूषयेत् ।
परस्य दण्डं नोद्यच्छेच्छिक्षार्थं पुत्त्रशिष्ययोः ॥ ४७ ॥
तद्वन्नोपविशेत् प्राज्ञः पादेनाक्रम्य चासनं ।
संयावं कृषरं मांसं नात्मार्थमुपसाधयेत् ॥ ४८ ॥
सायं प्रातश्च भोक्तव्यं कृत्वा चातिथिपूजनं ।

प्राङ्मुखोदङ्मुखोवापि वाग्यतो दन्तधावनं ॥ ४९ ॥
कुर्व्वीत सततं वत्स वर्ज्जयेद्वर्ज्ज्यवीरुधः ।
नोदक्शिराः स्वपेज्जातु न च प्रत्यक्शिरा नरः ॥ ५० ॥
शिरस्यगस्त्यमास्थाय शयीताथ पुरन्दरं ।
न तु गन्धवतीष्वप्सु स्नायीत न तथा निशि ॥ ५१ ॥
उपरागे परं स्नानमृते दिनमुदाहृतं ।
अपमृज्यान्न चास्नातो गात्राण्यम्बरपाणिभिः ॥ ५२ ॥
न चापि धूनयेत्केशान् वाससी न च धूनयेत् ।
नानुलेपनमादद्यादस्नातः कर्हिचिद्बुधः ॥ ५३ ॥
न चापि रक्तवासाः स्याच्चित्रासितधरोऽपि वा ।
न च कुर्य्याद्विपर्य्यासं वाससोर्नापि भूषणे ॥ ५४ ॥
वर्ज्यञ्च विदशं वस्त्रमत्यन्तोपहतञ्च यत् ।
केशकीटावपन्नञ्च चुम्बां श्वभिरवेक्षितं ॥ ५५ ॥
अवलीढावपन्नञ्च सारोद्धरणदूषितं ।
पृष्ठमांसं वृथामांसं वर्ज्ज्यमांसञ्च पुत्रक ॥ ५६ ॥
न भक्षयीत सततं प्रत्यक्षलवणानि च ।
वर्ज्यं चिरोषितं पुत्र भक्तं पर्य्युषितञ्च यत् ॥ ५७ ॥
पिष्टशाकेक्षुपयसां विकारान्नृपनन्दन ।
तथा मांसविकारांश्च ते च वर्ज्याश्चिरोषिताः ॥ ५८ ॥
उदयास्तमने भानोः शयनञ्च विवर्जयेत् ।
नास्नातो नैव संविष्टो न चैवान्यमना नरः ॥ ५९ ॥
न चैव शयने नोर्व्व्यामुपविष्टो न शब्दवत् ।

न चैकवस्त्रो न वदन् प्रेक्षतामप्रदाय च ॥ ६० ॥
भुञ्जीत पुरुषः स्नातः सायं प्रातर्यथाविधि ।
परदारा न गन्तव्याः पुरुषेण विपश्चिता ॥ ६१ ॥
इष्टापूर्त्तायुषां हन्त्री परदारगतिर्न्नृणां ।
न हीदृशमनायुष्यं लोके किञ्चन विद्यते ॥ ६२ ॥
यादृशं पुरुषस्येह परदाराभिमर्षणं ।
देवार्च्चनाग्निकार्य्याणि तथा गुर्व्वभिवादनं ॥ ६३ ॥
कुर्व्वीत सम्यगाचम्य तद्वदन्नभुजिक्रियां ।
अफेनाभिरगन्धाभिरद्भिरच्छाभिरादरात् ॥ ६४ ॥
आचामेत् पुत्र पुण्याभिः प्राङ्मुखोदङ्मुखोऽपि वा ।
अन्तर्जलादावसथाद्वल्मीकान्मूषिकस्थलात् ॥ ६५ ॥
कृतशौचावशिष्टाश्च वर्जयेत् पञ्च वै मृदः ।
प्रक्षाल्य हस्तौ पादौ च समभ्युक्ष्य समाहितः ॥ ६६ ॥
अन्तर्जानुस्तथाचामेत्त्रिश्चतुर्व्वा पिवेदपः ।
परिमृज्य द्विरांस्यान्तं खानि मूर्द्धानमेव च ॥ ६७ ॥
सम्यगाचम्य तोयेन क्रियां कुर्व्वीत वै शुचिः ।
देवतानामृषीणाञ्च पितॄणाञ्चैव यत्नतः ॥ ६८ ॥
समाहितमना भूत्वा कुर्व्वीत सततं नरः ।
क्षुत्त्वा निष्ठीव्य वासश्च परिधायाचमेद्बुधः ॥ ६९ ॥
क्षुतेऽवलिढे वान्ते च तथा निष्ठीवनादिषु ।
कुर्य्यादाचमनं स्पर्शं गोपृष्ठस्यार्कदर्शनं ॥ ७० ॥
कुर्व्वीतालम्भनं चापि दक्षिणश्रवणस्य वै ।

यथा विभवतो ह्येतत् पूर्व्वाभावे ततः परं ॥ ७१ ॥
अविद्यमाने पूर्व्वोक्ते उत्तरप्राप्तिरिष्यते ।
न कुर्य्याद्दन्तसङ्घर्षं नात्मनो देहताडनं ॥ ७२ ॥
स्वप्नाध्ययनभोज्यानि सन्ध्ययोश्च विवर्जयेत् ।
सन्ध्यायां मैथुनञ्चापि तथा प्रस्थानमेव च ॥ ७३ ॥
पूर्व्वाह्णे तात देवानां मनुष्याणाञ्च मध्यमे ।
भक्त्या तथापराह्णे च कुर्व्वीत पितृपूजनं ॥ ७४ ॥
शिरःस्नातश्च कुर्व्वीत दैवं पैत्र्यमथापि वा ।
प्राङ्मुखोदङ्मुखो वापि श्मश्रुकर्म्म च कारयेत् ॥ ७५ ॥
व्यङ्गिनीं वर्जयेत् कन्यां कुलजामपि रोगिणीं ।
विकृतां पिङ्गलाञ्चैव वाचाटां सर्व्वदूषितां ॥ ७६ ॥
अव्यङ्गीं सौम्यनासाञ्च सर्व्वलक्षणलक्षितां ।
तादृशीमुद्वहेत् कन्यां श्रेयःकामो नरः सदा ॥ ७७ ॥
उद्वहेत् पितृमातृोश्च सप्तमीं पञ्चमीन्तथा ।
रक्षेद्दारान् त्यजेदीर्षां दिवा च स्वप्नमैथुने ॥ ७८ ॥
परोपतापकं कर्म्म जन्तुपीडाञ्च वर्जयेत् ।
उदक्या सर्व्ववर्णानां वर्ज्या रात्रिचतुष्टयं ॥ ७९ ॥
स्त्रीजन्मपरिहारार्थं पञ्चमीमपि वर्जयेत् ।
ततः षष्ठ्यां व्रजेद्रात्र्यां श्रेष्ठा युग्मासु पुत्रक ॥ ८० ॥
युग्मासु पुत्रा जायन्ते स्त्रियोऽयुग्मासु रात्रिषु ।
तस्माद्युग्मासु पुत्रार्थी संविशेत सदा नरः ॥ ८१ ॥
विधर्म्मिणोऽह्नि पूर्व्वाख्ये सन्ध्याकाले च पण्ड्काः ।

क्षुरकर्म्मणि वान्ते च स्त्रीसम्भोगे च पुत्त्रक ॥ ८२ ॥
स्नायीत चेलवान् प्राज्ञः कटभूमिमुपेत्य च ।
देववेदद्विजातीनां साधुसत्यमहात्मनां ॥ ८३ ॥
गुरोः पतिव्रतानाञ्च तथा यज्वितपस्विनां ।
परिवादं न कुर्व्वीत परिहासञ्च पुत्त्रक ॥ ८४ ॥
कुर्व्वतामविनीतानां न श्रोतव्यं कथञ्चन ।
नोत्कृष्टशय्यासनयोर्न्नापकृष्टस्य चारुहेत् ॥ ८५ ॥
न चामङ्गल्यवेशः स्यान्न चामङ्गल्यवाग्भवेत् ।
धवलाम्बरसंवीतः सितपुष्पविभूषितः ॥ ८६ ॥
नोद्धूतोन्मत्तमूढैश्च नाविनीतैश्च पण्डितः ।
गच्छेन्मैत्रीं न चाशीलैर्न च चौर्य्यादिदूषितैः ॥ ८७ ॥
न चातिव्ययशीलैश्च न लुब्धैर्नापि वैरिभिः ।
न बन्धकीभिर्न न्यूनैर्बन्धकीपतिभिस्तथा ॥ ८८ ॥
सार्द्धं न बलिभिः कुर्य्यान्न च न्यूनैर्न निन्दितैः ।
न सर्व्वशङ्किभिर्न्नित्यं न च दैवपरैर्नरैः ॥ ८९ ॥
कुर्व्वीत साधुभिर्मैत्रीं सदाचारावलम्बिभिः ।
प्राज्ञैरपिशुनैः शक्तैः कर्म्मण्युद्योगभागिभिः ॥ ॥ ९० ॥
सुहृद्दीक्षितभूपालस्नातकश्वशुरैः सह ।
ऋत्विगादीन् षडर्घार्हानर्च्चयेच्च गृहागतान् ॥ ९१ ॥
यथा विभवतः पुत्त्र द्विजान् संवत्सरोषितान् ।
अर्च्चयेन्मधुपर्केण यथाकालमतन्द्रितः ॥ ९२ ॥
तिष्ठेच्च शासने तेषां श्रेयस्कामो द्विजोत्तमः ।

न च तान् विवदेद्धीमानाक्रुष्टश्चापि तैः सदा ॥ ९३ ॥
सम्यग्गृहार्च्चनं कृत्वा यथास्थानमनुक्रमात् ।
सम्पूजयेत्ततो वह्निं दद्याच्चैवाहुतीः क्रमात् ॥ ९४ ॥
प्रथमां ब्रह्मणे दद्यात् प्रजानां पतये ततः ।
तृतीयाञ्चैव गुह्येभ्यः कश्यपाय तथापरां ॥ ९५ ॥
ततोऽनुमतये दत्त्वा दद्याद्गृहवलिन्ततः ।
पूर्व्वाख्यातं मया यत्ते नित्यकर्म्मक्रियाविधौ ॥ ९६ ॥
वैश्वदेवन्ततः कुर्य्याद्वलयस्तच मे शृणु ।
यथास्थानविभागन्तु देवानुद्दिश्य वै पृथक् ॥ ९७ ॥
पर्ज्जन्याय धरित्रीणां दद्याच्च मणके चयं ।
वायवे च प्रतिदिशं दिग्भ्यः प्राच्यादितः क्रमात् ॥ ९८ ॥
ब्रह्मणे चान्तरीक्षाय सूर्य्याय च यथाक्रमं ।
विश्वेभ्यश्चैव देवेभ्यो विश्वभूतेभ्य एव च ॥ ९९ ॥
उषसे भूतपतये दद्याच्चोत्तरतस्ततः ।
स्वधा नम इतीत्युक्त्वा पितृभ्यश्चापि दक्षिणे ॥ १०० ॥
कृत्वापसव्यं वायव्यां यक्ष्मैतत्तेति भाजनात् ।
अन्नावशेषमिच्छन् वै तोयं दद्याद्यथाविधि ॥ १०१ ॥
ततोऽन्नाग्रं समुद्धृत्य हन्तकारोपकल्पनं ।
यथाविधि यथान्यायं ब्राह्मणायोपपादयेत् ॥ १०२ ॥
कुर्य्यात् कर्म्माणि तीर्थेन स्वेन स्वेन यथाविधि ।
देवादीनान्तथा कुर्य्याद्ब्राह्मेणाचमनक्रियां ॥ १०३ ॥
अङ्गुष्ठोत्तरतो रेखा पाण्यां दक्षिणस्य तु ।

एतद्ब्राह्ममिति ख्यातं तीर्थमाचमनाय वै ॥ १०४ ॥
तर्ज्जन्यङ्गुष्ठयोरन्तः पैत्र्यं तीर्थमुदाहृतं ।
पितृणां तेन तोयादि दद्यान्नान्दीमखादृते ॥ १०५ ॥
अङ्गुल्यग्रे तथा दैवं तेन दिव्यक्रियाविधिः ।
तीर्थं कनिष्ठिकामूले कायं तेन प्रजापतेः ॥ १०६ ॥
एवमेभिः सदा तीर्थैर्द्देवानां पितृभिः सह ।
सदा कार्य्याणि कुर्व्वीत नान्यतीर्थेन कर्हिचित् ॥ १०७ ॥
ब्राह्मेणाचमनं शस्तं पित्र्यं पैत्र्येण सर्व्वदा ।
देवतीर्थेन देवानां प्राजापत्यं निजेन च ॥ १०८ ॥
नान्दीमुखानां कुर्व्वीत प्राज्ञः पिण्डोदकक्रियां ।
प्राजापत्येन तीर्थेन यच्च किञ्चित् प्रजापतेः ॥ १०९ ॥
युगपज्जलमग्निञ्च बिभृयान्न विचक्षणः ।
गुरुदेवान् प्रति तथा न च पादौ प्रसारयेत् ॥ ११० ॥
नाचक्षीत धयन्तीं गां जलं नाञ्जलिना पिबेत् ।
शौचकालेषु सर्व्वेषु गुरुष्वल्पेषु वा पुनः ॥ १११ ॥
न विलम्बेत शौचार्थं न मुखेनानलं धमेत् ।
तत्र पुत्र न वस्तव्यं यत्र नास्ति चतुष्टयं ॥ ११२ ॥
ऋणप्रदाता वैद्यश्च श्रोत्रियः सजला नदी ।
जितामित्रो नृपो यत्र बलवान् धर्म्मतत्परः ॥ ११३ ॥
तत्र नित्यं वसेत् प्राज्ञः कुतः कुनृपतौ सुखं ।
यत्राप्रधृष्यो नृपतिर्यत्र शस्यवती मही ॥ ११४ ॥
पौराः सुसंयता यत्र सततं न्यायवर्त्तिनः ।

यत्रामत्सरिणो लोकास्तत्र वासः सुखोदयः ॥ ११५ ॥
यस्मिन् कृषीबला राष्ट्रे प्रायशो नातिभोगिनः ।
यत्रौषधान्यशेषाणि वसेत्तत्र विचक्षणः ॥ ११६ ॥
तत्र पुत्र न वस्तव्यं यत्रैतत्त्रितयं सदा ।
जिगीषुः पूर्व्ववैरश्च जनश्च सततोत्सवः ॥ ११७ ॥
वसेन्नित्यं सुशीलेषु सहवासिषु पण्डितः ।
इत्येतत् कथितं पुत्र मया ते हितकाम्यया ॥ ११८ ॥

इति श्रीमार्कण्डेयपुराणे अलर्कानुशासने सदाचाराध्यायः ॥ ३४ ॥

पञ्चत्रिंशोऽध्यायः ॥

मदालसोवाच ॥

अतःपरं शृणुष्व त्वं वर्ज्यावर्ज्यप्रतिक्रियां ।
भोज्यमन्नं पर्य्युषितं स्नेहाक्तं चिरसम्भृतं ॥ १ ॥
अस्नेहाश्चापि गोधूमयवगोरसविक्रियाः ।
शशकः कच्छपो गोधा श्वावित् खड्गोऽथ पुत्रक ॥ २ ॥
भक्ष्या ह्येते तथा वर्ज्यौ ग्रामशूकरकुक्कुटौ ।
पितृदेवादिशेषश्च श्राद्धे ब्राह्मणकाम्यया ॥ ३ ॥
प्रोक्षितञ्चौषधार्थञ्च खादन्मांसं न दुष्यति ।
शङ्खाश्मस्वर्णरूप्याणां रज्जूनामथ वाससां ॥ ४ ॥

शाकमूलफलानाञ्च तथा विदलचर्म्मणां।
मणिवज्रप्रवालानान्तथा मुक्ताफलस्य च॥ ५॥
गात्राणाञ्च मनुष्याणामम्बुना शौचमिष्यते।
यथायसानां तोयेन ग्राव्णः संघर्षणेन च॥ ६॥
सस्नेहानाञ्च भाण्डानां शुद्धिरुष्णेन वारिणा।
सूर्पधान्याजिनानाञ्च मुषलोलूखलस्य च॥ ७॥
संहतानाञ्च वस्त्राणां प्रोक्षणात् सञ्चयस्य च।
वल्कलानामशेषाणामम्बुमृच्छौचमिष्यते॥ ८॥
तृणकाष्ठौषधीनाञ्च प्रोक्षणाच्छुद्धिरिष्यते।
आविकानां समस्तानां केशानाञ्चापि मेध्यता॥ ९॥
सिद्धार्थकानां कल्केन तिलकल्केन वा पुनः।
साम्बुना तात भवति उपघातवतां सदा॥ १०॥
तथा कार्पासिकानाञ्च विशुद्धिर्जलभस्मना।
दारुदन्तास्थिशृङ्गाणां तक्षणाच्छुद्धिरिष्यते॥ ११॥
पुनः पाकेन भाण्डानां पार्थिवानाञ्च मेध्यता।
शुचिर्भैक्षं कारुहस्तः पण्यं योषिन्मुखं तथा॥ १२॥
रथ्यागतमविज्ञातं दासवर्गादिनाहृतं।
वाक्प्रशस्तं चिरातीतमनेकान्तरितं लघु॥ १३॥
अतिप्रभूतं बालञ्च वृद्धातुरविचेष्टितं।
कर्म्मान्ताङ्गारशालाश्च स्तनन्धयसुताः स्त्रियः॥ १४॥
शुचिन्यश्च तथैवापः स्रवन्त्योऽगन्धबुद्बुदाः।
भूमिर्विशुध्यते कालाद्दहमार्जनगोक्रमैः॥ १५॥

लेपादुल्लेखनात् सेकाद्वेश्मसंमार्ज्जनार्च्चनात् ।
केशकीटावपन्ने च गोघ्राते मक्षिकान्विते ॥ १६ ॥
मृदम्बुभस्मना तात प्रोक्षितव्यं विशुद्धये ।
औदुम्बराणामम्लेन क्षारेण त्रपुसीसयोः ॥ १७ ॥
भस्माम्बुभिश्च कांस्यानां शुद्धिः प्लावा द्रवस्य च ।
अमेध्याक्तस्य मृत्तोयैर्गन्धापहरणेन च ॥ १८ ॥
अन्येषाञ्चैव तद्द्रव्यैर्वर्णगन्धापहारतः ।
शुचि गोतृप्तिकृत्तोयं प्रकृतिस्थं महीगतं ॥ १९ ॥
तथा मांसञ्च चण्डालक्रव्यादादिनिपातितं ।
रथ्यागतञ्च चेलादि तात वाताच्छुचि स्मृतं ॥ २० ॥
रजोऽग्निरश्वो गौश्छाया रश्मयः पवनो मही ।
विप्रुषो मक्षिकाद्याश्च दुष्टसङ्गाददोषिणः ॥ २१ ॥
अजाश्वौ मुखतो मेध्यौ न गोर्वत्सस्य चाननं ।
मातुः प्रस्रवणे मेध्यं शकुनिः फलपातने ॥ २२ ॥
आसनं शयनं यानं नावः पथि तृणानि च ।
सोमसूर्य्यांशुपवनैः शुध्यन्ते तानि पण्यवत् ॥ २३ ॥
रथ्यावसर्पणस्नानक्षुत्पानम्लानकर्म्मसु ।
आचामेत यथान्यायं वासो विपरिधाय च ॥ २४ ॥
स्पृष्टानामप्यसंसर्गैर्विरथ्याकर्द्दमाम्भसां ।
पक्वेष्टरचितानाञ्च मेध्यता वायुसङ्गमात् ॥ २५ ॥
प्रभूतोपहतादन्नादग्रमुद्धृत्य सन्त्यजेत् ।
शेषस्य प्रोक्षणं कुर्य्यादाचम्याद्भिस्तथा मृदा ॥ २६ ॥

उपवासस्त्रिरात्रन्तु दुष्टभक्ताशिनो भवेत् ।
अज्ञाते ज्ञानपूर्व्वन्तु तद्दोषोपशमेन तु ॥ २७ ॥
उदक्याश्वशृगालादीन् सुतिकान्त्यावसायिनः ।
स्पृष्ट्वा स्नायीत शौचार्थं तथैव मृतहारिणः ॥ २८ ॥
नारं स्पृष्ट्वास्थि सस्नेहं स्नातः शुद्ध्यति मानवः ।
आचम्यैव तु निःस्नेहं गामालभ्यार्कमीक्ष्य वा ॥ २९ ॥
न लङ्घयेत्तथैवासृक्ष्ठीवनोद्वर्त्तनानि च ।
नोद्यानादौ विकालेषु प्राज्ञस्तिष्ठेत् कदाचन ॥ ३० ॥
न चालपेज्जनद्विष्टां वीरहीनान्तथा स्त्रियं ।
गृहादुच्छिष्टविण्मूत्रपादाम्भांसि क्षिपेद्बहिः ॥ ३१ ॥
पञ्च पिण्डाननुद्धृत्य न स्नायात् परवारिणि ।
स्नायीत देवखातेषु गङ्गाह्रदसरित्सु च ॥ ३२ ॥
देवतापितृसच्छास्त्रयज्ञमन्त्रादिनिन्दकैः ।
कृत्वा तु स्पर्शनालापं शुद्ध्येतार्कावलोकनात् ॥ ३३ ॥
अवलोक्य तथोदक्यामन्त्यजं पतितं शवं ।
विधर्म्मिसूतिकाषण्डविवस्त्रान्त्यावसायिनः ॥ ३४ ॥
सूतनिर्यातकांश्चैव परदाररताश्च ये ।
एतदेव हि कर्त्तव्यं प्राज्ञैः शोधनमात्मनः ॥ ३५ ॥
अभोज्यं सूतिकाषण्डमार्जाराखुश्वकुक्कुटान् ।
पतिताविद्धचण्डालमृतहारांश्च धर्म्मवित् ॥ ३६ ॥
संस्पृश्य शुद्ध्यते स्नानादुदक्याग्रामशूकरौ ।
तद्वच्च सूतिकाशौचदूषितौ पुरुषावपि ॥ ३७ ॥

यस्य चानुदिनं हानिर्गृहे नित्यस्य कर्म्मणः ।
यश्च ब्राह्मणसन्त्यक्तः किल्बिषी स नराधमः ॥ ३८ ॥
नित्यस्य कर्म्मणो हानिं न कुर्व्वीत कदाचन ।
तस्य त्वकरणे बन्धः केवलं मृतजन्मसु ॥ ३९ ॥
दशाहं ब्राह्मणस्तिष्ठेद्दानहोमादिवर्जितः ।
क्षत्रियो द्वादशाहञ्च वैश्यो मासार्द्धमेव च ॥ ४० ॥
शूद्रस्तु मासमासीत निजकर्म्मविवर्जितः ।
ततः परं निजं कर्म्म कुर्य्युः सर्व्वे यथोदितं ॥ ४१ ॥
प्रेताय सलिलं देयं वह्निदग्धा तु गोत्रिकैः ।
प्रथमेऽह्नि चतुर्थे च सप्तमे नवमे तथा ॥ ४२ ॥
भस्मास्थिचयनं कार्य्यं चतुर्थे गोत्रिकैर्द्दिने ।
ऊर्द्ध्वं सञ्चयनात्तेषामङ्गस्पर्शो विधीयते ॥ ४३ ॥
सोदकैस्तु क्रियाः सर्व्वाः कार्य्याः सञ्चयनात्परं ।
स्पर्श एव सपिण्डानां मृताहनि तथोभयोः ॥ ४४ ॥
अन्वेकमृक्षमाशस्त्रतोयोद्वन्धनवह्निषु ।
विषप्रपातादिमृते प्रायो नाशकयोरपि ॥ ४५ ॥
बाले देशान्तरस्थे च तथा प्रव्रजिते मृते ।
सद्यःशौचमथान्यैश्च त्र्यहमुक्तमशौचकं ॥ ४६ ॥
सपिण्डानां सपिण्डस्तु मृतेऽन्यस्मिन्मृतो यदि ।
पूर्व्वाशौचसमाख्यातैः कार्य्यास्तत्र दिनैः क्रियाः ॥ ४७ ॥
एष एव विधिर्द्दृष्टो जन्मन्यपिहि सूतके ।
सपिण्डानां सपिण्डेषु यथावत्सोदकेषु च ॥ ४८ ॥

जाते पुत्रे पितुः स्नानं सचेलंतु विधीयते ।
तत्रापि यदि चान्यस्मिन् जाते जायेत चापरः ॥ ४९ ॥
तत्रापि शुद्धिरुद्दिष्टा पूर्व्वजन्मवतो दिनैः ।
दशद्वादशमासार्द्धमाससंख्यैर्दिनैर्गतैः ॥ ५० ॥
स्वाः स्वाः कर्म्मक्रियाः कुर्य्युः सर्व्वे वर्णा यथाविधि ।
प्रेतमुद्दिश्य कर्त्तव्यमेकोद्दिष्टं ततः परं ॥ ५१ ॥
दानानि चैव देयानि ब्राह्मणेभ्यो मनीषिभिः ।
यद्यदिष्टतमं लोके यच्चापि दयितं गृहे ॥ ५२ ॥
तत्तद्गुणवते देयं तदेवाक्षयमिच्छता ।
पूर्णैस्तु दिवसैः स्पृष्ट्वा सलिलं वाहनायुधं ॥ ५३ ॥
प्रतोददण्डौ च तथा सम्यग्वर्णाः कृतक्रियाः ।
स्ववर्णधर्म्मनिर्द्दिष्टमुपादानं तथा क्रियाः ॥ ५४ ॥
कुर्य्युः समस्ताः शुचिनः परत्रेह च भूतिदाः ।
अध्येतव्या त्रयी नित्यं भवितव्यं विपश्चिता ॥ ५५ ॥
धर्म्मतो धनमाहार्य्यं यष्टव्यञ्चापि यत्नतः ।
यच्चापि कुर्व्वतो नात्मा जुगुप्सामेति पुत्रक ॥ ५६ ॥
तत्कर्त्तव्यमशङ्केन यन्न गोप्यं महाजने ।
एवमाचरतो वत्स पुरुषस्य गृहे सतः ॥
धर्म्मार्थकामसंप्राप्त्या परत्रेह च शोभनं ॥ ५७ ॥

इति श्रीमार्कण्डेयपुराणेऽलर्कानुशासने वर्ज्यावर्ज्याध्यायः ॥ ३५ ॥

षट्त्रिंशोऽध्यायः ॥

जड उवाच ॥

स एवमनुशिष्टः सन् मात्रा संप्राप्य यौवनं ।
ऋतध्वजसुतश्चक्रे सम्यग्दारपरिग्रहं ॥ १ ॥
पुत्रांश्चोत्पादयामास यज्ञैश्चाप्ययजद्विभुः ।
पितुश्च सर्व्वकालेषु चकाराज्ञानुपालनं ॥ २ ॥
ततः कालेन महता संप्राप्य चरमं वयः ।
चक्रेऽभिषेकं पुत्रस्य तस्य राज्ये ऋतध्वजः ॥ ३ ॥
भार्य्यया सह धर्म्मात्मा यियासुस्तपसे वनं ।
अवतीर्णो महाराज्ञो महाभागो महीपतिः ॥ ४ ॥
मदालसा च तनयं प्राहेदं पश्चिमं वचः ।
कामोपभोगसंसर्गप्रहाणाय सुतस्य वै ॥ ५ ॥

मदालसोवाच ॥

यदा दुःखमसह्यं ते प्रियबन्धुवियोगजं ।
शत्रुबाधोद्भवं वापि वित्तनाशात्मसम्भवं ॥ ६ ॥
भवेत्तत्कुर्व्वतो राज्यं गृहधर्म्मावलम्बिनः ।
दुःखायतनभूतो हि ममत्वालम्बिनो गृही ॥ ७ ॥
तदास्मात् पुत्र निष्कृष्य मद्दत्तादङ्गुलीयकात् ।
वाच्यन्ते शासनं पट्टे सूक्ष्माक्षरनिवेशितं ॥ ८ ।

जड उवाच ॥

इत्युक्ता प्रददौ तस्मै सौवर्णं साङ्गुलीयकं ।

आशिषश्चापि या योग्याः पुरुषस्य गृहे सतः ॥ ९ ॥
ततः कुवलयाश्वोऽसौ सा च देवी मदालसा ।
पुत्राय दत्वा तद्राज्यं तपसे काननं गतः ॥ १० ॥

इति श्रीमार्कण्डेयपुराणे मदालसोपाख्यानं ॥ ३६ ॥

सप्तत्रिंशोऽध्यायः ॥

जड उवाच ॥

सोऽप्यलर्कों यथान्यायं पुत्रवन्मुदिताः प्रजाः ।
पालयामास धर्म्मात्मा स्वे स्वे कर्म्मण्यवस्थिताः ॥ १ ॥
दुष्टेषु दण्डं शिष्टेषु सम्यक् च परिपालनं ।
कुर्व्वन् परां मुदं लेभे इयाज च महामखैः ॥ २ ॥
अजायन्त सुताश्चास्य महाबलपराक्रमाः ।
धर्म्मात्मानो महात्मानो विमार्गपरिपन्थिनः ॥ ३ ॥
चकार सोऽर्थं धर्म्मेण धर्म्ममर्थेन वा पुनः ।
तयोश्चैवाविरोधेन बुभुजे विषयानपि ॥ ४ ॥
एवं बहूणि वर्षाणि तस्य पालयतो महीं ।
धर्म्मार्थकामसक्तस्य जग्मुरेकमहर्यथा ॥ ५ ॥
वैराग्यं नास्य सञ्जज्ञे भुञ्जतो विषयान् प्रियान् ।
न चाप्यलमभूत्तस्य धर्म्मार्थोपार्ज्जनं प्रति ॥ ६ ॥

तं तथा भोगसंसर्गप्रमत्तमजितेन्द्रियं ।
सुबाहुर्नाम शुश्राव भ्राता तस्य वनेचरः ॥ ७ ॥
तं बुबोधयिषुः सोऽथ चिरं ध्यात्वा महीपतिः ।
तद्वैरिसंश्रयं तस्य श्रेयोऽमन्यत भूपतेः ॥ ८ ॥
ततः स काशिभूपालमुदीर्णबलवाहनं ।
स्वराज्यं प्राप्तुमागच्छद्बहुशः शरणं कृती ॥ ९ ॥
सोऽपि चक्रे बलोद्योगमलर्कं प्रति पार्थिवः ।
दूतञ्च प्रेषयामास राज्यमस्मै प्रदीयतां ॥ १० ॥
सोऽपि नैच्छत्तदा दातुमाज्ञापूर्वं स्वधर्म्मवित् ।
प्रत्युवाच च तं दूतमलर्कः काशिभूभृतः ॥ ११ ॥
मामेवाभ्येत्य हार्द्देन याचतां राज्यमग्रजः ।
नाक्रान्त्या संप्रदास्यामि भयेनाल्पामपि क्षितिं ॥ १२ ॥
सुबाहुरपि नो याच्ञाञ्चकार मतिमांस्तदा ।
न धर्म्मः क्षत्रियस्येति याच्ञा वीर्य्यधनो हि सः ॥ १३ ॥
ततः समस्तसैन्येन काशीशः परिवारितः ।
आक्रान्तुमभ्यगाद्राष्ट्रमलर्कस्य महीपतेः ॥ १४ ॥
अनन्तरैश्च संश्लेषमभ्येत्य तदनन्तरं ।
तेषामन्यतमैर्भृत्यैः समाक्रम्यानयद्वशं ॥ १५ ॥
अपीडयंश्च सामन्तांस्तस्य राष्ट्रोपरोधनैः ।
तथा दुर्गानुपालांश्च चक्रे चाटविकान् वशे ॥ १६ ॥
कांश्चिच्चोपप्रदानेन कांश्चिद्भेदेन पार्थिवान् ।
साम्नैवान्यान् वशं निन्ये निभृतास्तस्य येऽभवन् ॥ १७ ॥

ततः सोऽल्पबलो राजा परचक्रावपीडितः ।
कोषक्षयमवापोच्चैः पुरञ्चारुध्यतारिणा ॥ १८ ॥
इत्थं सम्पीड्यमानस्तु क्षीणकोषो दिने दिने ।
विषादमागात्परमं व्याकुलत्वञ्च चेतसः ॥ १९ ॥
आर्त्तिं स परमां प्राप्य तत्संस्माराङ्गुरीयकं ।
यदुद्दिश्य पुरा प्राह माता तस्य मदालसा ॥ २० ॥
ततः स्नातः शुचिर्भूत्वा वाचयित्वा द्विजोत्तमान् ।
निष्कृष्य शासनं तस्माद्ददृशे प्रस्फुटाक्षरं ॥ २१ ॥
तत्रैव लिखितं मात्रा वाचयामास पार्थिवः ।
प्रकाशपुलकाङ्गोऽसौ प्रहर्षोत्फुल्ललोचनः ॥ २२ ॥
सङ्गः सर्व्वात्मना त्याज्यः स चेत्त्यक्तुं न शक्यते ।
स सद्भिः सह कर्त्तव्यः सतां सङ्गो हि भेषजं ॥ २३ ॥
कामः सर्व्वात्मना हेयो हातुञ्चेच्छक्यते न सः ।
मुमुक्षां प्रति तत्कार्य्यं सैव तस्यापि भेषजं ॥ २४ ॥
वाचयित्वा तु बहुशो न्नृणां श्रेयः कथं त्विति ।
मुमुक्षयेति निश्चित्य सा च तत्सङ्गतो यतः ॥ २५ ॥
ततः स साधुसम्पर्कं चिन्तयन् पृथिवीपतिः ।
दत्तात्रेयं महाभागमगच्छत् परमार्त्तिमान् ॥ २६ ॥
तं समेत्य महात्मानमकल्मषमसङ्गिनं ।
प्रणिपत्याभिसम्पूज्य यथान्यायमभाषत ॥ २७ ॥
ब्रह्मन् कुरु प्रसादं मे शरणं शरणार्थिनां ।
दुःखापहार कुरु मे दुःखार्त्तस्यातिकामिनः ॥ २८ ॥

दत्तात्रेय उवाच ॥

दुःखापहारमद्यैव करोमि तव पार्थिव ।
सत्यं ब्रूहि किमर्थं ते दुःखं तत्पृथिवीपते ॥ २९ ॥

जड उवाच ॥

इत्युक्तश्चिन्तयामास स राजा तेन धीमता ।
त्रिविधस्यापि दुःखस्य स्थानमात्मानमेव च ॥ ३० ॥
स विमृष्य चिरं राजा पुनःपुनरुदारधीः ।
आत्मानमात्मना धीरः प्रहस्येदमथाब्रवीत् ॥ ३१ ॥
नाहमुर्व्वी न सलिलं न ज्योतिरनिलो न च ।
नाकाशं किन्तु शारीरं समेत्य सुखमिष्यते ॥ ३२ ॥
न्यूनातिरिक्ततां याति पञ्चकेऽस्मिन् सुखासुखं ।
यदि स्यान्मम किन्न स्यादन्यस्थेऽपि हितं मयि ॥ ३३ ॥
नित्यप्रभूतसद्भावे न्यूनाधिक्यान्नतोन्नते ।
तथाच ममतात्यक्तो विशेषेणोपलभ्यते ॥ ३४ ॥
तन्मात्रावस्थिते सूक्ष्मे तृतीयांशे च पश्यतः ।
तथैव भूतसद्भावं शारीरं किं सुखासुखं ॥ ३५ ॥
मनस्यवस्थितं दुःखं सुखं वा मानसञ्च यत् ।
यतस्ततो न मे दुःखं सुखं वा नह्यहं मनः ॥ ३६ ॥
नाहङ्कारो न च मनो बुद्धिर्नाहं यतस्ततः ।
अन्तःकरणजं दुःखं पारक्यं मम तत्कथं ॥ ३७ ॥

नाहं शरीरं न मनो यतोऽहं
पृथक् शरीरान्मनसस्तथाहं ।

तत्स्तु चेतस्यथवापि देहे
सुखानि दुःखानि च किं ममात्र ॥ ३८ ॥
राज्यस्य वाञ्छां कुरुतेऽग्रजोऽस्य
देहस्य चेत् पञ्चमयः स राशिः ।
गुणप्रवृत्त्या मम किन्नु तत्र
तत्स्थः स चाहञ्च शरीरतोऽन्यः ॥ ३९ ॥
न यस्य हस्तादिकमप्यशेषं
मांसं न चास्थीनि शिराविभागः ।
कस्तस्य नागाश्वरथादिकोषैः
स्वल्पोऽपि सम्बन्ध इहास्ति पुंसः ॥ ४० ॥
तस्मान्न मेऽरिर्न्न च मेऽस्ति दुःखं
न मे सुखं नापि पुरं न कोषं ।
न चाश्वनागादि बलं न तस्य
नान्यस्य वा कस्य चिद्वा ममास्ति ॥ ४१ ॥
यथा घटीकुम्भकमण्डलुस्थ-
माकाशमेकं बहुधा हि दृष्टं ।
तथा सुबाहुः स च काशिपोऽहं
मन्ये च देहेषु शरीरभेदैः ॥ ४२ ॥

इति श्रीमार्कण्डेयपुराणे पितापुत्रसंवादे आत्मविवेकोऽध्यायः ॥ ३७ ॥

अष्टत्रिंशोऽध्यायः ॥

जड उवाच ॥

दत्तात्रेयं ततो विप्रं प्रणिपत्य स पार्थिवः ।
प्रत्युवाच महात्मानं प्रश्रयावनतो वचः ॥ १ ॥
सम्यक् प्रपश्यतो ब्रह्मन् मम दुःखं न किञ्चन ।
असम्यग्दर्शिनो मग्नाः सर्व्वदैवासुखार्णवे ॥ २ ॥
यस्मिन् यस्मिन्ममासक्ता बुद्धिः पुंसः प्रजायते ।
ततस्ततः समादाय दुःखान्येव प्रयच्छति ॥ ३ ॥
मार्जारभक्षिते दुःखं यादृशं गृहकुक्कुटे ।
न तादृङ्ममताशून्ये कलविङ्केऽथ मूषिके ॥ ४ ॥
सोऽहं न दुःखी न सुखी यतोऽहं प्रकृतेः परः ।
यो भूताभिभवो भूतैः सुखदुःखात्मको हि सः ॥ ५ ॥

दत्तात्रेय उवाच ॥

एवमेतन्नरव्याघ्र यथैतद्व्याहृतं त्वया ।
ममेति मूलं दुःखस्य न ममेति च निर्वृतेः ॥ ६ ॥
मत्प्रश्नादेव ते ज्ञानमुत्पन्नमिदमुत्तमं ।
ममेति प्रत्ययो येन क्षिप्तः शाल्मलितूलवत् ॥ ७ ॥
अहमित्यङ्कुरोत्पन्नो ममेति स्कन्धवान् महान् ।
गृहक्षेत्रोच्चशाखाश्च पुत्त्रदारादिपल्लवः ॥ ८ ॥
धनधान्यमहापत्रो नैककालप्रवर्द्धितः ।

पुण्यापुण्याग्रपुष्पश्च सुखदुःखमहाफलः ॥ ९ ॥
तत्र मुक्तिपथव्यापी मूढसम्पर्कसेचनः ।
विधित्साभृङ्गमालाढ्यो कृत्यज्ञानमहातरुः ॥ १० ॥
संसाराध्वपरिश्रान्ता ये तच्छायां समाश्रिताः ।
भ्रान्तिज्ञानसुखाधीनास्तेषामात्यन्तिकं कुतः ॥ ११ ॥
यैस्तु सत्सङ्गपाषाणशितेन ममतातरुः ।
छिन्नो विद्याकुठारेण ते गतास्तेन वर्त्मना ॥ १२ ॥
प्राप्य ब्रह्मवनं शीतं नीरजस्कमकण्टकं ।
प्राप्नुवन्ति परां प्राज्ञा निर्वृतिं वृत्तिवर्जिताः ॥ १३ ॥
भूतेन्द्रियमयं स्थूलं न त्वं राजन्न चाप्यहं ।
न तन्मात्रं मया वाच्यं नैवान्तःकरणात्मकौ ॥ १४ ॥
कं वा पश्यामि राजेन्द्र प्रधानमिदमावयोः ।
यतः परो हि क्षेत्रज्ञः संघातो हि गुणात्मकः ॥ १५ ॥
मशकोडुम्बरेषीकामुञ्जमत्स्याम्भसां यथा ।
एकत्वेऽपि पृथग्भावस्तथा क्षेत्रात्मनोर्नृप ॥ १६ ॥

अलर्क उवाच ॥

भगवंस्त्वत्प्रसादेन ममाविर्भूतमुत्तमं ।
ज्ञानं प्रधानच्चिच्छक्तिविवेककरमीदृशं ॥ १७ ॥
किन्त्वत्र विषयाक्रान्ते स्थैर्य्यवत्त्वं न चेतसि ।
न चापि वेद्मि मुच्येयं कथं प्रकृतिबन्धनात् ॥ १८ ॥
कथं न भूयां भूयश्च कथं निर्गुणतामियां ।
कथञ्च ब्रह्मणैकत्वं व्रजेयं शाश्वतेन वै ॥ १९ ॥

तन्मे योगन्तथा ब्रह्मन् प्रणतायाभियाचते ।
सम्यग्ब्रूहि महाप्राज्ञ सत्सङ्गो ह्युपकृन्नृणां ॥ २० ॥

इति श्रीमार्कण्डेयपुराणे पितापुत्रसंवादे प्रश्नाध्यायः ॥ ३८ ॥

ऊनचत्वारिंशोऽध्यायः ॥

दत्तात्रेय उवाच ॥

ज्ञानपूर्व्वो वियोगो योऽज्ञानेन सह योगिनः ।
सा मुक्तिर्ब्रह्मणा चैक्यमनैक्यं प्राकृतैर्गुणैः ॥ १ ॥
मुक्तिर्योगात्तथा योगः सम्यग् ज्ञानान्महीपते ।
ज्ञानं दुःखोद्भवं दुःखं ममत्वासक्तचेतसां ॥ २ ॥
तस्मात् सङ्गं प्रयत्नेन मुमुक्षुः सन्त्यजेन्नरः ।
सङ्गाभावे ममेत्यस्याः ख्यातेर्हानिः प्रजायते ॥ ३ ॥
निर्म्ममत्वं सुखायैव वैराग्याद्दोषदर्शनं ।
ज्ञानादेव च वैराग्यं ज्ञानं वैराग्यपूर्व्वकं ॥ ४ ॥
तद्गृहं यत्र वसतिस्तद्भोज्यं येन जीवति ।
यन्मुक्तये तदेवोक्तं ज्ञानमज्ञानमन्यथा ॥ ५ ॥
उपभोगेन पुण्यानामपुण्यानाञ्च पार्थिव ।
कर्त्तव्यानाञ्च नित्यानामकामकरणात्तथा ॥ ६ ॥

असञ्चयादपूर्व्वस्य क्षयात् पूर्व्वार्जितस्य च ।
कर्म्मणो बन्धमाप्नोति शारीरं न पुनः पुनः ॥ ७ ॥
एतत्ते कथितं राजन् योगं चेमं निबोध मे ।
यं प्राप्य ब्रह्मणो योगी शाश्वतान्नान्यतां व्रजेत् ॥ ८ ॥
प्रागेवात्मात्मना जेयो योगिनां स हि दुर्ज्जयः ।
कुर्व्वीत तज्जये यत्नं तस्योपायं शृणुष्व मे ॥ ९ ॥
प्राणायामैर्द्दहेद्दोषान् धारणाभिश्च किल्बिषं ।
प्रत्याहारेण विषयान् ध्यानेनानीश्वरान् गुणान् ॥ १० ॥
यथा पर्व्वतधातूनां दोषा दह्यन्ति धाम्यतां ।
तथेन्द्रियकृता दोषा दह्यन्ते प्राणनिग्रहात् ॥ ११ ॥
प्रथमं साधनं कुर्य्यात् प्राणायामस्य योगवित् ।
प्राणापाननिरोधस्तु प्राणायाम उदाहृतः ॥ १२ ॥
लघुमध्योत्तरीयाख्यः प्राणायामस्त्रिधोदितः ।
तस्य प्रमाणं वक्ष्यामि तदलर्क शृणुष्व मे ॥ १३ ॥
लघुर्द्वादशमात्रस्तु द्विगुणः स तु मध्यमः ।
त्रिगुणाभिस्तु मात्राभिरुत्तमः परिकीर्त्तितः ॥ १४ ॥
निमेषोन्मेषणे मात्राकालो लघ्वक्षरस्तथा ।
प्राणायामस्य सङ्ख्यार्थं स्मृतो द्वादशमात्रिकः ॥ १५ ॥
प्रथमेन जयेत् स्वेदं मध्यमेन च वेपथुं ।
विषादं हि तृतीयेन जयेद्दोषाननुक्रमात् ॥ १६ ॥
मृदुत्वं सेव्यमानास्तु सिंहशार्दूलकुञ्जराः ।
यथा यान्ति तथा प्राणो वश्यो भवति योगिनः ॥ १७ ॥

वश्यं मत्तं यथेच्छातो नागं नयति हस्तिपः ।
तथैव योगी सच्छन्दः प्राणं नयति साधितं ॥ १८ ॥
यथा हि साधितः सिंहो मृगान् हन्ति न मानवान् ।
तद्वन्निषिद्धपवनः किल्बिषं न नृणां तनुं ॥ १९ ॥
तस्माद्युक्तः सदा योगी प्राणायामपरो भवेत् ।
श्रूयतां मुक्तिफलदं तस्यावस्थाचतुष्टयं ॥ २० ॥
ध्वस्तिः प्राप्तिस्तथा संवित् प्रसादश्च महीपते ।
स्वरूपं शृणु चैतेषां कथ्यमानमनुक्रमात् ॥ २१ ॥
कर्म्मणामिष्टदुष्टानां जायते फलसंक्षयः ।
चेतसोऽपकषायत्वं यत्र सा ध्वस्तिरुच्यते ॥ २२ ॥
ऐहिकामुष्मिकान् कामान् लोभमोहात्मकान् स्वयं ।
निरुध्यास्ते सदा योगी प्राप्तिः सा सार्व्वकालिकी ॥ २३ ॥
अतीतानागतानर्थान् विप्रकृष्टतिरोहितान् ।
विजानातीन्दुसूर्य्यर्क्षग्रहाणां ज्ञानसम्पदा ॥ २४ ॥
तुल्यप्रभावस्तु यदा योगी प्राप्नोति सम्पदं ।
तदा संविदिति ख्याता प्राणायामस्य संस्थितिः ॥ २५ ॥
यान्ति प्रसादं येनास्य मनः पञ्च च वायवः ।
इन्द्रियाणीन्द्रियार्थाश्च स प्रसाद इति स्मृतः ॥ २६ ॥
शृणुष्व च महीपाल प्राणायामस्य लक्षणं ।
युञ्जतश्च सदा योगं यादृग्विहितमासनं ॥ २७ ॥
पद्ममर्द्धासनञ्चापि तथा स्वस्तिकमासनं ।
आस्थाय योगं युञ्जीत कृत्वा च प्रणवं हृदि ॥ २८ ॥

समः समासनो भूत्वा संहृत्य चरणावुभौ ।
संवृतास्यस्तथैवोरू सम्यग्विष्टभ्य चाग्रतः ॥ २९ ॥
पार्ष्णिभ्यां लिङ्गवृषणावस्पृशन् प्रयतः स्थितः ।
किञ्चिदुन्नामितशिरा दन्तैर्दन्तान्न संस्पृशेत् ॥ ३० ॥
संपश्यन्नासिकाग्रं स्वं दिशश्चानवलोकयन् ।
रजसा तमसो वृत्तिं सत्त्वेन रजसस्तथा ॥ ३१ ॥
सञ्छाद्य निर्म्मले सत्त्वे स्थितो युञ्जीत योगवित् ।
इन्द्रियाणीन्द्रियार्थेभ्यः प्राणादीन्मन एव च ॥ ३२ ॥
निगृह्य समवायेन प्रत्याहारमुपक्रमेत् ।
यस्तु प्रत्याहरेत्कामान् सर्व्वाङ्गानीव कच्छपः ॥ ३३ ॥
सदात्मरतिरेकस्थः पश्यत्यात्मानमात्मनि ।
स वाह्याभ्यन्तरं शौचं निष्पाद्याकण्ठनाभितः ॥ ३४ ॥
पूरयित्वा बुधो देहं प्रत्याहारमुपक्रमेत् ।
प्राणायामा दश द्वौ च धारणा साभिधीयते ॥ ३५ ॥
द्वे धारणे स्मृते योगे योगिभिस्तत्त्वदृष्टिभिः ।
तथा वै योगयुक्तस्य योगिनो नियतात्मनः ॥ ३६ ॥
सर्व्वे दोषाः प्रणश्यन्ति स्वस्थश्चैवोपजायते ।
वीक्षते च परं ब्रह्म प्राकृतांश्च गुणान् पृथक् ॥ ३७ ॥
व्योमादिपरमाणूंश्च तथात्मानमकल्मषं ।
इत्थं योगी यताहारः प्राणायामपरायणः ॥ ३८ ॥
जितां जितां शनैर्भूमिमारोहेत यथा गृहं ।
दोषान् व्याधींस्तथा मोहमाक्रान्ता भूरनिर्जिता ॥ ३९ ॥

विवर्द्धयति नारोहैंत्तस्माद्भूमिमनिर्ज्जिताम् ।
प्राणानामुपसंरोधात्प्राणायाम इति स्मृतः ॥ ४० ॥
धारणेत्युच्यते चेयं धार्य्यते यन्मनो यया ।
शब्दादिभ्यः प्रवृत्तानि यदक्षानि यतात्मभिः ॥ ४१ ॥
प्रत्याह्रियन्ते योगेन प्रत्याहारस्ततः स्मृतः ।
उपायश्चात्र कथितो योगिभिः परमर्षिभिः ॥ ४२ ॥
येन व्याध्यादयो दोषा न जायन्ते हि योगिनः ।
यथा तोयार्थिनस्तोयं यन्त्रनालादिभिः शनैः ॥ ४३ ॥
आपिबेयुस्तथा वायुं पिबेद्योगी जितश्रमः ।
प्राङ्नाभ्यां हृदये चात्र तृतीये च तथोरसि ॥ ४४ ॥
कण्ठे मुखे नासिकाग्रे नेत्रभ्रूमध्यमूर्द्धसु ।
किञ्च तस्मात्परस्मिंश्च धारणा परमा स्मृता ॥ ४५ ॥
दशैता धारणाः प्राप्य प्राप्नोत्यक्षरसाम्यताम् ।
नाध्मातः क्षुधितः श्रान्तो नच व्याकुलचेतनः ॥ ४६ ॥
युञ्जीत योगं राजेन्द्र योगी सिद्ध्यर्थमादृतः ।
नातिशीते नचोष्णे वै न द्वन्द्वेनानिलात्मके ॥ ४७ ॥
कालेष्वेतेषु युञ्जीत न योगं ध्यानतत्परः ।
सशब्दाग्निजलाभ्यासे जीर्णगोष्ठे चतुष्पथे ॥ ४८ ॥
शुष्कपर्णचये नद्यां श्मशाने ससरीसृपे ।
सभये कूपतीरे वा चैत्यवल्मीकसञ्चये ॥ ४९ ॥
देशेष्वेतेषु तत्त्वज्ञो योगाभ्यासं विवर्ज्जयेत् ।
सत्त्वस्यानुपपत्तौ च देशकालं विवर्ज्जयेत् ॥ ५० ॥

नासतो दर्शनं योगे तस्मात्तत्परिवर्ज्जयेत् ।
देशानेताननादृत्य मूढत्वाद्यो युनक्ति वै ॥ ५१ ॥
विघ्नाय तस्य वै दोषा जायन्ते तन्निबोध मे ।
बाधिर्य्यं जडता लोपः स्मृतेर्मूकत्वमन्धता ॥ ५२ ॥
ज्वरश्च जायते सद्यस्तत्तदज्ञानयोगिनः ।
प्रमादाद्योगिनो दोषा यद्येते स्युश्चिकित्सितं ॥ ५३ ॥
तेषां नाशाय कर्त्तव्यं योगिनां तन्निबोध मे ।
स्निग्धां यवागूमत्युष्णां भुक्त्वा तत्रैव धारयेत् ॥ ५४ ॥
वातगुल्मप्रशान्त्यर्थमुदावर्त्ते तथोदरे ।
यवागूं वापि पवनं वायुग्रन्थिं प्रतिक्षिपेत् ॥ ५५ ॥
तद्वत्कम्पे महाशैलं स्थिरं मनसि धारयेत् ।
विघाते वचसो वाचं बाधिर्य्ये श्रवणेन्द्रियं ॥ ५६ ॥
यथैवाम्रफलं ध्यायेत् तृष्णार्त्तो रसनेन्द्रिये ।
यस्मिन् यस्मिन्रुजा देहे तस्मिंस्तदुपकारिणीं ॥ ५७ ॥
धारयेद्धारणामुष्णे शीतां शीते च दाहिनीं ।
कीलं शिरसि संस्थाप्य काष्ठं काष्ठेन ताडयेत् ॥ ५८ ॥
लुप्तस्मृतेः स्मृतिः सद्यो योगिनस्तेन जायते ।
द्यावापृथिव्यौ वाय्वग्नी व्यापिनावपि धारयेत् ॥ ५९ ॥
अमानुषात् सत्त्वजाद्वा बाधास्त्वेताश्चिकित्सिताः ।
अमानुषं सत्त्वमन्तर्योगिनं प्रविशेद्यदि ॥ ६० ॥
वाय्वग्निधारणेनैनं देहसंस्थं विनिर्दहेत् ।
एवं सर्व्वात्मना रक्षा कार्य्या योगविदा नृप ॥ ६१ ॥

धर्म्मार्थकाममोक्षाणां शरीरं साधनं यतः ।
प्रवृत्तिलक्षणाख्यानाद्योगिनो विस्मयात्तथा ॥
विज्ञानं विलयं याति तस्माद्गोप्याः प्रवृत्तयः ॥ ६२ ॥

आलोल्यमारोग्यमनिष्ठुरत्वं
गन्धः शुभो मूत्रपुरीषमल्पं ।
कान्तिः प्रसादः स्वरसौम्यता च
योगप्रवृत्तेः प्रथमं हि चिह्नं ॥ ६३ ॥

अनुरागी जनो याति परोक्षे गुणकीर्त्तनं ।
न बिभ्यति च सत्त्वानि सिद्धेर्लक्षणमुत्तमं ॥ ६४ ॥
शीतोष्णादिभिरत्युग्रैर्यस्य बाधा न विद्यते ।
न भीतिमेति चान्येभ्यस्तस्य सिद्धिरुपस्थिता ॥ ६५ ॥

इति श्रीमार्कण्डेयपुराणे जडोपाख्याने योगाध्यायः ॥ ३९ ॥

चत्वारिंशोऽध्यायः ॥

दत्तात्रेय उवाच ॥

उपसर्गाः प्रवर्त्तन्ते दृष्टे ह्यात्मनि योगिनः ।
ये तांस्ते संप्रवक्ष्यामि समासेन निबोध मे ॥ १ ॥
काम्याः क्रियास्तथा कामान् मानुषानभिवाञ्छति ।
स्त्रियो दानफलं विद्यां मायां कुप्यं धनं दिवं ॥ २ ॥

देवत्वममरेशत्वं रसायनचयः क्रियाः ।
मरुत्प्रपतनं यज्ञं जलाग्न्यावेशनन्तथा ॥ ३ ॥
श्राद्धानां सर्व्वदानानां फलानि नियमांस्तथा ।
तथोपवासात् पूर्त्ताच्च देवताभ्यर्च्चनादपि ॥ ४ ॥
तेभ्यस्तेभ्यश्च कर्म्मभ्य उपसृष्टोऽभिवाञ्छति ।
चित्तमित्थं वर्त्तमानं यत्नाद्योगी निवर्त्तयेत् ॥ ५ ॥
ब्रह्मसङ्गि मनः कुर्व्वन्नुपसर्गात् प्रमुच्यते ।
उपसर्गैर्जितैरेभिरुपसर्गास्ततः पुनः ॥ ६ ॥
योगिनः संप्रवर्त्तन्ते सात्त्वराजसतामसाः ।
प्रातिभः श्रावणो दैवो भ्रमावर्त्तौ तथापरौ ॥ ७ ॥
पञ्चैते योगिनां योगविघ्नाय कटुकोदयाः ।
वेदार्थाः काव्यशास्त्रार्थाः विद्याशिल्पान्यशेषतः ॥ ८ ॥
प्रतिभान्ति यदस्येति प्रातिभः स तु योगिनः ।
शब्दार्थानखिलान् वेत्ति शब्दं गृह्णाति चैव यत् ॥ ९ ॥
योजनानां सहस्रेभ्यः श्रावणः सोऽभिधीयते ।
समन्ताद्वीक्षते चाष्टौ स यदा देवतोपमः ॥ १० ॥
उपसर्गन्तमप्याहुर्दैवमुन्मत्तवद्बुधाः ।
भ्राम्यते यन्निरालम्बं मनो दोषेण योगिनः ॥ ११ ॥
समस्ताचारविभ्रंशाद्भ्रमः स परिकीर्त्तितः ।
आवर्त्त इव तोयस्य ज्ञानावर्त्तो यदाकुलः ॥ १२ ॥
नाशयेच्चित्तमावर्त्त उपसर्गः स उच्यते ।
एतैर्नाशितयोगास्तु सकला देवयोनयः ॥ १३ ॥

उपसर्गैर्म्महाघोरैरावर्त्तन्ते पुनःपुनः ।
प्रावृत्य कम्बलं शुक्लं योगी तस्मान्मनोमयं ॥ १४ ॥
चिन्तयेत् परमं ब्रह्म कृत्वा तत्प्रवणं मनः ।
योगयुक्तः सदा योगी लघ्वाहारो जितेन्द्रियः ॥ १५ ॥
सूक्ष्मास्तु धारणाः सप्त भूराद्या मुर्द्धि धारयेत् ।
धरित्रीं धारयेद्योगी तत् सौख्यं प्रतिपद्यते ॥ १६ ॥
आत्मानं मन्यते चोर्व्वीं तद्वन्धञ्च जहाति सः ।
तथैवाप्सु रसं सूक्ष्मं तद्वद्रूपञ्च तेजसि ॥ १७ ॥
स्पर्शं वायौ तथा तद्वद्बिभ्रतस्तस्य धारणां ।
व्योम्नः सूक्ष्मां प्रवृत्तिञ्च शब्दं तद्वज्जहाति सः ॥ १८ ॥
मनसा सर्व्वभूतानां मनस्याविशते यदा ।
मानसीं धारणां बिभ्रन्मनः सूक्ष्मञ्च जायते ॥ १९ ॥
तद्वद्बुद्धिमशेषाणां सत्त्वानामेत्य योगवित् ।
परित्यजति सम्प्राप्य बुद्धिसौक्ष्ममनुत्तमं ॥ २० ॥
परित्यजति सूक्ष्माणि सप्त त्वेतानि योगवित् ।
सम्यग्विज्ञाय योऽलर्क तस्यावृत्तिर्न विद्यते ॥ २१ ॥
एतासां धारणानान्तु सप्तानां सौक्ष्ममात्मवान् ।
दृष्ट्वा दृष्ट्वा ततः सिद्धिं त्यक्त्वा त्यक्त्वा परां व्रजेत् ॥ २२ ॥
यस्मिन् यस्मिंश्च कुरुते भूते रागं महीपते ।
तस्मिंस्तस्मिन् समासक्तिं संप्राप्य स विनश्यति ॥ २३ ॥
तस्माद्विदित्वा सूक्ष्माणि संसक्तानि परस्परं ।
परित्यजति यो देही स परं प्राप्नुयात् पदं ॥ २४ ॥

एतान्येव तु सन्धाय सप्त सूक्ष्माणि पार्थिव ।
भूतादीनां विरागोऽच सद्भावज्ञस्य मुक्तये ॥ २५ ॥
गन्धादिषु समासक्तिं सम्प्राप्य स विनश्यति ।
पुनरावर्त्तते भूप स ब्रह्मापरमानुषं ॥ २६ ॥
सप्तैता धारणा योगी समतीत्य यदिच्छति ।
तस्मिंस्तस्मिंल्लयं सूक्ष्मे भूते याति नरेश्वर ॥ २७ ॥
देवानामसुराणां वा गन्धर्व्वोरगरक्षसां ।
देहेषु लयमायाति सङ्गं नाप्नोति च क्वचित् ॥ २८ ॥
अणिमा लघिमा चैव महिमा प्राप्तिरेव च ।
प्राकाम्यञ्च तथेशित्वं वशित्वञ्च तथापरं ॥ २९ ॥
यच्च कामावशायित्वं गुणानेतांस्तथैश्वरान् ।
प्राप्नोत्यष्टौ नरव्याघ्र परं निर्व्वाणसूचकान् ॥ ३० ॥
सूक्ष्मात्सूक्ष्मतमोऽणीयान् शीघ्रत्वं लघिमा गुणः ।
महिमाशेषपूज्यत्वात् प्राप्तिर्नाप्राप्यमस्य यत् ॥ ३१ ॥
प्राकाम्यमस्य व्यापित्वादीशित्वञ्चेश्वरो यतः ।
वशित्वाद्वशिमा नाम योगिनः सप्तमो गुणः ॥ ३२ ॥
यत्रेच्छास्थानमप्युक्तं यच्च कामावशायिता ।
ऐश्वर्य्यकारणैरेभिर्योगिनः प्रोक्तमष्टधा ॥ ३३ ॥
मुक्तिसंसूचकं भूप परं निर्व्वाणमात्मनः ।
ततो न जायते नैव वर्द्धते न विनश्यति ॥ ३४ ॥
नापि क्षयमवाप्नोति परिणामं न गच्छति ।
छेदं क्लेदं तथा दाहं शोषं भूरादितो नच ॥ ३५ ॥

भूतवर्गादवाप्नोति शब्दाद्यैः ह्रियते नच ।
नचास्य सन्ति शब्दाद्यास्तद्भोक्ता तैर्न युज्यते ॥ ३६ ॥
यथाहि कनकं खण्डमपद्रव्यवदग्निना ।
दग्धदोषं द्वितीयेन खण्डेनैक्यं व्रजन्नृप ॥ ३७ ॥
न विशेषमवाप्नोति तद्वद्योगाग्निना यतिः ।
निर्दग्धदोषस्तेनैक्यं प्रयाति ब्रह्मणा सह ॥ ३८ ॥
यथाग्निरग्नौ संक्षिप्तः समानत्वमनुव्रजेत् ।
तदाख्यस्तन्मयो भूतो न गृह्येत विशेषतः ॥ ३९ ॥
परेण ब्रह्मणा तद्वत्प्राप्यैक्यं दग्धकिल्बिषः ।
योगी याति पृथग्भावं न कदाचिन्महीपते ॥ ४० ॥
यथा जलं जलेनैक्यं निक्षिप्तमुपगच्छति ।
तथात्मा साम्यमभ्येति योगिनः परमात्मनि ॥ ४१ ॥

इति श्रीमार्कण्डेयपुराणे योगिसिद्धिर्नामाध्यायः ॥ ४० ॥

एकचत्वारिंशोऽध्यायः ॥

अलर्क उवाच ॥

भगवन् योगिनश्चर्य्यां श्रोतुमिच्छामि तत्त्वतः ।
ब्रह्मवर्त्मन्यनुसरन् यथा योगी न सीदति ॥ १ ॥

दत्तात्रेय उवाच ॥

मानापमानौ यावेतौ प्रीत्युद्वेगकरौ नृणां ।

तावेव विपरीतार्थौ योगिनः सिद्धिकारकौ ॥ २ ॥
मानापमानौ यावेतौ तावेवाहुर्विषामृते ।
अपमानोऽमृतं तत्र मानस्तु विषमं विषं ॥ ३ ॥
चक्षुःपूतं न्यसेत्पादं वस्त्रपूतं जलं पिबेत् ।
सत्यपूतां वदेद्वाणीं बुद्धिपूतञ्च चिन्तयेत् ॥ ४ ॥
आतिथ्यश्राद्धयज्ञेषु देवयात्रोत्सवेषु च ।
महाजनञ्च सिद्ध्यर्थं न गच्छेद्योगवित् क्वचित् ॥ ५ ॥
व्यस्ते विधूमे व्यङ्गारे सर्व्वस्मिन् भुक्तवज्जने ।
अटेत योगविद्भैक्ष्यं नतु त्रिष्वेव नित्यशः ॥ ६ ॥
यथैवमवमन्यन्ते जनाः परिभवन्ति च ।
तथा युक्तश्चरेद्योगी सतां वर्त्म न दूषयन् ॥ ७ ॥
भैक्ष्यञ्चरेद्गृहस्थेषु यायावरगृहेषु च ।
श्रेष्ठा तु प्रथमा चेति वृत्तिरस्योपदिश्यते ॥ ८ ॥
अथ नित्यं गृहस्थेषु शालीनेषु चरेद्यतिः ।
श्रद्दधानेषु दान्तेषु श्रोत्रियेषु महात्मसु ॥ ९ ॥
अत ऊर्द्ध्वं पुनश्चापि अदुष्टापतितेषु च ।
भैक्ष्यचर्य्या विवर्णेषु जघन्या वृत्तिरिष्यते ॥ १० ॥
भैक्ष्यं यवागूं तक्रं वा पयोयावकमेव वा ।
फलं मूलं प्रियङ्गुं वा कणपिण्याकशक्तवः ॥ ११ ॥
इत्येते च शुभाहारा योगिनः सिद्धिकारकाः ।
तत्प्रयुञ्ज्यान्मुनिर्भक्त्या परमेण समाधिना ॥ १२ ॥
अपः पूर्व्वं सकृत् प्राश्य तूष्णीं भूत्वा समाहितः ।

प्राणायेति ततस्तस्य प्रथमा ह्याहुतिः स्मृता ॥ १३ ॥
अपानाय द्वितीया तु समानायेति चापरा ।
उदानाय चतुर्थी स्याद्व्यानायेति च पञ्चमी ॥ १४ ॥
प्राणायामैः पृथक् कृत्वा शेषं भुञ्जीत कामतः ।
अपः पुनः सकृत्प्राश्य आचम्य हृदयं स्पृशेत् ॥ १५ ॥
अस्तेयं ब्रह्मचर्य्यञ्च त्यागोऽलोभस्तथैव च ।
व्रतानि पञ्च भिक्षूणामहिंसापरमाणि वै ॥ १६ ॥
अक्रोधो गुरुशुश्रूषा शौचमाहारलाघवं ।
नित्यस्वाध्याय इत्येते नियमाः पञ्च कीर्त्तिताः ॥ १७ ॥
सारभूतमुपासीत ज्ञानं यत्कार्य्यसाधकं ।
ज्ञानानां बहुता येयं योगविघ्नकरा हि सा ॥ १८ ॥
इदं ज्ञेयमिदं ज्ञेयमिति यस्तृषितश्चरेत् ।
अपि कल्पसहस्रेषु नैव ज्ञेयमवाप्नुयात् ॥ १९ ॥
त्यक्तसङ्गो जितक्रोधो लघ्वाहारो जितेन्द्रियः ।
विधाय बुद्ध्या द्वाराणि मनो ध्याने निवेशयेत् ॥ २० ॥
शून्येष्वेवावकाशेषु गुहासु च वनेषु च ।
नित्ययुक्तः सदा योगी ध्यानं सम्यगुपक्रमेत् ॥ २१ ॥
वाग्दण्डः कर्म्मदण्डश्च मनोदण्डश्च ते त्रयः ।
यस्यैते नियता दण्डाः स त्रिदण्डी महायतिः ॥ २२ ॥
सर्व्वमात्ममयं यस्य सदसज्जगदीदृशं ।
गुणागुणमयन्तस्य कः प्रियः को नृपाप्रियः ॥ २३ ॥

विशुद्धबुद्धिः समलोष्ट्रकाञ्चनः

समस्तभूतेषु च तत्समाहितः ।
स्थानं परं शाश्वतमव्ययञ्च
परं हि मत्वा न पुनः प्रजायते ॥ २४ ॥
वेदाः श्रेष्ठाः सर्व्वयज्ञक्रियाश्च
यज्ञाज्जप्यं ज्ञानमार्गश्च जप्यात् ।
ज्ञानाद्ध्यानं सङ्गरागव्यपेतं
तस्मिन् प्राप्ते शाश्वतस्योपलब्धिः ॥ २५ ॥
समाहितो ब्रह्मपरोऽप्रमादी
शुचिस्तथैकान्तरतिर्यतेन्द्रियः ।
समाप्नुयाद्योगमिमं महात्मा
विमुक्तिमाप्नोति ततः स्वयोगतः ॥ २६ ॥

इति श्रीमार्कण्डेयपुराणे योगिचर्य्याध्यायः ॥ ४१ ॥

द्विचत्वारिंशोऽध्यायः ॥

दत्तात्रेय उवाच ॥

एवं यो वर्त्तते योगी सम्यग्योगव्यवस्थितः ।
न स व्यावर्त्तितुं शक्यो जन्मान्तरशतैरपि ॥ १ ॥
दृष्ट्वा च परमात्मानं प्रत्यक्षं विश्वरूपिणं ।
विश्वपादशिरोग्रीवं विश्वेशं विश्वभावनं ॥ २ ॥
तत्प्राप्तये महत्पुण्यमोमित्येकाक्षरं जपेत् ।

तदेवाध्ययनं तस्य स्वरूपं शृणुतः परं ॥ ३ ॥
अकारश्च तथोकारो मकारश्चाक्षरत्रयं ।
एताएव त्रयो मात्राः सात्त्वराजसतामसाः ॥ ४ ॥
निर्गुणा योगिगम्यान्या चार्द्धमात्रोर्द्धसंस्थिता ।
गान्धारीति च विज्ञेया गान्धारस्वरसंश्रया ॥ ५ ॥
पिपीलिकागतिस्पर्शा प्रयुक्ता मूर्द्ध्नि लक्ष्यते ।
यथा प्रयुक्त ओङ्कारः प्रतिनिर्याति मूर्द्धनि ॥ ६ ॥
तथोङ्कारमयो योगी त्वक्षरे त्वक्षरो भवेत् ।
प्राणोधनुः शरोह्यात्मा ब्रह्म वेध्यमनुत्तमं ॥ ७ ॥
अप्रमत्तेन वेद्धव्यं शरवत्तन्मयो भवेत् ।
ओमित्येतत्त्रयो वेदास्त्रयो लोकास्त्रयोऽग्नयः ॥ ८ ॥
विष्णुर्ब्रह्मा हरश्चैव ऋक्सामानि यजूंषि च ।
मात्राः सार्द्धाश्च तिस्रश्च विज्ञेयाः परमार्थतः ॥ ९ ॥
तत्र युक्तस्तु यो योगी स तल्लयमवाप्नुयात् ।
अकारस्त्वथ भूर्लोक उकारश्चोच्यते भुवः ॥ १० ॥
सव्यञ्जनो मकारश्च स्वर्लोकः परिकल्प्यते ।
व्यक्ता तु प्रथमा मात्रा द्वितीयाव्यक्तसंज्ञिता ॥ ११ ॥
मात्रा तृतीया चिच्छक्तिरर्द्धमात्रा परं पदं ।
अनेनैव क्रमेणैता विज्ञेया योगभूमयः ॥ १२ ॥
ओमित्युच्चारणात् सर्व्वं गृहीतं सदसद्भवेत् ।
ह्रस्वा तु प्रथमा मात्रा द्वितीया दैर्घ्यसंयुता ॥ १३ ॥
तृतीया च प्लुतार्द्धाख्या वचसः सा न गोचरा ।

इत्येतदक्षरं ब्रह्म परमोङ्कारसंज्ञितं ॥ १४ ॥
यस्तु वेद नरः सम्यक् तथा ध्यायति वा पुनः ।
संसारचक्रमुत्सृज्य त्यक्तत्रिविधबन्धनः ॥ १५ ॥
प्राप्नोति ब्रह्मणि लयं परमे परमात्मनि ।
अक्षीणकर्म्मबन्धश्च ज्ञात्वा मृत्युमरिष्टतः ॥ १६ ॥
उत्क्रान्तिकाले संस्मृत्य पुनर्योगित्वमृच्छति ।
तस्मादसिद्धयोगेन सिद्धयोगेन वा पुनः ॥
ज्ञेयान्यरिष्टानि सदा येनोत्क्रान्तौ न सीदति ॥ १७ ॥

इति श्रीमार्कण्डेयपुराणे योगधर्म्मे ओङ्काराध्यायः ॥ ४२ ॥

त्रिचत्वारिंशोऽध्यायः ॥

दत्तात्रेय उवाच ॥

अरिष्टानि महाराज शृणु वक्ष्यामि तानि ते ।
येषामालोकनान्मृत्युं निजं जानाति योगवित् ॥ १ ॥
देवमार्गं ध्रुवं शुक्रं सोमच्छायामरुन्धतीं ।
यो न पश्येन्न जीवेत् स नरः संवत्सरात्परं ॥ २ ॥
अरश्मि विम्बं सूर्य्यस्य वह्निं चैवांशुमालिनं ।
दृष्ट्वैकादशमासात्तु नरो नोर्द्धं तु जीवति ॥ ३ ॥
वान्ते मूत्रपुरीषे च यः स्वर्णं रजतं तथा ।
प्रत्यक्षं कुरुते स्वप्ने जीवेत् स दशमासिकं ॥ ४ ॥

दृष्ट्वा प्रेतपिशाचादीन् गन्धर्व्वनगराणि च ।
सुवर्णवर्णान् वृक्षांश्च नव मासान् स जीवति ॥ ५ ॥
स्थूलः कृशः कृशः स्थूलो योऽकस्मादेव जायते ।
प्रकृतेश्च निवर्त्तेत तस्यायुश्चाष्टमासिकं ॥ ६ ॥
खण्डं यस्य पदं पार्ष्ण्यां पादस्याग्रे च वा भवेत् ।
पांशुकर्दमयोर्मध्ये सप्त मासान् स जीवति ॥ ७ ॥
गृध्रः कपोतः काकोलो वायसो वापि मूर्द्धनि ।
क्रव्यादो वा खगो नीलः षण्मासायुःप्रदर्शकः ॥ ८ ॥
हन्यते काकपङ्क्तीभिः पांशुवर्षेण वा नरः ।
स्वां छायामन्यथा दृष्ट्वा चतुः पञ्च स जीवति ॥ ९ ॥
अनभ्रे विद्युतं दृष्ट्वा दक्षिणां दिशमाश्रितां ।
रात्राविन्द्रधनुश्चापि जीवितं द्वित्रिमासिकं ॥ १० ॥
घृते तैले तथादर्शे तोये वा नात्मनस्तनुं ।
यः पश्येदशिरस्कां वा मासादूर्द्ध्वं न जीवति ॥ ११ ॥
यस्य वस्तसमो गन्धो गात्रे शवसमोऽपिवा ।
तस्यार्द्धमासिकं ज्ञेयं योगिनो नृप जीवितं ॥ १२ ॥
यस्य वै स्नातमात्रस्य हृत्पादमवशुष्यते ।
पिवतश्च जलं शोषो दशाहं सोऽपि जीवति ॥ १३ ॥
सम्भिन्नो मारुतो यस्य मर्म्मस्थानानि कृन्तति ।
हृष्यते नाम्बुसंस्पर्शात् तस्य मृत्युरुपस्थितः ॥ १४ ॥
ऋक्षवानरयानस्थो गायन् यो दक्षिणां दिशं ।
स्वप्ने प्रयाति तस्यापि न मृत्युः कालमिच्छति ॥ १५ ॥

रक्तकृष्णाम्बरधरा गायन्ती हसती च यं।
दक्षिणाशान्नयेन्नारी स्वप्ने सोऽपि न जीवति ॥ १६ ॥
नग्नं क्षपणकं स्वप्ने हसमानं महाबलं।
एकं संवीक्ष्य वल्गन्तं विद्यान्मृत्युमुपस्थितं ॥ १७ ॥
आमस्तकतलाद्यस्तु निमग्नं पङ्कसागरे।
स्वप्ने पश्यत्यथात्मानं स सद्यो म्रियते नरः ॥ १८ ॥
केशाङ्गारांस्तथा भस्म भुजङ्गान्निर्जलां नदीं।
दृष्ट्वा स्वप्ने दशाहात्तु मृत्युरेकादशे दिने ॥ १९ ॥
करालैर्विकटैः कृष्णैः पुरुषैरुद्यतायुधैः।
पाषाणैस्ताडितः स्वप्ने सद्यो मृत्युं लभेन्नरः ॥ २० ॥
सूर्य्योदये यस्य शिवा क्रोशन्ती याति सम्मुखं।
विपरीतं परीतं वा स सद्यो मृत्युमृच्छति ॥ २१ ॥
यस्य वै भुक्तमात्रस्य हृदयं बाधते क्षुधा।
जायते दन्तघर्षश्च स गतायुर्न्न संशयं ॥ २२ ॥
दीपगन्धं नयो वेत्ति त्रस्यत्यह्नि तथा निशि।
नात्मानं परनेत्रस्थं वीक्षते न स जीवति ॥ २३ ॥
शक्रायुधं चार्द्धरात्रे दिवा ग्रहगणन्तथा।
दृष्ट्वा मन्येत संक्षीणमात्मजीवितमात्मवित् ॥ २४ ॥
नासिका वक्रतामेति कर्णयोर्न्नमनोन्नती।
नेत्रञ्च वामं स्रवति यस्य तस्यायुरुद्गतं ॥ २५ ॥
आरक्ततामेति मुखं जिह्वा वा श्यामतां यदा।
तदा प्राज्ञो विजानीयान्मृत्युमासन्नमात्मनः ॥ २६ ॥

उष्ट्ररासभयानेन यः स्वप्ने दक्षिणां दिशं।
प्रयाति तञ्च जानीयात् सद्योमृत्युं न संशयः ॥ २७ ॥
पिधाय कर्णौ निर्घोषं न शृणोत्यात्मसम्भवं।
नश्यते चक्षुषोर्ज्योतिर्यस्य सोऽपि न जीवति ॥ २८ ॥
पततो यस्य वै गर्त्ते स्वप्ने द्वारं पिधीयते।
नचोत्तिष्ठति यः श्वभ्रात्तदन्तं तस्य जीवितं ॥ २९ ॥

ऊर्द्धा च दृष्टिर्न च संप्रतिष्ठा
रक्ता पुनः संपरिवर्त्तमाना।
मुखस्य चोष्मा शुषिरञ्च नाभेः
शंसन्ति पुंसामपरं शरीरं ॥ ३० ॥

स्वप्नेऽग्निं प्रविशेद्यस्तु न च निष्क्रमते पुनः।
जलप्रवेशादपि वा तदन्तं तस्य जीवितं ॥ ३१ ॥
यश्चाभिहन्यते दुष्टैर्भूतैराचावथो दिवा।
स मृत्युं सप्तरात्र्यन्ते नरः प्राप्नोत्यसंशयं ॥ ३२ ॥
स्ववस्त्रममलं शुक्लं रक्तं पश्यत्यथासितं।
यः पुमान् मृत्युमासन्नं तस्यापि हि विनिर्दिशेत् ॥ ३३ ॥
स्वभाववैपरीत्यन्तु प्रकृतेश्च विपर्य्ययः।
कथयन्ति मनुष्याणां सदासन्नौ यमान्तकौ ॥ ३४ ॥
येषां विनीतः सततं येऽस्य पूज्यतमा मताः।
तानेव चावजानाति तानेव च विनिन्दति ॥ ३५ ॥
देवान्नार्चयते वृद्धान् गुरून् विप्रांश्च निन्दति।
मातापित्रोर्न सत्कारं जामातॄणां करोति च ॥ ३६ ॥

योगिनां ज्ञानविदुषामन्येषाञ्च महात्मनां ।
प्राप्ते तु काले पुरुषस्तद्विज्ञेयं विचक्षणैः ॥ ३७ ॥
योगिनां सततं यत्नादरिष्टान्यवनीपते ।
संवत्सरान्ते तज्ज्ञेयं फलदानि दिवानिशं ॥ ३८ ॥
विलोक्या विशदा चैषां फलपंक्तिः सुभीषणा ।
विज्ञाय कार्य्यों मनसि स च कालो नरेश्वर ॥ ३९ ॥
ज्ञात्वा कालञ्च तं सम्यगभयस्थानमाश्रितः ।
युञ्जीत योगी कालोऽसौ यथा नास्याफलो भवेत् ॥ ४० ॥
दृष्ट्वारिष्टं तथा योगी त्यक्त्वा मरणजं भयं ।
तत्स्वभावं तदालोक्य काले यावत्युपागतं ॥ ४१ ॥
तस्य भागे तथैवाह्नो योगं युञ्जीत योगवित् ।
पूर्व्वाह्णे चापराह्णे च मध्याह्णे चापि तद्दिने ॥ ४२ ॥
यत्र वा रजनीभागे तदरिष्टं निरीक्षितं ।
तत्रैव तावद्युञ्जीत यावत्प्राप्तं हि तद्दिनं ॥ ४३ ॥
ततस्त्यक्त्वा भयं सर्व्वं जित्वा तं कालमात्मवान् ।
तत्रैवावसथे स्थित्वा यत्र वा स्थैर्य्यमात्मनः ॥ ४४ ॥
युञ्जीत योगं निर्जित्य त्रीन् गुणान् परमात्मनि ।
तन्मयश्चात्मना भूत्वा चिद्वृत्तिमपि सन्त्यजेत् ॥ ४५ ॥
ततः परमनिर्व्वाणमतीन्द्रियमगोचरं ।
यद्बुद्धेर्यन्न चाख्यातुं शक्यते तत्समश्नुते ॥ ४६ ॥
एतत्सर्व्वं समाख्यातं तवालर्क यथार्थवत् ।
प्राप्स्यसे येन तद्ब्रह्म संक्षेपात्तन्निबोध मे ॥ ४७ ॥

शशाङ्करश्मिसंयोगाच्चन्द्रकान्तमणिः पयः ।
समुत्सृजति नायुक्तः सोपमा योगिनः स्मृता ॥ ४८ ॥
यथार्करश्मिसंयोगादर्ककान्तो हुताशनं ।
आविष्करोति नैकः सन्नुपमा सापि योगिनः ॥ ४९ ॥
पिपीलिकाखुनकुलगृहगोधाकपिञ्जलाः ।
वसन्ति स्वामिवद्गेहे ध्वस्ते यान्ति ततोऽन्यतः ॥ ५० ॥
दुःखन्तु स्वामिनो ध्वंसे तस्य तेषां न किञ्चन ।
वेश्मनो यत्र राजेन्द्र सोपमा योगसिद्धये ॥ ५१ ॥
मृद्देहिकाल्पदेहापि मुखाग्रेणाप्यणीयसा ।
करोति मृद्भारचयमुपदेशः स योगिनः ॥ ५२ ॥
पशुपक्षिमनुष्याद्यैः पत्रपुष्पफलान्वितं ।
वृक्षं विलुप्यमानन्तु दृष्ट्वा सिद्ध्यन्ति योगिनः ॥ ५३ ॥
रुरुशावविषाणाग्रमालक्ष्य तिलकाकृतिं ।
सह तेन विवर्द्धन्तं योगी सिद्धिमवाप्नुयात् ॥ ५४ ॥
द्रवपूर्णमुपादाय पात्रमारोहतो भुवः ।
तुङ्गमङ्गं विलोक्योच्चैर्विज्ञातं किं न योगिना ॥ ५५ ॥
सर्व्वस्वं जीवनायालं निखाते पुरुषस्य या ।
चेष्टा तां तत्त्वतो ज्ञात्वा योगिनः कृतकृत्यता ॥ ५६ ॥
तद्गृहं यत्र वसति तद्भोज्यं येन जीवति ।
येन सम्पद्यते चार्थस्तत्सुखं ममताच का ॥ ५७ ॥
अभ्यर्थितोऽपि तैः कार्य्यं करोति करणैर्यथा ।
तथा बुद्ध्यादिभिर्योगी पारक्यैः साधयेत्परं ॥ ५८ ॥

जड उवाच ॥

ततः प्रणम्याचिपुत्त्रमलर्कः स महीपतिः ।
प्रश्रयावनतो वाक्यमुवाचातिमुदान्वितः ॥ ५९ ॥

अलर्क उवाच ॥

दिष्ट्या दैवैरिदं ब्रह्मन् पराभिभवसम्भवं ।
उपपादितमत्युग्रं प्राणसन्देहदम्भयं ॥ ६० ॥
दिष्ट्या काशिपतेर्भूरिबलसम्पत्पराक्रमः ।
यदुच्छेदादिहायातः स युष्मत्सङ्गदो मम ॥ ६१ ॥
दिष्ट्या मन्दबलश्चाहं दिष्ट्या भृत्याश्च मे हताः ।
दिष्ट्या कोषः क्षयं यातो दिष्ट्याहं भीतिमागतः ॥ ६२ ॥
दिष्ट्या त्वत्पादयुगलं मम स्मृतिपथं गतं ।
दिष्ट्या त्वदुक्तयः सर्वा मम चेतसि संस्थिताः ॥ ६३ ॥
दिष्ट्या ज्ञानं ममोत्पन्नं भवतश्च समागमात् ।
भवता चैव कारुण्यं दिष्ट्या ब्रह्मन् कृतं मम ॥ ६४ ॥
अनर्थोऽप्यर्थतां याति पुरुषस्य शुभोदये ।
यथेदमुपकाराय व्यसनं सङ्गमात्तव ॥ ६५ ॥
सुबाहुरुपकारी मे स च काशिपतिः प्रभो ।
ययोः कृतेऽहं संप्राप्तो योगीश भवतोऽन्तिकं ॥ ६६ ॥
सोऽहन्तव प्रसादाग्निनिर्दग्धाज्ञानकिल्बिषः ।
तथा यतिष्ये येनेदृङ् भूयां दुःखभाजनं ॥ ६७ ॥
परित्यजिष्ये गार्हस्थ्यमार्त्तिपादपकाननं ।
त्वत्तोऽनुज्ञां समासाद्य ज्ञानदातुर्म्महात्मनः ॥ ६८ ॥

दत्तात्रेय उवाच ॥

गच्छ राजेन्द्र भद्रं ते यथा ते कथितं मया ।
निर्म्ममो निरहङ्कारस्तथा चर विमुक्तये ॥ ६९ ॥

जड उवाच ॥

एवमुक्तः प्रणम्यैनमाजगाम त्वरान्वितः ।
यत्र काशिपतिर्भ्राता सुबाहुश्चास्य सोऽग्रजः ॥ ७० ॥
समुत्पत्य महाबाहुं सोऽलर्कः काशिभूपतिं ।
सुबाहोरग्रतो वीरमुवाच प्रहसन्निव ॥ ७१ ॥
राज्यकामुक काशीश भुज्यतां राज्यमूर्जितं ।
तथा च रोचते तद्वत् सुबाहोः संप्रयच्छ वा ॥ ७२ ॥

काशिराज उवाच ॥

किमलर्क परित्यक्तं राज्यन्ते संयुगं विना ।
क्षत्रियस्य न धर्म्मोऽयं भवांश्च क्षत्रधर्म्मवित् ॥ ७३ ॥
निर्जितामात्यवर्गस्तु त्यक्त्वा मरणजं भयं ।
सन्दधीत शरं राजा लक्ष्यमुद्दिश्य वैरिणां ॥ ७४ ॥
तं जित्वा नृपतिर्भोगान् यथाभिलषितान् वरान् ।
भुञ्जीत परमं सिद्ध्यै यजेत च महामखैः ॥ ७५ ॥

अलर्क उवाच ॥

एवमीदृशकं वीर ममाप्यासीन्मनः पुरा ।
साम्प्रतं विपरीतार्थं शृणु चाप्यत्र कारणं ॥ ७६ ॥
यथायं भौतिकः सङ्घस्तथान्तःकरणं नृणां ।
गुणास्तु सकलास्तद्वदशेषेष्वेव जन्तुषु ॥ ७७ ॥

चिच्छक्तिरेकएवायं यदा नान्योऽस्ति कश्चन ।
तदा का नृपते ज्ञानान्मित्रारिप्रभुभृत्यता ॥ ७८ ॥
तन्मया दुःखमासाद्य त्वद्भयोद्भवमुत्तमं ।
दत्तात्रेयप्रसादेन ज्ञानं प्राप्तं नरेश्वर ॥ ७९ ॥
निर्जितेन्द्रियवर्गस्तु त्यक्त्वा सङ्गमशेषतः ।
मनो ब्रह्मणि सन्धाय तज्जये परमो जयः ॥ ८० ॥
संसाध्यमन्यत्तत्सिद्धौ यतः किञ्चिन्न विद्यते ।
इन्द्रियाणि च संयम्य ततः सिद्धिं नियच्छति ॥ ८१ ॥

सोऽहं न तेऽरिर्न ममासि शत्रुः
सुबाहुरेषो न ममापकारी ।
दृष्टं मया सर्व्वमिदं यथात्मा
अन्विष्यतां भूप रिपुस्त्वयान्यः ॥ ८२ ॥
इत्थं स तेनाभिहितो नरेन्द्रो
हृष्टः समुत्थाय ततः सुबाहुः ।
दिष्ट्येति तं भ्रातरमाभिनन्द्य
काशीश्वरं वाक्यमिदं बभाषे ॥ ८३ ॥

इति श्रीमार्कण्डेयपुराणेऽरिष्टाध्यायः ॥ ४३ ॥

चतुश्चत्वारिंशोऽध्यायः ॥

सुबाहुरुवाच ॥

यदर्थं नृपशार्दूल त्वामहं शरणं गतः ।
तन्मया सकलं प्राप्तं यास्यामि त्वं सुखी भव ॥ १ ॥

काशिराज उवाच ॥

किन्निमित्तं भवान् प्राप्तो निष्पन्नोऽर्थश्च कस्तव ।
सुबाहो तन्ममाचक्ष परं कौतूहलं हि मे ॥ २ ॥
समाक्रान्तमलर्केण पितृपैतामहं महत् ।
राज्यं देहीति निर्जित्य त्वयाहमभिचोदितः ॥ ३ ॥
ततो मया समाक्रम्य राज्यमस्यानुजस्य ते ।
एतत्ते बलमानीतं तद्भुङ्क्ष्व कुलोचितं ॥ ४ ॥

सुबाहुरुवाच ॥

काशिराज निबोध त्वं यदर्थमयमुद्यमः ।
कृतो मया भवांश्चैव कारितोऽत्यन्तमुद्यमं ॥ ५ ॥
भ्राता ममायं ग्राम्येषु शक्तो भोगेषु तत्त्ववित् ।
विमूढौ बोधवन्तौ च भ्रातरावग्रजौ मम ॥ ६ ॥
तयोर्मम च यन्माता बाल्ये स्तन्यं यथा मुखे ।
तथावबोधो विन्यस्तः कर्णयोरवनीपते ॥ ७ ॥
तयोर्मम च विज्ञेयाः पदार्था ये मता नृभिः ।
प्रकाश्यमनसो नीतास्ते माता नास्य पार्थिवं ॥ ८ ॥

यथैकमर्थं यातानामेकस्मिन्नवसीदति ।
दुःखं भवति साधूनां तथास्माकं महीपते ॥ ९ ॥
गार्हस्थ्यमोहमापन्ने सीदत्यस्मिन्नरेश्वर ।
सम्बन्धिन्यस्य देहस्य बिभ्रति भ्रातृकल्पनां ॥ १० ॥
ततो मया विनिश्चित्य दुःखाद्वैराग्यभावना ।
भविष्यतीत्यस्य भवानित्युद्योगाय संश्रितः ॥ ११ ॥
तदस्य दुःखाद्वैराग्यं संबोधादवनीपते ।
समुद्भूतं कृतं कार्य्यं भद्रं तेऽस्तु व्रजाम्यहं ॥ १२ ॥
उष्ट्वा मदालसागर्भे पीत्वा तस्यास्तथा स्तनं ।
नान्यनारीसुतैर्यातं वर्त्म यात्विति पार्थिव ॥ १३ ॥
विचार्य्यं तन्मया सर्व्वं युष्मत्संश्रयपूर्व्वकं ।
कृतं तच्चापि निष्पन्नं प्रयास्ये सिद्धये पुनः ॥ १४ ॥
उपेक्ष्यते सीदमानः स्वजनो बान्धवः सुहृत् ।
यैर्न्नरेन्द्र न तान् मन्ये सेन्द्रिया विकला हि ते ॥ १५ ॥
सुहृदि स्वजने बन्धौ समर्थे योऽवसीदति ।
धर्म्मार्थकाममोक्षेभ्यो वाच्यास्ते तत्र न त्वसौ ॥ १६ ॥
एतत् त्वत्सङ्गमाद् भूप मया कार्य्यं महत्कृतं ।
स्वस्ति तेऽस्तु गमिष्यामि ज्ञानभाग्भव सत्तम ॥ १७ ॥

काशिराज उवाच ॥

उपकारस्त्वया साधोरलर्कस्य कृतो महान् ।
ममोपकाराय कथं न करोषि स्वमानसं ॥ १८ ॥
फलदायी सतां सद्भिः सङ्गमो नाफलो यतः ।

तस्मात्त्वत्संश्रयाद्युक्ता मया प्राप्ता समुन्नतिः ॥ १९ ॥

सुबाहुरुवाच ॥

धर्म्मार्थकाममोक्षाख्यं पुरुषार्थचतुष्टयं ।
तत्र धर्म्मार्थकामास्ते सकला हीयतेऽपरः ॥ २० ॥
तत्ते सङ्क्षेपतो वक्ष्ये तदिहैकमनाः शृणु ।
श्रुत्वा च सम्यगालोच्य यतेथाः श्रेयसे नृप ॥ २१ ॥
ममेतिप्रत्ययो भूप न कार्य्योऽहमिति त्वया ।
सम्यगालोच्य धर्म्मो हि धर्म्माभावे निराश्रयः ॥ २२ ॥
कस्याहमिति सञ्ज्ञेयमित्यालोच्य त्वयात्मना ।
वाह्यान्तर्गतमालोच्यमालोच्यापररात्रिषु ॥ २३ ॥
अव्यक्तादिविशेषान्तमविकारमचेतनं ।
व्यक्ताव्यक्तं त्वया ज्ञेयं ज्ञाता कश्चाहमित्युत ॥ २४ ॥
एतस्मिन्नेव विज्ञाते विज्ञातमखिलं त्वया ।
अनात्मन्यात्मविज्ञानमस्वे स्वमिति मूढता ॥ २५ ॥
सोऽहं सर्व्वगतो भूप लोकसंव्यवहारतः ।
मयेदमुच्यते सर्व्वं त्वया पृष्टो व्रजाम्यहं ॥ २६ ॥
एवमुक्त्वा ययौ धीमान् सुबाहुः काशिभूमिपं ।
काशिराजोऽपि संपूज्य सोऽलर्क्कं स्वपुरं ययौ ॥ २७ ॥
अलर्कोऽपि सुतं ज्येष्ठमभिषिच्य नराधिपं ।
वनं जगाम सन्त्यक्तसर्व्वसङ्गः स्वसिद्धये ॥ २८ ॥
ततः कालेन महता निर्द्वन्द्वो निष्परिग्रहः ।
प्राप्य योगर्द्धिमतुलां परं निर्व्वाणमाप्तवान् ॥ २९ ॥

पश्यन् जगदिदं सर्व्वं सदेवासुरमानुषं ।
पाशैर्गुणमयैर्बद्धं बध्यमानञ्च नित्यशः ॥ ३० ॥
पुत्त्रादिभ्रातृपुत्त्रादिस्वपारक्यादिभावितैः ।
आकृष्यमाणं करणैर्दुःखार्त्तं भिन्नदर्शनं ॥ ३१ ॥
अज्ञानपङ्कगर्भस्थमनुद्धारं महामतिः ।
आत्मानञ्च समुत्तीर्णं गाथामेतामगायत ॥ ३२ ॥
अहो कष्टं यदस्माभिः पूर्व्वं राज्यमनुष्ठितं ।
इति पश्चान्मया ज्ञातं योगान्नास्ति परं सुखं ॥ ३३ ॥

जड उवाच ॥

तातैनं त्वं समातिष्ठ मुक्तये योगमुत्तमं ।
प्राप्स्यसे येन तद्ब्रह्म यत्र गत्वा न शोचसि ॥ ३४ ॥
ततोऽहमपि यास्यामि किं यज्ञैः किं जपेन मे ।
कृतकृत्यस्य करणं ब्रह्मभावाय कल्पते ॥ ३५ ॥
त्वत्तोऽनुज्ञामवाप्याहं निर्द्वन्द्वो निष्परिग्रहः ।
प्रयतिष्ये तथा मुक्तौ यथा यास्यामि निर्वृतिं ॥ ३६ ॥

पक्षिण ऊचुः ॥

एवमुक्त्वा स पितरं प्राप्यानुज्ञां ततश्च सः ।
ब्रह्मन् जगाम मेधावी परित्यक्तपरिग्रहः ॥ ३७ ॥
सोऽपि तस्य पिता तद्वत् क्रमेण सुमहामतिः ।
वानप्रस्थं समास्थाय चतुर्थाश्रममभ्यगात् ॥ ३८ ॥
तत्रात्मजं समासाद्य हित्वा बन्धं गुणादिकं ।
प्राप सिद्धिं परां प्राज्ञस्तत्कालोपात्तसंमतिः ॥ ३९ ॥

एतत्ते कथितं ब्रह्मन् यत्पृष्टा भवता वयं ।
सुविस्तरं यथावच्च किमन्यच्छ्रोतुमिच्छसि ॥ ४० ॥

इति श्रीमार्कण्डेयपुराणे पितापुत्त्रसंवादे जडोपाख्यनं समाप्तं ॥ ४४ ॥

पञ्चचत्वारिंशोऽध्यायः ॥

जैमिनिरुवाच

सम्यगेतन्ममाख्यातं भवद्भिर्द्विजसत्तमाः ।
प्रवृत्तिश्च निवृत्तिश्च द्विविधं कर्म्म वैदिकं ॥ १ ॥
अहो पितृप्रसादेन भवतां ज्ञानमीदृशं ।
येन तिर्य्यक्त्वमप्येतत्प्राप्य मोहस्तिरस्कृतः ॥ २ ॥
धन्या भवन्तः संसिद्धौ प्रागवस्थास्थितं यतः ।
भवतां विषयोद्भूतैर्न्न मोहैश्चाल्यते मनः ॥ ३ ॥
दिष्ट्या भगवता तेन मार्कण्डेयेन धीमता ।
भवन्तो वै समाख्याताः सर्व्वसन्देहहृत्तमाः ॥ ४ ॥
संसारेऽस्मिन्मनुष्याणां भ्रमतामतिसङ्कटे ।
भवद्विधैः समं सङ्गो जायते न तपस्विनां ॥ ५ ॥
यद्यहं सङ्गमासाद्य भवद्भिर्ज्ञानदृष्टिभिः ।
न स्यां कृतार्थस्तन्नूनं न मेऽन्यत्र कृतार्थता ॥ ६ ॥
प्रवृत्ते च निवृत्ते च भवतां ज्ञानकर्म्मणि ।

मतिमस्तमलां मन्ये यथा नान्यस्य कस्यचित् ॥ ७ ॥
यदि त्वनुग्रहवती मयि बुद्धिर्द्विजोत्तमाः ।
भवतां तत्समाख्यातुमर्हतेदमशेषतः ॥ ८ ॥
कथमेतत्समुद्भूतं जगत् स्थावरजङ्गमं ।
कथञ्च प्रलयं काले पुनर्यास्यति सत्तमाः ॥ ९ ॥
कथञ्च वंशाद्देवर्षिपितृभूतादिसम्भवाः ।
मन्वन्तराणि च कथं वंशानुचरितञ्च यत् ॥ १० ॥
यावत्यः सृष्टयश्चैव यावन्तः प्रलयास्तथा ।
यथा कल्पविभागश्च या च मन्वन्तरस्थितिः ॥ ११ ॥
यथा च क्षितिसंस्थानं यत्प्रमाणञ्च वै भुवः ।
यथास्थिति समुद्राद्रिनिम्नगाः काननानि च ॥ १२ ॥
भूर्लोकादिस्वर्लोकानां गणः पातालसंश्रयः ।
गतिस्तथार्कसोमादिग्रहर्चज्योतिषामपि ॥ १३ ॥
श्रोतुमिच्छाम्यहं सर्व्वमेतदाहूतसंप्लव ।
उपसंहृते च यच्छेषं जगत्यस्मिन् भविष्यति ॥ १४ ॥

पक्षिण ऊचुः ॥

प्रश्नभारोऽयमतुलो यस्त्वया मुनिसत्तम ।
पृष्टस्तन्ते प्रवक्ष्यामस्तत् शृणुष्वेह जैमिने ॥ १५ ॥
मार्कण्डेयेन कथितं पुरा क्रौष्टुकये यथा ।
द्विजपुत्राय शान्ताय व्रतस्नाताय धीमते ॥ १६ ॥
मार्कण्डेयं महात्मानमुपासीनं द्विजोत्तमैः ।
क्रौष्टुकिः परिपप्रच्छ यदेतत्पृष्टवान् प्रभो ॥ १७ ॥

तस्य चाकथयत् प्रीत्या यन्मुनिर्भृगुनन्दनः ।
तत्ते प्रकथयिष्यामः शृणु त्वं द्विजसत्तम ॥ १८ ॥
प्रणिपत्य जगन्नाथं पद्मयोनिं पितामहं ।
जगद्योनिं स्थितं सृष्टौ स्थितौ विष्णुस्वरूपिणं ॥
प्रलये चान्तकर्त्तारं रौद्रं रुद्रस्वरूपिणं ॥ १९ ॥

मार्कण्डेय उवाच ॥

उत्पन्नमात्रस्य पुरा ब्रह्मणोऽव्यक्तजन्मनः ।
पुराणमेतद्वेदाश्च मुखेभ्योऽनुविनिःसृताः ॥ २० ॥
पुराणसंहिताश्चक्रुर्ब्बहुलाः परमर्षयः ।
वेदानां प्रविभागश्च कृतस्तैस्तु सहस्रशः ॥ २१ ॥
धर्म्मंज्ञानञ्च वैराग्यमैश्वर्य्यञ्च महात्मनः ।
तस्योपदेशेन विना न हि सिद्धञ्चतुष्टयं ॥ २२ ॥
वेदान् सप्तर्षयस्तस्माज्जगृहुस्तस्य मानसाः ।
पुराणं जगृहुश्चाद्या मुनयस्तस्य मानसाः ॥ २३ ॥
भृगोः सकाशाच्च्यवनस्तेनोक्तञ्च द्विजन्मनां ।
ऋषिभिश्चापि दक्षाय प्रोक्तमेतन्महात्मभिः ॥ २४ ॥
दक्षेण चापि कथितमिदमासीत्तदा मम ।
तत्तुभ्यं कथयाम्यद्य कलिकल्मषनाशनं ॥ २५ ॥
सर्व्वमेतन्महाभाग श्रूयतां मे समाधिना ।
यथाश्रुतं मया पूर्व्वं दक्षस्य गदतो मुने ॥ २६ ॥
प्रणिपत्य जगद्योनिमजमव्ययमाश्रयं ।
चराचरस्य जगतो धातारं परमं पदं ॥ २७ ॥

ब्रह्माणमादिपुरुषमुत्पत्तिस्थितिसंयमे ।
यत्कारणमनौरस्यं यत्र सर्व्वं प्रतिष्ठितं ॥ २८ ॥
तस्मै हिरण्यगर्भ्भाय लोकतन्त्राय धीमते ।
प्रणम्य सम्यग्वक्ष्यामि भूतवर्गमनुत्तमं ॥ २९ ॥
महदाद्यं विशेषान्तं सवैरूप्यं सलक्षणं ।
प्रमाणैः पञ्चभिर्गम्यं स्रोतोभिः सद्भिरन्वितं ॥ ३० ॥
पुरुषाधिष्ठितं नित्यमनित्यमिव च स्थितं ।
तच्छ्रूयतां महाभाग परमेण समाधिना ॥ ३१ ॥
प्रधानं कारणं यत्तदव्यक्ताख्यं महर्षयः ।
यदाहुः प्रकृतिं सूक्ष्मां नित्यां सदसदात्मिकां ॥ ३२ ॥
ध्रुवमक्षय्यमजरममेयं नान्यसंश्रयं ।
गन्धरूपरसैर्हीनं शब्दस्पर्शविवर्ज्जितं ॥ ३३ ॥
अनाद्यन्तं जगद्योनिं त्रिगुणप्रभवाप्ययं ।
असाम्प्रतमविज्ञेयं ब्रह्माग्रे समवर्त्तत ॥ ३४ ॥
प्रलयस्यानु तेनेदं व्याप्तमासीदशेषतः ।
गुणसाम्यात्ततस्तस्मात् क्षेत्रज्ञाधिष्ठितान्मुने ॥ ३५ ॥
गुणभावात्सृज्यमानात् सर्गकाले ततः पुनः ।
प्रधानं तत्त्वमुद्भूतं महान्तं तत्समावृणोत् ॥ ३६ ॥
यथा वीजं त्वचा तद्वदव्यक्तेनावृतो महान् ।
सात्त्विको राजसश्चैव तामसश्च त्रिधोदितः ॥ ३७ ॥
ततस्तस्मादहङ्कारस्त्रिविधो वै व्यजायत ।
वैकारिकस्तैजसश्च भूतादिश्च सतामसः ॥ ३८ ॥

महता चावृतः सोऽपि यथाव्यक्तेन वै महान् ।
भूतादिस्तु विकुर्व्वाणः शब्दतन्मात्रकन्ततः ॥ ३९ ॥
ससर्ज शब्दतन्मात्रादाकाशं शब्दलक्षणं ।
आकाशं शब्दमात्रन्तु भूतादिश्चावृणोत्ततः ॥ ४० ॥
स्पर्शतन्मात्रमेवेह जायते नात्र संशयः ।
बलवान् जायते वायुस्तस्य स्पर्शगुणो मतः ॥ ४१ ॥
वायुश्चापि विकुर्व्वाणो रूपमात्रं ससर्ज ह ।
ज्योतिरुत्पद्यते वायोस्तद्रूपगुणमुच्यते ॥ ४२ ॥
स्पर्शमात्रस्तु वै वायू रूपमात्रं समावृणोत् ।
ज्योतिश्चापि विकुर्व्वाणं रसमात्रं ससर्ज ह ॥ ४३ ॥
सम्भवन्ति ततो ह्यापश्चासन् वै ता रसात्मिकाः ।
रसमात्रन्तु ताह्यापो रूपमात्रं समावृणोत् ॥ ४४ ॥
आपश्चापि विकुर्व्वत्यो गन्धमात्रं ससर्ज्जिरे ।
सङ्घातो जायते तस्मात्तस्य गन्धो गुणो मतः ॥ ४५ ॥
तस्मिंस्तस्मिंस्तु तन्मात्रं तेन तन्मात्रता स्मृता ।
अविशेषवाचकत्वादविशेषास्ततश्च ते ॥ ४६ ॥
न शान्ता नापि घोरास्ते न मूढाश्चाविशेषतः ।
भूततन्मात्रसर्गोऽयमहङ्कारात्तु तामसात् ॥ ४७ ॥
वैकारिकादहङ्कारात् सत्त्वोद्रिक्तात्तु सात्त्विकात् ।
वैकारिकः स सर्गस्तु युगपत् सम्प्रवर्त्तते ॥ ४८ ॥
बुद्धीन्द्रियाणि पञ्चैव पञ्च कर्म्मेन्द्रियाणि च ।
तैजसानीन्द्रियाण्याहुर्द्देवा वैकारिका दश ॥ ४९ ॥

एकादशं मनस्तत्र देवा वैकारिकाः स्मृताः।
श्रोत्रं त्वक्चक्षुषी जिह्वा नासिका चैव पञ्चमी॥ ५०॥
शब्दादीनामवाप्त्यर्थं बुद्धियुक्तानि वक्ष्यते।
पादौ पायुरुपस्थश्च हस्तौ वाक् पञ्चमी भवेत्॥ ५१॥
गतिर्विसर्गो ह्यानन्दः शिल्पं वाक्यञ्च कर्म्म तत्।
आकाशं शब्दमात्रन्तु स्पर्शमात्रं समाविशत्॥ ५२॥
द्विगुणो जायते वायुस्तस्य स्पर्शो गुणो मतः।
रूपन्तथैवाविशतः शब्दस्पर्शगुणावुभौ॥ ५३॥
द्विगुणस्तु ततश्चाग्निः स शब्दस्पर्शरूपवान्।
शब्दः स्पर्शश्च रूपञ्च रसमात्रं समाविशत्॥ ५४॥
तस्माच्चतुर्गुणा ह्यापो विज्ञेयास्ता रसात्मिकाः।
शब्दः स्पर्शश्च रूपञ्च रसो गन्धं समाविशत्॥ ५५॥
संहता गन्धमात्रेण आवृण्वंस्ते महीमिमां।
तस्मात् पञ्चगुणा भूमिः स्थूला भूतेषु दृश्यते॥ ५६॥
शान्ता घोराश्च मूढाश्च विशेषास्तेन ते स्मृताः।
परस्परानुप्रवेशाद्धारयन्ति परस्परं॥ ५७॥
भूमेरन्तस्त्विमं सर्व्वं लोकालोकं घनावृतं।
विशेषाश्चेन्द्रियग्राह्या नियतत्वाच्च ते स्मृताः॥ ५८॥
गुणं पूर्व्वस्य पूर्व्वस्य प्राप्नुवन्त्युत्तरोत्तरं।
नानावीर्य्याः पृथग्भूताः सप्तैते संहतिं विना॥ ५९॥
नाशक्नुवन् प्रजाः स्रष्टुमसमागम्य कृत्स्नशः।
समेत्यान्योन्यसंयोगमन्योन्याश्रयिनश्च ते॥ ६०॥

एकसंघातचिह्नाश्च संप्राप्यैक्यमशेषतः ।
पुरुषाधिष्ठितत्वाच्च अव्यक्तानुग्रहेण च ॥ ६१ ॥
महदाद्या विशेषान्ता ह्यण्डमुत्पादयन्ति ते ।
जलबुद्बुदवत्तच्च क्रमाद्वै वृद्धिमागतं ॥ ६२ ॥
भूतेभ्योऽण्डं महाबुद्धे वृहत्तदुदकेशयं ।
प्राकृतेऽण्डे विवृद्धः सन् क्षेत्रज्ञो ब्रह्मसंज्ञितः ॥ ६३ ॥
स वै शरीरी प्रथमः स वै पुरुष उच्यते ।
आदिकर्त्ता च भूतानां ब्रह्माग्रे समवर्त्तत ॥ ६४ ॥
तेन सर्व्वमिदं व्याप्तं त्रैलोक्यं सचराचरं ।
मेरुस्तस्यानुसम्भूतो जरायुश्चापि पर्व्वताः ॥ ६५ ॥
समुद्रा गर्ब्भसलिलं तस्याण्डस्य महात्मनः ।
तस्मिन्नण्डे जगत्सर्व्वं सदेवासुरमानुषं ॥ ६६ ॥
द्वीपाद्यद्रिसमुद्राश्च सज्योतिर्लोकसंग्रहः ।
जलानिलानलाकाशैस्ततो भूतादिना वहिः ॥ ६७ ॥
वृतमण्डं दशगुणैरेकैकत्वेन तैः पुनः ।
महता तत्प्रमाणेन सहैवानेन वेष्टितः ॥ ६८ ॥
महांस्तैः सहितः सर्व्वैरव्यक्तेन समावृतः ।
एभिरावरणैरण्डं सप्तभिः प्राकृतैर्वृतं ॥ ६९ ॥
अन्योन्यमावृतवता अष्टौ प्रकृतयः स्थिताः ।
एषा सा प्रकृतिर्न्नित्या तदन्तः पुरुषश्च सः ॥ ७० ॥
ब्रह्माख्यः कथितो यस्ते समासात् श्रूयतां पुनः ।
यथा मग्नो जले कश्चिदुन्मज्जन् जलसम्भवं ॥ ७१ ॥

जलञ्च क्षिपति ब्रह्मा स तथा प्रकृतिर्विभुः ।
अव्यक्तं क्षेत्रमुद्दिष्टं ब्रह्मा क्षेत्रज्ञ उच्यते ॥ ७२ ॥
एतत्समस्तं जानीयात् क्षेत्रक्षेत्रज्ञलक्षणं ।
इत्येष प्राकृतः सर्गः क्षेत्रज्ञाधिष्ठितस्तु सः ॥
अबुद्धिपूर्व्वः प्रथमः प्रादुर्भूतस्तडिद्यथा ॥ ७३ ॥

इति श्रीमार्कण्डेयपुराणे ब्रह्मोत्पत्तिर्नाम ॥ ४५ ॥

षट्चत्वारिंशोऽध्यायः ॥

क्रौष्टुकिरुवाच ॥

भगवंस्त्वण्डसम्भूतिर्यथावत् कथिता मम ।
ब्रह्माण्डे ब्रह्मणो जन्म तथाचोक्तं महात्मनः ॥ १ ॥
एतदिच्छाम्यहं श्रोतुं त्वत्तो भृगुकुलोद्भव ।
यदा न सृष्टिर्भूतानामस्ति किन्नु न चास्ति वा ॥
काले वै प्रलयस्यान्ते सर्व्वस्मिन्नुपसंहृते ॥ २ ॥

मार्कण्डेय उवाच ॥

यदा तु प्रकृतौ याति लयं विश्वमिदं जगत् ।
तदोच्यते प्राकृतोऽयं विद्वद्भिः प्रतिसञ्चरः ॥ ३ ॥
स्वात्मन्यवस्थितेऽव्यक्ते विकारे प्रतिसंहृते ।
प्रकृतिः पुरुषश्चैव साधर्म्म्येणावतिष्ठतः ॥ ४ ॥

तदा तमश्च सत्त्वञ्च समत्वेन व्यवस्थितौ ।
अनुद्रिक्तावनूनौ च तत्प्रोतौ च परस्परं ॥ ५ ॥
तिलेषु वा यथा तैलं घृतं पयसि वा स्थितं ।
तथा तमसि सत्त्वे च रजोऽप्यनुसृतं स्थितं ॥ ६ ॥
उत्पत्तिर्ब्रह्मणो यावदायुषो द्विपरार्द्धिकं ।
तावद्दिनं परेशस्य तत्समा संयमे निशा ॥ ७ ॥
अहर्मुखे प्रबुद्धस्तु जगदादिरनादिमान् ।
सर्व्वहेतुरचिन्त्यात्मा परः कोऽप्यपरक्रियः ॥ ८ ॥
प्रकृतिं पुरुषञ्चैव प्रविश्याशु जगत्पतिः ।
क्षोभयामास योगेन परेण परमेश्वरः ॥ ९ ॥
यथा मदो नवस्त्रीणां यथा वा माधवानिलः ।
अनुप्रविष्टः क्षोभाय तथासौ योगमूर्त्तिमान् ॥ १० ॥
प्रधाने क्षोभ्यमाने तु स देवो ब्रह्मसंज्ञितः ।
समुत्पन्नोऽण्डकोषस्थो यथा ते कथितं मया ॥ ११ ॥
स एव क्षोभकः पूर्व्वं स क्षोभ्यः प्रकृतेः पतिः ।
स संकोचविकाशाभ्यां प्रधानत्वेऽपि च स्थितः ॥ १२ ॥
उत्पन्नः स जगद्योनिरगुणोऽपि रजोगुणं ।
भुञ्जन् प्रवर्त्तते सर्गे ब्रह्मत्वं समुपाश्रितः ॥ १३ ॥
ब्रह्मत्वे स प्रजाः सृष्ट्वा ततः सत्त्वातिरेकवान ।
विष्णुत्वमेत्य धर्म्मेण कुरुते परिपालनं ॥ १४ ॥
ततस्तमोगुणोद्रिक्तो रुद्रत्वे चाखिलं जगत् ।
उपसंहृत्य वै शेते त्रैलोक्यं त्रिगुणोऽगुणः ॥ १५ ॥

यथा प्राग्व्यापकः क्षेत्री पालको लावकस्तथा ।
तथा स संज्ञामायाति ब्रह्मविष्णवीशकारिणीं ॥ १६ ॥
ब्रह्मत्वे सृजते लोकान् रुद्रत्वे संहरत्यपि ।
विष्णुत्वे चाप्युदासीनस्तिस्रोऽवस्थाः स्वयम्भुवः ॥ १७ ॥
रजोब्रह्मा तमो रुद्रो विष्णुः सत्त्वं जगत्पतिः ।
एत एव त्रयो देवा एत एव त्रयो गुणाः ॥ १८ ॥
अन्योन्यमिथुना ह्येते अन्योन्याश्रयिणस्तथा ।
क्षणं वियोगो न ह्येषां न त्यजन्ति परस्परं ॥ १९ ॥
एवं ब्रह्मा जगत्पूर्व्वो देवदेवश्चतुर्मुखः ।
रजोगुणं समाश्रित्य स्रष्टृत्वे स व्यवस्थितः ॥ २० ॥
हिरण्यगर्ब्भो देवादिरनादिरुपचारतः ।
भूपद्मकर्णिकासंस्थो ब्रह्माग्रे समजायत ॥ २१ ॥
तस्य वर्षशतं त्वेकं परमायुर्महात्मनः ।
ब्राह्मेणैव हि मानेन तस्य संख्यां निबोध मे ॥ २२ ॥
निमेषैर्दशभिः काष्ठा तथा पञ्चभिरुच्यते ।
कलास्त्रिंशच्च वै काष्ठा मुहूर्त्तं त्रिंशत्ताः कलाः ॥ २३ ॥
अहोरात्रं मुहूर्त्तानां नृणां त्रिंशत्तु वै स्मृतं ।
अहोरात्रैश्च त्रिंशद्भिः पक्षौ द्वौ मास उच्यते ॥ २४ ॥
तैः षड्भिरयनं वर्षं द्वेऽयने दक्षिणोत्तरे ।
तद्देवानामहोरात्रं दिनं तत्रोत्तरायणं ॥ २५ ॥
दिव्यैर्वर्षसहस्रैस्तु कृतत्रेतादिसंज्ञितं ।
चतुर्युगं द्वादशभिस्तद्विभागं शृणुष्व मे ॥ २६ ॥

चत्वारि तु सहस्राणि वर्षाणां कृतमुच्यते ।
शतानि सन्ध्या चत्वारि सन्ध्यांशश्च तथाविधः ॥ २७ ॥
त्रेता त्रीणि सहस्राणि दिव्याब्दानां शतत्रयं ।
तत्सन्ध्या तत्समा चैव सन्ध्यांशश्च तथाविधः ॥ २८ ॥
द्वापरं द्वे सहस्रे तु वर्षाणां द्वे शते तथा ।
तस्य सन्ध्या समाख्याता द्वे शताब्दे तदंशकः ॥ २९ ॥
कलिः सहस्रं दिव्यानामब्दानां द्विजसत्तम ।
सन्ध्या सन्ध्यांशकश्चैव शतकौ समुदाहृतौ ॥ ३० ॥
एषा द्वादशसाहस्री युगाख्या कविभिः कृता ।
एतत् सहस्रगुणितमहो ब्राह्मयमुदाहृतं ॥ ३१ ॥
ब्रह्मणो दिवसे ब्रह्मन् मनवः स्युश्चतुर्द्दश ।
भवन्ति भागशस्तेषां सहस्रं तद्विभज्यते ॥ ३२ ॥
देवाः सप्तर्षयः सेन्द्रा मनुस्तत्सूनवो नृपाः ।
मनुना सह सृज्यन्ते संह्रियन्ते च पूर्व्ववत् ॥ ३३ ॥
चतुर्युगानां संख्याता साधिका ह्येकसप्ततिः ।
मन्वन्तरं तस्य संख्यां मानुषाब्दैर्निबोध मे ॥ ३४ ॥
त्रिंशत् कोट्यस्तु संपूर्णाः संख्याताः संख्यया द्विज ।
सप्तषष्टिस्तथान्यानि नियुतानि च संख्यया ॥ ३५ ॥
विंशतिश्च सहस्राणि कालोऽयं साधिकं विना ।
एतन्मन्वन्तरं प्रोक्तं दिव्यैर्वर्षैर्निबोध मे ॥ ३६ ॥
अष्टौ वर्षसहस्राणि दिव्यया संख्यया युतं ।
द्विपञ्चाशत्तथान्यानि सहस्राण्यधिकानि तु ॥ ३७ ॥

चतुर्द्दशगुणो ह्येष कालो ब्राह्ममहः स्मृतं ।
तस्यान्ते प्रलयः प्रोक्तो ब्रह्मन् नैमित्तिको बुधैः ॥ ३८ ॥
भूर्लोकोऽथ भुवर्ल्लोकः स्वर्लोकश्च विनाशिनः ।
तथा विनाशमायाति महर्लोकश्च तिष्ठति ॥ ३९ ॥
तद्वासिनोऽपि तापेन जनलोकं प्रयान्ति वै ।
एकार्णवे च त्रैलोक्ये ब्रह्मा स्वपिति वै निशि ॥ ४० ॥
तत्प्रमाणैव सा रात्रिस्तदन्ते सृज्यते पुनः ।
एवन्तु ब्रह्मणो वर्षमेकं वर्षशतन्तु तत् ॥ ४१ ॥
शतं हि तस्य वर्षाणां परमित्यभिधीयते ।
पञ्चाशद्भिस्तथा वर्षैः परार्द्धमिति कीर्त्त्यते ॥ ४२ ॥
एवमस्य परार्द्धन्तु व्यतीतं द्विजसत्तम ।
यस्यान्तेऽभून्महाकल्पः पाद्मइत्यभिविश्रुतः ॥ ४३ ॥
द्वितीयस्य परार्द्धस्य वर्त्तमानस्य वै द्विज ।
वाराह इति कल्पोऽयं प्रथमः परिकल्पितः ॥ ४४ ॥

इति श्रीमार्कण्डेयपुराणे ब्रह्मायुः प्रमाणं ॥ ४६ ॥

सप्तचत्वारिंशोऽध्यायः ॥

क्रौष्टुकिरुवाच ॥

यथा ससर्ज वै ब्रह्मा भगवानादिकृत्प्रजाः ।
प्रजापतिः पतिर्द्देवस्तन्मे विस्तरतो वद ॥ १ ॥

मार्कण्डेय उवाच ॥

कथयाम्येष ते ब्रह्मन् ससर्ज भगवान् यथा ।
लोककृच्छाश्वतः कृत्स्नं जगत् स्थावरजङ्गमं ॥ २ ॥
पद्मावसाने प्रलये निशासुप्तोत्थितः प्रभुः ।
सत्त्वोद्रिक्तस्तदा ब्रह्मा शून्यं लोकमवैक्षत ॥ ३ ॥
इमञ्चोदाहरन्त्यत्र श्लोकं नारायणं प्रति ।
ब्रह्मस्वरूपिणं देवं जगतः प्रभवाव्ययं ॥ ४ ॥
आपो नारा वै तनव इत्यपां नाम शुश्रुम ।
तासु शेते स यस्माच्च तेन नारायणः स्मृतः ॥ ५ ॥
विबुद्धः सलिले तस्मिन् विज्ञायान्तर्गतां महीं ।
अनुमानात् समुद्धारं कर्त्तुकामस्तदा क्षितेः ॥ ६ ॥
अकरोत् स तनूरन्याः कल्पादिषु यथा पुरा ।
मत्स्यकूर्म्मादिकास्तद्वद्वाराहं वपुरास्थितः ॥ ७ ॥
वेदयज्ञमयं दिव्यं वेदयज्ञमयो विभुः ।
रूपं कृत्वा विवेशाप्सु सर्व्वगः सर्व्वसम्भवः ॥ ८ ॥
समुद्धृत्य च पातालान्मुमोच सलिले भुवं ।
जनलोकस्थितैः सिद्धैश्चिन्त्यमानो जगत्पतिः ॥ ९ ॥
तस्योपरि जलौघस्य महती नौरिव स्थिता ।
विततत्वात्तु देहस्य न मही याति संप्लवं ॥ १० ॥
ततः क्षितिं समीकृत्य पृथिव्यां सोऽसृजद्गिरीन् ।
प्राक् सर्गे दह्यमाने तु तदा सम्वर्त्तकाग्निना ॥ ११ ॥
तेनाग्निना विशीर्णास्ते पर्व्वता भुवि सर्व्वशः ।

शैला एकार्णवे मग्ना वायुनापस्तु संहृताः ॥ १२ ॥
निषक्ता यत्र यत्रासंस्तत्र तत्राचला भवन् ।
भूविभागन्ततः कृत्वा सप्तद्वीपोपशोभितं ॥ १३ ॥
भूराद्यांश्चतुरो लोकान् पूर्व्ववत् समकल्पयत् ।
सृष्टिञ्चिन्तयतस्तस्य कल्पादिषु यथा पुरा ॥ १४ ॥
अबुद्धिपूर्व्वकस्तस्मात् प्रादुर्भूतस्तमोमयः ।
तमो मोहो महामोहस्तामिस्रो ह्यन्धसंज्ञितः ॥ १५ ॥
अविद्या पञ्चपूर्व्वैषा प्रादुर्भूता महात्मनः ।
पञ्चधावस्थितः सर्गो ध्यायतोऽप्रतिबोधवान् ॥ १६ ॥
वहिरन्तश्चाप्रकाशः संवृतात्मा नगात्मकः ।
मुख्या नगा यतश्चोक्ता मुख्यसर्गस्ततस्त्वयं ॥ १७ ॥
तं दृष्ट्वा साधकं सर्गममन्यदपरं पुनः ।
तस्याभिध्यायतः सर्गं तिर्य्यक्स्रोतो ह्यवर्त्तत ॥ १८ ॥
यस्मात्तिर्य्यक्प्रवृत्तिः सा तिर्य्यक्स्रोतस्ततः स्मृतः ।
पश्वादयस्ते विख्यातास्तमःप्राया ह्यवेदिनः ॥ १९ ॥
उत्पथग्राहिणश्चैव तेऽज्ञाने ज्ञानमानिनः ।
अहंकृता अहंमाना अष्टाविंशद्विधात्मकाः ॥ २० ॥
अन्तःप्रकाशास्ते सर्व्वे आवृतास्तु परस्परं ।
तमप्यसाधकं मत्वा ध्यायतोऽन्यस्ततोऽभवत् ॥ २१ ॥
ऊर्द्ध्वस्रोतस्तृतीयस्तु सात्त्विकोर्द्ध्वमवर्त्तत ।
ते सुखप्रीतिबहुला वहिरन्तस्त्वनावृताः ॥ २२ ॥
प्रकाशा वहिरन्तश्च ऊर्द्ध्वस्रोतःसमुद्भवाः ।

तुष्टात्मनस्तृतीयस्तु देवसर्गो हि स स्मृतः ॥ २३ ॥
तस्मिन् सर्गेऽभवत् प्रीतिर्निष्पन्ने ब्रह्मणस्तदा ।
ततोऽन्यं स तदा दध्यौ साधकं सर्गमुत्तमं ॥ २४ ॥
तथाभिध्यायतस्तस्य सत्याभिध्यायिनस्ततः ।
प्रादुर्बभौ तदाव्यक्तादर्वाक्स्रोतस्तु साधकः ॥ २५ ॥
यस्मादर्व्वाग्व्यवर्त्तन्त ततोऽर्वाक्स्रोतसस्तु त ।
ते च प्रकाशबहुलास्तमोद्रिक्ता रजोऽधिकाः ॥ २६ ॥
तस्मात्ते दुःखबहुला भूयोभूयश्च कारिणः ।
प्रकाशा वहिरन्तश्च मनुष्याः साधकाश्च ते ॥ २७ ॥
पञ्चमोऽनुग्रहः सर्गः स चतुर्द्धा व्यवस्थितः ।
विपर्य्ययेण सिद्ध्या च शान्त्या तुष्ट्या तथैव च ॥ २८ ॥
निर्वृत्तं वर्त्तमानञ्च तेऽर्थं जानन्ति वै पुनः ।
भूतादिकानां भूतानां षष्ठः सर्गः स उच्यते ॥ २९ ॥
ते परिग्रहिणः सर्व्वे संविभागरतास्तथा ।
चोदनाश्चाप्यशीलाश्च ज्ञेया भूतादिकाश्च ते ॥ ३० ॥
प्रथमो महतः सर्गो विज्ञेयो ब्रह्मणस्तु सः ।
तन्मात्राणां द्वितीयस्तु भूतसर्गः स उच्यते ॥ ३१ ॥
वैकारिकस्तृतीयस्तु सर्गश्चैन्द्रियकः स्मृतः ।
इत्येष प्राकृतः सर्गः संभूतो बुद्धिपूर्व्वकः ॥ ३२ ॥
मुख्यः सर्गश्चतुर्थस्तु मुख्या वै स्थावराः स्मृताः ।
तिर्य्यक्स्रोतस्तु यः प्रोक्तस्तैर्य्यग्योन्यः स पञ्चमः ॥ ३३ ॥
ततोऽर्द्धस्रोतसां षष्ठो देवसर्गस्तु स स्मृतः ।

ततोर्व्वाकस्रोतसां सर्गः सप्तमः स तु मानुषः ॥ ३४ ॥
अष्टमोऽनुग्रहः सर्गः सात्त्विकस्तामसश्च सः ।
पञ्चैते वैकृताः सर्गाः प्राकृतास्तु त्रयः स्मृताः ॥ ३५ ॥
प्राकृतो वैकृतश्चैव कौमारो नवमः स्मृतः ।
इत्येते वै समाख्याता नव सर्गाः प्रजापतेः ॥ ३६ ॥

इति श्रीमार्कण्डेयपुराणे प्राकृतवैकृतसर्गः ॥ ४७ ॥

अष्टचत्वारिंशोऽध्यायः ॥

क्रौष्टुकिरुवाच ॥

समासात् कथिता सृष्टिः सम्यग्भगवता मम ।
देवादीनां भवं ब्रह्मन् विस्तरात्तु ब्रवीहि मे ॥ १ ॥

मार्कण्डेय उवाच ॥

कुशला कुशलैर्ब्रह्मन् भाविता पूर्व्वकर्म्मभिः ।
ख्याता तया ह्यनिर्मुक्ताः प्रलये ह्युपसंहृताः ॥ २ ॥
देवाद्याः स्थावरान्ताश्च प्रजा ब्रह्मंश्चतुर्व्विधाः ।
ब्रह्मणः कुर्व्वतः सृष्टिं जज्ञिरे मानसास्तदा ॥ ३ ॥
ततो देवासुरपितॄन् मानुषांश्च चतुष्टयं ।
सिसृक्षुरम्भांस्येतानि स्वमात्मानमयूयुजत् ॥ ४ ॥
युक्तात्मनस्तमोमात्रा उद्रिक्ताभूत् प्रजापतेः ।

सिसृक्षोर्जघनात् पूर्वमसुरा जज्ञिरे ततः ॥ ५ ॥
उत्ससर्ज ततस्तान्तु तमोमात्रात्मिकां तनुं ।
सापविद्धा तनुस्तेन सद्यो रात्रिरजायत ॥ ६ ॥
अन्यां तनुमुपादाय सिसृक्षुः प्रीतिमाप सः ।
सत्त्वोद्रेकास्ततो देवा मुखतस्तस्य जज्ञिरे ॥ ७ ॥
उत्ससर्ज च भूतेशस्तनुं तामप्यसौ विभुः ।
सा चापविद्धा दिवसं सत्त्वप्रायमजायत ॥ ८ ॥
सत्त्वमात्रात्मिकामेव ततोऽन्यां जगृहे तनुं ।
पितृवन्मन्यमानस्य पितरस्तस्य जज्ञिरे ॥ ९ ॥
सृष्ट्वा पितॄनुत्ससर्ज तनुं तामपि स प्रभुः ।
सा चोत्सृष्टाभवत् सन्ध्या दिननक्तान्तरस्थिता ॥ १० ॥
रजोमात्रात्मिकामन्यां तनुं भेजेऽथ स प्रभुः ।
ततो मनुष्याः सम्भूता रजोमात्रासमुद्भवाः ॥ ११ ॥
सृष्ट्वा मनुष्यान् स विभुरुत्ससर्ज तनुं ततः ।
ज्योत्स्ना समभवत् सा च नक्तान्तेऽहर्मुखे च या ॥ १२ ॥
इत्येतास्तनवस्तस्य देवदेवस्य धीमतः ।
ख्याता रात्र्यहनी चैव सन्ध्या ज्योत्स्ना च वै द्विज ॥ १३ ॥
ज्योत्स्ना सन्ध्या तथैवाहः सत्त्वमात्रात्मकं त्रयं ।
तमोमात्रात्मिका रात्रिः सा वै तस्मात् त्रियामिका ॥ १४ ॥
तस्माद्देवा दिवा रात्रावसुरास्तु बलान्विताः ।
ज्योत्स्नागमे च मनुजाः सन्ध्यायां पितरस्तथा ॥ १५ ॥
भवन्ति बलिनोऽधृष्या विपक्षाणां न संशयः ।

तद्विपर्य्ययमासाद्य प्रयान्ति च विपर्य्ययं ॥ १६ ॥
ज्योत्स्ना राच्यहनी सन्ध्या चत्वार्य्येतानि वै प्रभोः ।
ब्रह्मणस्तु शरीराणि त्रिगुणोपश्रितानि तु ॥ १७ ॥
चत्वार्य्येतान्यथोत्पाद्य तनुमन्यां प्रजापतिः ।
रजस्तमोमयीं रात्रौ जगृहे क्षुत्तृडन्वितः ॥ १८ ॥
तदन्धकारे क्षुत्क्षामानसृजद्भगवानजः ।
विरूपान् श्मश्रुलानत्तुमारब्धास्ते च तां तनुं ॥ १९ ॥
रक्षाम इति तेभ्योऽन्ये य ऊचुस्ते तु राक्षसाः ।
खादाम इति ये चोचुस्ते यक्षा यक्षणात् द्विज ॥ २० ॥
तान् दृष्ट्वा ह्यप्रियेणास्य केशाः शीर्य्यन्त वेधसः ।
समारोहणहीनाश्च शिरसो ब्रह्मणस्तु ते ॥ २१ ॥
सर्पणात्तेऽभवन् सर्पा हीनत्वादहयः स्मृताः ।
सर्पान् दृष्ट्वा ततः क्रोधात् क्रोधात्मानो विनिर्म्ममे ॥ २२ ॥
वर्णेन कपिलेनोग्रास्ते भूताः पिशिताशनाः ।
ध्यायतो गां ततस्तस्य गन्धर्व्वा जज्ञिरे सुताः ॥ २३ ॥
जज्ञिरे पिवतो वाचं गन्धर्व्वास्तेन ते स्मृताः ।
अष्टास्वेतासु सृष्टासु देवयोनिषु स प्रभुः ॥ २४ ॥
ततः स्वदेहतोऽन्यानि वयांसि पशवोऽसृजत् ।
मुखतोऽजाः ससर्ज्जाथ वक्षसश्चावयोऽसृजत् ॥ २५ ॥
गावश्चैवोदराद्ब्रह्मा पार्श्वाभ्याञ्च विनिर्म्ममे ।
पद्भ्याञ्चाश्वान् समातङ्गान्रासभान् शशकान् मृगान् ॥ २६ ॥
उष्ट्रानश्वतरांश्चैव नानारूपाश्च जातयः ।

ओषध्यः फलमूलिन्यो रोमभ्यस्तस्य जज्ञिरे ॥ २७ ॥
एवं पश्वोषधीः सृष्ट्वा ह्ययजच्चाध्वरे विभुः ।
तस्मादादौ तु कल्पस्य त्रेतायुगमुखे तदा ॥ २८ ॥
गौरजः पुरुषो मेषो अश्वाश्वतरगर्द्दभाः ।
एतान् ग्राम्यान् पशूनाहुरारण्यांश्च निबोध मे ॥ २९ ॥
श्वापदं द्विखुरं हस्ती वानराः पक्षिपञ्चमाः ।
औदकाः पशवः षष्ठाः सप्तमास्तु सरीसृपाः ॥ ३० ॥
गायत्रीञ्च ऋचञ्चैव त्रिवृत् साम रथन्तरं ।
अग्निष्टोमञ्च यज्ञानां निर्म्ममे प्रथमान्मुखात् ॥ ३१ ॥
यजूंषि त्रैष्टुभं छन्दः स्तोमं पञ्चदशन्तथा ।
बृहत् साम तथोक्थञ्च दक्षिणादसृजन्मुखात् ॥ ३२ ॥
सामानि जगतीछन्दः स्तोमं पञ्चदशन्तथा ।
वैरूपमतिरात्रञ्च निर्म्ममे पश्चिमान्मुखात् ॥ ३३ ॥
एकविंशमथर्व्वाणमाप्तोर्य्यामाणमेव च ।
अनुष्टुभं सवैराजमुत्तरादसृजन्मुखात् ॥ ३४ ॥
विद्युतोऽशनिमेघाश्च रोहितेन्द्रधनूंषि च ।
वयांसि च ससर्ज्जादौ कल्पस्य भगवान् विभुः ॥ ३५ ॥
उच्चावचानि भूतानि गात्रेभ्यस्तस्य जज्ञिरे ।
सृष्ट्वा चतुष्टयं पूर्व्वं देवासुरपितॄन् प्रजाः ॥ ३६ ॥
ततोऽसृजत् स भूतानि स्थावराणि चराणि च ।
यक्षान् पिशाचान् गन्धर्व्वांस्तथैवाप्सरसाङ्गणान् ॥ ३७ ॥
नरकिन्नररक्षांसि वयःपशुमृगोरगान् ।

अव्ययञ्च व्ययञ्चैव यदिदं स्थाणुजङ्गमं ॥ ३८ ॥
तेषां ये यानि कर्म्माणि प्राक् सृष्टेः प्रतिपेदिरे ।
तान्येव प्रतिपद्यन्ते सृज्यमानाः पुनः पुनः ॥ ३९ ॥
हिंस्राहिंस्रे मृदुक्रूरे धर्म्माधर्म्मावृतानृते ।
तद्भाविताः प्रपद्यन्ते तस्मात्तत्तस्य रोचते ॥ ४० ॥
इन्द्रियार्थेषु भूतेषु शरीरेषु च स प्रभुः ।
नानात्वं विनियोगञ्च धातैव व्यदधात् स्वयं ॥ ४१ ॥
नामरूपञ्च भूतानां कृत्यानाञ्च प्रपञ्चनं ।
वेदशब्देभ्य एवादौ देवादीनाञ्चकार सः ॥ ४२ ॥
ऋषीणां नामधेयानि याश्च देवेषु सृष्टयः ।
सर्व्वर्य्यन्ते प्रसूतानामन्येषाञ्च ददाति सः ॥ ४३ ॥
यथार्त्तावृतुलिङ्गानि नानारूपाणि पर्य्यये ।
दृश्यन्ते तानि तान्येव तथा भावा युगादिषु ॥ ४४ ॥
एवंविधाः सृष्टयस्तु ब्रह्मणोऽव्यक्तजन्मनः ।
सर्व्वर्य्यन्ते प्रबुद्धस्य कल्पे कल्पे भवन्ति वै ॥ ४५ ॥

इति श्रीमार्कण्डेयपुराणे सृष्टिप्रकरणे ॥ ४८ ॥

ऊनपञ्चाशोऽध्यायः ॥

क्रौष्टुकिरुवाच ।

अर्व्वाक्स्रोतस्तु कथितो भवता यस्तु मानुषः ।
ब्रह्मन् विस्तरतो ब्रूहि ब्रह्मा समसृजद्यथा ॥ १ ॥

यथा च वर्णानसृजद्यद्गुणांश्च महामते ।
यच्च येषां स्मृतं कर्म्म विप्रादीनां वदस्व तत् ॥ २ ॥

मार्कण्डेय उवाच ।

ब्रह्मणः सृजतः पूर्व्वं सत्याभिध्यायिनस्तथा ।
मिथुनानां सहस्रन्तु मुखात्सोऽथासृजन्मुने ॥ ३ ॥
जातास्ते ह्युपपद्यन्ते सत्त्वोद्रिक्ताः स्वतेजसः ।
सहस्रमन्यद्वक्षसो मिथुनानां ससर्ज्ज ह ॥ ४ ॥
ते सर्व्वे रजसोद्रिक्ताः शुष्मिणश्चाप्यमर्षिणः ।
ससर्जान्यत् सहस्रन्तु द्वःस्थानां मरुतः पुनः ॥ ५ ॥
रजस्तमोभ्यामुद्रिक्ता ईहाशीलास्तु ते स्मृताः ।
पद्भ्यां सहस्रमन्यच्च मिथुनानां ससर्ज ह ॥ ६ ॥
उद्रिक्तास्तमसा सर्व्वे निश्रीका ह्यल्पचेतसः ।
ततः संहर्षमानास्ते द्वन्द्वोत्पन्नास्तु प्राणिनः ॥ ७ ॥
अन्योन्यहृच्छयाविष्टा मैथुनायोपचक्रमुः ।
ततः प्रभृति कल्पेऽस्मिन् मिथुनानां हि सम्भवः ॥ ८ ॥
मासि मास्यार्त्तवं यत्तु न तदासीत्तु योषितां ।
तस्मात्तदा न सुषुवुः सेवितैरपि मैथुनैः ॥ ९ ॥
आयुषोऽन्ते प्रसूयन्ते मिथुनान्येव ताः सकृत् ।
ततः प्रभृति कल्पेऽस्मिन् मिथुनानां हि सम्भवः ॥ १० ॥
ध्यानेन मनसा तासां प्रजानां जायते सकृत् ।
शब्दादिर्विषयः शुद्धः प्रत्येकं पञ्चलक्षणं ॥ ११ ॥
इत्येषा मानुषी सृष्टिर्या पूर्व्वं वै प्रजापतेः ।

तस्यान्ववायसम्भूता यैरिदं पूजितं जगत् ॥ १२ ॥
सरित्सरःसमुद्रांश्च सेवन्ते पर्व्वतानपि ।
तास्तदा ह्यल्पशीतोष्णा युगे तस्मिंश्चरन्ति वै ॥ १३ ॥
तृप्तिं स्वाभाविकीं प्राप्ता विषयेषु महामते ।
न तासां प्रतिघातोऽस्ति न द्वेषो नापि मत्सरः ॥ १४ ॥
पर्व्वतोदधिसेविन्यो ह्यनिकेतास्तु सर्व्वशः ।
ता वै निष्कामचारिण्यो नित्यं मुदितमानसाः ॥ १५ ॥
पिशाचोरगरक्षांसि तथा मत्सरिणो जनाः ।
पशवः पक्षिणश्चैव नक्रा मत्स्याः सरीसृपाः ॥ १६ ॥
अवारका ह्यण्डजा वा ते ह्यधर्म्मप्रसूतयः ।
न मूलफलपुष्पाणि नार्त्तवा वत्सराणि च ॥ १७ ॥
सर्व्वकालसुखः कालो नात्यर्थं घर्म्मशीतता ।
कालेन गच्छता तेषां चित्ता सिद्धिरजायत ॥ १८ ॥
ततश्च तेषां पूर्व्वाह्णे मध्याह्ने च वितृप्तता ।
पुनस्तथेच्छतां तृप्तिरनायासेन साभवत् ॥ १९ ॥
इच्छताञ्च तथायासो मनसः समजायत ।
अपां सौक्ष्म्यं ततस्तासां सिद्धिर्न्नाम्नावयो न सा ॥ २० ॥
समजायत चैवान्या सर्व्वकामप्रदायिनी ।
असंस्कार्य्यैः शरीरैश्च प्रजास्ताः स्थिरयौवनाः ॥ २१ ॥
तासां विना तु संकल्पं जायन्ते मिथुनाः प्रजाः ।
समं जन्म च रूपञ्च म्रियन्ते चैव ताः समं ॥ २२ ॥
अनिच्छाद्वेषसंयुक्ता वर्त्तन्ते तु परस्परं ।

तुल्यरूपायुषः सर्व्वा अधमोत्तमतां विना ॥ २३ ॥
चत्वारि तु सहस्राणि वर्षाणां मानुषाणि तु ।
आयुःप्रमाणं जीवन्ति न च क्लेशाद्विपत्तयः ॥ २४ ॥
क्वचित्क्वचित्पुनः साभूत् क्षितिर्भाग्येन सर्व्वशः ।
कालेन गच्छता नाशमुपयान्ति यथा प्रजाः ॥ २५ ॥
तथा ताः क्रमशो नाशं जग्मुः सर्व्वत्र सिद्धयः ।
तासु सर्व्वासु नष्टासु नभसः प्रच्युता नराः ॥ २६ ॥
प्रायशः कल्पवृक्षास्ते सम्भूता गृहसंज्ञिताः ।
सर्व्वे प्रत्युपभोगाश्च तासां तेभ्यः प्रजायते ॥ २७ ॥
वर्त्तयन्ति स्म तेभ्यस्तास्त्रेतायुगमुखे तदा ।
ततः कालेन वै रागस्तासामाकस्मिकोऽभवत् ॥ १८ ॥
मासि मास्यार्त्तवोत्पत्त्या गर्भोत्पत्तिः पुनः पुनः ।
रागोत्पत्त्या ततस्तासां वृक्षास्ते गृहसंज्ञिताः ॥ २९ ॥
ब्रह्मन्नन्वपरेषान्तु पेतुः शाखा महीरुहां ।
वस्त्राणि च प्रसूयन्ते फलेष्वाभरणानि च ॥ ३० ॥
तेष्वेव जायते तेषां गन्धवर्णरसान्वितं ।
अमाक्षिकं महावीर्य्यं पुटके पुटके मधु ॥ ३१ ॥
तेन ता वर्त्तयन्ति स्म मुखे त्रेतायुगस्य वै ।
ततः कालान्तरेणैव पुनर्लोभान्वितास्तु ताः ॥ ३२ ॥
वृक्षास्ताः पर्य्यगृह्णन्त ममत्वाविष्टचेतसः ।
नेशुस्तेनापचारेण तेऽपि तासां महीरुहाः ॥ ३३ ॥
ततो द्वन्द्वान्यजायन्त शीतोष्णक्षुन्मुखानि वै ।

तास्तद्वन्धोपघातार्थं चक्रुः पूर्व्वं पुराणि तु ॥ ३४ ॥
मरुधन्वषु दुर्गेषु पर्व्वतेषु दरीषु च ।
संश्रयन्ति च दुर्गाणि वार्क्षं पार्व्वतमौदकं ॥ ३५ ॥
कृत्रिमञ्च तथा दुर्गं मित्वा मित्वात्मनोऽङ्गुलैः ।
मानार्थानि प्रमाणानि तास्तु पूर्व्वं प्रचक्रिरे ॥ ३६ ॥
परमाणुः परं सूक्ष्मं त्रसरेणुर्महीरजः ।
बालाग्रञ्चैव निष्कां च यूकां चाथ यवोदरं ॥ ३७ ॥
एकादशगुणं तेषां यवमध्यं तथाङ्गुलं ।
षड़ङ्गुलं पदन्तच्च वितस्तिर्द्विगुणं स्मृतं ॥ ३८ ॥
द्वे वितस्ती तथा हस्तो ब्राह्मतीर्थादिवेष्टनं ।
चतुर्हस्तं धनुर्दण्डो नाड़िकायुगमेव च ॥ ३९ ॥
धनुषां द्वे सहस्रे तु गव्यूतिस्तच्चतुर्गुणं ।
प्रोक्तञ्च योजनं प्राज्ञैः संख्यानार्थमिदं परं ॥ ४० ॥
चतुर्णामथ दुर्गाणां स्वसमुत्थानि त्रीणि तु ।
चतुर्थं कृत्रिमं दुर्गं तच्च कुर्य्यात् सतस्तु ते ॥ ४१ ॥
पुरञ्च खेटकञ्चैव तद्वद्द्रोणीमुखं द्विजः ।
शाखानगरकञ्चापि तथा कर्व्वटकं त्रयी ॥ ४२ ॥
ग्रामसंघोषविन्यासं तेषु चावसथान् पृथक् ।
सोत्सेधवप्रकारञ्च सर्व्वतः परिखावृतं ॥ ४३ ॥
योजनार्द्धार्द्धविष्कम्भमष्टभागायतं पुरं ।
प्रागुदक्प्लवनं शस्तं शुद्धवंशवहिर्गमं ॥ ४४ ॥
तदर्द्धेन तथा खेटं तत्पादेन च कर्व्वटं ।

न्यूनं द्रोणीमुखं तस्मादन्तभागेन चोच्यते ॥ ४५ ॥
प्राकारं परिखाहीनं पुरं वर्म्मवदुच्यते ।
शाखानगरकञ्चान्यन्मन्त्रिसामन्तभुक्तिमत् ॥ ४६ ॥
तथा शूद्रजलप्रायाः स्वसमृद्धिकृषीबलाः ।
क्षेत्रोपभोग्यभूमध्ये वसतिर्ग्रामसंज्ञिता ॥ ४७ ॥
अन्यस्मान्नगरादेर्या कार्य्यमुद्दिश्य मानवैः ।
क्रियते वसतिः सा वै विज्ञेया वसतिर्नवैः ॥ ४८ ॥
दुष्टप्रायो विना क्षेत्रैः परभूमिचरो बली ।
ग्रामएवाक्रिमीसंज्ञो राजवल्लभसंश्रयः ॥ ४९ ॥
शकटारूढभाण्डैश्च गोपालैर्व्विपणं विना ।
गोसमूहस्तथा घोषो यत्रेच्छा भूमिकेतनः ॥ ५० ॥
तएवं नगरादींस्तु कृत्वा वासार्थमात्मनः ।
निकेतनानि द्वन्द्वानां चक्रुरावसथाय वै ॥ ५१ ॥
गृहाकारा यथा पूर्व्वं तेषामासन्महीरुहाः ।
तथा संस्मृत्य तत्सर्व्वं चक्रुर्व्वेश्मानि ताः प्रजाः ॥ ५२ ॥
वृक्षस्यैवङ्गताः शाखास्तथैवञ्चापरा गताः ।
नताश्चैवोन्नताश्चैव तद्वच्छाखाः प्रचक्रिरे ॥ ५३ ॥
याः शाखाः कल्पवृक्षाणां पूर्व्वमासन् द्विजोत्तम ।
ताएव शाखा गेहानां शालात्वं तेन तासु तत् ॥ ५४ ॥
कृत्वा द्वन्द्वोपघातन्ते वार्त्तोपायमचिन्तयत् ।
नष्टेषु मधुना सार्द्धं कल्पवृक्षेष्वशेषतः ॥ ५५ ॥
विषादव्याकुलास्ता वै प्रजास्तृष्णाक्षुधार्द्दिताः ।

ततः प्रादुर्बभौ तासां सिद्धिस्त्रेतामुखे तदा ॥ ५६ ॥
वार्त्तास्वसाधिता ह्यन्या वृष्टिस्तासां निकामतः ।
तासां वृष्ट्युदकानीह यानि निम्नगतानि वै ॥ ५७ ॥
वृष्ट्यावरुद्धैरभवत् स्रोतःखातानि निम्नगाः ।
ये पुरस्तादपां स्तोका आपन्नाः पृथिवीतले ॥ ५८ ॥
ततो भूमेश्च संयोगादोषध्यस्तास्तदाभवन् ।
अफालकृष्टाश्चानुप्ता ग्राम्यारण्याश्चतुर्द्दश ॥ ५९ ॥
ऋतुपुष्पफलाश्चैव वृक्षा गुल्माश्च जज्ञिरे ।
प्रादुर्भावस्तु त्रेतायामाद्योऽयमौषधस्य तु ॥ ६० ॥
तेनौषधेन वर्त्तन्ते प्रजास्त्रेतायुगे मुने ।
रागलोभौ समासाद्य प्रजाश्चाकस्मिकौ तदा ॥ ६१ ॥
ततस्ताः पर्य्यगृह्णन्त नदीक्षेत्राणि पर्व्वतान् ।
वृक्षगुल्मौषधीश्चैवमात्मन्यायाद्यथा बलं ॥ ६२ ॥
तेन दोषेण ता नेशुरौषध्यो मिषतां द्विजः ।
अग्रसद्भूर्युगपत्तास्तदौषध्यो महामते ॥ ६३ ॥
पुनस्तासु प्रणष्टासु विभ्रान्तास्ताः पुनः प्रजाः ।
ब्रह्माणं शरणं जग्मुः क्षुधार्त्ताः परमेष्ठिनं ॥ ६४ ॥
स चापि तत्त्वतो ज्ञात्वा तदा ग्रस्तां वसुन्धरां ।
वत्सं कृत्वा सुमेरुन्तु दुदोह भगवान् विभुः ॥ ६५ ॥
दुग्धेयं गौस्तदा तेन सस्यानि पृथिवीतले ।
जज्ञिरे तानि बीजानि ग्राम्यारण्यास्तु ताः पुनः ॥ ६६ ॥
ओषध्यः फलपाकान्ता गणाः सप्तदश स्मृताः ।

व्रीहयश्च यवाश्चैव गोधूमा अणवस्तिलाः ॥ ६७ ॥
प्रियङ्गवो ह्युदाराश्च कोरदूषाः सचीनकाः ।
माषा मुद्गा मसूराश्च निष्पावाः सकुलत्थकाः ॥ ६८ ॥
आढकाश्चनकाश्चैव गणाः सप्तदश स्मृताः ।
इत्येता ओषधीनान्तु ग्राम्याणां जातयः पुरा ॥ ६९ ॥
ओषध्यो यज्ञियाश्चैव ग्राम्यारण्याश्चतुर्द्दश ।
व्रीहयश्च यवाश्चैव गोधूमा अणवस्तिलाः ॥ ७० ॥
प्रियङ्गुसप्तमा ह्येते अष्टमास्तु कुलत्थकाः ।
श्यामाकास्त्वथ नीवारा यत्तिला सगवेधुकाः ॥ ७१ ॥
कुरुविन्दा मर्कटकास्तथावेणुयवाश्च ये ।
ग्राम्यारण्याः स्मृता ह्येता ओषध्यश्च चतुर्द्दश ॥ ७२ ॥
यदा प्रसृष्टा ओषध्यो न प्ररोहन्ति ताः पुनः ।
ततः स तासां वृद्ध्यर्थं वार्त्तोपायञ्चकार ह ॥ ७३ ॥
ब्रह्मा स्वयम्भुर्भगवान् हस्तसिद्धिञ्च कर्म्मजां ।
ततः प्रभृत्यथौषध्यः कृष्टपच्यास्तु जज्ञिरे ॥ ७४ ॥
संसिद्धायान्तु वार्त्तायां ततस्तासां स्वयं प्रभुः ।
मर्य्यादां स्थापयामास यथान्यायं यथागुणं ॥ ७५ ॥
वर्णानामाश्रमाणाञ्च धर्म्मान् धर्म्मभृतांवर ।
लोकानां सर्व्ववर्णानां सम्यक्धर्म्मार्थपालिनां ॥ ७६ ॥
प्राजापत्यं ब्राह्मणानां स्मृतं स्थानं क्रियावतां ।
स्थानमैन्द्रं क्षत्रियाणां संग्रामेष्वपलायिनां ॥ ७७ ॥
वैश्यानां मारुतं स्थानं स्वधर्म्ममनुवर्त्ततां ।

गान्धर्व्वं शूद्रजातीनां परिचर्य्यानुवर्त्ततां॥ ७८॥
अष्टाशीतिसहस्राणामृषीणामूर्द्ध्वरेतसां।
स्मृतं तेषान्तु यत् स्थानं तदेव गुरुवासिनां॥ ७९॥
सप्तर्षीणान्तु यत् स्थानं स्मृतं तद्वै वनौकसां।
प्राजापत्यं गृहस्थानां न्यासिनां ब्रह्मणः क्षयं॥
योगिनाममृतं स्थानमिति वै स्थानकल्पना॥ ८०॥

इति श्रीमार्कण्डेयपुराणे सृष्टिप्रकरणे॥ ४९॥

पञ्चाशोऽध्यायः॥

मार्कण्डेय उवाच॥

ततोऽभिध्यायतस्तस्य जज्ञिरे मानसीः प्रजाः।
तच्छरीरसमुत्पन्नैः कार्य्यैस्तैः कारणैः सह॥ १॥
क्षेत्रज्ञाः समवर्त्तन्त गात्रेभ्यस्तस्य धीमतः।
ते सर्व्वे समवर्त्तन्त ये मया प्रागुदाहृताः॥ २॥
देवाद्याः स्थावरान्ताश्च त्रैगुण्यविषयाः स्मृताः।
एवम्भूतानि सृष्टानि स्थावराणि चराणि च॥ ३॥
यदास्य ताः प्रजाः सर्व्वा न व्यवर्द्धन्त धीमतः।
अथान्यान्मानसान् पुत्रान् सदृशानात्मनोऽसृजत्॥ ४॥
भृगुं पुलस्त्यं पुलहं क्रतुमङ्गिरसन्तथा।
मरीचिं दक्षमत्रिञ्च वशिष्ठञ्चैव मानसं॥ ५॥

नव ब्रह्मण इत्येते पुराणे निश्चयङ्गताः ।
ततोऽसृजत् पुनर्ब्रह्मा रुद्रं क्रोधात्मसम्भवं ॥ ६ ॥
सङ्कल्पञ्चैव धर्म्मञ्च पूर्व्वेषामपि-पूर्व्वजं ।
सनन्दनादयो ये च पूर्व्वं सृष्टाः स्वयम्भुवा ॥ ७ ॥
न ते लोकेषु सज्जन्तो निरपेक्षाः समाहिताः ।
सर्व्वे तेऽनागतज्ञाना वीतरागा विमत्सराः ॥ ८ ॥
तेष्वेवं निरपेक्षेषु लोकसृष्टौ महात्मनः ।
ब्रह्मणोऽभून्महाक्रोधस्तत्रोत्पन्नोऽर्कसन्निभः ॥ ९ ॥
अर्द्धनारीनरवपुः पुरुषोऽतिशरीरवान् ।
विभजात्मानमित्युक्ता स तदान्तर्दधे ततः ॥ १० ॥
स चोक्तो वै पृथक् स्त्रीत्वं पुरुषत्वं तथाकरोत् ।
बिभेद पुरुषत्वञ्च दशधा चैकधा तु सः ॥ ११ ॥
सौम्यासौम्यैस्तथा शान्तैः पुंस्त्वं स्त्रीत्वञ्च स प्रभुः ।
बिभेद बहुधा देवः पुरुषैरसितैः सितैः ॥ १२ ॥
ततो ब्रह्मात्मसम्भूतं पूर्व्वं स्वायम्भुवं प्रभुः ।
आत्मनः सदृशं कृत्वा प्रजापालो मनुं द्विजः ॥ १३ ॥
शतरूपाञ्च तां नारीं तपोनिर्धूतकल्मषां ।
स्वायम्भुवो मनुर्द्देवः पत्नीत्वे जगृहे विभुः ॥ १४ ॥
तस्माच्च पुरुषात्पुत्रौ शतरूपा व्यजायत ।
प्रियव्रतोत्तानपादौ प्रख्यातावात्मकर्म्मभिः ॥ १५ ॥
कन्ये द्वे च तथाऋद्धिं प्रसूतिञ्च ततः पिता ।
ददौ प्रसूतिं दक्षाय तथा ऋद्धिं रुचेः पुरा ॥ १६ ॥

प्रजापतिः स जग्राह तयोर्यज्ञः सदक्षिणः ।
पुत्रो जज्ञे महाभाग दम्पतीमिथुनं ततः ॥ १७ ॥
यज्ञस्य दक्षिणायान्तु पुत्रा द्वादश जज्ञिरे ।
यामाइति समाख्याता देवाः स्वायम्भुवोऽन्तरे ॥ १८ ॥
तस्य पुत्रास्तु यज्ञस्य दक्षिणायां सभास्वराः ।
प्रसूत्याञ्च तथा दक्षश्चतस्रो विंशतिस्तथा ॥ १९ ॥
ससर्ज्ज कन्यास्तासाञ्च सम्यङ्नामानि मे शृणु ।
श्रद्धा लक्ष्मीर्धृतिस्तुष्टिः पुष्टिर्मेधा क्रिया तथा ॥ २० ॥
बुद्धिर्लज्जा वपुः शान्तिः सिद्धिः कीर्त्तिस्त्रयोदशी ।
पत्न्यर्थे प्रतिजग्राह धर्म्मो दाक्षायणीः प्रभुः ॥ २१ ॥
ताभ्यः शिष्टा यवीयस्य एकादश सुलोचनाः ।
ख्यातिः सत्यथ सम्भूतिः स्मृतिः प्रीतिस्तथा क्षमा ॥ २२ ॥
सन्ततिश्चानसूया च ऊर्ज्जा स्वाहा स्वधा तथा ।
भृगुर्भवो मरीचिश्च तथा चैवाङ्गिरा मुनिः ॥ २३ ॥
पुलस्त्यः पुलहश्चैव क्रतुश्च ऋषयस्तथा ।
वशिष्ठोऽत्रिस्तथा वह्निः पितरश्च यथा क्रमं ॥ २४ ॥
ख्यात्याद्या जगृहुः कन्या मुनयो मुनिसत्तमाः ।
श्रद्धा कामं श्रीश्च दर्प्पं नियमं धृतिरात्मजं ॥ २५ ॥
सन्तोषञ्च तथा तुष्टिर्लोभं पुष्टिरजायत ।
मेधा श्रुतं क्रिया दण्डं नयं विनयमेव च ॥ २६ ॥
बोधं बुद्धिस्तथा लज्जा विनयं वपुरात्मजं ।
व्यवसायं प्रजज्ञे वै क्षेमं शान्तिरसूयत ॥ २७ ॥

सुखं सिद्धिर्यशः कीर्त्तिरित्येते धर्म्मयोनयः ।
कामाद्रतिमुदं हर्षं धर्म्मपौत्त्रमसूयत ॥ २८ ॥
हिंसा भार्य्या त्वधर्म्मस्य तस्यां जज्ञे तथानृतं ।
कन्या च निर्ऋतिस्तस्यां सुतौ द्वौ नरकं भयं ॥ २९ ॥
माया च वेदना चैव मिथुनं द्वयमेतयोः ।
तयोर्जज्ञेऽथ वै माया मृत्युं भूतापहारिणं ॥ ३० ॥
वेदनात्मसुतश्चापि दुःखं जज्ञेऽथ रौरवात् ।
मृत्योर्व्याधिजराशोकतृष्णाक्रोधाश्च जज्ञिरे ॥ ३१ ॥
दुःखोद्भवाः स्मृता ह्येते सर्व्वे वाधर्म्मलक्षणाः ।
नैषां भार्य्यास्ति पुत्त्रो वा सर्व्वे ते ह्यूर्द्ध्वरेतसः ॥ ३२ ॥
निर्ऋतिश्च तथा चान्या मृत्योर्भार्य्याभवन्मुने ।
अलक्ष्मीर्नाम तस्याञ्च मृत्योः पुत्त्राश्चतुर्द्दश ॥ ३३ ॥
अलक्ष्मीपुत्त्रका ह्येते मृत्योरादेशकारिणः ।
विनाशकालेषु नरान् भजन्त्येते शृणुष्व तान् ॥ ३४ ॥
इन्द्रियेषु दशस्वेते तथा मनसि च स्थिताः ।
स्वे स्वे नरं स्त्रियं वापि विषये योजयन्ति हि ॥ ३५ ॥
अथेन्द्रियाणि चाक्रम्य रागक्रोधादिभिर्नरान् ।
योजयन्ति यथा हानिं यान्त्यधर्म्मादिभिर्द्विज ॥ ३६ ॥
अहङ्कारगतश्चान्यस्तथान्यो बुद्धिसंस्थितः ।
विनाशाय नराः स्त्रीणां यतन्ते मोहसंश्रिताः ॥ ३७ ॥
तथैवान्ये गृहे पुंसां दुःसहो नाम विश्रुतः ।
क्षुत्क्षामोऽधोमुखो नग्नश्चीरी काकसमस्वनः ॥ ३८ ॥

स सर्व्वान् खादितुं सृष्टो ब्रह्मणा तपसो निधिः ।
दंष्ट्राकरालमत्यर्थं विवृतास्यं सुभैरवं ॥ ३९ ॥
तमत्तुकाममाहेदं ब्रह्मा लोकपितामहः ।
सर्व्वब्रह्ममयः शुद्धः कारणं जगतोऽव्ययः ॥ ४० ॥

ब्रह्मोवाच ॥

नात्तव्यन्ते जगदिदं जहि कोपं शमं व्रज ।
त्यजैनान्तामसीं वृत्तिमपास्य रजसः कलां ॥ ४१ ॥

दुःसह उवाच ॥

क्षुत्क्षामोऽस्मि जगन्नाथ पिपासुश्चापि दुर्ब्बलः ।
कथं तृप्तिमियान्नाथ भवेयं बलवान् कथं ॥
कश्चाश्रयो ममाख्याहि वर्त्तेयं यत्र निर्वृतः ॥ ४२ ॥

ब्रह्मोवाच ॥

तवाश्रयो गृहं पुंसां जनश्चाधार्म्मिको बलं ।
पुष्टिं नित्यक्रियाहान्या भवान् वत्स गमिष्यति ॥ ४३ ॥
वृथा स्फोटाश्च ते वस्त्रमाहरञ्च ददामि ते ।
क्षतं कीटावपन्नञ्च तथा श्वभिरवेक्षितं ॥ ४४ ॥
भग्नभाण्डगतन्तद्वत् मुखवातोपशामितं ।
उच्छिष्टापक्वमस्विन्नमवलीढमसंस्कृतं ॥ ४५ ॥
भग्नासनस्थितैर्भुक्तमासन्नागतमेव च ।
विदिङ्मुखं सन्ध्ययोश्च नृत्यवाद्यस्वरोत्तमं ॥ ४६ ॥
उदक्योपहतं भुक्तमुदक्या दृष्टमेव च ।
यच्चोपघातवत् किञ्चित् भक्ष्यं पेयमथापि वा ॥ ४७ ॥

एतानि तव पुष्ट्यर्थमन्यच्चापि ददामि ते ।
अश्रद्धया हुतं दत्तमस्नातैर्यदवज्ञया ॥ ४८ ॥
यन्नाम्बुपूर्व्वकं क्षिप्तमनर्थीकृतमेव च ।
त्यक्तुमाविष्कृतं यत्तु दत्तं चैवातिविस्मयात् ॥ ४९ ॥
दुष्टं क्रुद्धार्त्तदत्तञ्च यक्ष तद्भागि तत्फलं ।
यच्च पौनर्भवः किञ्चित् करोत्यामुष्मिकं क्रमं ॥ ५० ॥
यच्च पौनर्भवा योषित् तद्यक्ष तव तृप्तये ।
कन्या शुल्कोपधानाय समुपास्ते धनक्रियाः ॥ ५१ ॥
तथैव यक्ष पुष्ट्यर्थमसच्छास्त्रक्रियाश्च याः ।
यश्चार्थं निर्हृतं किञ्चिदधीतं यच्च सत्यतः ॥ ५२ ॥
तत्सर्व्वं तव कालांश्च ददामि तव सिद्धये ।
गुर्व्विण्यभिगमे सन्ध्यानित्यकार्य्यव्यतिक्रमे ॥ ५३ ॥
असच्छास्त्रक्रियालापदूषितेषु च दुःसह ।
तवाभिभवसामर्थ्यं भविष्यति सदा नृषु ॥ ५४ ॥
पङ्क्तिभेदे वृथापाके पाकभेदे तथा क्रिया ।
नित्यञ्च गेहकलहे भविता वसतिस्तव ॥ ५५ ॥
अपोष्यमाणे च तथा बद्धे गोवाहनादिके ।
असन्ध्याभ्युक्षितागारे काले त्वत्तो भयं नृणां ॥ ५६ ॥
नक्षत्रग्रहपीड़ासु त्रिविधोत्पातदर्शने ।
अशान्तिकपरान् यक्ष नरानभिभविष्यसि ॥ ५७ ॥
वृथोपवासिनो मर्त्या द्यूतस्त्रीषु सदा रताः ।
त्वद्भाषणोपकर्त्तारो वैड़ालव्रतिकाश्च ये ॥ ५८ ॥

अब्रह्मचारिणाधीतमिज्या चाविदुषा कृता ।
तपोवने ग्राम्यभुजां तथैवानिर्जितात्मनां ॥ ५९ ॥
ब्राह्मणक्षत्रियविशां शूद्राणाञ्च स्वकर्म्मतः ।
परिच्युतानां या चेष्टा परलोकार्थमिप्सतां ॥ ६० ॥
तस्याश्च यत्फलं सर्व्वं तत्ते यक्ष भविष्यति ।
अन्यच्च ते प्रयच्छामि पुष्ट्यर्थं सन्निबोध तत् ॥ ६१ ॥
भवतो वैश्वदेवान्ते नामोच्चारणपूर्व्वकं ।
एतत्तवेति दास्यन्ति भवतो वलिमूर्ज्जितं ॥ ६२ ॥
यः संस्कृताशी विधिवच्छुचिरन्तस्तथा वहिः ।
अलोलुपोऽजितस्त्रीकस्तद्गेहमपवर्ज्जय ॥ ६३ ॥
पूज्यन्ते हव्यकव्याभ्यां देवताः पितरस्तथा ।
यामयोऽतिथयश्चापि तद्गेहं यक्ष वर्ज्जय ॥ ६४ ॥
यत्र मैत्रीगृहे बालवृद्धयोषिन्नरेषु च ।
तथा स्वजनवर्गेषु गृहं तच्चापि वर्जय ॥ ६५ ॥
योषितोऽभिरता यत्र न वहिर्गमनोत्सुकाः ।
लज्जान्विताः सदा गेहं यक्ष तत्परिवर्जय ॥ ६६ ॥
वयःसम्बन्धयोग्यानि शयनान्यशनानि च ।
यत्र गेहे त्वया यक्ष तद्वर्ज्ज्यं वचनान्मम ॥ ६७ ॥
यत्र कारुणिका नित्यं साधुकर्म्मण्यवस्थिताः ।
सामान्योपस्करैर्य्युक्तास्त्यजेथा यच्च तद्गृहं ॥ ६८ ॥
यत्रासनस्थास्तिष्ठत्सु गुरुवृद्धद्विजातिषु ।
न तिष्ठन्ति गृहं तच्च वर्ज्ज्यं यक्ष त्वया सदा ॥ ६९ ॥

तरुगुल्मादिभिर्द्वारं न विद्धं यस्य वेश्मनः ।
मर्म्मभेदोऽथवा पुंसस्तच्छ्रेयो भवनं न ते ॥ ७० ॥
देवतापितृमर्त्त्यानामतिथीनाञ्च वर्त्तनं ।
यस्यावशिष्टेनान्नेन पुंसस्तस्य गृहं त्यज ॥ ७१ ॥
सत्यवाक्यान् क्षमाशीलानहिंस्रान्नानुतापिनः ।
पुरुषानीदृशान् यच्च त्यजेथाश्चानसूयकान् ॥ ७२ ॥
भर्त्तृशुश्रूषणे युक्तामसत्स्त्रीसङ्गवर्जितां ।
कुटुम्बभर्त्तृशेषान्नपुष्टाञ्च त्यज योषितं ॥ ७३ ॥
यजनाध्ययनाभ्यासदानासक्तमतिं सदा ।
याजनाध्यापनादानकृतवृत्तिं द्विजं त्यज ॥ ७४ ॥
दानाध्ययनयज्ञेषु सदोद्युक्तञ्च दुःसह ।
क्षत्त्रियं त्यज सच्छुल्कशस्त्राजीवात्तवेतनं ॥ ७५ ॥
त्रिभिः पूर्व्वगुणैर्युक्तं पाशुपाल्यवणिज्ययोः ।
कृषेश्चावाप्तवृत्तिञ्च त्यज वैश्यमकल्मषं ॥ ७६ ॥
दानेज्याद्विजशुश्रूषातत्परं यक्ष सन्त्यज ।
शूद्रञ्च ब्राह्मणादीनां शुश्रूषावृत्तिपोषकं ॥ ७७ ॥
श्रुतिस्मृत्यविरोधेन कृतवृत्तिर्गृहे गृही ।
यत्र तत्र च तत्पत्नी तस्यैवानुगतात्मिका ॥ ७८ ॥
यत्र पुत्रो गुरोः पूजां देवानाञ्च तथा पितुः ।
पत्नी च भर्त्तुः कुरुते तत्रालक्ष्मीभयं कुतः ॥ ७९ ॥
यदानुलिप्तं सन्ध्यासु गृहमम्बुसमुक्षितं ।
कृतपुष्पबलिं यत्र न त्वं शक्नोषि वीक्षितुं ॥ ८० ॥

भास्कराद्दृष्टशय्यानि नित्याग्निसलिलानि च ।
सूर्य्यावलोकदीपानि लक्ष्म्या गेहानि भाजनं ॥ ८१ ॥
यत्रोक्षा चन्दनं वीणा आदर्शौ मधुसर्पिषी ।
विषाज्यताम्रपात्राणि तद्गृहं न तवाश्रयः ॥ ८२ ॥
यत्र कण्टकिनो वृक्षा यत्र निष्पाववल्लरी ।
भार्य्या पुनर्भूर्वल्मीकस्तद्यच्च तव मन्दिरं ॥ ८३ ॥
यस्मिन् गृहे नराः पञ्च स्त्रीत्रयं तावतीश्च गाः ।
अन्धकारेन्धनाग्निश्च तद्गृहं वसतिस्तव ॥ ८४ ॥
एकच्छागं द्विवालेयं त्रिगवं पञ्चमाहिषं ।
षडश्वं सप्तमातङ्गं गृहं यक्षाशु शोषय ॥ ८५ ॥
कुद्दालदात्रपिटकं तद्वत् स्थाल्यादिभाजनं ।
यत्र तत्रैव क्षिप्तानि तव दद्युः प्रतिश्रयं ॥ ८६ ॥
मुषलोदूखले स्त्रीणामास्या तद्वदुदुम्बरे ।
अवस्करे मन्त्रणञ्च यच्चैतदुपकृत् तव ॥ ८७ ॥
लङ्घ्यन्ते यत्र धान्यानि पक्वापक्वानि वेश्मनि ।
तद्वच्छास्त्राणि तत्र त्वं यथेष्टं चर दुःसह ॥ ८८ ॥
स्थालीपिधाने यत्राग्निर्दत्तो दर्व्वीफलेन वा ।
गृहे तत्र हि रिष्टानामशेषाणां समाश्रयः ॥ ८९ ॥
मानुषास्थि गृहे यत्र दिवारात्रं मृतस्थितिः ।
तत्र यत्र तवावासस्तथान्येषाञ्च रक्षसां ॥ ९० ॥
अदत्वा भुञ्जते ये वै बन्धोः पिण्डं तथोदकं ।
सपिण्डान् सोदकांश्चैव तत्काले तान् नरान् भज ॥ ९१ ॥

यत्र पद्ममहापद्मौ युवती मोदकाशिनी ।
वृषभैरावतो यत्र कल्प्यते तद्गृहं त्यज ॥ ९२ ॥
अशस्त्रा देवता यत्र सशस्त्राश्चाहवं विना ।
कल्प्यन्ते मनुजैरर्च्चास्तत्परित्यज मन्दिरं ॥ ९३ ॥
पौरजानपदा यत्र प्राक्प्रसिद्धमहोत्सवाः ।
क्रियन्ते पूर्व्ववद्गेहे न त्वं तत्र गृहे चर ॥ ९४ ॥
शूर्पवातघटाम्भोभिः स्नानं वस्त्राम्बुविप्रुषैः ।
नखाग्रसलिलैश्चैव तान् याहि हतलक्षणान् ॥ ९५ ॥

देशाचारान् समयान् ज्ञातिधर्म्मं
जयं होमं मङ्गलं देवतेष्टिं ।
सम्यक् शौचं विधिवल्लोकवादान्
पुंसस्त्वया कुर्व्वतो माऽस्तु सङ्गः ॥ ९६ ॥

मार्कण्डेय उवाच ॥

इत्युक्ता दुःसहं ब्रह्मा तत्रैवान्तरधीयत ।
चकार शासनं सोऽपि तथा पङ्कजजन्मनः ॥ ९७ ॥

इति श्रीमार्कण्डेयपुराणे यक्ष्मानुशासनं नाम पञ्चाशोऽध्यायः ॥ ५० ॥

एकपञ्चाशोऽध्यायः ॥

मार्कण्डेय उवाच ॥

दुःसहस्याभवद्भार्य्या निर्म्माष्टिर्नाम नामतः ।
जाता कलेस्तु भार्य्यायामृतौ चाण्डालदर्शनात् ॥ १ ॥
तयोरपत्यान्यभवन् जगद्व्यापीनि षोड़श ।
अष्टौ कुमाराः कन्याश्च तथाष्टावतिभीषणाः ॥ २ ॥
दन्ताकृष्टिस्तथोक्तिश्च परिवर्त्तस्तथापरः ।
अङ्गधृक् शकुनिश्चैव गण्डप्रान्तरतिस्तथा ॥ ३ ॥
गर्भहा सस्यहा चान्यः कुमारास्तनयास्तयोः ।
कन्याश्चान्यास्तथैवाष्टौ तासां नामानि मे शृणु ॥ ४ ॥
नियोजिका वै प्रथमा तथैवान्या विरोधिनी ।
स्वयंहारकरी चैव भ्रामणी ऋतुहारिका ॥ ५ ॥
स्मृतिवीजहरे चान्ये तयोः कन्येऽतिदारुणे ।
विद्वेषण्यष्टमी नाम कन्या लोकभयावहा ॥ ६ ॥
एतासां कर्म्म वच्यामि दोषप्रशमनञ्च यत् ।
अष्टानाञ्च कुमाराणां श्रूयतां द्विजसत्तम ॥ ७ ॥
दन्ताकृष्टिः प्रसूतानां बालानां दशनस्थितः ।
करोति संहर्षमतो चिकीर्षुर्दुःसहागमं ॥ ८ ॥
तस्योपशमनं कार्य्यं सुप्तस्य सितसर्षपैः ।
शयनस्योपरि क्षिप्तैर्मानुषैर्दशनोपरि ॥ ९ ॥

सुवर्च्चसौषधीस्नानात्तथा सच्छास्त्रकीर्त्तनात् ।
उष्ट्रकण्टकखड्गास्थिक्षौमवस्त्रविधारणात् ॥ १० ॥
तिष्ठत्यन्यकुमारस्तु तथास्त्वित्यसकृद्ब्रुवन् ।
शुभाशुभे नृणां युंक्ते तथोक्तिस्तच्च नान्यथा ॥ ११ ॥
तस्मादहृष्टं मङ्गल्यं वक्तव्यं पण्डितैः सदा ।
दुष्टे श्रुते तथैवोक्ते कीर्त्तनीयो जनार्द्दनः ॥ १२ ॥
चराचरगुरुर्ब्रह्मा या यस्य कुलदेवता ।
अन्यगर्ब्भे परान् गर्ब्भान् सदैव परिवर्त्तयन् ॥ १३ ॥
रतिमाप्नोति वाक्यञ्च विवक्षोरन्यदेव यत् ।
परिवर्त्तकसंज्ञोऽयं तस्यापि सितसर्षपैः ॥ १४ ॥
रक्षोघ्नमन्त्रजप्यैश्च रक्षां कुर्व्वीत तत्त्ववित् ।
अन्यश्चानिलवन्नृणामङ्गेषु स्फुरणोदितं ॥ १५ ॥
शुभाशुभं समाचष्टे कुशैस्तस्याङ्कताड़नं ।
काकादिपक्षिसंस्थोऽन्यः खादेन खगतोऽपिवा ॥ १६ ॥
शुभाशुभञ्च कुशलैः कुमारोऽन्यो ब्रवीति वै ।
तत्रापि दुष्टे व्याक्षेपः प्रारम्भत्यागएव च ॥ १७ ॥
शुभे द्रुततरं कार्य्यमिति प्राह प्रजापतिः ।
गण्डान्तेषु स्थितश्चान्यो मुहूर्त्तार्द्धं द्विजोत्तम ॥ १८ ॥
सर्व्वारम्भान् कुमारोऽत्ति शस्तताञ्चानसूयतां ।
विप्रोक्त्या देवतास्तुत्या मूलोत्खातेन च द्विज ॥ १९ ॥
गोमूत्रसर्षपस्नानैस्तद्दलग्रहपूजनैः ।
पुनश्च धर्म्मोपनिषत्करणैः शस्त्रदर्शनैः ॥ २० ॥

अवज्ञया जन्मनश्च प्रशमं याति गण्डवान् ।
गर्भस्त्रीणां तथाऽन्यस्तु फलनाशी सुदारुणः ॥ २१ ॥
तस्य रक्षा सदा कार्य्या नित्यं शौचनिषेवणात् ।
प्रसिद्धमन्त्रलिखनाच्छस्तमाल्यादिधारणात् ॥ २२ ॥
विशुद्धगेहावसथादनायासाच्च वै द्विज ।
तथैव सस्यहा चान्यः सस्यर्द्धिमुपहन्ति यः ॥ २३ ॥
तस्यापि रक्षां कुर्व्वीत जीर्णोपानद्विधारणात् ।
तथापसव्यगमनाच्चाण्डालस्य प्रवेशनात् ॥ २४ ॥
वहिर्बलिप्रदानाच्च सोमाम्बुपरिकीर्त्तनात् ।
परदारपरद्रव्यहरणादिषु मानवान् ॥ २५ ॥
नियोजयति चैवान्यान् कन्या सा च नियोजिका ।
तस्याः पवित्रपठनात् क्रोधलोभादिवर्ज्जनात् ॥ २६ ॥
नियोजयति मामेषु विरोधाच्च विवर्ज्जनं ।
आकृष्टोऽन्येन मन्येत ताडितो वा नियोजिका ॥ २७ ॥
नियोजयत्येनमिति न गच्छेत्तद्वशं बुधः ।
परदारादिसंसर्गे चित्तमात्मानमेव च ॥ २८ ॥
नियोजयत्यच सा मामिति प्राज्ञो विचिन्तयेत् ।
विरोधं कुरुते चान्या दम्पत्योः प्रीयमाणयोः ॥ २९ ॥
बन्धूनां सुहृदां पित्रोः पुत्रैः सावर्णिकैश्च या ।
विरोधिनी सा तद्रक्षां कुर्व्वीत वलिकर्म्मणा ॥ ३० ॥
तथातिवादसहनाच्छास्त्राचारनिषेवणात् ।
धान्यं खलाद्गृहाद्गोभ्यः पयः सर्पिस्तथापरा ॥ ३१ ॥

सम्वृद्धिमृद्धिमद्‌द्रव्यादपहन्ति च कन्यका ।
सा स्वयंहारिकेत्युक्ता सदान्तर्धानतत्परा ॥ ३२ ॥
महानसादर्द्धसिद्धमन्नागारस्थितं तथा ।
परिविश्यमाणञ्च सदा सार्द्धं भुङ्क्ते च भुञ्जता ॥ ३३ ॥
उच्छेषणं मनुष्याणां हरत्यन्नञ्च दुर्हरा ।
कर्म्मान्तागारशालाभ्यः सिद्धर्द्धिं हरति द्विज ॥ ३४ ॥
गोस्त्रीस्तनेभ्यश्च पयः क्षीरहारी सदैव सा ।
दध्नो घृतं तिलात्तैलं सुरागारात्तथा सुरां ॥ ३५ ॥
रागं कुसम्भुकादीनां कार्पासात् सूत्रमेव च ।
सा स्वयंहारिका नाम हरत्यविरतं द्विज ॥ ३६ ॥
कुर्य्याच्छिखण्डिनो द्वन्द्वं रक्षार्थं कृत्रिमां स्त्रियं ।
रक्षाश्चैव गृहे लख्या वर्ज्या च सोष्मता तथा ॥ ३७ ॥
होमाग्निदेवताधूपभस्मना च परिष्क्रिया ।
कार्य्या क्षीरादिभाण्डानामेव तद्रक्षणं स्मृतं ॥ ३८ ॥
उद्वेगं जनयत्यन्या एकस्थाननिवासिनः ।
पुरुषस्य तु या प्रोक्ता भ्रामणी सा तु कन्यका ॥ ३९ ॥
तस्याथ रक्षां कुर्व्वीत विक्षिप्तैः सितसर्षपैः ।
आसने शयने चोर्व्व्यां यत्रास्ते स तु मानवः ॥ ४० ॥
चिन्तयेच्च नरः पापा मामेषा दुष्टचेतना ।
भ्रामयत्यसकृज्जप्यं भुवः सूक्तं समाधिना ॥ ४१ ॥
स्त्रीणां पुष्पं हरत्यन्या प्रवृत्तं सा तु कन्यका ।
अथ प्रवृत्तं सा ज्ञेया दौःसहा ऋतुहारिका ॥ ४२ ॥

कुर्व्वीत तीर्थदेवौकश्चैत्यपर्व्वतसानुषु।
नदीसङ्गमखातेषु स्नपनं तत्प्रशान्तये॥ ४३॥
मन्त्रवित् कृततत्त्वज्ञः पर्व्वमूषसि च द्विज।
चिकित्साज्ञश्च वै वैद्यः संप्रयुक्तैर्वरौषधैः॥ ४४॥
स्मृतिञ्चापहरत्यन्या स्त्रीणां सा स्मृतिहारिका।
विविक्तदेशसेवित्वात्तस्याश्चोपशमो भवेत्॥ ४५॥
वीजापहारिणी चान्या स्त्रीपुंसोरतिभीषणा।
मेध्यान्नभोजनैः स्नानैस्तस्याश्चोपशमो भवेत्॥ ४६॥
अष्टमी द्वेषणी नाम कन्या लोकभयावहा।
या करोति नवद्विष्टं नरं नारीमथापिवा॥ ४७॥
मधुक्षीरघृताक्तांस्तु शान्त्यर्थं होमयेत्तिलान्।
कुर्व्वीत मित्रबिन्दाञ्च तथेष्टिन्तत्प्रशान्तये॥ ४८॥
एतेषान्तु कुमाराणां कन्यानां द्विजसत्तम।
अष्टत्रिंशदपत्यानि तेषां नामानि मे शृणु॥ ४९॥
दन्ताकृष्टेरभूत् कन्या विजल्पा कलहा तथा।
अवज्ञान्ततदुष्टोक्तिर्विजल्पा तत्प्रशान्तये॥ ५०॥
तामेव चिन्तयेत् प्राज्ञः प्रयतश्च गृही भवेत्।
कलहा कलहं गेहे करोत्यविरतं न्नृणां॥ ५१॥
कुटुम्बनाशहेतुः सा तत्प्रशान्तिं निशामय।
दूर्व्वाङ्कुरान्मधुघृतक्षीराक्तान् बलिकर्म्मणि॥ ५२॥
विक्षिपेज्जुहुयाच्चैवानलं मित्रञ्च कीर्त्तयेत्।
भूतानां मातृभिः सार्द्धं बालकानान्तु शान्तये॥ ५३॥

विद्यानां तपसाञ्चैव संयमस्य यमस्य च ।
कृष्यां वाणिज्यलाभे च शान्तिं कुर्व्वन्तु मे सदा ॥ ५४ ॥
पूजिताश्च यथान्यायं तुष्टिं गच्छन्तु सर्व्वशः ।
कुष्माण्डा यातुधानाश्च ये चान्ये गणसंज्ञिताः ॥ ५५ ॥
महादेवप्रसादेन महेश्वरमतेन च ।
सर्व्व एते न्नृणां नित्यं तुष्टिमाशु व्रजन्तु ते ॥ ५६ ॥
तुष्टाः सर्व्वं निरस्यन्तु दुष्कृतं दुरनुष्ठितं ।
महापातकजं सर्व्वं यच्चान्यद्विघ्नकारणं ॥ ५७ ॥
तेषामेव प्रसादेन विघ्ना नश्यन्तु सर्व्वशः ।
उद्वाहेषु च सर्व्वेषु वृद्धिकर्म्मसु चैव हि ॥ ५८ ॥
पुण्यानुष्ठानयोगेषु गुरुदेवार्च्चनेषु च ।
जपयज्ञविधानेषु यात्रासु च चतुर्द्दश ॥ ५९ ॥
शरीरारोग्यभोग्येषु सुखदानधनेषु च ।
वृद्धबालातुरेष्वेव शान्तिं कुर्व्वन्तु मे सदा ॥ ६० ॥
सोमाम्बुपौ तथाम्भोधिः सविता चानिलानलौ ।
तथोक्तः कालजिह्वोऽभूत् पुत्रस्तालनिकेतनः ॥ ६१ ॥
स येषां जननीसंस्थस्तानसाधून् विबाधते ।
परिवर्त्तसुतौ द्वौ तु विरूपविकृतौ द्विज ॥ ६२ ॥
तौ तु वृत्ताग्रपरिखाप्राकाराम्भोधिसंश्रयौ ।
गुर्व्विण्याः परिवर्त्तन्तौ कुरुतः पादपादिषु ॥ ६३ ॥
क्रौष्टुके परिवर्त्तन्त्या गर्ब्भस्यान्योदरात्ततः ।
न वृक्षं चैव नैवाट्टं न प्राकारं महोदधिं ॥ ६४ ॥

परिखां वा समाक्रामेदबला गर्ब्भधारिणी।
अङ्गधृक् तनयं लेभे पिशुनं नाम नामतः ॥ ६५ ॥
सोऽस्थिमज्जागतः पुंसां बलमत्त्यजितात्मनां।
श्येनकाककपोतांश्च गृध्रोलूकैश्च वै सुतान् ॥ ६६ ॥
अवाप शकुनिः पञ्च जगृहुस्तान् सुरासुराः।
श्येनं जग्राह मृत्युश्च काकं कालो गृहीतवान् ॥ ६७ ॥
उलूकं निर्ऋतिश्चैव जग्राहातिभयावहं।
गृध्रं व्याधिस्तदीशोऽथ कपोतं च स्वयं यमः ॥ ६८ ॥
एतेषामेव चैवोक्ता भूताः पापोपपादने।
तस्माच्छ्येनादयो यस्य निलीयेयुः शिरस्यथ ॥ ६९ ॥
तेनात्मरक्षणायालं शान्तिं कुर्य्याद्द्विजोत्तम।
गेहे प्रसूतिरेतेषां तद्वन्नीड़निवेशनं ॥ ७० ॥
नरस्तं वर्ज्जयेद्गेहं कपोताक्रान्तमस्तकं।
श्येनः कपोतो गृध्रश्च काकोलूकौ गृहे द्विज ॥ ७१ ॥
प्रविष्टः कथयेदन्तं वसतां तत्र वेश्मनि।
ईदृक् परित्यजेद्गेहं शान्तिं कुर्य्याच्च पण्डितः ॥ ७२ ॥
स्वप्नेऽपि हि कपोतस्य दर्शनं न प्रशस्यते।
षडपत्यानि कथ्यन्ते गण्डप्रान्तरतेस्तथा ॥ ७३ ॥
स्त्रीणां रजस्यवस्थानं तेषां कालांश्च मे शृणु।
चत्वार्य्यहानि पूर्व्वानि तथैवान्यत् त्रयोदश ॥ ७४ ॥
एकादश तथैवान्यदपत्यं तस्य वै दिने।
अन्यद्दिनाभिगमने श्राद्धदाने तथापरे ॥ ७५ ॥

पर्व्वस्वथान्यत् तस्मात्तु वर्ज्ज्यान्येतानि पण्डितैः ।
गर्भहन्तुः सुतो निघ्नो मोहनी चापि कन्यका ॥ ७६ ॥
प्रविश्य गर्भमत्त्येको भुक्त्वा मोहयतेऽपरा ।
जायन्ते मोहनात्तस्याः सर्पमण्डूककच्छपाः ॥ ७७ ॥
सरीसृपाणि चान्यानि पुरीषमथवा पुनः ।
षण्मासान् गुर्व्विणीमांसमश्नुवानामसंयतां ॥ ७८ ॥
वृक्षच्छायाश्रयां रात्रावथवा चितुष्पथे ।
श्मशानकटभूमिष्ठामुत्तरीयविवर्ज्जितां ॥ ७९ ॥
रुद्यमानां निशीथेऽथ आविशेत्तामसौ स्त्रियं ।
सस्यहन्तुस्तथैवैकः क्षुद्रको नाम नामतः ॥ ८० ॥
सस्यर्द्धिं स सदा हन्ति लब्ध्वा रन्ध्रं शृणुष्व तत् ।
अमङ्गल्यदिनारम्भे सुतृप्तो वपते च यः ॥ ८१ ॥
क्षेत्रेष्वनुप्रवेशं वै करोत्यन्तोपसङ्गिषु ।
तस्मात् कल्यः सुप्रशस्ते दिनेऽभ्यर्च्च्य निशाकरं ॥ ८२ ॥
कुर्य्यादारम्भमुत्सिच्य हृष्टस्तुष्टः सहायवान् ।
नियोजिकेति या कन्या दुःसहस्य मयोदिता ॥ ८३ ॥
जातं प्रचोदिकासंज्ञं तस्याः कन्याचतुष्टयं ।
मत्तोन्मत्तप्रमत्तास्तु नवा नार्य्यस्तु ताः सदा ॥ ८४ ॥
समाविशन्ति नाशाय चोदयन्तीह दारुणं ।
अधर्म्मं धर्म्मरूपेण कामञ्चाकामरूपिणं ॥ ८५ ॥
अनर्थञ्चार्थरूपेण मोक्षञ्चामोक्षरूपिणं ।
दुर्विनीता विना शौचं दर्शयन्ति पृथङ्नरान् ॥ ८६ ॥

भ्राम्यन्ते ताभिरष्टाभिः पुरुषार्थात् पृथङ्नराः ।
तासां प्रवेशश्च गृहे सन्ध्यर्च्चेषु उदुम्बरे ॥ ८७ ॥
धाताविधाचोश्च बलिर्यच काले न दीयते ।
भुञ्जतां पिवतां वापि सङ्गिभिर्जलविप्रुषैः ॥ ८८ ॥
नवनारीषु संक्रान्तिस्तासामास्वभिजायते ।
विरोधिन्यास्त्रयः पुत्राश्चोदकग्राहकस्तथा ॥ ८९ ॥
तमःप्रछादकश्चान्यस्तत्स्वरूपं शृणुष्व मे ।
प्रदीपतैलसंसर्गदूषिते लङ्घिते तथा ॥ ९० ॥
मुषलोलूखले यच पादुके वासने स्त्रियः ।
सूर्पदाचादिकं यच पदाकृष्य तथासनं ॥ ९१ ॥
यचोपलिप्तश्चानर्च्चंत्र विहारः क्रियते गृहे ।
दर्व्वीमुखेन यचाग्निराहृतोऽन्यच नीयते ॥ ९२ ॥
विरोधिनीसुतास्तच विजृम्भन्ते प्रचोदिताः ।
एको जिह्वागतः पुंसां स्त्रीणाञ्चालीकसत्यवान् ॥ ९३ ॥
चोदको नाम स प्रोक्तः पैशुन्यं कुरुते गृहे ।
अवधानकृतश्चान्यः श्रवणस्थोऽतिदुर्म्मतिः ॥ ९४ ॥
करोति ग्रहणन्तेषां वचसां ग्राहकस्तु सः ।
आक्रम्यान्यो मनो नृणां तमसाछाद्य दुर्म्मतिः ॥ ९५ ॥
क्रोधं जनयते यस्तु तमःप्रछादकस्तु सः ।
स्वयंहार्य्यास्तु चौर्य्येन जनितन्तनयचयं ॥ ९६ ॥
सर्व्वहार्य्यर्द्धहारी च वीर्य्यहारी तथैव च ।
अनाचान्तगृहेष्वेते मन्दाचारगृहेषु च ॥ ९७ ॥

अप्रक्षालितपादेषु प्रविशत्सु महानसं।
खलेषु गोष्ठेषु च वै द्रोहो येषु गृहेषु वै॥ ९८॥
तेषु सर्व्वं यथान्यायं विहरन्ति रमन्ति च।
ग्रामण्यास्तनयस्त्वेकः काकजङ्घ इति स्मृतः॥ ९९॥
तेनाविष्टो रतिं सर्व्वो नैव प्राप्नोति वै पुरे।
भुञ्जन् यो गायते मैचे गायते हसते च यः॥ १००॥
सन्ध्यामैथुनिनञ्चैव नरमाविशति द्विज।
कन्याचयं प्रसूता सा या कन्या ऋतुहारिणी॥ १०१॥
एका कुचहरा कन्या अन्या व्यञ्जनहारिका।
तृतीया तु समाख्याता कन्यका जातहारिणी॥ १०२॥
यस्या न क्रियते सर्व्वः सम्यक् वैवाहिको विधिः।
कालातीतोऽथवा तस्या हरत्येका कुचद्वयं॥ १०३॥
सम्यक् श्राद्धमदत्त्वा च तथानर्च्चय च मातरं।
विवाहितायाः कन्याया हरति व्यञ्जनं तथा॥ १०४॥
अग्न्यम्बुशून्ये च तथा विधूपे सूतिकागृहे।
अदीपशस्त्रमुषले भूतिसर्षपवर्जिते॥ १०५॥
अनुप्रविश्य सा जातमपहृत्यात्मसम्भवं।
क्षणप्रसविनी बालं तत्रैवोत्सृजते द्विज॥ १०६॥
सा जातहारिणी नाम सुघोरा पिशिताशना।
तस्मात् संरक्षणं कार्य्यं यत्नतः सूतिकागृहे॥ १०७॥
स्मृतिञ्चाप्रयतानाञ्च शून्यागारनिषेवणात्।
अपहन्ति सुतस्तस्याः प्रचण्डो नाम नामतः॥ १०८॥

पौत्रेभ्यस्तस्य सम्भूता लोकाः शतसहस्रशः ।
चण्डालयोनयश्चाष्टौ दण्डपाशातिभीषणाः ॥ १०९ ॥
क्षुधाविष्टास्ततो लोकास्ताश्च चण्डालयोनयः ।
अभ्यधावन्त चान्योन्यमत्तुकामाः परस्परं ॥ ११० ॥
प्रचण्डो वारयित्वा तु तास्ताश्चण्डालयोनयः ।
समये स्थापयामास यादृशे तादृशं शृणु ॥ १११ ॥
अद्य प्रभृति लोकानामावासं यो हि दास्यति ।
दण्डं तस्याहमतुलं पातयिष्ये न संशयः ॥ ११२ ॥
चण्डालयोन्योऽवसथे लोका या प्रसविष्यति ।
तस्याश्च सन्ततिः पूर्व्वा साच सद्यो न शिष्यति ॥ ११३ ॥
प्रसूते कन्यके द्वे तु स्त्रीपुंसोर्वीजहारिणी ।
वातरूपामरूपाञ्च तस्याः प्रहरणन्तु ते ॥ ११४ ॥
वातरूपा निषेकान्ते सा यस्मै क्षिपते सुतं ।
स पुमान् वातशुक्रत्वं प्रयाति वनितापि वा ॥ ११५ ॥
तथैव गच्छतः सद्यो निर्वीजत्वमरूपया ।
अस्नाताशी नरो योऽसौ तथा चापि वियोगिनः ॥ ११६ ॥
विद्वेषिणी तु या कन्या भृकुटीकुटिलानना ।
तस्या द्वौ तनयौ पुंसामपकारप्रकाशकौ ॥ ११७ ॥
निर्वीजत्वं नरो याति नारी वा शौचवर्ज्जिता ।
पैशुन्याभिरतं लोलमसज्जलनिषेवणं ॥ ११८ ॥
पुरुषद्वेषिणश्चैतौ नरमाक्रम्य तिष्ठतः ।
मात्रा भ्रात्रा तथा मित्रैरभीष्टैः स्वजनैः परैः ॥ ११९ ॥

विद्विष्टो नाशमायाति पुरुषो धर्म्मतोऽर्थतः ।
एकस्तु स्वगुणाँल्लोके प्रकाशयति पापकृत् ॥ १२० ॥
द्वितीयस्तु गुणान् मैत्रीं लोकस्थामपकर्षति ।
इत्येते दौःसहाः सर्व्वे यक्ष्मणः सन्ततावथ ॥
पापाचाराः समाख्याता यैर्व्याप्तमखिलं जगत् ॥१२१ ॥

इति श्रीमार्कण्डेयपुराणे दौःसहोत्पत्तिसमापनं नाम ॥ ५१ ॥

द्विपञ्चाशोऽध्यायः ॥

मार्कण्डेय उवाच ॥

इत्येष तामसः सर्गो ब्रह्मणोऽव्यक्तजन्मनः ।
रुद्रसर्गं प्रवक्ष्यामि तन्मे निगदतः शृणु ॥ १ ॥
तनयाश्च तथैवाष्टौ पत्न्यः पुत्राश्च ते तथा ।
कल्पादावात्मनस्तुल्यं सुतं प्रध्यायतः प्रभोः ॥ २ ॥
प्रादुरासीदथाङ्केऽस्य कुमारो नीललोहितः ।
रुरोद सुस्वरं सोऽथ द्रवंश्च द्विजसत्तम ॥ ३ ॥
किं रोदिषीति तं ब्रह्मा रुदन्तं प्रत्युवाच ह ।
नाम देहीति तं सोऽथ प्रत्युवाच जगत्पतिं ॥ ४ ॥
रुद्रस्त्वं देव नाम्नासि मा रोदीर्धैर्य्यमावह ।
एवमुक्तस्ततः सोऽथ सप्तकृत्वो रुरोद ह ॥ ५ ॥

ततोऽन्यानि ददौ तस्मै सप्त नामानि वै प्रभुः ।
स्थानानि चैषामष्टानां पत्नीः पुत्रांश्च वै द्विज ॥ ६ ॥
भवं सर्व्वं तथेशानं तथा पशुपतिं प्रभुः ।
भीममुग्रं महादेवमुवाच स पितामहः ॥ ७ ॥
चक्रे नामान्यथैतानि स्थानान्येषाञ्चकार ह ।
सूर्य्यो जलं मही वह्निर्व्वायुराकाशमेव च ॥ ८ ॥
दीक्षितो ब्राह्मणः सोम इत्येतास्तनवः क्रमात् ।
सुवर्च्चना तथैवोमा विकेशी चापरा स्वधा ॥ ९ ॥
स्वाहा दिशस्तथा दीक्षा रोहिणी च यथाक्रमं ।
सूर्य्यादीनां द्विजश्रेष्ठ रुद्राद्यैर्नामभिः सह ॥ १० ॥
शनैश्चरस्तथा शुक्रो लोहिताङ्गो मनोजवः ।
स्कन्दः सर्गोऽथ सन्तानो बुधश्चानुक्रमात् सुतः ॥ ११ ॥
एवम्प्रकारो रुद्रोऽसौ सतीं भार्य्यामविन्दत ।
दक्षकोपाच्च तत्याज सा सती स्वं कलेवरं ॥ १२ ॥
हिमवद्दुहिता साभून्मेनायां द्विजसत्तम ।
तस्या भ्राता तु मैनाकः सखाम्भोधेरनुत्तमः ॥ १३ ॥
उपयेमे पुनश्चैनामनन्यां भगवान् भवः ।
देवौ धाताविधातारौ भृगोः ख्यातिरसूयत ॥ १४ ॥
श्रियञ्च देवदेवस्य पत्नी नारायणस्य या ।
आयतिर्नियतिश्चैव मेरोः कन्ये महात्मनः ॥ १५ ॥
धाताविधात्रोस्ते भार्य्ये तयोर्ज्जातौ सुतावुभौ ।
प्राणश्चैव मृकण्डुश्च पिता मम महायशाः ॥ १६ ॥

मनस्विन्यामहं तस्मात् पुत्त्रो वेदशिरा मम ।
धूम्रवत्यां समभवत् प्राणस्यापि निबोध मे ॥ १७ ॥
प्राणस्य द्युतिमान् पुत्त्र उत्पन्नस्तस्य चात्मजः ।
अजराश्च तयोः पुत्त्राः पौत्त्राश्च बहवोऽभवन् ॥ १८ ॥
पत्नी मरीचेः सम्भूतिः पौर्णमासमसूयत ।
विरजाः पर्व्वतश्चैव तस्य पुत्त्रौ महात्मनः ॥ १९ ॥
तयोः पुत्त्रांस्तु वक्ष्यामि वंशसंकीर्त्तने द्विज ।
स्मृतिश्चाङ्गिरसः पत्नी प्रसूता कन्यकास्तथा ॥ २० ॥
शिनीवाली कुहुश्चैव राका भानुमती तथा ।
अनुसूया तथैवात्रेर्जज्ञे पुत्त्रानकल्मषान् ॥ २१ ॥
सोमं दुर्व्वाससञ्चैव दत्तात्रेयञ्च योगिनं ।
प्रीत्यां पुलस्त्यभार्य्यायां दत्तोलिस्तत्सुतोऽभवत् ॥ २२ ॥
पूर्व्वजन्मनि सोऽगस्त्यः स्मृतः स्वायम्भुवेऽन्तरे ।
कर्द्दमश्चार्व्ववीरश्च सहिष्णुश्च सुतत्रयं ॥ २३ ॥
क्षमा तु सुषुवे भार्य्या पुलहस्य प्रजापतेः ।
क्रतोस्तु सन्नतिर्भार्य्या बालिखिल्यानसूयत ॥ २४ ॥
षष्टिर्यानि सहस्राणि ऋषीणामूर्द्ध्वरेतसां ।
उर्ज्जायान्तु वशिष्ठस्य सप्ताजायन्त वै सुताः ॥ २५ ॥
रजोगात्रोर्द्ध्वबाहुश्च सबलश्चानघस्तथा ।
सुतपाः शुक्रइत्येते सर्व्वे सप्तर्षयः स्मृताः ॥ २६ ॥
योऽसावग्निरभीमानी ब्रह्मणस्तनयोऽग्रजः ।
तस्मात् स्वाहा सुतान् लेभे त्रीनुदारौजसो द्विज ॥ २७ ॥

पावकं पवमानञ्च शुचिञ्चापि जलाशिनं ।
तेषान्तु सन्ततावन्ये चत्वारिंशच्च पञ्च च ॥ २८ ॥
कथ्यन्ते बहुशश्चैते पिता पुत्त्रचयञ्च यत् ।
एवमेकोनपञ्चाशद्वर्ज्जयाः परिकीर्त्तिताः ॥ २९ ॥
पितरो ब्रह्मणा सृष्टा ये व्याख्याता मया तव ।
अग्निस्वात्ता वर्हिषदोऽनग्नयः साग्नयश्च ये ॥ ३० ॥
तेभ्यः स्वधा सुते जज्ञे मेनां वै धारिणीं तथा ।
ते उभे ब्रह्मवादिन्यौ योगिन्यौ चाप्युभे द्विज ॥ ३१ ॥

इति श्रीमार्कण्डेयपुराणे रुद्रसर्गाभिधानो नाम ॥ ५२ ॥

त्रिपञ्चाशोऽध्यायः ॥

क्रोष्टुकिरुवाच ॥

स्वायम्भुवं त्वयाख्यातमेतन्मन्वन्तरञ्च यत् ।
तदहं भगवन् सम्यक् श्रोतुमिच्छामि कथ्यतां ॥ १ ॥
मन्वन्तरप्रमाणञ्च देवा देवर्षयस्तथा ।
ये च क्षितीशा भगवन् देवेन्द्रश्चैव यस्तथा ॥ २ ॥

मार्कण्डेय उवाच ॥

मन्वन्तराणां संख्याता साधिका ह्येकसप्ततिः ।
मानुषेण प्रमाणेन शृणु मन्वन्तरञ्च मे ॥ ३ ॥

त्रिंशत्कोट्यस्तु संख्याताः सहस्राणि च विंशतिः ।
सप्तषष्टिस्तथान्यानि नियुतानि च संख्यया ॥ ४ ॥
मन्वन्तरप्रमाणञ्च इत्येतत् साधिकं विना ।
अष्टौ शतसहस्राणि दिव्यया संख्यया स्मृतं ॥ ५ ॥
द्विपञ्चाशत्तथान्यानि सहस्राण्यधिकानि च ।
स्वायम्भुवो मनुः पूर्व्वं मनुः स्वारोचिषस्तथा ॥ ६ ॥
औत्तमस्तामसश्चैव रैवतश्चाक्षुषस्तथा ।
षडेते मनवोऽतीतास्तथा वैवस्वतोऽधुना ॥ ७ ॥
सावर्णाः पञ्च रौच्याश्च भौत्याश्चागमिनस्त्वमी ।
एतेषां विस्तरं भूयो मन्वन्तरपरिग्रहे ॥ ८ ॥
वक्ष्ये देवानृषींश्चैव यक्षेन्द्राः पितरश्च ये ।
उत्पत्तिं संग्रहं ब्रह्मन् श्रूयतामस्य सन्ततिः ॥ ९ ॥
यत्र तेषामभूत् क्षेत्रं तत्पुत्राणां महात्मनां ।
मनोःस्वायम्भुवस्यासन् दश पुत्रास्तु तत्समाः ॥ १० ॥
यैरियं पृथिवी सर्व्वा सप्तद्वीपा सपर्व्वता ।
ससमुद्रा करवती प्रतिवर्षं निवेशिता ॥ ११ ॥
स्वायम्भुवेऽन्तरे पूर्व्वमाद्ये त्रेतायुगे तथा ।
प्रियव्रतस्य पुत्रैस्तैः पौत्रैः स्वायम्भुवस्य च ॥ १२ ॥
प्रियव्रतात् प्रजावत्यां वीरात् कन्या व्यजायत ।
कन्या सा तु महाभागा कर्द्दमस्य प्रजापतेः ॥ १३ ॥
कन्ये द्वे दश पुत्रांश्च सम्राट्कुक्षी च ते उभे ।
तयोर्वै भ्रातरः शूराः प्रजापतिसमा दश ॥ १४ ॥

अग्नीध्रो मेधातिथिश्च वपुष्मांश्च तथापरः ।
ज्योतिष्मान्द्युतिमान् भव्यः सवनः सप्त एव ते ॥ १५ ॥
प्रियव्रतोऽभ्यषिञ्चत्तान् सप्त सप्तसु पार्थिवान् ।
द्वीपेषु तेन धर्म्मेण द्वीपांश्चैव निबोध मे ॥ १६ ॥
जम्बुद्वीपे तथाग्नीध्रं राजानं कृतवान् पिता ।
प्लक्षद्वीपेश्वरश्चापि तेन मेधातिथिः कृतः ॥ १७ ॥
शाल्मलेस्तु वपुष्मन्तं ज्योतिष्मन्तं कुशाह्वये ।
क्रौञ्चद्वीपे द्युतिमन्तं भव्यं शाकाह्वयेश्वरं ॥ १८ ॥
पुष्कराधिपतिञ्चापि सवनं कृतवान् सुतं ।
महावीतो धातकिश्च पुष्कराधिपतेः सुतौ ॥ १९ ॥
द्विधा कृत्वा तयोर्वर्षं पुष्करः सन्न्यवेशयत् ।
भव्यस्य पुत्राः सप्तासन्नामतस्तान्निबोध मे ॥ २० ॥
जलदश्च कुमारश्च सुकुमारो मनीवकः ।
कुशोत्तरोऽथ मेधावी सप्तमस्तु महाद्रुमः ॥ २१ ॥
तन्नामकानि वर्षाणि शाकद्वीपे चकार सः ।
तथा द्युतिमतः सप्त पुत्रास्तांश्च निबोध मे ॥ २२ ॥
कुशलो मनुगश्चोष्णः प्राकरश्चार्थकारकः ।
मुनिश्च दुन्दुभिश्चैव सप्तमः परिकीर्त्तितः ॥ २३ ॥
तेषां स्वनामधेयानि क्रौञ्चद्वीपे तथाभवन् ।
ज्योतिष्मतः कुशद्वीपे पुत्रनामाङ्कितानि वै ॥ २४ ॥
तत्रापि सप्त वर्षाणि तेषां नामानि मे शृणु ।
उद्भिदं वैणवञ्चैव सुरथं लम्बनं तथा ॥ २५ ॥

धृतिमत् प्राकरञ्चैव कापिलं चापि सप्तमं।
वपुष्मतः सुताः सप्त शाल्मलेशस्य चाभवन्॥ २६॥
श्वेतश्च हरितश्चैव जीमूतो रोहितस्तथा।
वैद्युतो मानसश्चैव केतुमान् सप्तमस्तथा॥ २७॥
तथैव शाल्मलेस्तेषां समनामानि सप्त वै।
सप्त मेधातिथेः पुत्राः प्लक्षद्वीपेश्वरस्य वै॥ २८॥
येषां नामाङ्कितैर्वर्षैः प्लक्षद्वीपस्तु सप्तधा।
पूर्वं शाकभवं वर्षं शिशिरन्तु सुखोदयं॥ २९॥
आनन्दञ्च शिवञ्चैव क्षेमकञ्च ध्रुवन्तथा।
प्लक्षद्वीपादिभूतेषु शाकद्वीपान्तिमेषु वै॥ ३०॥
ज्ञेयः पञ्चसु धर्म्मश्च वर्णाश्रमविभागजः।
नित्यः स्वाभाविकश्चैव अहिंसाविधिवर्ज्जितः॥ ३१॥
पञ्चस्वेतेषु वर्षेषु सर्व्वसाधारणः स्मृतः।
अग्नीध्राय पिता पूर्व्वं जम्बुद्वीपं ददौ द्विज॥ ३२॥
तस्य पुत्रा बभूवुर्हि प्रजापतिसमा नव।
ज्येष्ठो नाभिरिति ख्यातस्तस्य किंपुरुषोऽनुजः॥ ३३॥
हरिवर्षस्तृतीयस्तु चतुर्थोऽभूदिलावृतः।
वश्यश्च पञ्चमः पुत्रो हिरण्यःषष्ठ उच्यते॥ ३४॥
कुरुस्तु सप्तमस्तेषां भद्राश्वश्चाष्टमः स्मृतः।
नवमः केतुमालश्च तन्नाम्ना वर्षसंस्थितिः॥ ३५॥
यानि किंपुरुषाख्यानि वर्ज्जयित्वा हिमाह्वयं।
तेषां स्वभावतः सिद्धिः सुखप्राया ह्ययत्नतः॥ ३६॥

विपर्य्ययो न तेष्वस्ति जरामृत्युभयं न च ।
धर्म्माधर्म्मौ न तेष्वास्तां नोत्तमाधममध्यमाः ॥ ३७ ॥
न वै चतुर्युगावस्था नार्त्तवा ऋतवो न च ।
अग्नीध्रसूनोर्नाभेस्तु ऋषभोऽभूत्सुतो द्विज ॥ ३८ ॥
ऋषभाद्भरतो जज्ञे वीरः पुत्रशताद्वरः ।
सोऽभिषिच्यर्षभः पुत्रं महाप्राव्राज्यमास्थितः ॥ ३९ ॥
तपस्तेपे महाभागः पुलहाश्रमसंश्रयः ।
हिमाह्वं दक्षिणं वर्षं भरताय पिता ददौ ॥ ४० ॥
तस्मात्तु भारतं वर्षं तस्य नाम्ना महात्मनः ।
भरतस्याप्यभूत्पुत्रः सुमतिर्नाम धार्म्मिकः ॥ ४१ ॥
तस्मिन्राज्यं समावेश्य भरतोऽपि वनं ययौ ।
एतेषां पुत्रपौत्रैस्तु सप्तद्वीपा वसुन्धरा ॥ ४२ ॥
प्रियव्रतस्य पुत्रैस्तु भुक्ता स्वायम्भुवेऽन्तरे ।
एष स्वायम्भुवः सर्गः कथितस्ते द्विजोत्तम ॥ ४३ ॥
पूर्व्वमन्वन्तरे सम्यक् किमन्यत् कथयामि ते ॥ ४४ ॥

इति श्रीमार्कण्डेय पुराणे मन्वन्तरकथनं नाम ॥ ५३ ॥

चतुःपञ्चाशोऽध्यायः ॥

क्रोष्टुकिरुवाच ॥

कति द्वीपाः समुद्रा वा पर्व्वता वा कति द्विज ।
कियन्ति चैव वर्षाणि तेषां नद्यश्च का मुने ॥ १ ॥

महाभूतप्रमाणञ्च लोकालोकन्तथैव च ।
पर्य्यासं परिमाणञ्च गतिञ्चन्द्रार्कयोरपि ॥ २ ॥
एतत् प्रब्रूहि मे सर्व्वं विस्तरेण महामुने ॥ ३ ॥

मार्कण्डेय उवाच ॥

शतार्द्धकोटिविस्तारा पृथिवी कृत्स्नशो द्विज ।
तस्या हि स्थानमखिलं कथयामि शृणुष्व तत् ॥ ४ ॥
ये ते द्वीपा मया प्रोक्ता जम्बुद्वीपादयो द्विज ।
पुष्करान्ता महाभाग शृण्वेषां विस्तरं पुनः ॥ ५ ॥
द्वीपात्तु द्विगुणो द्वीपो जम्बुः प्लक्षोऽथ शाल्मलः ।
कुशः क्रौञ्चस्तथा शाकः पुष्करद्वीप एव च ॥ ६ ॥
लवणेक्षुसुरासर्पिर्द्दधिदुग्धजलाब्धिभिः ।
द्विगुणैर्द्विगुणैर्वृद्ध्या सर्व्वतः परिवेष्टिताः ॥ ७ ॥
जम्बुद्वीपस्य संस्थानं प्रवक्ष्येऽहं निबोध मे ।
लक्षमेकं योजनानां वृत्तो विस्तारदैर्घतः ॥ ८ ॥
हिमवान् हेमकूटश्च ऋषभो मेरुरेव च ।
नीलः श्वेतस्तथा शृङ्गी सप्तास्मिन् वर्षपर्व्वताः ॥ ९ ॥
द्वौ लक्षयोजनायामौ मध्ये तत्र महाचलौ ।
तयोर्द्दक्षिणतो यौ तु यौ तथोत्तरतो गिरी ॥ १० ॥
दशभिर्द्दशभिर्न्यूनैः सहस्रैस्तैः परस्परं ।
द्विसाहस्रोच्छ्रयाः सर्व्वे तावद्विस्तारिणश्च ते ॥ ११ ॥
समुद्रान्तःप्रविष्टाश्च षड़स्मिन् वर्षपर्व्वताः ।
दक्षिणोत्तरतो निम्ना मध्ये तुङ्गायता क्षितिः ॥ १२ ॥

वेद्यर्द्धे दक्षिणे चीणि चीणि वर्षाणि चोत्तरे ।
इलावृतं तयोर्म्मध्ये चन्द्रार्द्धाकारवत् स्थितं ॥ १३ ॥
ततः पूर्व्वेण भद्राश्वं केतुमालञ्च पश्चिमे ।
इलावृतस्य मध्ये तु मेरुः कनकपर्व्वतः ॥ १४ ॥
चतुरसीतिसाहस्रस्तस्योच्छ्रायो महागिरेः ।
प्रविष्टः षोड़शाधस्ताद्विस्तीर्णः शोड़शैव तु ॥ १५ ॥
शरावसंस्थितत्वाच्च द्वाचिंशन्मूर्द्ध्नि विस्तृतः ।
शुक्लः पीतोऽसितो रक्तः प्राच्यादिषु यथाक्रमं ॥ १६ ॥
विप्रो वैश्यस्तथा शूद्रः क्षचियश्च सवर्णतः ।
तस्योपरि तथैवाष्टौ पूर्व्वादिषु यथाक्रमं ॥ १७ ॥
इन्द्रादिलोकपालानां तन्मध्ये ब्रह्मणः सभा ।
योजनानां सहस्राणि चतुर्द्दश समुच्छ्रिता ॥ १८ ॥
अयुतोच्छ्रायस्तस्याधस्तथा विष्कम्भपर्व्वतः ।
प्राच्यादिषु क्रमेणैव मन्दरो गन्धमादनः ॥ १९ ॥
विपुलश्च सुपार्श्वश्च केतुपादपशोभिताः ।
कदम्बो मन्दरे केतुर्जम्बुर्व्वै गन्धमादने ॥ २० ॥
विपुले च तथाश्वत्थः सुपार्श्वे च वटो महान् ।
एकादशशतायामा योजनानामिमे नगाः ॥ २१ ॥
जठरो देवकूटश्च पूर्व्वस्यां दिशि पर्व्वतौ ।
आनीलनिषधौ प्राप्तौ परस्परनिरन्तरौ ॥ २२ ॥
निषधः पारिपाचश्च मेरोः पार्श्वे तु पश्चिमे ।
यथा पूर्व्वौ तथाचैतावानीलनिषधायतौ ॥ २३ ॥

कैलासो हिमवांश्चैव दक्षिणेन महाचलौ ।
पूर्व्वपश्चायतावेतावर्ण्णवान्तर्व्यवस्थितौ ॥ २४ ॥
शृङ्गवान् जारुधिश्चैव तथैवोत्तरपर्व्वतौ ।
यथैव दक्षिणे तद्वदन्तर्वान्तर्व्यवस्थितौ ॥ २५ ॥
मर्य्यादपर्व्वता ह्येते कथ्यन्तेऽष्टौ द्विजोत्तम ।
हिमवद्धेमकूटादिपर्व्वतानां परस्परं ॥ २६ ॥
नव योजनसाहस्रं प्रागुदग्दक्षिणोत्तरं ।
मेरोरिलावृते तद्वदन्तरे वै चतुर्द्दिशं ॥ २७ ॥
फलानि यानि वै जम्बा गन्धमादनपर्व्वते ।
गजदेहप्रमाणानि पतन्ति गिरिमूर्द्धनि ॥ २८ ॥
तेषां स्रावात् प्रभवति ख्याता जम्बूनदीतिवै ।
यच जाम्बूनदं नाम कनकं सम्प्रजायते ॥ २९ ॥
सा परिक्रम्य वै मेरुं जम्बूमूलं पुनर्नदी ।
विशति द्विजशार्दूल पीयमाना जनैश्च तैः ॥ ३० ॥
भद्राश्वेऽश्वशिरा विष्णुर्भारिते कूर्म्मसंस्थितिः ।
वराहः केतुमाले च मत्स्यरूपस्तथोत्तरे ॥ ३१ ॥
तेषु नक्षत्रविन्यासाद्विषयाः समवस्थिताः ।
चतुर्ष्वपि द्विजश्रेष्ठ ग्रहाभिभवपाठकाः ॥ ३२ ॥

इति श्रीमार्कण्डेय पुराणे भुवनकोषे जम्बूद्वीपवर्णनं नाम ॥ ५४ ॥

पञ्चपञ्चाशोऽध्यायः ॥

मार्कण्डेय उवाच ॥

शैलेषु मन्दराद्येषु चतुर्ष्वेव द्विजोत्तम ।
वनानि यानि चत्वारि सरांसि च निबोध मे ॥ १ ॥
पूर्व्वं चैत्ररथं नाम दक्षिणे नन्दनं वनं ।
वैभ्राजं पश्चिमे शैले सावित्रं चोत्तराचले ॥ २ ॥
अरुणोदं सरः पूर्व्वं मानसं दक्षिणे तथा ।
शीतोदं पश्चिमे मेरोर्महाभद्रं तथोत्तरे ॥ ३ ॥
शीतार्त्तश्चक्रमुञ्जश्च कुलीरोऽथ सुकङ्कवान् ।
मणिशैलोऽथ वृषवान् महानीलो भवाचलः ॥ ४ ॥
सबिन्दुर्मन्दरो वेणुस्तामसो निषधस्तथा ।
देवशैलश्च पूर्व्वेण मन्दरस्य महाचलः ॥ ५ ॥
त्रिकूटशिखराद्रिश्च कलिङ्गोऽथ पतङ्गकः ।
रुचकः सानुमांश्चाद्रिस्ताम्रकोऽथ विशाखवान् ॥ ६ ॥
श्वेतोदरः समूलश्च वसुधारश्च रत्नवान् ।
एकशृङ्गो महाशैलो राजशैलः पिपाठकः ॥ ७ ॥
पञ्चशैलोऽथ कैलासो हिमवांश्चाचलोत्तमः ।
इत्येते दक्षिणे पार्श्वे मेरोः प्रोक्ता महाचलाः ॥ ८ ॥
सुरक्षः शिशिराक्षश्च वैदुर्य्यः कपिलस्तथा ।
पिञ्जरोऽथ महाभद्रः सुरसः कपिलो मधुः ॥ ९ ॥

अञ्जनः कुक्कुटः कृष्णः पाण्डरश्चाचलोत्तमः ।
सहस्रशिखरश्चाद्रिः पारिपात्रः सशृङ्गवान् ॥ १० ॥
पश्चिमेन तथा मेरोर्विस्कम्भात् पश्चिमाद्बहिः ।
एतेऽचलाः समाख्याताः शृणुष्वान्यांस्तथोत्तरान् ॥ ११ ॥
शङ्खकूटोऽथ वृषभो हंसनाभस्तथाचलः ।
कपिलेन्द्रस्तथा शैलः सानुमान् नील एव च ॥ १२ ॥
स्वर्णशृङ्गी शातशृङ्गी पुष्पको मेघपर्व्वतः ।
विरजाक्षो वराहाद्रिर्मयूरो जारुधिस्तथा ॥ १३ ॥
इत्येते कथिता ब्रह्मन् मेरोरुत्तरतो नगाः ।
एतेषां पर्व्वतानान्तु द्रोन्योऽतीवमनोहराः ॥ १४ ॥
वनैरमलपानीयैः सरोभिरुपशोभिताः ।
तासु पुण्यकृतां जन्म मनुष्याणां द्विजोत्तम ॥ १५ ॥
एते भौमा द्विजश्रेष्ठ स्वर्गाः स्वर्गगुणाधिकाः ।
न तासु पुण्यपापानामपूर्व्वानामुपार्ज्जनं ॥ १६ ॥
पुण्योपभोगा एवोक्ता देवानामपि तास्वपि ।
शीतान्ताद्येषु चैतेषु शैलेषु द्विजसत्तम ॥ १७ ॥
विद्याधराणां यक्षाणां किन्नरोरगरक्षसां ।
देवानाञ्च महावासा गन्धर्व्वाणां च शोभनाः ॥ १८ ॥
महापुण्या मनोज्ञैश्च सदेवोपवनैर्युताः ।
सरांसि च मनोज्ञानि सर्व्वर्त्तुसुखदोऽनिलः ॥ १९ ॥
न चैतेषु मनुष्याणां वैमनस्यानि कुत्रचित् ।
तदेवं पार्थिवं पद्मं चतुष्पत्रं मयोदितं ॥ २० ॥

भद्राश्वभारताद्यानि पत्रान्यस्य चतुर्द्दिशं ।
भारतं नाम यद्वर्षं दक्षिणेन मयोदितं ॥ २१ ॥
तत् कर्म्मभूमिर्नान्यत्र संप्राप्तिः पुण्यपापयोः ।
एतत् प्रधानं विज्ञेयं यत्र सर्व्वं प्रतिष्ठितं ॥ २२ ॥
तस्मात् स्वर्गापवर्गौ च मानुष्यनारकावपि ।
तिर्य्यक्त्वमथवाप्यन्यत् नरः प्राप्नोति वै द्विज ॥ २३ ॥

इति श्रीमार्कण्डेय पुराणे भुवनकोषे ॥ ५५ ॥

षट्पञ्चाशोऽध्यायः ॥

मार्कण्डेय उवाच ॥

धराधारं जगद्योनिं पदं नारायणस्य च ।
ततः प्रवृत्ता या देवी गङ्गा त्रिपथगामिनी ॥ १ ॥
सा प्रविश्य सुधायोनिं सोममाधारमम्भसां ।
ततः सम्वध्यमानार्करश्मिसङ्गतिपावनी ॥ २ ॥
पपात मेरुपृष्ठे च सा चतुर्द्धा ततो ययौ ।
मेरुकूटतटान्तेभ्यो निपतन्ती विवर्त्तिता ॥ ३ ॥
विकीर्य्यमाणसलिला निरालम्बा पपात सा ।
मन्दराद्येषु पादेषु प्रविभक्तोदका समं ॥ ४ ॥
चतुर्ष्वपि पपाताम्बुविभिन्नाङ्घ्रिशिलोच्चया ।
पूर्व्वाशीतेऽतिविख्याता ययौ चैत्ररथं वनं ॥ ५ ॥

तत्प्लावयित्वा च ययौ वरुणोदं सरोवरं ।
शीतान्तञ्च गिरिं तस्मात्ततश्चान्यान् गिरीन् क्रमात् ॥ ६ ॥
गत्वा भुवं समासाद्य भद्राश्वाज्जलधिं गता ।
तथैवालकनन्दाख्यं दक्षिणे गन्धमादने ॥ ७ ॥
मेरुपादवनं गत्वा नन्दनं देवनन्दनं ।
मानसञ्च महावेगात् प्लावयित्वा सरोवरं ॥ ८ ॥
आसाद्य शैलराजानं रम्यं हि शिखरन्तथा ।
तस्माच्च पर्व्वतान् सर्व्वान् दक्षिणोपक्रमोदितान् ॥ ९ ॥
तान् प्लावयित्वा संप्राप्ता हिमवन्तं महागिरिं ।
दधार तत्र तां शम्भुर्न मुमोच वृषध्वजः ॥ १० ॥
भगीरथेनोपवासैः स्तुत्या चाराधितो विभुः ।
तत्र मुक्ता च शर्व्वेन सप्तधा दक्षिणोदधिं ॥ ११ ॥
प्रविवेश त्रिधा प्राच्यां प्लावयन्ती महानदी ।
भगीरथरथस्यानु स्रोतसैकेन दक्षिणां ॥ १२ ॥
तथैव पश्चिमे पादे विपुले सा महानदी ।
स्वरक्षुरिति विख्याता वैभ्राजं साचलं ययौ ॥ १३ ॥
शीतोदञ्च सरस्तस्मात् प्लावयन्ती महानदी ।
स्वरक्षुः पर्व्वतं प्राप्ता ततश्च त्रिशिखं गता ॥ १४ ॥
तस्मात् क्रमेण चाद्रीणां शिखरेषु निपत्य सा ।
केतुमालं समासाद्य प्रविष्टा लवणोदधिं ॥ १५ ॥
सुपार्श्वन्तु तथैवाद्रिं मेरुपादं हि सा गता ।
तत्र सोमेति विख्याता सा ययौ सवितुर्वनं ॥ १६ ॥

तत्पावयन्ती संप्राप्ता महाभद्रं सरोवरं ।
ततश्च शङ्खकूटं सा प्रयाता वै महानदी ॥ १७ ॥
तस्माच्च वृषभादीन् सा क्रमात् प्राप्य शिलोच्चयान् ।
महार्णवमनुप्राप्ता प्लावयित्वोत्तरान् कुरून् ॥ १८ ॥
एवमेषा मया गङ्गा कथिता ते द्विजर्षभ ।
जम्बुद्वीपनिवेशाश्च वर्षाणि च यथातथं ॥ १९ ॥
वसन्ति तेषु सर्व्वेषु प्रजाः किंपुरुषादिषु ।
सुखप्राया निरातङ्का न्यूनतोत्कर्षवर्ज्जिताः ॥ २० ॥
नवस्वपि च वर्षेषु सप्त सप्त कुलाचलाः ।
एकैकस्मिंस्तदा देशे नद्यश्चाद्रिविनिःसृताः ॥ २१ ॥
यानि किंपुरुषाद्यानि वर्षाण्यष्टौ द्विजोत्तम ।
तेषूद्भिदानि तोयानि मेघवार्य्यंच भारते ॥ २२ ॥
वार्क्षी स्वाभाविकी देश्या तोयोत्था मानसी तथा ।
कर्म्मजा च नृणां सिद्धिर्व्वर्षेष्वेतेषु चाष्टसु ॥ २३ ॥
कामप्रदेभ्यो वृक्षेभ्यो वार्क्षी सिद्धिः स्वभावजा ।
स्वाभाविकी समाख्याता तृप्तिर्देश्या च दैशिकी ॥ २४ ॥
अपां सौक्ष्म्याच्च तोयात्था ध्यानोपेता च मानसी ।
उपासनादिकार्य्याच्तु धर्म्मजा साप्युदाहृता ॥ २५ ॥
न चैतेषु युगावस्था नाधयो व्याधयो न च ।
पुण्यापुण्यसमारम्भो नैव तेषु द्विजोत्तम ॥ २६ ॥

इति श्रीमार्कण्डेयपुराणे गङ्गावतारो नाम ॥ ५६ ॥